Religion and Religions

Interfaith Treasures Uncovered

Under this Series, the Publishers endeavor to focus on Comparative Studies pertaining to Christian Faith & Living in the central matrix and Hinduism, Buddhism, Sikhism, Islam, Judaism, etc., on the peripheral. The Studies shall cover topics like Literature & Poetry, Indigenous Philosophizing, Ethical response towards Agriculture, Health & Healing, Science & Technology, Ecofeminist Theology, Sociological approach towards Human Rights, Law & Politics, Arts, History of Ideas, Ancient Civilizations, Cultural Contiguity, Religious Cosmologies & Mysticism, Footsteps of famous Theologians, World Peace & Harmony, Global Capitalism, Network Marketing, Cybertheology, Population & Demographics, Epigraphic Studies, Contextualized Education, and many others. We welcome a Mss. on any topic/s mentioned, whether they are original works, scholarly monographs, collections of conference papers, revised dissertations, or translations of historical documents. Through the Series, we are striving to put forward published works that may help Institutions, Academic Bodies, Researchers, Scholars and the World at large in furthering their respective knowledge and understanding on the concerned subject. We welcome your comments on our efforts and further suggestions on how we can foster the upcoming books on parallel interfaces between and among Christianity and other religions.

Interfaith Treasures Uncovered - 13

Religion and Religions

An Interfaith Perspective

Israel Selvanayagam

CWI

Christian World Imprints™

First Published in 2018 by

Christian World Imprints™
Christian Publishing & Books from India
H-12 Bali Nagar, **New Delhi-110015**
info@christianworldimprints.com
www.ChristianWorldImprints.com
Phone: +91 11 25465925

ISBN 13: 978-93-5148-269-7 ISBN 10: 93-5148-269-3

Cataloging in Publication Data--DK
Courtesy: D.K. Agencies (P) Ltd. <docinfo@dkagencies.com>

Celvanāyakam, Israyēl, author.
Religion and religions : an interfaith perspective / Israel Selvanayagam.
pages cm. -- (Interfaith treasures uncovered ; 13)
Includes bibliographical references.
ISBN 9351482693
ISBN 9789351482697

1. Christianity and other religions--India. 2. Religions--Relations. 3. Implicit religion--India. 4. Religious pluralism--India. I. Title. II. Series: Interfaith treasures uncovered ; 13.

LCC BR127.C45 2018 | DDC 261.2 23

Printed in India

TO

Eric J. Lott

Contents

Foreword

I am indeed honoured and pleased to write this foreword to the very insightful and meaningful book produced by Dr. Israel Selvanayagam. In this book, he brings together his life's work of both scholarly and personal journey in understanding the issues of religion/s and their study by both theologians and historians of religions. First, the value of the book lies in the fact that he unpacks carefully the methodological and theoretical issues in dealing with religions of the world, but also very significantly he engages the definition of religion by locating it in the lives of people rather than in the abstract philosophical debates. Secondly, he writes with the intention of exposing the western study and engagement with religion to the non-western context, such as India and in doing so, he teases out the difficulties in ignoring the non-western discourses on religion. By offering comprehensive reviews of relevant literature in each chapter, Dr. Selvanayagam offers useful guidelines to readers for further investigation and research. He combines his strong roots in Christian theology with the study of religion comparatively by focusing on how religious ideas such as God and soul in different religions may be comparable, albeit he limits his analysis to the Abrahamic and Indian religions. As a theologian, he is committed to questions of meaning, interfaith dialogue, justice and peace. These issues are discussed pervasively in the book. He makes clear of his intention to push for the study of religion centred around people's daily experience rather than relying solely on religious texts. The key significance of this book is that here Dr. Selvanayagam reflects closely from his Indian experience, especially on issues of secularism, pluralism and dialogue, thereby filling the gap in scholarship that is mostly from a western perspective. In his discussion on the question of religious 'truth' drawing from the earlier Indian and western Christian theologians, he locates it in the concrete realities of the world where issues of caste, poverty and inequality matter, moving away from the abstract discussions of philosophers and theologians. He has offered relevant and useful guidelines in the discussion on inter-religious dialogue by emphasising on religious commitment and willingness to learn from others and openness to accept differences. The book is a very useful contribution to both students of theology and religious studies who are interested in the broader questions of inter-religious relations. He writes with a sense of purpose and advocacy that does not at the same time compromise rational discussion. He expresses his view candidly and gracefully. I strongly recommend this book to scholars and researchers who are in their quest to understand the Indian Christian context on issues of pluralism, conversion, and dialogue.

P. Pratap Kumar
Emeritus Professor
School of Religion, Philosophy and Classics
University of KwaZulu-Natal
South Africa

Acknowledgement

I have acknowledged below parts or summaries of some of the materials have been used by me in meetings and publications. Eric Lott, from the Bangalore days in 1981, has been a consultant. His contribution to methodology of the study of religion with its integral relationship with theology is well known in India and elsewhere. He lent me many materials of foundational nature. He read earlier drafts of at least half of the chapters and offered comments and correction. It is fitting that Dr. P. Pratap Kumar has kindly provided a 'Foreword' for we had many sessions together with Eric Lott on issues in the study of religion during our Masters at United Theological College, Bangalore, during 1981-1983. Thanks are due to him. Then I have more than one reason for dedicating this book to Eric Lott with a great sense of gratitude.

The final draft was seen and checked by William Allberry, a long-standing friend, a priest of the Church of England and a regular visiting teacher of English to the Tamilnadu Theological Seminary, Madurai. I am immensely grateful to him. Thanks are due also to the publisher, Mr. Sudhanshu Kanda, Christian World Imprints, for his friendly approach, prompt correspondence and perfect workmanship.

A note on inclusive language and style: While maintaining an inclusive style with gender equality I have not attempted to synchronize in the quotes nor leave the text full of *sic* notes!

This book is unusual in its style and structure. There are familiar ideas and novel ones too. My intention is that the scientific studies of religion have certain gaps, and it is my hope that some of the themes of this book will clarify and fill them. Also it gives an easy entry for those who want to take up the study of religion either for personal enrichment or for academic recognition, and removes the fear of those who are still doubtful about the significance of informed interfaith engagement in today's world.

Introduction

'Now I am tasting a slice of mango; I only know its taste; so also the taste of God in Christ. Likewise you can taste God. There is no surety without tasting it!' As a teenager I heard this from a Christian preacher in my local congregation. Many questions arose in my mind. For example, why he could not share a slice of mango with every one of that poor congregation? My southern Indian village is known for a variety of mangoes; some are sweet while some others are sweeter; some are sour while some others are sweet and sour! In all cases the taste depends on the ripeness of the fruit. In religious terms, while some Christians claim to be in the sweet presence of Christ always, in practice others find them too sour. But at the same time, in that multifaith village there were exceptional individuals from other faiths who were known to be sweet. Were they deceptive and pretending to be sweet as some Christian enthusiasts claimed? This justified their preaching the gospel to the non-Christians. This is enough for a start!

After teaching and coordinating a new programme of interfaith dialogue at the Tamilnadu Theological Seminary in Madurai (a famous temple town in southern India) for four years, I joined the United Theological College in Bangalore in 1981 to do my Masters in the field of Religions with a special focus on Hinduism. 'Methods in the Study of Religion' was a required course. Herbert Jaisingh, an Indian who had lived in Chicago for several years, was the teacher of this course. What was obvious was that he depended completely on books produced in the English language. He took pains to explain certain terms used in different approaches to the study of religion. We did not fail to notice that the term 'methodology' was the most frequent yet the most ambiguous word to grapple. The reason was that different writers used it in different senses. However, such factors could not dampen my interest in the study of religion.

Later in 1996 when I moved to England to teach religions and guide interfaith exposure at various institutions I started reading more and watching the way the study of religion was done there. It was striking that the study of religion itself is known by different terms, the most common ones being science of religion, scientific study of religion, history of religion, comparative religion, phenomenology of religion, religious studies and interfaith studies.

During 2001-2006 I had the privilege of being the Principal of the United College of the Ascension situated in Selly Oak, Birmingham. Selly Oak with several mission colleges became the hub of mission thinkers, researchers and church leaders from across the world. One of the responsibilities of me and my colleagues was to help and guide postgraduate students from overseas to formulate, develop and complete their research in time. They were normally good in stating basic facts about their subject. Just introduced to the British academic context (Birmingham is a university city), they struggled to grasp the meaning of certain terms, the most popular being 'methodology'. At the same time, I was not sure as what the best way of helping them was.

Further, during this period, I was associated with the study network of Implicit Religion and Contemporary Spirituality. A new definition of religion (commitment, common concern and sacred focus, either one of them or together) was repeated as originally proposed by the founder Edward Bailey. Exposure to the annual Denton Conference (Salisbury, 2016), reading the articles of the Journal and discussions with research scholars and Bailey himself and making a few presentations myself increased my growing understanding of religion, its orientations and expressions. I mustered the confidence to write a book which developed slowly and it was growing very slowly.

From 2010 to 2016, I was teaching aspects of religion and religions for the postgraduate students of the Gurukul Theological College and Research Institute. More than those who took the Hinduism specialization, students of other disciplines were taking the Methodology seminar for a week. We provided different definitions of the word 'methodology' both its common and subject specific meanings. While we marvelled at the variety of definitions and explanations of the application of the analytical tools, for the young generation of Indian theological students who are already overloaded by the variety and volumes of materials in English, their relevance to the Indian situation seemed very limited. In one seminar I suggested the following.

'As the uses of the words "method" and "methodology" are confusing, after consultation with the Senate, they may be replaced by the terms "perspectives" and "procedures". "Perspective" (Latin *perspicere* = to inspect carefully) has the meaning of angles and viewpoints. For example, a road accident is viewed and assessed differently by police, lawyers, medical personnel, poets, philosophers and theologians. Each category of people has a set of parameters to assess and analyze the situation, and to write reports or reflections. "Procedure" means the practical side of the research, whether reading in libraries or field work (empirical and case studies).'

An average Indian scholar of religion based in church-related institutions of theological education and ministerial training is placed in a peculiar position. They do not have the privilege of holding an academic post in a secular institution as in the West or in a department of philosophy in an Indian university. They are indirectly forced to hang in a balance between commitment and openness, between their ministerial obligation of helping the candidates for ministry and mission and striving to maintain independent scholarship and research. It is extraordinary indeed if one is able to maintain this balance steady and healthy. A few of them who have had opportunities to study in the western universities are not encouraged to research with a free mind and inform their faith community. Of course more than any other country India has a rich and diverse heritage of religions, but Indian scholars have not been able to study them in a detailed and systematic manner as western scholars do. And since the secular Indian universities are pre-occupied with the study of Indian philosophies and are not interested in the study of religion and religions in a comprehensive sense, Christian students hardly have scholarly partnership. At the same time a few of them have started to study aspects of Indian religious traditions in India, but while relying on western materials introduce western study methods, part or full, and study aspects of particular religious traditions (primal/tribal/Dalit and diverse popular cults). Further, they struggle to find adequate financial resources and have to write in a language which is foreign to them.

A pitfall in the western studies of religion is that Indian contributions are hardly recognized. Great names such as S. Radhakrishnan may have been mentioned but not Rabindranath Tagore, Swami Vivekananda and B.R. Ambedkar who have defined religion in their own way and formed opinions about world religions. This shows either ignorance, prejudice or judgment about noteworthiness. In this book I have mentioned many of them. This does not mean that western scholars of religion are always cognizant of their colleagues across the continents. There are areas where the position of 'one hand not knowing what the other hand is doing' and some of them are exposed in this study. Inter-continental ignorance in the study of religion is no secret for those who study comparatively and comprehensively. Those who study them from the Third World have the advantage of finding the gaps and filling them if possible. But the issues are many more than a study of this kind can point out.

Major Approaches to the Study of Religion

Apart from the history of the science of religion starting from Max Muller (1823-1900), known as the pioneer, a student of religion is supposed to study different approaches known in the field. Normally they are the following:

1. Historical – locating the origins and studying particular irreversible sequences, decisive moments of change and structures, beliefs and practices.
2. Psychological – locating the seat of consciousness of religious experience in the human mind or psyche and studying impulses, reactions and ecstatic expressions.

3. Philosophical – critical examination of the truth value of immense material of myths, symbols and rites and analysis of the main contents of religious experience including the transcendental dimension of human life.
4. Sociological – study of the interrelation of religion and society and the forms of interaction between them identifying social forces that influence impulses and ideas.
5. Anthropological – closely related to the above but concentrating mainly on the primal traditions and societies with special reference to beliefs and behaviour.
6. Phenomenological – trying to understand the meaning of religious expressions by classifying their types like prayer and sacrifice through detached observation and value free judgment.
7. Dialogical – inter-disciplinary with interaction between past and present, between scriptures and modern interpretation and between tradition and living people. Theology of religions and perspectives of inter-faith dialogue are related concerns.

This study takes the last one for obvious reasons but uses relevant insights from the others. All the other approaches, sometimes with novel combinations, are overdone as evident from the flood of fresh materials in libraries and bookshops. However, a comprehensive and systematic text-book on the study of religion is yet to emerge. Of course there is no claim that this book will fill all the gap, but many of its ingredients may be incorporated. Also from my own study, scholarly interaction, practice of interfaith dialogue and inter-disciplinary study, it comes with conviction and is indispensable. There is no concealment of my Christian identity but there is the avowed obligation that 'I shall not bear false witness against my neighbour.'

The chapters of this book were developed over more than a decade. If any of them was presented in conferences or published it will be noted below.

The *first* chapter brings together the classical and some casual definitions of religion. A preliminary form was presented at the Denton Conference in 2002. Some teachers of Religious Studies were after the paper as they found it to be somewhat exhaustive of definitions. Part of the paper was published ("What is Religion? A Summary of an inconclusive Discussion" in *Harmony Flame Spreads Across India,* Edited by Gnana Robinson, Kanyakumari: Kanyakumari Peace and Justice Publications, 2009, 120-133; *permission received*). Later, I realized that the definitions of religion not only exposed different perspectives and approaches to the study of religion, but also indirectly presented their significance for theology.

The *second* chapter on dimensions and dynamics of religion took me through an exciting journey. I identified different enumerations of dimensions and interpretations, and the number grew from six to eleven. When part of my study was presented in the Denton Conference in 2004 the participants appreciated my work, but my suggestion of a further dimension of culture with two components (sacred geography and sacred language) evoked different opinions. Since then I revised that part, and it is up to the reader to make his/her opinion on the present form. It emerged that dynamic process had been proposed by Eric Lott as one dimension in every religious life. I have made an attempt to work out creative interaction between religious traditions and the emergence of new ones. I have taken the examples of the Semitic and Indian religious traditions.

Implicit religion and its variety form the *third* chapter. I have noted the so called quasi-religions in the background. Though Edward Bailey, the exponent of this concept, suggested implicit religion after an empirical study, it came to be a field without boundaries. The religion of the sports is an obvious example of implicit religion. The Princess Diana syndrome has attracted much scholarly attention, and the idea of implicit religion received a great boost. But at the same time implicit religion befriended sociology of religion and consequently the latter dominated in studies in the name of the former. The Journal *Implicit Religion* carries articles from various fields and in many cases one may ask 'what is implicit here?' However, like the Denton Conferences (now Salisbury) it provides a meeting point for those who want to interact with a group of international scholars of different disciplines.

The *fourth* chapter explicates the nature, need and parameters of a dialogical approach to the study of religion. It starts with a critical view of W.C. Smith towards the scientific study of religion. For him religious persons and communities are there not to give fodder to the ever devouring scholars with their attractive tools of analysis. Smith calls for the recognition of persons and their inherent faith which is different from the cumulative tradition including ritual and belief. G. Flood criticizes the claims of objective study by phenomenology. Taking insights from the Russian philosopher M. M. Bakhtin's dialogism, he points out that utterances acquire meaning only in dialogue. Person, interaction and reassessment form a rhythm of dialogue and communication. Then Flood argues that while some claim that religious experience is ineffable, it is in its utterability and dialogical relationship that it is built and grown. With specialization in the study of Indian religious traditions Stanley Samartha once surprised Tillich by introducing to him S. Radhakrishnan's concept of the concrete Spirit which was not far different from Tillich's. He studied 'Hindu responses to the unbound Christ' and made his own assessment. The climax was his engagement in interfaith dialogue and taught the Christian world about its significance. For Samartha, dialogue could be the most authentic way of understanding other religions.

'Naming the Transcendence' is the title of the *fifth* chapter. There is no unanimity about the essence of religious life. Sacred, sacred power, transcendence, truth, mystery etc. are used by those who studied aspects of religious life. They are abstract and colourless. But the major religious traditions have maintained in their communal life, with metal image or mental image, a God, Goddess or the Supreme. This 'revelation' did not happen instantly. There have been changes of visions, traditions and interpretations and in the case of the last there has been fierce confrontation as well. In the Indian religious traditions, from Vedic polytheism to curious speculations of uncertainty to monotheism to avatars and monism there are many traditions with or without interactions between them. Buddhism and Jainism do believe in the plurality of gods and goddesses, but not in a supreme creator God, although in certain traditions the title 'Highest God' is used. The Abrahamic faiths share in common visions and ideas of one God. Judaism's idea of God with the enigmatic name Yahweh existed side by side with God in general. Christians took it forward up to the vision of trinity which appeared to create some confusion in the other monotheistic faiths of Judaism and Islam. To make things complex Sikhism emerged with elements from Hinduism and Islam. Thus by naming the transcendence in such dynamic ways specific meanings are gained, and an awareness of this fact may encourage interfaith dialogue.

The *sixth* chapter deals with the meanings of meaning. The question has been asked from the beginning of humanity but the answer is varied. One may want to marvel at the way 'meaning' is defined in philology and philosophy. It is often held that the ultimate concern gives meaning to a culture. But as history has shown, there is no guarantee for its consistent progress. We have witnessed downfalls. One important question is whether a sense of meaning is possible within an individual without any intercourse with a community. An imperfect community cannot ensure a readymade sense of meaning. Therefore there should be a critical yet positive interaction between individuals and the society. At the same time they make meaning for each other. This chapter explores religious traditions as meaning systems but not without tension. Understanding of the inner being (soul!) and its future position plays an important role for one's meaning. The missionary religions with a claim of a developed culture think that they have a message to other religions but without understanding what they mean by meaning. Now such cultures of traditional missionary societies are found to be wanting if not actually having become pagan. This calls for a new approach, and interfaith dialogue can help. As studies show, humans continue to search for meaning out of their existential struggle with finitude and decay. Every moment of pleasure is fleeting, and to observe how religious traditions respond to this situation is quite exciting.

The process of secularization and its impact on religion is dealt with in the *seventh* chapter. At one time religions tried to rule supreme in different contexts of the world, following Enlightenment, and along with the scientific revolution and urbanization, secular ideas and structures erupted and spread all over the world. Humanist and atheistic movements challenged the claims of religions, and the latter appear to be in decline in the western world. But in due course there were interesting developments. Dimensions of religion could not be avoided in the celebration of national and secular holidays. Some secular movements drifted to fascist quasi-religions. The two World Wars in the twentieth century raised questions about the development of humanity, particularly its moral stability and social responsibility. Some religious traditions incorporated some of the liberative insights of secularism and reinterpreted the traditional dichotomies such as sacred and profane. Also secular experiments and new configurations have proved to be un-enduring. Most notably the collapse of the Soviet Union disclosed the stable life of religion in Russia and a revival of it in the other countries of the Union. Everywhere there is a search for spirituality and there are cases of dialogue between religious thinkers and secular exponents of freedom. No one seems to have denied that human life can be defined by only material resources and intellectual satisfaction.

The *eighth* chapter explores the Truth and truths of religion. A preliminary draft was published ("TRUTH and truths in Inter-faith Dialogue", *Religion and Society*, 46/1-2, March-June, 1999, 37-64; *permission received*). The word 'truth' was suspended in religious studies for a long time. The genuine feat was that a particular perception or conviction of truth may colour the value judgment of religious data. However, it is realized that the question of truth cannot be suspended permanently. The word Truth is used in almost all religions and interfaith dialogues. Basically, questions about Truth may be cynical and non-committal as was the case of Pilate, the Roman governor who tried Jesus. Jesus had said that he was the truth and that he witnessed to the truth, and in both sayings he never meant a metaphysical capsule but the powerful in-breaking of the kingdom of God. This came to be taken further in discussions on Christian mission and evaluation of religions. In a remarkable study which is ignored in interreligious discussions, D.G. Moses has dealt with different species of truth and aspects of religious truth. Also there are sayings like 'One Truth–different names' (Rigveda), 'God's name is Truth' (Sikhism), 'Truth is God' (Gandhi) and so on. The contexts of these sayings merit a close look so that their connotations become clear. In interfaith discussions the word 'Truth' is referred to in different senses including the above, but obviously confusion overcomes clarity. A careful study would reveal that Truth can be defined by a set of truths, which are meaningful for human life. Above all while being based on rock-like foundations that have sustained the life of millions for several generations, being open to the unfolding of Truth may prove to be reforming and maturing.

The *ninth* chapter presents a summary of the relationship between the study of religion, religious pluralism and interfaith dialogue. It is beyond doubt that the study of religion, along with international events such as the World Parliament of Religions, missionary encounters with world religions and early theologies of religious pluralism, contributed to interreligious dialogue. The word 'faith' came to be interchangeable with 'religion'. Samartha transformed commitment to mission into engagement in interfaith dialogue but not without Christian witness, and his legacy in the World Council of Churches continues to bear fruit. Thereby he redefined both mission and dialogue. On the age-long Christian approaches and attitudes to people of other faiths and paradigms of religious pluralism I have written at some length. Here I have used the summary of two articles ("Theological Positions in Christian Approach to Religious Pluralism – The Fourth Way", *Arasaradi Journal of Theological Reflection*, XVII/1, Jan-June, 2004, 1-23; "Paradigms of Religious Pluralism: A Clarification", *Ariopagus: Journal of the Association of Faculty for Religion, Philosophy and Culture*, Vol. 1, 2011, 75-84). The popular triple model of the theologies of religious pluralism – exclusivism, inclusivism, pluralism – is shown as shaky and too limited as it has not taken into account different strands of each. Again, perhaps, for the first time we recognize eight paradigms of religious pluralism. Finally, the vexed question about the possibility of religious conversion in the process of interfaith dialogue is taken for a concise discussion. It depends on how serious and committed are those who partner in dialogue and how prepared are they for strong commitment and boundless openness.

Chapter 1

Defining Religion
Attempts and Conclusions

A Significant Realisation

What is religion? Ask this question at the beginning of a class on any study of religion or religions. The answers will vary from simple forms of ritual or prayer, to sophisticated definitions, perhaps including the words 'spirituality', 'faith' and 'moral life'. This may lead you to sidetrack for a while, and ask for a clearer defining of 'spirituality'. If you stick to the question, 'what is religion?' you will encounter a strange moment of silence, bewilderment, mental struggle etc. Then someone in the class might ask you, the teacher, for the answer. If you are honest, you will eventually say, 'I don't know the answer; religion is almost impossible to define conclusively.' This will certainly evoke some amusement, even laughter. To reassure the class and help them realise that this is an important point in the study of religion, you might quote a few scholars. For example, Eric Sharpe, one of the well-known historians of comparative religion, before making a survey of efforts to define religion, observes:

> To spend time discussing definitions of religions might therefore appear to be time wasted, were it not for the fact that one soon discovers in reading or discussion that there is very real disagreement, among believers and students alike, about where religion actually begins and ends. Time and time again, a writer on religion will begin by saying in effect, 'Before I get on my subject, let me tell you what I understand by religion.' A day's work in an average library would produce several dozen statements resulting from this need for explicitness.[1]

[1] Eric Sharpe, *Understanding Religion*, London: Duckworth, 1983, 33.

If one shares this classroom discussion with an ardent devotee or mystic, s/he might ridicule it as quite futile to understand religion by way of definition, claiming it to be an essentially indefinable experience. Then what does a student of religion do? Unless they are wavering enough merely to be immediately initiated into a particular form of mystical experience, with greater humility they will try to understand what the basic characteristics of religious experience are. The student of religion may be tempted to accept generalising claims, such as that in essence and experience all religions are the same. However, if they overcome this temptation and pursue their enquiry they will be amazed by the variety of ways in which mystics of particular religious traditions express their experience and interpret it in relation to other aspects of their religious life – its symbols, myths, rituals and so on.

The recognition that religions are distinctive and that a definition of religion is elusive might look very strange in today's world of religions as well as in the field of religious studies or comparative study of religion. Why is it so, when religion is such an obvious and integral part of human life as history reveals? Whether people affirm the enduring value of religion – despite shattering conflicts of religious history – or pronounce it dead, though with its burial delayed, or see it as a poison for humanity as some social critics proclaim, the persistence of religion in one form or another in the life of individuals and societies is a fact as frustrating for some as it is fascinating for others. In any case, whether as the starting-point of a rigorous study of religion using all the methodological tools developed in the field, or as the basis for a theological investigation into the perplexing reality of religious pluralism, it has to be acknowledged that religion is solidly embedded in the life of millions through the ages, yet is so slippery, evading any definite grasp of its nature and content. The purpose of this chapter is to demonstrate simply and clearly, and press for its acknowledgement, that religion is both elusive and inescapable.

Concrete Terms and Complex Meanings

The Latin word *religio* is the root of the word for religion in many European languages including English. Again, there is no one clear meaning. For example, *The New Shorter Oxford English Dictionary* (1993) gives six meanings.[1] Interestingly, *Webster's Third New International Dictionary* of the same year (1993) gives slightly different sets of meanings.[2] If we consult the secondary meanings

[1] 1. A state of life bound by religious vows; the condition of belonging to a religious order; 2. A peculiar monastic or religious order or rule; 3. Belief in or sensing of some superhuman controlling power or powers, entitled to obedience, reverence, and worship, or in a system defining a code of living; 4. A particular system of such belief; 5. Devotion, fidelity, consciousness and pious attachment; and 6. The sanction or obligation of an oath.

[2] They include: 1. The personal commitment to and serving of God or a god with worshipful devotion, conduct in accord with divine commands as found in accepted sacred writings or declared by authoritative teachers, a way of life recognized as incumbent on true believers, and

and extended meanings given in such dictionaries, the whole exercise will become unbearably cumbersome. Sometimes we come across interpretive meanings of the word 'religion', such as 'that which binds everything together.' Is this meaning of 'religion' only the case with European languages?

There is an initial methodological problem here in importing the word 'religion' into a non-European context. But it is still a useful exercise in exploring how religion is understood as 'a binding force' in other cultures. The Arabic word for religion, *Dīn,* 'covers a semantic range which includes religion, judgment and conduct.' Religion 'rests ultimately on faith (*Imān*), faith that the values and understanding upon which a religious system is based are ultimately trustworthy and true. The root of *Imān* implies 'security, firmness' and ultimately refers to a deep conviction that a particular system of values or worldview is worth staking your life on.'[1] The Muslim focus of faith of course is on Almighty God to whom human beings should submit by way of worshipping and obeying his commands. In this connection the word *Sharī'ah* deserves attention. It originally means 'the path' or 'the way.' 'Within the Islamic religious framework it refers to the way of life to which Muslims should commit themselves, the prescribed set of rules, laws, values, criteria, behavioural patterns and worship practices which are supposed to organize and guide Muslim life both individually and collectively'.[2] There is a binding responsibility on individuals as well as on collective organisations like the state.

In the Indian religious traditions, a different set of terms is used. In Vedic life, which is the most ancient written tradition, two terms are popular. One is *Darśana* which means 'vision'. It signifies the vision of a 'cosmotheandric reality' (to use the coinage of R. Panikkar) in which the universe, gods and human beings co-operate to sustain the complex nexus of life in the universe. The ritual sacrifice is central to the realisation of this vision. The six orthodox metaphysical traditions of Brahmanic Hinduism are also called *Darśana*s. The other word is *Dharma* which, in a comprehensive sense, means 'righteous order' based on the above vision. Regular performance of sacrifice to secure the proper functioning of gods and universe and the stratification of society on the basis of *varna* (the proto-type of the caste system) constitute *dharma*. Later, when God the Supreme became the

---

typically the relating of oneself to an organized body of believers; 2. The state of a religious (e.g. nun); 3. One of the systems of faith and worship including institutionalised expressions, sacred beliefs, observances and social practices found within a given cultural context; 4. The profession or practice of religious beliefs; 5. Scrupulous conformity; 6. A personal awareness or conviction of the existence of a supreme being or of supernatural powers or influences controlling one's own, humanity's or all nature's destiny; and 7. A cause, principle, system of tenets held with ardour, devotion, consciousness, and faith.

[1] Bert F. Breiner, "Secularism and Religion – Alternative Bases for the Quest for a Genuine Pluralism" in *Religion, Law and Society: A Christian-Muslim Discussion*, ed. by Tarek Mitri, Geneva: WCC Publications, 1995, 92f.

[2] Walid Saif, "*Sharī'ah* and Modernity" in Ibid., 11.

ultimate focus of human devotion and action, different ways (*mārgas)* of reaching him were categorised. Traditionally they are three: way of action (karma), both ritual and moral, way of knowledge (jñāna) and way of devotion (bhakti). The priority, sequence or combination is a matter of interpretation. Thus, in Vedic Hindu tradition too religion has binding inclusiveness in its ramifications.

Buddhism inherited the word 'dharma' (*dhamma)* and interpreted it in new ways of which remaining in the path of enlightenment is essential. The emphasis is much more on an interior vision as opposed to the Vedic vision of a ritual-centred universe. A Buddhist commitment requires surrender to Dhamma, Buddha and Sangha (the monastic community). The words 'way' and 'path' are also used in Buddhist circles. Again, the 'way' is inclusive and, 'binding', though such commitment is now made paradoxical – as indeed in the 'end of Vedic religion' (or Vedanta) – for there is an absolute emphasis on interiority and inner liberation.

The words used for religion in different regions and languages of India might shed more light on its meaning. For instance, the Tamil word *camayam* is interpreted in various ways ranging from religious systems or sects to cooking ingredients together, to cultivating persons and societies for adopting good values and some sort of oneness.

It is interesting to note that 'religion' is not a popular word in the Bible although a variety of things we have mentioned above appear in its body. The Greek word (*thrēskeia*) translated as 'religion' occurs only three times in the whole of the New Testament: in the first instance it refers to Judaism (Acts 26: 5), and in the second and third instance it occurs together with an interpretation distinguishing between futile religion that is merely talkative and pure religion which finds expression in looking after orphans and widows in trouble and keeps the practitioner untarnished by the world (Jas. 1: 26, 27). This distinction has become connected with the fierce social critique of religion in the modern world and, consequently, there are not many who are comfortable with the word 'religion'. It has become a dirty word even for those who take religious life seriously. It is frequently claimed that theirs is not a religion but a way of life. We often come across such persons in all religious traditions.

Yet there is another sense in which the term 'religion' is used. This is to do with indicating the majority religion of a particular context or the particular tradition within a religion one belongs to. For example, Henry Fielding in his novel *Tom Jones* makes Parson Thwackum say that 'when I mention religion, I mean the Christian religion; not only the Christian religion but Protestant religion; not only the Protestant religion but the Church of England.' It is taken for granted that when an average European uses the word religion, it invariably means Christianity though it has been changing. This is applicable to the popular use of the word by a Muslim living in a part of the 'Muslim world', so also by a Hindu, Buddhist and so on.

If the story of the meaning of the term 'religion' presents such a diverse picture, how then are we to understand religion? What looks obvious is that religious life is immensely complex, but is also endlessly fascinating as we see in the life and practice of millions of people around the world. The complexity increases when, as is inevitable, we relate religion to culture – another fundamental aspect of human life. Some, for example, see religion as merely part of culture, while others see culture as part of religion. All such perplexing factors must guard anyone against using such terms as 'religion' and 'culture' without explaining the particular meaning with which they are used. With this humble recognition, we turn to the scholarly world of comparative religion or science of religion for understanding further the difficulty of defining religion.

Scholarly Definitions from Particular Perspectives

Our scope is limited to point out only the most typical definitions. For example, one could start from the classical Greek philosopher Plato for whom religion is an *instinct for reality*. All the subsequent searches for reality have something to say about religion. And people who have had penny-dropping, heart-warming or life-transforming experiences have seen in them profound aspects of religion. Although, they might be scholars in their own right in different disciplines, they will not necessarily be scholars of comparative religion. Yet they feel justified in identifying some profound experience as having 'religious' dimension.

There are many casual and passing definitions of religion. For example, in the context of a study of 'sex and sex worship' the following definition is proposed: 'A religion is the form or embodiment which the devotion of a religious mind assumes towards God; it consists of certain rites or ceremonials practised in the worship of God. Cicero defined religion to be reverence for the gods, the fear of God connected with a careful pondering of divine things, piety, religion.'[1] It is not uncommon that ordinary people in their casual conversations, if religion is mentioned, instantly define it in some way, often referring to the sayings of their favourite sages or thinkers.

There are definitions of religion that display different ideological/theological/philosophical biases. For example, Karl Marx (1818-1883), from an extreme socio-economic analytical viewpoint declared that 'Religious distress is at the same time the **expression** of real distress and the **protest** against real distress. Religion is the sigh of the oppressed creature, the heart of a heartless world, just as it is the spirit of a spiritless situation. It is the *opium* of the people.'[2] In a similar spirit, but from the viewpoint of the sole divine revelation being from God, the 'Wholly Other', through Jesus Christ, without any regard for the human capacity to perceive and comprehend but merely to accept with an outstretched

[1] O.A. Wall, *Sex and Sex Worship in the World*, Delhi: Inter-India Publications, 1979, 6.

[2] Quoted, Bas Wielenga, *Introduction to Marxism*, Bangalore: Centre for Social Action, 1984, 338f.

hand, Karl Barth (1886-1968), while recognising the vitality of human life but not being interested in suggesting a comprehensive definition as was in the case of Marx, declared that *religion is unbelief,* it is human rebellion against God. He saw the divine revelation in Jesus Christ beyond religion.[1] For the Process philosopher A.N. Whitehead (1861-1947), 'Religion is what the individual does in his solitariness'. Two German theologians were influenced by two different philosophies. While Romanticism made F. Schleiermacher (1768-1834) say that religion is the feeling of 'absolute dependence', an existentialist bias led P. Tillich (1886-1965) to view it as 'ultimate concern.' From an inter-faith perspective, S.J. Samartha (1920-2001), an Indian scholar, theologian and pioneer of interfaith dialogue, sees the great religious traditions of humanity as different 'responses to the Mystery.' The flow of such position-based definitions has not stopped.

Coming to the notable scholars in the field of comparative religion, not all of them struggle to find a definition of religion. But their search into the origins and essence of religion might provide insights for such a pursuit. Therefore, it would be helpful to distinguish between indirect definitions and direct definitions. First we will briefly point out examples of the first category which are reflected in the way some scholars identified the origin or essence of religion, again depending on the particular perspective from which they have approached the subject, and the data they have handled which came from a particular geographical background.

Herbert Spencer (1820-1904) used the principles of evolution to understand the origin of religion, and origins are presumed to define what is essential. Because he suggested a belief in the continuing existence of the *spirit of ancestors,* his is called the 'ghost theory of the origin of religion.' His simple assertion was: "The rudimentary form of all religions is the propitiation of dead ancestors, who are supposed to be still existing, and to be capable of working good or evil to their descendants."[2] From the perspective of anthropological data and religious speculation, John Lubbock (1834-1913) found *fetishism* as the origin of religion which was succeeded by the stages of totemism, shamanism, anthropomorphism and finally ethical monotheism. In this order it is worth mentioning Edward Tylor's (1832-1917) animism, Andrew Lang's (1844-1912) 'an inscrutable mystery', Robert Marrett's (1866-1943) 'pre-animistic' religion which 'stands for a certain composite or concrete state of mind wherein various emotions and ideas are directly provocative of action.' As an anthropologist, Marrett chose to apply the Melanasian term *mana* to the phenomenon of 'impersonal power' which was later reasserted by phenomenologists like Van der Leeuw (1890-1950). Akin to this is the idea of *Holy* proposed by Rudolf Otto (1869-1937), a phenomenon

---

[1] See J. Hick and B. Hebblethwaite (ed.), *Christianity and Other Religions*, Glasgow: William Collins, 1980, 32-51.

[2] Quoted, Eric Sharpe, *Comparative Religion: A History*, London: Duckworth, 1975, 34; the same ('The Origin of Animal Worship' in *Essays* (1874) source is referred to in the following summary; particularly, see 51f, 61, 66ff, 90, 110 and 208ff.

experienced as both fascinating and terrifying, as a number of biblical narratives illustrate. James Frazer (1854-1941) built on the anthropological school when he suggested *magic* as the origin of religion, this being closely associated with the idea of divine kingship and the concept of the dying and rising god or goddess of vegetation.

The psychological school recognised the human *psyche* as the original seat of religion and of the highly varied forms of religious experience. For example, William James (1842-1910) claimed that even if there was a source of inspiration on high, 'the neurotic temperament would furnish the chief condition of the requisite receptivity.' For Sigmund Freud (1856-1938), from a psychoanalytical point of view, religion originated from 'the projection of infantile dependencies upon imagined super-human beings' which led to feelings of guilt and remorse, the solution of which was found in marking a totem animal. Combining psychology and alchemy, Carl Jung (1875-1961) revealed the existence of 'collective unconscious' which handles the overpowering and destructive *anima* and helps to explore the immemorial treasures of myths, symbols and icons. More recently, scholars like Mercea Eliade (1907-1986) have further built on this revelation combining depth psychology, anthropology and concern for dialogue between different religious traditions.

While the above explorations have brought out profound insights for an understanding of religion in its variety and complexity, and have assumed that their originating source points to religion's defining essence, not all of them have attempted a formal definition as such. Therefore a consultation of a few direct definitions of religion will be in order. Max Müller (1823-1900) is known as the pioneer of the comparative religion or scientific study of religion. Influenced by the streams of German romantic idealism, comparative Indo-European philology and post-Hegelian philosophy of history, Müller found myth to be a disease of language when humans felt constrained by the forces of natural phenomenon. 'Religion', therefore is, 'the perception of the infinite under such manifestations as are able to influence the moral character of man.'[1] Emile Durkheim (1858-1917), who laid the foundation for the sociology of religion has defined religion as 'a unified system of beliefs and practices relative to sacred things, that is to say, things set apart and forbidden – beliefs and practices which unite into one single moral community called a church, all those who adhere to them.'[2] In contrast to this, William James (1842-1910), from a psychological viewpoint, defines religion as, 'the feelings, acts, and experiences of individual men in their solitude, so far as they apprehend themselves to stand in relation to whatever they consider the divine.'[3] Striking a balance between the excesses of individualism

[1] Müller, F.M., *Natural Religion*, New Delhi: Asian Educational Services, 1979, 169.

[2] Durkheim, E., *The Elementary Form of Religious Life* (Eng. tr. 1915, 47); quoted, Sharpe, op.cit., 85.

[3] James, W., *The Varieties of Religious* Experience (1902), 31; quoted, Ibid., p. 111.

and social emphasis, James Pratt (1875-1944) defines religion as 'the serious and social attitude of individuals or communities toward the power or powers which they conceive as having ultimate control over their interests and destinies.'[1] These definitions provide a minimum of examples of attempts to define religion from different perspectives in the early phase of the science of religion. Later developments of these perspectives and more rigorous methods that may make for further refinement would not give a simpler or clearer view of religion.

As distinct disciplinary approaches to the study of religion developed more fully, few have dared to suggest a comprehensive definition of religion, adequate for all religions and for all times. What is usually acknowledged is the possibility of a definition only from a particular perspective. While recognising this fact, Alan Richardson, in his attempt to give a summary of the contemporary debate on religion, in his introductory section gives this definition: 'From an anthropological or sociological standpoint it would be adequate to define religion as man's response to the exigency of the human condition, in which he is driven to seek security, status and permanence by identifying himself with a reality greater, more worthy and more durable than himself.'[2] More recently, from a cultural-linguistic perspective, George Lindbeck has suggested that religion should be seen as

> a comprehensive interpretive scheme, usually embodied in myths or narratives and heavily ritualised, which structure human experience and understanding of self and world...Stated more technically, a religion can be viewed as a kind of cultural and / or linguistic framework or medium that shapes the entirety of life and thought ... Its doctrines, cosmic stories or myths, and ethical directives are integrally related to the rituals it practices, the sentiments or experiences it evokes, the actions it recommends, and the institutional forms it develops.[3]

Cultural anthropologist Clifford Geertz (b. 1926) defines religion as 'a system of symbols which acts to establish powerful, pervasive, and long-lasting moods and motivations in men by formulating conceptions of a general order of existence and clothing these conceptions with such an aura of factuality that the moods and motivations seem uniquely realistic.'[4] The readers must already feel overloaded with overlapping definitions. Certainly some definitions are more comprehensive than others, but the question of full adequacy will continue to remain as long as scholars do not recognise the need for a sense of awe and wonder,

---

[1] Quoted, Ibid., 114.

[2] Alan Richardson, *Religion in Contemporary Debate*, London: SCM Press, 1968, 16.

[3] George Lindbeck, *The Nature of Doctrine*, London: SPCK, 1984, 33f.

[4] C. Geertz, *The Interpretation of Cultures*, London: Fontana, 1993, 90.

the need always to move on with sincere openness instead of pushing through one definition as either the best or one that is most comprehensive.

'Philosophy of Religion' is yet another popular branch of scholarly study. Meaning 'love for wisdom' it asks questions about ways of knowing, coherence of argument and consistency with empirical reality. In this respect it borders with theology, and some famous philosophers are theologians of religions as well. As an example, we briefly mention the approach and views of John Hick (1922-2012), a Christian minister-turned philosopher of religion and theologian of religious pluralism. His influential book *An Interpretation of Religion* (1991) is sub-titled *Human Responses to the Transcendent.* The shift or slip from a definition of religion to theology of religions is evident in this title. For him two definitions of religion could be religious and naturalistic. He recognizes the difficulty of bringing Theravada in as a religion, and is unjustly selective in referring to traditions within a religion or strands within a tradition. This is evident in his treatment of Hinduism as he has taken the tiny philosophical traditions leaving the devotional popular traditions the majority of Indians adhere to. But in general, he is open to the perceptions of the phenomenology of religion. After an extensive discussion on philosophical issues, he concludes the above book with the following words:

> My conclusion, then, is that the differences between the root concepts and experiences of the different religions, their different and often conflicting historical and trans-historical beliefs, their incommensurable mythologies, and the diverse and ramifying belief-systems into which all these are built, are compatible with the pluralistic hypothesis that the great world traditions constitute different conceptions and perceptions of, and responses to, the Real from within the different cultural ways of being human.[1]

Hick's use of alternative words God, Real, Ultimate, Being and Truth is the result of his grappling with the ultimate, cohering centres which he encountered and betrays his Christian starting point and end with an indefinable Real as held by some philosophies.

Building on other views about the indispensable social function of religion and that all religious beliefs are symbolic, Hick notes the functions of religious symbols are fourfold: 'to stimulate the will to moral activity; to bind a community together through its common symbols; to communicate quality of experience which can only be expressed by poetry and symbol; and to open our eyes to the "order of splendor" in the world, comprising nature's more elusive depths

---

[1] J. Hick, *An Interpretation of Religion: Human Responses to the Transcendent*, London: Macmillan, 1991, 375f.

and mysteries.'[1] Perhaps how one's eye is opened is a question for comparative religionists and theologians.

Indian Attempts

First of all, it must be recognised that science of religion has never been a discipline in India though it was the cradle of some of the world's major religious traditions. What is happening, however, particularly in Christian study circles, is that western methods and presuppositions are applied to the study of Indian religious traditions. It has its own limitations, and we have yet to see a distinctive Indian, Asian, or even for that matter African approach to the study of religion. There have been attempts to introduce western methods including a discussion on the definition of religion. For example, Eric Lott, a western scholar who encountered the Indian religious traditions with passionate involvement, has suggested a tool for approaching India's religious traditions. In his opening essay in a volume of this nature, he first raised a warning about the problem of defining religion. He then, however, tentatively suggested a definition that might be 'both sufficiently inclusive and sufficiently focussed to be of some methodological use:'

> Religion is the way humans experience and relate to some sacred Focus (or foci). It is an experience transmitted as a community tradition with sacred symbols, places, times, people and (sometimes) scriptures; it is expressed in rituals, myths, doctrines, and ethical-cultural values; by participating in this constantly adapting tradition perceived human limitations and threats to existence are experienced and overcome or transcended.[2]

Whether or in what way this definition has influenced or guided each essay in the volume is a different question. Even if one is not able to find out the connection, it is revealing that western tools are introduced in the context of the study of Indian religious traditions with special emphasis informed by a long and passionate interaction with those traditions. In due course, however, the same author moved from struggling to give a formal definition to identifying different dimensions of religious life.

At the same time the emphasis on 'experience' in Lott's definition is very relevant in the Indian context where, even in study circles, experience is repeated as the essence of religious life without taking any effort to analyse the nature of that experience. In one of the few attempts to bring together Indian approaches

---

[1] P. Badham (ed.), *A John Hick Reader*, London: Macmillan, 1990, 21 (from "Religion as Fact-Asserting", published originally as two articles in *Theology Today* (1961) and *Theology* (1968). The complete article was included in *God and the Universe of Faiths* (1973, 1988).

[2] Eric J. Lott, "Approaching a Religious Tradition" in *Religious Traditions of India*, ed. by P.S. Daniel, David C. Scott and G.R. Singh, Senate of Serampore College: Indian Theological Library, 1988, 2.

to the study of religion, the participants of the project categorically maintain that experience is the essential core of religious life. It is either re-experiencing an ancient spirituality based on certain sacred acts, or experiencing afresh the fountains of life, which would transcend all logic. There is an assertion that no one can understand religion if one is not having a religious experience oneself.[1] Then it is unrealistic to expect rigorous studies of the 'varieties of religious experience' as done in the West. Indian thinkers seem to call for a different approach not only because of the specific nature of the religious traditions cradled in the sub-continent, but also because of peculiar ways of trying to absorb conflicting differences into a single framework such as life-soul, transcendence, supreme reality or absolute mystery. We will illustrate with the positions of well-known and fairly recent Indian thinkers, most of whom are also Hindu apologists.

Swami Vivekananda (1863-1902) who interpreted the Hindu Vedantic thought for the reformation of the Indian society and who founded the Ramakrishna Mission, had a view of universal religion based on the divinity endowed in every human being. 'Each soul is potentially divine. The goal is to manifest this divinity within by controlling nature, external and internal. Do this either by work or worship or psychic control or philosophy – by one or more or all of these – and be free. This is the whole of religion. Doctrines or dogmas or rituals or books or temples or forms are but secondary details.'[2] Through the experience of a transcendental meditation one can see the unity in all multiplicity. That is the test of true knowledge as well. At the level of personal devotion, Vivekananda held that God is the absolute truth and that truth can be judged by truth alone.

M.K. Gandhi (1869-1948) combined his religious vision with political independence and a just economic structure. For him Hinduism with its essential message of non-violence was the most glorious religion. By means of non-violence only can one attain the goal that is God or Truth. Truth cannot be confined to a perceived fact, accuracy, veracity of statements or logical truth reached by deduction from accepted premises. 'Truth is the sovereign principle which includes numerous other principles. This truth is not only truthfulness in word, but truthfulness in thought also and not only the relative truth of our conception but the absolute Truth, the Eternal principle, that is God.'[3] Non-violence is not only abstaining from harming but also engaging in loving action and is not only the essence of Hinduism but also the essence of all true religion. It is the supreme manifestation of Truth. 'The ultimate definition of religion may be said to be obedience to the law of God. God and his law are synonymous terms. Therefore

---

[1] See the essays in *Approaches to the Study of Religion*, ed. by Harbans Singh, Patiala: Gobindsingh Department of Religious Studies (year not given).

[2] *What Religion is in the Words of Swami Vivekananda*, ed. by Swami Vidyatmananda, Calcutta: Advaita Ashrama, 1998.

[3] M.K. Gandhi, *Autobiography: Or the Story of My Experiments with Truth*, Ahmedabad: Navajivan, 1927/1991, xi.

God signifies an unchanging and living law. No one has really found him. But *avatars* and prophets have, by means of their *tapasya*, given to mankind a faint glimpse of the eternal law.'[1] Gandhi viewed religion from his particular Vaishnava Hindu tradition.

B.R. Ambedkar (1891-1956), a Hindu 'untouchable' was at loggerheads with Gandhi on the question of caste and converted to Buddhism along with millions of his followers. According to a summary of his views on religion,[2] the foundation of it as the vital force or live wire is essential to the life and practices of society. Religion is desirable when it motivates people to establish a society based on liberty, equality and fraternity as components of democracy as noted in the Preamble to the Indian Constitution which he drafted. It stands for an ideal divine governance mediated to create a social and moral order. He refers to Burke who has said, true religion is the foundation of society, the basis on which all true civil government rests. Religion enforces cultural values and promotes nationalism free of exploitation. The aspiration of the masses of India in this regard is reflected in their conversion to Christianity and Islam though Ambedkar himself preferred an indigenous religion such as Buddhism or Sikhism. He first called for reformation within Hinduism, purging it particularly of caste prejudices and structural untouchability. When such legitimate change was not possible, religious conversion was inevitable.

As a poet and thinker Rabindranath Tagore (1861-1941) saw religion as a constant struggle for balance in the spiritual arena of human beings. For him religion in essence is a harmonious whole which cannot be exhausted by its partial manifestations or dimensions. The Vedic orientation and the Bengali Vaishnava tradition helped him to see the ultimate harmony of religious life that includes intense form of devotion. Religion is 'the creative principle of unity, the divine mystery of existence.'[3] God is the Supreme Being in whom all things human in knowledge, will and action, are comprehended and who is the ultimate goal. Self-realisation and devotion are fundamental means to achieve this goal.

Aurobindo Ghose (1872-1950), a spiritual hero and political activist, interpreted religion in terms of integral yoga. He based his ideas on the Upanishadic teaching of Brahman, the transcendental unity and stability lying behind the phenomenal variety and flux. Growing self-awareness with constant recognition of the Supreme Self permeates all areas of life. 'We acknowledge that nothing is likely to become a universal and master impulse in India which is not identified with religion. The obvious course is to recognise that politics is religion and infuse it with the spirit of religion; for that is the true patriotism which sees God as

---

[1] M.K. Gandhi, *India of My Dreams*, New Delhi: Navajivan Publishing House, 1995 (Collection of articles that appeared in *Young India* in 1930s), 75.

[2] See P. Mohan Larbeer, *Abedkar on Religion: A Liberative Perspective*, New Delhi: ISPCK, 2003, 160-185.

[3] R. Tagore, *The Religion of Man*, Boston: Beacon Press, 1961, p. 14f.

the Mother in our country, God as *sakti* in the mass of our countrymen, and religiously devotes itself to their service and their liberation from present suffering and servitude.'[1] Integral yoga helps one to achieve a supreme consciousness oneself and the Supreme Self in the evolutional path towards the Super Mind.

S. Radhakrishnan (1888-1975), a Hindu philosopher and apologetic who held the Spalding Chair in Oxford and came to be the President of India, saw religion as the soul of civilization. For him, 'Religion has been from the beginning the bearer of human culture. It is the supreme achievement of man's profound experience. It is the deepest kind of life reflecting the different phases, complex and conflicting, of human living. Millions of minds, their thoughts and dreams, go to make a religion. A large part of the world received its religious education from India. In spite of continuous struggle with superstition and theological baggage, India has held fast for centuries to the ideals of spirit.'[2] These words are seminal which are explained and interpreted voluminously. Radhakrishnan claims that Hinduism represents best the essence of a world religion with its complex variety yet leading to the concrete spirit or the Absolute real. For him the non-dualist world-view and experience provide most authentic framework for a unified spirituality and universal religion.

All these five Hindu thinkers have viewed religion from the perspective of the pan-mythic religious traditions of India which, in their view, culminate in the mystical experience of oneness with the supreme being. They do not show any interest to study the nature and phenomenal variety of religious experience as has been attempted in the scholarly tradition of the West. While western scholarship has taken the Hindu religious traditions seriously, on the whole, the Hindu side has remained faithful to the position of the above thinkers repeating words such as essence, way of life and spiritual experience. One may argue that the main reason for these thinkers holding on tightly to the Vedantic view of ultimate unity was to counter the claims of Islam and Christianity for 'one truth-one religion' in their distinctive ways. The framework of one truth-many religions is most popular among people of the sub-continent ranging from illiterate masses to educated thinkers. In a veiled form this framework has influenced some Indian Christian theologians as well. For example, Stanley Samartha (1920-2001), taking insights from Vedantic responses to Christ which he studied thoroughly, western views of religious pluralism and interfaith dialogue of which he was a pioneer in the ecumenical movement, has written for a controversial book. Noting the claims and counter-claims of different religions about their truth-value, he says:

[1] Sri Aurobindo, *Birth Centenary Library*, Pondicherry: Sri Aurobindo Ashram Trust, 1971, Vol. 1, 235.

[2] S. Radhakrishnan, *Eastern Religions and Western Thought*, New Delhi: Oxford University Press, 2000 (ninth impression), 116.

> And yet for new relationships between different religious communities it is not just a matter of political adjustments or redistribution of economic resources. Deep down, it is a theological question seeking to relate different responses to the Mystery of Truth.[1]

Can one establish that different religious traditions and their quests are different responses to the same 'mystery of truth'? We will elaborate this question later. What we observe here is that such frameworks or positions give no motivation to study and define one's own religion and understand the distinctiveness of other religious traditions. Nowhere else is it prevalent as in India. It may be argued that if there can be interreligious understanding there can very well be interreligious attempts to define religion as well.

Miscellaneous Definitions and a New Suggestion

It has been customary to give or quote a definition of religion in materials on religion in general and religions in particular. Writers seem to be keen on consulting definitions even if they may not suit their particular perspective (if at all there is one) and interpretation. For example, as early as 1935 R.E. Hume writing on living religions opened the discussion with his own definition of religion:

> Religion is so simple that any intelligible child, as well as an adult, may have a religious experience. Religion is also so inclusive and complex that it needs to be analyzed, so as to be completely understood and fully enjoyed. It may be defined in simple terms as that aspect of a person's experience, including his thoughts, feelings, and actions, whereby he endeavours to live in relationship with what he deems to be the Divine, *i.e.,* the supremely worthful Power controlling in the world ... From a psychological point of view, religion is partly intellectual, partly emotional, and partly an act of will. But religion involves more than merely a subjective experience. It always has some reference to an object of faith and of worship. What constitutes a person's religion is his belief in some God, or gods, and his experience of that God, or gods. What differentiates one particular religion from another is the kind of deity in which its adherents believe and the kind of human experience which appropriately follows from that belief.[2]

Hume then quotes nine definitions by others. Apart from the central foci we have already given, the following are significant: mental faculty to apprehend the Infinite; worship of higher powers from the sense of need; synthesis between destiny and opposing influences; consciousness of the highest social values;

[1] S.J. Samartha, "The Cross and the Rainbow: Christ in a Multireligious Culture" in *The Myth of Christian Uniqueness*, ed. by J. Hick and P. Knitter, London: SCM Press, 1987, 72.

[2] R.E. Hume, *The World's Living Religions*, New York: Charles Scribner's Sons, 1935, 2f.

individual experience of the divine; whole bearing of humans towards what seems to them the Greatest; and togetherness of dependence, responsibility and communion.[1] In the light of several other definitions in this chapter and analysis in the whole book one cannot but surmise that significant strides have been made in the study of religion made since the above was observed.

Consulting definitions, both old and new, have continued in modern presentations of religion. While introducing the study of religion a group of five teachers of religion have reproduced the following definitions (one or two we have seen earlier) in a box at the beginning of which they give the question: 'Analyze the definitions which follow, and if possible and discuss them with another person. After reading each definition consider: does the definition accord with the way you have been accustomed to think about religion? Why, or why not? Would you be able to use it as a framework for describing the religious experience of people you know? Why, or why not?

1. Religion is a "feeling of absolute independence." Religion is "the consciousness that the whole of our spontaneous activity comes from a source outside of us."
   (Friedrich Schleiermacher, 1768-1834, theologian)
2. Religion is "an institution of culturally patterned interaction with culturally postulated superhuman beings."
   (Melford Spiro, contemporary anthropologist)
3. "Religion is the aspect of depth in the totality of the human spirit." "Religion is an expression of ultimate concern."
   (Paul Tillich, 1886-1965, theologian and philosopher)
4. Religion is "the recognition of all duties as divine commands."
   (Immanuel Kant, 1724-1804, philosopher)
5. Religion is "a set of symbolic forms and acts that relate man to the ultimate conditions of his existence."
   (Robert Bellah, contemporary sociologist)'[2]

It will be an enriching experience to hear or read their answers to the given questions about these definitions. 'This book is an introductory college text book on the study of religion' in the American context. It will be rewarding to collect and analyze such definitions in flooding the books on the study of religion. Compared to the definitions we referred to earlier, the above definitions cover very limited concerns. Can we formulate a comprehensive definition of religions which will cover the experiences and expressions of all religious communities in all regions and all ages? We are already feeling the finitude of search and research.

---

[1] Ibid., 5f.

[2] N.C. Ring et.al., *Introduction to the Study of Religion*, Maryknoll: Orbis Books, 1998, 63.

Finally, a decade ago there appeared in America a huge volume entitled *Religion, Beyond a Concept* containing the result of the most extensive study of contemporary approaches to religion, its definition and various aspects. It is acknowledged that religion is complex, perplexing and unpredictable. In his 98 page long introduction the editor notes:

> This much is certain: no simple linear narrative or causal explanation, least of all a logic of progressive mythologization, disenchantment, and secularization is capable of assigning a clear universal designation to any 'concept' of religion. A different logic of attribution and acknowledgement can be found at work in the redistribution of its meaning, uses, and abuses, at least now, at the outset of the twenty-first century.[1]

A fuller understanding of religion can be achieved only by an interdisciplinary approach with an international outlook. As acknowledged, religion is a 'saturated' phenomenon, and yet is beyond the full grasp of its perplexing manifestations. It is clear that consulting various definitions of religion does not make the issue simpler as the word is used to indicate wide ranging phenomena, from fetish belief to political nationalism. The perceived essence and manifestation of religion by phenomenology has not escaped scrutiny. Every particular location needs a distinctive method which requires responsibility and openness.

As observed, in modernity multiple forms in a global system are already emerging. 'Under conditions of globalization, moreover, all the world religions draw not only upon their own traditions but also increasingly upon one another. Inter-civilizational encounters, cultural imitations and borrowings, hybridity, creolization, and cross-cultural hyphenations are as much part and parcel of global life as present Western hegemony, cosmopolitan homogenization, religious fundamentalism, or the clash of civilizations.'[2] These develop side by side with provincialising God and untranslatable religious experiences. There is an ambivalent movement of religion from the past to the present, with aspirations for the future also evident. While the question of 'after theism' is raised on the one hand, there are also strong affirmations concerning the active presence of God in the world and individual lives, on the other.

Further study is recommended to find out how spirituality is socially constructed and transmitted when it is introduced to the public domain. On the whole the volume may be seen as a commentary on the statement: 'religion is immensely complex and immeasurably varied' (Eric Lott). However, the book furthers modern interpretations of religion which border around what is known

---

[1] Hent de Vries (ed.), *Religion, Beyond a Concept*, New York: Fordham University Press, 2008, 2.

[2] Ibid., 119.

as 'implicit religion.' However, thankfully, there is no claim that this in any way exhausts the subject.

Concluding Remarks

Even the limited survey we have made on attempts to define religion from different perspectives shows that religious life is immensely complex and immeasurably varied. While 'religion' still evades most satisfying definition, there are attempts to identify and explain different dimensions of religion such as ritual, mythical, experiential and ethical as we will see in the next chapter. Again a separate study of these attempts would reveal the difficulty of finding their coherence within each religion as well as in comparison with others. Further, because some 'secular' world-views and practices share some fundamental dimensions of religion they have been called 'quasi-religions'; communism, fascism and nationalism are primary examples. In the context of people leaving the established and explicit religion, as noticed worldwide, there is a search for transcendental meaning, the words 'implicit religion' and 'secular spirituality' and even 'no religion' are becoming popular. We have devoted a chapter for this type of religion.

While attempts to define religion from different perspectives are continuing, inter-faith relations promise a great contribution. True inter-faith relations are based on commitment and openness. While each partner in this relationship remains deeply committed to his/her own grounding and starting point of religious life guided by particular visions, experiences and traditions, they honestly search for the new avenues of the unfolding of the Concrete Spirit, Absolute Reality or God. Neither nominal members of a particular religion, nor fanatics of a particular movement are appropriate candidates for such a pursuit. In a safe space with independence there should be an urge to pursue what religion is or it can be. On the whole, at the moment, the fundamental essence of religion is still elusive, but different manifestations are observable and sharable. It is reasonable to conclude that the origin and essential nature of religion remains a mystery for scholarly study, as well as for lay understanding of religion, just as does the origin and purpose of human life for science. However, transcendental awareness or sacred focus or spiritual dimension, if held to be obvious and non-negotiable, it seems that scientific study of religion itself may not be adequate for a lively expression and convincing interpretation. It has to be left to be experienced within a particular religious grounding and theological interpretation unless it is done as an academic exercise just as many cases of sociology of religion appear. That requires a separate discussion.

Chapter 2

Dimensions and Dynamics of Religion

Yet Another Way of Looking at Religion

Efforts at precisely defining religion continue, and approaches to the study of religion continue to grow. Religious life is immeasurably complex, and attempts to simplify it result in further complication rather than clarification. As such, another attempt has been made, that is to identify and illustrate the basic aspects, modes, or, more popularly, *dimensions* of religion. Again there is no promise of consistency among scholars. As we will point out, there have been changes in the understanding even by a particular scholar.

In this chapter, we will first consult different enumerations of the essential 'dimensions' of religion, and in passing pointing out some illustrations of these. Then we will look at how uniquely complex are developments within the Semitic and Indian traditions. This would suggest that simple classification of religion's 'dimensions' could miss out important dynamics within a particular religious tradition. Throughout we will point out tendencies towards reductionism with regard to these dimensions. In other words, in the name of Truth, spirituality, experience or ethics, religious life has tended to be understood essentially in terms of one or more of its complex aspects.

The Enumeration of 'Dimensions'

Scholars differ in what they recognise as the essential dimensions of religion. For example, 'Frederick Streng describes religion in terms of its three primary dimensions: the personal, the cultural and the ultimate,' while sociologists 'Charles Glock and Rodney Stark identify five distinct dimensions: the experiential, the ideological, the ritualistic, the intellectual and the consequential.'[1]

---

[1] Referred, Peter Connolly (ed.), *Approaches to the Study of Religion*, London: Cassell, 1999, 6.

Eric Sharpe describes four 'modes' of religion: existential, intellectual, institutional and ethical.[1] Before he presents these 'modes', he refers to Ninian Smart's highly popular and original classification of six dimensions of religion: doctrinal, mythological, ethical, ritual, experiential and social. Though he acknowledges that these represent 'a new and creative way of looking at the totality of religious belief and practice' as often quoted approvingly, Sharpe expresses his unhappiness with it. This is for two reasons. The first is that the way in which it is set out leads one to suppose 'that the lower the number, the more important the element in question: the parahistorical appears to be more important than the historical, doctrine more important than myth and ethics, and so on.' Second, more seriously, he wonders whether all of these 'dimensions' in fact fall into the same type of category. Two of them at least, the mythological and ritual dimensions, appear to him 'to be more matters of *content* than do the other four'. If myth and ritual are to be accepted as 'dimensions' of religion, then, for him, there are other, similar 'dimensions', which deserve serious consideration as well. 'It could be said, for instance, that there is a legal dimension, a musical dimension, a symbolical dimension, a spatial dimension, and many more such dimensions. But it would be hard to maintain that there is a musical or a legal *mode*, which is an intrinsic part of the structure of religion, without which it cannot be understood.'[2] For Sharpe, myth and ritual can be taken out of religion altogether as they are observable phenomena, which can be analysed in his scheme of functional modes.

Sharpe presents four modes: existential, intellectual, institutional and ethical. They are interrelated in the sense that each would include the other. He observes that all modes cannot be equal because a mode such as dealing with the supernatural or transcendent may be more dominant than or the gateway to others. In his explanation he calls the existential mode 'the circle of faith' as it is purely the individual aspect of religion including faith and all forms of experience. The intellectual mode he calls 'the circle of beliefs' as it is 'the formulation of statements *about* the supernatural or the transcendent order.' The creeds of the Christian Church fall into this category. The institutional mode he calls 'the circle of organisations.' They are both natural organisations beginning with original families, tribes or castes, and voluntary organisations, assemblies of individuals and families who have at some stage chosen to join them at conversion or migration. The ethical mode Sharpe calls 'the circle of duties' which focus on human conduct in response to a transcendental vision. None of the four modes, he emphasises, exists in total isolation from the others. Though it is not easy, the particular student has to choose to study what s/he is attracted to or interested in.

Comparison between different classifications of dimensions or modes of religion might complicate the matter and therefore it is profitable to keep

[1] E.J. Sharpe, *Understanding Religion,* London: Duckworth, 1983, 95ff.

[2] Ibid., 94.

Smart's enumeration as basic. Interestingly we notice change and expansion in his enumeration. But first we shall look at a few attempts to build on Smart's early classification. Eric Lott, who accepts his teacher Smart's original list of six, adds five further essential modes of religion.[1] Religion, he argues, is invariably characterised by organic structure, dynamic process, by a symbolist and aesthetic character, and by the central role of some sacred object or sacred focus. Of these the organic structure closely relates to Smart's social dimension and Sharpe's organisational mode, though Lott's point more concerns the integrated interconnecting of all other 'dimensions'. Symbolic and aesthetic dimensions are newly recognised although they can be seen in part as connected to Smart's myth and experience. Similarly sacred object or sacred focus may be taken for granted as fundamental and permeating all religious life and experience, though it has to be said that it is precisely why Lott lists these aspects of religion as irreducible dimensions that are often *not* taken for granted. What is most significant in Lott's additions is what he describes as the 'dynamic process' invariably characterising religion, and we will come back to this later.

More recently, Frank Whaling in his essay on theological approaches to religion mentions in passing eight elements of each religious tradition, acknowledging the need for different orders of priority depending on the different weight given in a particular tradition. They are: community, ritual, ethics, social and political involvement, scripture, concepts or doctrines, aesthetics and spirituality.[2] Apart from a few new terms used there is no dimension that is entirely new. So, instead of proceeding with such listing, for the sake of clarity and brevity we return to Smart's enumeration of the dimensions of religion.

As we have already indicated, there was a change or growth in the way Smart himself identified the dimensions of religion. In 1969, in his seminal publication on religious life, Smart mentions six dimensions as noted above.[3] In a publication twenty years later, he put a combination or alternative word for each of the six dimensions and introduced a seventh. The six dimensions are: the practical or ritual, experiential and emotional, narrative or mythic, doctrinal and philosophical, ethical and legal, and the social and institutional. The seventh one newly introduced is the material dimension meaning the material forms such as buildings, works of art, icons and other creations.[4] Yet seven years later, in

---

[1] E.J. Lott, *Vision, Tradition, Interpretation: Theology, Religion and the Study of Religion*, Berlin: Mouton de Gruyter, 1987, 30ff.

[2] F. Whaling, "Theological Approaches" in P. Connolly (ed.), op. cit., 233.

[3] N. Smart, *The Religious Experience of Mankind*, Glasgow: Collins Fount Paperbacks, 1969, 15ff.

[4] N. Smart, *The World's Religions*, Cambridge: Press Syndicate of the University of Cambridge, 1995 (reprint), 12-21.

his book sketching an inventory of what he calls 'Dimensions of the Sacred,'[1] more extensive than all he had written before on the subject, Smart adds two dimensions which for him are most basic: the political and economic. But strangely, in this book the final chapter is on the political effects of religion, and the whole economic dimension is left out! However, there are passing references to attitudes and exchange of economics, which we will point out in due course.

Now the question is whether Smart's inventory exhausts all the dimensions of religion. Before we survey the illustrative elucidation of his eight dimensions and offer some explanation of the ninth, I want to suggest two more dimensions of religion, which are important. One relates to *geography*, the other to *language*. The places of the origin of a religion or a cult are held as special by the respective religious communities. Thus Sarnath is important for the Buddhists, Varanasi for the Hindus, Jerusalem for Jews and Christians (also Muslims), Mecca for the Muslims and Amritsar for the Sikhs. Further, there are several places marked as the birthplaces of gods in Hinduism such as Ayodhya (Rama) and Brindavan (Krishna) or sacred places of pilgrimage. Similarly, there is the idea of holy language. Sanskrit, Pali, Hebrew, Greek, Latin, Arabic and Gurmukhi come to the mind. Where translations are now accepted as equally authentic as the original, reciting or hearing the original is given special significance.

Dimensional Analysis with Illustrative Elucidation

To start with we will follow the order and treatment of dimensions mentioned in Smart's *Dimensions of the Sacred*, particularly that of the chapters which, again interestingly, is different from the listing in the 'Introduction.'[2] This will be followed by a brief introduction to other dimensions we have mentioned above. We have place only to list the correlations Smart makes and a summary of the explanatory theses he provides. Our evaluation of such a pattern of treatment will be part of the next section.

---

[1] N. Smart, *Dimensions of the Sacred: An Anatomy of the World's Beliefs*, London: Fontana Press, 1996.

[2] The 'Introduction' mentions the ritual or practical dimension, the doctrinal or philosophical dimension, the mythic or narrative dimension, the experiential or emotional dimension, the ethical or legal dimensions, the organisational or social component, the material or artistic dimension. After mentioning some orthodox Christian themes, Smart notes seven religious dimensions evident in the nationalism of the United States. Then he discusses the relationship of the dimensions to the following disciplines: textual and philosophical studies, anthropology and sociology, psychology and psychoanalysis, history, philosophy, art history and the material dimension, theology, political science, and economics and various exchanges. After raising questions about ancient and modern, he introduces his attempts to 'supply correlations ... offering incipient explanatory theses' with a view not to make things tidy but to make them better patterned'. See ibid., 1-25. But the chapters follow the following order: 'doctrine, philosophy & 'some dimensions', the ritual dimension, the mythic or narrative dimension, the experiential & emotional dimension, the ethical & legal dimension, the social dimension, the material dimension, the political effects of religion.

1. Smart's treatment of 'doctrine, philosophy and some dimensions' starts with a clarification of the relationship between religion and theism. Theism is not a natural and consistent corollary to religion as is evident in the Theravada sect and Madhyamika, one of the mainstream forms of Mahayana Buddhism, which does not believe in God as the supreme. The Dalai Lama has openly declared, 'We Buddhists are atheists.' At the same time such Buddhists extol spirituality and transcendental awareness. And there is no dearth of mythic narratives of celestial beings, including gods of various rank and order, with devotion and rituals related to them, in the Buddhist traditions. This is true of the Jaina traditions as well.

There are two doctrines that relate to the supreme beings and to ethics and outlooks on life, in ways which are comparable between traditions. Thus, Christians have a vision of Trinity signifying the intimacy of the three Persons, to express perfect love and inspire Christians to grow towards intimate *communion with this triune God.* The three-body or three-aspect doctrine (*trikāya*) of Mahayana Buddhism stands for the unification of three 'decks' of focus and practice. The bottom deck is the world of rebirth in a chain of several births; at the next deck some Buddhas are celestial beings like gods having the power to bless their devotees; finally at the uppermost deck there is the truth body of the Buddha, which is identifiable with emptiness. Mythic narratives find berths in the first two decks, as the final form and experience are ineffable. Trinity and Trikāya are comparable but caution needs to be exercised. Similarly there are doctrines about creation, soul and afterlife, with internal variety, as in the case of the Hindu religious traditions. So, there is the possibility of external comparison with such doctrines of other religions.

2. The ritual dimension too relates to other dimensions of religious life. There are many types of ritual, the most important being 'focused' ritual and 'harnessing' ritual or yogic ritual. In the first type the ritual activity is addressed to sacred beings, such as gods or ancestors. The second type helps to control the body and senses and leads to the achieving of higher states of consciousness. There is a manipulative character in ritual and religious traditions, which have developed a counter force to check this.

One theory of ritual is that in a communal context of rivalry, tensions can be mitigated if aggressive impulses are directed towards a scapegoat. Then the scapegoat becomes sacred and saviour. Jesus is compared to a scapegoat whose death became an atoning sacrifice. Some rituals re-enact the cosmic process of creation and recreation while others help transformation in the passing stages of human life; the latter are called the rites of passage. Some rituals not only help devotion but also themselves become devotional acts. Where scripture is ritualised by giving special place and honour, the very veneration of the scripture leads to a moral life according to its prescriptions. Thus, in varying ways the ritual dimension interlocks with other dimensions in religious life.

3. Myths, despite various interpretations, primarily stand for imaginative narratives of the past including primordial time and particular periods in sacred, sacralised history. There are fanciful myths creating a sense of awe and wonder about the primordial and its perplexing reality, and there are factual myths, which give new meanings to an event. One theme connected with myth is that of space containing a sky that is low down and inhabited by God in order to be close to the human race, as projected by a number of African myths. Mythic narratives provide motivation for existential concerns and models for imitation.

4. The experiential and emotional dimension manifests in different ways. For example, it can be a *mysterium tremendum et fascinans* that is just a feeling of the Other, or as inspiring obedience to act, or it can be a feeling of oneness with the supreme being and her world as closely related or embodied. Thus there are three primary varieties of religious experience – the numinous, the panenhenic and monistic. Although, some claim that all mystics speak the same language as a supportive point for reiterating the theology of 'one truth or essence – many religions', as far as we can observe, their religious orientation, growth and expression are different depending on the particular religious traditions they belong to and on the particular contexts in which they have lived.

5. The ethical and legal dimension is as popular as it is diverse. Every religion, through its scriptures and traditions, prescribes certain rules or commandments to regulate their life in the world. We have morals applicable to individual life and ethical values applicable to the religious community concerned. On the basis of these morals and ethical values legal systems are created and they operate differently in different contexts. There are common values such as love, justice and peace owned by all religions. However, the way each of such values is understood and embodied in a legal system depends on the situation. They may be interpreted differently by different sects or experts of the same sect. In contexts such as India there is a division of Criminal Law and certain aspects of Civil Law, and Personal Law. The former governs all people while the latter is different between major religious traditions – Hindu, Christian, Muslim – as it is used to govern matters of family, inheritance and marriage. Buddhists, Jains and Sikhs are governed by the Hindu Personal Law and this has created tension in the context of the search for distinctive identities. There are certain issues, which create dilemmas and difference of opinion in every religious tradition such as the use of violence, birth control, abortion methods, prolongation of life, the discrimination of sex in babies before birth and transplants of vital organs. Ethics motivated by religious teachings continue to be debated with reference to war, foreign policy, trade rules, medical ethics and so on.

6. The social dimension has to do with living together as a religious community, with group feeling or vision, and the method of organisation and governance. Some religious traditions celebrate the founders – prophets, leaders, prophets, sages and teachers. The way their movement developed, the dilemma

it faced and the structure it established are interesting topics for study. There are new sets of figures to nurture and lead the present communities, and they include priests, preachers, pastors, teachers and imams. Some religious communities insist on or prefer theocracy while others are content to live in a secular and multi-religious atmosphere. There are different forms of monarchy, and similarly there are different forms of democracy as well. Decisive moments of changes or reformation can be traced in every religious tradition. In today's world finding the best form of religious identity continues to be a struggle along with the search for the best form of polity.

7. As we have already noted, in addition to the above, and representing a certain modification and elaboration of the six dimensions he identified in 1969, Ninian Smart introduced a new one called the 'material dimension.' In the introduction to his *The Dimensions of the Sacred* he mentions 'the material or artistic dimension' as the seventh one, and the seventh chapter is titled 'material dimension' and starts by mentioning idols, symbols, sacraments, sacrifice, focal points of worship and the deification of certain aspects of the environment (mountain, sea, wind etc.), aniconic religions and natural objects.

Where he first introduced the material dimension[1] as the seventh one Smart saw the material form as an incarnation of the 'social or institutional dimension' of religion. It includes buildings, works of art, and other creations, which find expression in a wide range of ways from simple forms without representations to an elaborate array of icons and idols. Other important material expressions of religion, for Smart, are those natural features of the world which are singled out as being of special sacredness and meaning – the river Ganges, the Jordan, the sacred mountains of China, Mount Fuji in Japan, Ayers Rock in Australia, the Mount of Olives, Mount Sinai, and so forth. Sometimes of course these sacred landmarks combine with more direct human creations, such as the holy city of Jerusalem, the sacred shrines of Banaras, or the temple at Bodh Gaya which commemorates the Buddha's Enlightenment.

We will come back to some of these 'material facts' when we introduce the geographic dimension. In *Dimensions of the Sacred,* however, Smart mentions the material dimension as comprised of various aspects such as buildings for worship and ritual, sanctuary and paintings, the uniform and vestments of priests, books, amulets, graves, burning-ghats, sacrificial animals and the like. He also briefly discusses royal patronage to religions, patterns of temples, synagogues, churches and mosques, pilgrimage places, the significance of holy books, paintings and sculptures. He concludes the section with the following words:

> It is obvious that the richer the ritual and the stronger the demand for art works to decorate religious buildings, the greater the importance of wealth for rulers who patronize religion and the greater the need

[1] N. Smart, *The World's Religions,* 20f.

> for contributions to sacred causes. It is an interesting irony that it was this demand which led to the unveiling of Catholic corruption which sparked off the Protestant revolt and with it the Reformation. It is also clear that the more impressive the demand for royal temples enhancing the ritual links between heaven and earth, the stronger the ideology of cosmic kingship needs to be. The material dimension is a reinforcement of cosmology. The impressiveness of the institution is registered through vestments, relics, jewels, glittering divinities, glorious statues, soaring buildings. In effect the material dimension is both congealed ritual and conceptual hardware.[1]

Actually, as promised in the introduction, economic and political dimensions are newly introduced as eighth and ninth in his progressive identification of dimensions of religion, but are treated rather at random. As is clear in the foregoing, some of the economic aspects are mentioned in the material dimension.

Smart has mentioned 'Economics and various exchanges' as closely associated with dimensions of religion, and they are closely related to the material dimension.

Although, religionists have not much interested themselves in economics it is a fruitful subject in relation to worldviews, ranging from such expansive theses as Weber's concerning Protestantism and the rise of Capitalism to current thinking about Confucian values in the East Asian economic upsurge. But it also embraces deeper questions of exchange: for example, consider ways in which lay Buddhists give material goods such as robes and food to monks in exchange for moral instruction and enhancement of their own merit.[2]

There is great scope to develop a more thorough understanding of the economic dimension since no religion or religious movement, even the most austere one, is free from money and property in its structural or institutional life. Then the question will be, how much they own, how do they mobilise material resources and how do they connect it with religious commitment and spirituality?

8. The political dimension also is treated by Smart somewhat randomly. We have already mentioned some aspects of it when we mentioned the social or organisational dimension and the material dimension. Political science deals with partly the connection of religious traditions with politics and the political ideologies they have developed. The modern phenomenon of religion's both positive and manipulative play in politics is studied by those working in the field of sociology of religion. Smart mentions in passing the political structure in the aura of which major religions were born and flourished such as imperial Rome and

[1] N. Smart, *Dimensions of the Sacred,* 287f.

[2] Ibid., 21.

its modern equivalent. More passionately, he observes the demographic changes in the heartlands, the change of balance of the south and north in Christianity, the religion of migrants and the diaspora, and the new tension and conflicts emerging. At the same time he asks for a more dialogical existence trying to see the possibility of creating a dialogical faith (especially between Christians and Muslims) and working together to narrow down the widening gap between the rich and the poor.

We leave Smart at this point in our discussion of the dimensions of religion. Though he deserves the credit for initiating this way of looking at religion his is not the most systematic treatment, nor does he claim it to be so. He is generous in acknowledging that his is one way of approaching the religious life and in encouraging other ways of doing so. One scholar who directly builds on Smart's enumeration of dimensions is his student Lott as we have noted. We have already mentioned his elaboration of these dimensions. To tidy up the order of dimensions I want to suggest that his seventh one on organic structure and interdependence or interconnectedness may be included in the social or organisation dimension. Even if one takes the interlocking of dimensions as another aspect of interconnectedness, it is almost impossible to find the same links and sequences are evident as common in all religious traditions. The ninth on religion's symbolist character and the tenth on its aesthetic character are included in the material dimension by Smart. The eleventh concerning the central role of some sacred object or sacred focus seems a general feature that permeates all dimensions of religious life in one way or another, though Lott himself claims that because the study of religion so often ignores this essential and identifiable factor in religious life, a viable methodology somehow needs systematically to draw attention to it. My own assessment is that the most important dimension (eighth) Lott mentions is that of religion's *dynamic process*. We will elaborate this in the next section.

In the meantime, as we noted earlier, we have to recognise two important dimensions – geographical and linguistic – and they will be tenth and eleventh, following the enumeration of Smart. Sometimes, these two are mentioned as parts of the cultural dimension, which is integral to religion. Therefore it is in order to discuss briefly the nature and meanings of culture, which not only relates to religion in an integral way, but also includes geography and language as two major focal points.

9. We come now to the cultural dimension. Though Smart mentions 'cultural blocks' with geographical boundaries where religions hold identities of varying magnitude, he does not discuss culture in relation to religion in any detail. Earlier, Eric Sharpe initiated a discussion of 'religions and cultures.'[1] He argues that if 'we narrow down religion to its existential mode, claiming it to be entirely a matter of the individual's relationship on the spiritual plane with the power which created and which governs the universe, then there is no particularly compelling

[1] This is the title of chapter nine of E. Sharpe, *Understanding Religion*, 125-142.

reason why religion … should have any cultural dimension at all'. Though one cannot but touch on religion's cultural plane for a reasonable account of religion, the way the relationship between the two operates is difficult to discern. 'On the opposite wing of opinion are those who maintain with equal force that nothing … observable in religion can be separated from the cultural forms in which it expresses itself.' But whether components of a culture such as ideas, rituals, customs etc. contribute to the formation of a religious tradition or the other way round is hard to generalise. The basic problem is to achieve a precise definition of culture. As Sharpe observes,

> It is almost as difficult to arrive at an adequate definition of culture as it is of religion. In a 1960 article Albert C. Cafagna quoted a large number of sociological definitions, most of which had at least this much in common, that they saw culture as a type of learned behaviour, a matter of transmitted social learning', involving the passing on of ideas by various means – verbal, symbolical, imitation, and so on. Ideas are therefore of central importance … (as in) the German … definition of *Kultur* as 'the totality of typical life-forms of a community, including its spiritual/intellectual system … and especially its scale of values.[1]

Compared to an Indian attempt at collecting various definitions of culture, both western and Indian, this is very minimal.[2] Moreover, as pointed out by Sharpe, 'cultures are no more static than are religion, and they must not be approached as though they were fixed, permanently formed entities, each having its own immutable shape and content.' This is not to deny strands of resistance to changes within and without. We will elaborate this point when we discuss the dynamic process.

The constituent elements of culture include religion or a sect, geography, history, language, music, arts and architecture and forms of ethical and moral values as well as certain nuances expressed in conversations and jokes. One has to take a particular issue for discussion so that the enigmatic and changing connection between that aspect of religion and culture becomes clear. For example, as Sharpe points out, the German Lutheran missionaries in Hindu India saw caste as a 'social, cultural institution having religious overtones,' whereas British missionaries on the whole saw it 'as a religious institution which apparently denied the idea of the universal brotherhood of man.' The consequence of these views and their continued effect in the Indian church is a different story.

More than any other religious traditions, Christianity has initiated discussions on faith or gospel and culture. Ecumenically, in recent discussions

[1] Ibid., 126.

[2] See K.P. Aleaz, *The Gospel of Indian Culture*, Calcutta: Punthi Pustak, 1994, 1-96.

on the gospel and culture,[1] western culture is identified with the gospel, and 'cultures' are normally the cultures of the 'Third World.' Nevertheless it has been clarified that the gospel was never culture-free and that while there are gospel-friendly values being cherished in other cultures, western culture has acquired many characteristics, which are unfriendly to the gospel. Some theologians have even used the term 'the pagan west' concerning the post-modern world. Hence, the growing movement of 'the gospel and contemporary culture.'[2] And also in the wake of globalisation there is an attempt to homogenise one politically and economically dominant culture as though it is of cosmic standard (e.g. Macdonaldisation). At the same time, interestingly, using its advantages, some traditionally 'alien cultures' (like India's) are busy selling their emotional and behavioural products such as dietary regulations and yoga in the name of holistic health and art of living.

This is not the place to discuss the impact of secularisation on religion as there is a chapter devoted to it. What is noteworthy, however, is that its impact on culture and its relationship with religion provide an interesting scenario for students and researchers of religion. Sharpe observes:

> For as secularisation advances, cultures become more and more fragmented and unstable; old authorities are challenged; mobility increases; functions previously performed by religion (education, Medicine, some degree of political control, the transmission of unquestioned values) are shifted to newer, secular agencies; priest-kings are replaced by constitutional monarchs or elected representatives; decisions are arrived at (at least in theory) by popular consensus. Religion then becomes only one part of the totality we call culture, but very often an isolated part which, however hard it may try to maintain contact with other parts of the totality, often fails precisely because those who run the remainder have either lost touch with the world of religion altogether or view it too narrowly.[3]

This observation of course comes from the west. The Asian and African situations, while being affected by the process of secularisation, have responded to its effect differently. The revival of African traditional religions, of the Orthodox Church in the former Communist block and of Hinduism in the name of cultural nationalism are examples. And religious traditions that have moved from their homeland to other lands through migration, trade, imitation, conquest, mission and the like have responded in yet another way by keeping the original almost intact and using the advantages of the Diaspora world.

---

[1] See a series of pamphlets starting from W. Wesley Ariarajah, *Gospel and Culture: An Ongoing Discussion Within the Ecumenical Movement*, Geneva: WCC Publications, 1995.

[2] Hugh Montefiore (ed.), *The Gospel and Contemporary Culture*, London: Mowbray, 1992.

[3] Sharpe, *Understanding Religion*, 134.

Today Cultural Studies is a separate branch in the academic world and is dominated by the presuppositions and methods of anthropology. However, the relationship between religion and culture is not more clearly defined. A recent essay notes that the idea of 'cultural studies' can dissolve into 'all studies with a foot somewhere in the humanities' as culture permeates the whole social fabric although it especially valorises literature and art. The question, 'is culture a subset of religion or vice versa?' is answered as 'we cannot ride both these definitional horses at the same time.' After illustrating how the field of religion and culture has both overlapping consensus and confusing conflict, it suggests a multi-level dialogue to be carried by many kinds of scholars and the religious practitioners they study. 'This dialogue, it is noted, 'is not neutral with respect to values. Rather it is a process of cultural contestation focusing on what the study of religion should be: what it is good for, and for whom.' In other words, this raises the question of what are the criteria for being 'good.' This well-written essay concludes with the words, 'we need to learn how to choose wisely among approaches to culture. It is because such choices are important in people's lives – as applied toward specific goals in concrete cases – that the field of religion and culture matters and we need good maps to navigate it with.'[1] It is unfortunate that in the complex enumeration of dimensions of religion arts, symbols, pilgrim centres, architecture and music have to be included in the broad category of culture or as Smart has done in the material dimension. However, as we have already noted, geographic and linguistic dimensions deserve a separate and somewhat detailed treatment.

10. Following the later addition of three dimensions as recognised by Smart further to his original six, and if we take culture as too broad to pin down to a particular dimension, then we should newly recognise *geography* or 'sacred geography' as a tenth dimension of religious life. A few attempts to study religion in relation to geography in fact concentrate on the material distribution of religions through a long historical process and mention briefly the significance of sacred places and sacred spaces.[2] But we are concerned with the geographical factors that have influenced the general character of a religious tradition and the attitudes of its people. The Abrahamic religions, for example, emerged in the context of the desert, and it is no wonder that the Israelites believed they were journeying towards a promised land where honey and milk flowed, signifying fertility and natural resources like trees, water and fruits. The Christian vision for the new world had a place for 'the river of the water of life, sparkling like crystal flowing from the throne … down the middle of the city's street. On either side of the river stood a tree of life, which yields twelve crops of fruit, one for each month of the year. The leaves of the trees are for the healing of the nations'. Similarly, the

[1] Mark Hulsether, "Religion and Culture" in J.R. Hinnels (ed.), *The Routledge Companion to the Study of Religion*, London: Routledge, 2005, 504.

[2] E.g. see Chris Park, "Religion and Geography" in Ibid., 439-455.

Qur'ānic picture of paradise resembles an oasis in a desert. Not only the fauna and flora but also important geographical locations are popular in these traditions.

Eastern religions have their own distinctive landscape and names of locations. Religions of the 'Indo-Gangetic hearth' are based on the lowland plains of the Indian subcontinent that are drained by the Indus and Ganges rivers. Scriptural descriptions are full of the beautiful sights of nature. Further, the tribal religions and other folk religions of the villages share common beliefs in animism and the worship of trees, stones and animals. Whatever may be the central deities, the guarding and protecting deities are equally important as the people in these landscapes were subject to many kinds of danger.

Because of their own cultural values and notions, it is claimed by Asian theologians that they are in an easy position to understand the biblical values of, for example, the family, as the Bible was a West Asian book. And the life ethos of Jesus as a wandering teacher and prophet too is easily understandable. Hence, as the Sri Lankan Jesuit theologian Aloysius Pieris voices for reclaiming of Jesus, an Asian monk who was hijacked by the Europeans and reintroduced into India as a white tribal god! Likewise, there are many proverbial images (e.g.stone -and grass-denoting the insignificant and downtrodden people as used by John the Baptist), which are easily understandable in Asian countries.

More interestingly, as suggested in discussions on interfaith relations, there is a connection between people's attitude to others and the nature of the geography of their religious tradition's birth and growth. At least two Indian Christian theologians contrast the desert-based Semitic religions with the river bed-based Indian religious traditions that account for their attitude to reality and to people of other faiths.[1] The former tend to be intolerant and dogmatic while the latter is flexible and non-dogmatic, although there is the possibility for the one to adopt from the other either positively or negatively. Some of us may find it odd but there is no reason to doubt an element of truth. Kosuke Koyama, a Japanese theologian's *Mount Fuji and Mount Sinai* (1984) is an elaboration of his proposal to bring together the hot Yahweh (zealous and burning god, impatient to change the society and establish justice) and the cool *arhant* (the one who has achieved the goal of life following the pioneer Buddha, unperturbed even in the midst of stormy situation), in his seminal and fascinating book *Water Buffalo Theology* (1974). The image water buffalo itself became his focus of reflection on God's resourcefulness, speed and way of working as he daily encountered this stirring animal on paddy fields on his way to teach in a seminary in Thailand.

We have already mentioned, certain locations associated with religious traditions have become famous pilgrim centres. Even traditions that least bothered

[1] See S.J. Samartha, "The Causes and Consequences of Religious Fundamentalism" in *Fundamentalism and Secularism: The Indian Predicament*, ed. Andreas Nehring, Madras: Gurukul, 1994, 42; A. George Ninan in his *Selected Speeches on Church and Society*, eds. Rajendra Sail and Akshay Sail, Mumbai: BUILD & RCDRC, 1999, 241.

about practices like pilgrimage later came to mark centres of pilgrimage. Even the non-conformist Methodists with simple piety and structures, for example, have made John Wesley's birth place and his old chapel in Bristol (called New Room, near Charles Wesley's house) major centres of world Methodist pilgrimage. By visiting these places the devotees relive their history and experience renewal by imagining the past with emotional fervour.

Some places become focal points of prayer and devotion, like Jerusalem for Jews and Mecca for Muslims. Local Hindu shrines not only represent a moment of revelation or miracle in the past but also become the centre of the universe (*locus mundi*), where God dances, creates and recreates, and bestows his grace. Since historical upheavals changed the location and meaning of some spots of a religious community, their revival is marked by their struggle to reclaim those spots. For instance, the Babri Masjid, a mosque built in honour of the Muslim ruler Baber in Ayodhya, a temple town in the state of Uttar Pradesh, North India, was demolished by Hindu extremists in 1992 with the claim that it was originally built by the invading Muslim ruler on the rubbles of a temple marking the birthplace of Rama, one of the divine-heroes and incarnations of Vaishnava Hinduism. Lamentable developments since the event testify that a sacred spot can be the tinderbox of communal conflicts. This is in spite of the fact that of more than five hundred temples in the small town Ayodhya about twenty are claimed to have been built on the actual birthplace of Rama. Similarly, the ongoing fight for ownership of Jerusalem by Jews, Christians and Muslims not only represents an ambiguous history with political complications, but also the underlying significance of geographical locations and the emotional attachment of devotees.

11. The next addition, eleventh in the overall list, is the *linguistic dimension*. Each religious tradition has a distinctive original language in which its scripture is written and worship held. Sanskrit is the sacred language in brahmanic Hinduism. Even where transformation is evident in the course of a transition from orthodoxy to modernity, where the vernacular is passionately promoted, preference to the use of Sanskrit in Hindu worship persists.[1] Where Vedic ritual persists in Hindu temples, recitation of Sanskrit mantras by a Brahmin priest, taken from the Vedas and Agamas, is vital. That is the reason that Hindus in the Diaspora bring such priests from India to do the worship even if they do not have adequate knowledge of the meaning and even if they are not able to interact with the wider community of their profession. Further, more than understanding, hearing the scripture recited in its original language evokes a unique experience for the Hindus concerned. Likewise Pali in the Buddhist tradition and Gurmukhi in the Sikh tradition are preferred in worship and in study of scripture.

[1] For the case of a Saiva Math in south India see I. Selvanayagam, "From Orthodoxy to Modernity: The Transition of a Saiva Math in South India", *Humanitas: The Journal of George Bell Institute*, 3/1 October 2001, 20-43; *Religion and Society*, 47/2 June 2000, 5-25.

Biblical Hebrew continues to be used in worship in Jewish Synagogues. Hebrew and Greek were the sacred languages for Christians as they are languages of their scripture. When the Bible was translated into Latin in the fourth century, the language of Italy, became the sacred language of the Roman Catholic Church throughout the world and even today Latin is preferred for Mass in certain pockets of the non-western world. Translating the Bible into other European languages was resisted for centuries and around the time of the Reformation a few lost their lives for daring to do so. However, today more than any other religious community Protestant Christians are comfortable with translations of the Bible in the vernacular. In the case of Muslims, the Arabic language in which the Qur'ān was revealed and recorded has been regarded as sacred. For a long time translating it into other languages was strictly prohibited. When the first translations appeared they were called 'The Meaning of the Holy Qur'ān' rather than the scripture itself. Though the situation is slowly changing Muslims are unique in preserving Arabic as their holy language as evident in their worship. Doing things in the original language seems to give a feeling of being connected with the original revelation and its geographical location.

Dynamics, Dilemmas and Divisions

Each religious tradition functions as a dynamic process, and this fact has been highlighted by Eric Lott. 'Whatever significant continuities there may be in each tradition', he writes, 'as it appropriates its past heritage, there are also continual changes, transitions, one might even speak of "mutations". In general this mutable, processive character of a religion's ongoing life has tended to be overlooked by comparative religionists almost as much as it will probably be denied by the devotees of a tradition.'[1] Lott mentions dharma in Hinduism and the Qur'ān/ Hadith in Islam as examples of conservative believers regarding their tradition as immutable and unchanging. Consciously or unconsciously, though, he points out that, in spite of the guardians of orthodoxy, every generation is part of a process of historical change, and that some traditions – such as Buddhism with its view of the eternal flux of life – find such change easier to respond to than others.

Lott, then, does not claim that this dynamic process in each religious tradition is of the same pattern of change and continuity. This is important to emphasise because this will challenge a possible phenomenological reductionism that gives too much weight to certain dimensions only. Such an approach may well also lead to a kind of relativism and pluralism (found even in theologies of religious pluralism) that in turn has encouraged people of one religious tradition to take seriously the particular historical journey or dynamic process experienced by those of other traditions. Of course both the proposition of religious pluralism and its denial will remain theoretical if we do not substantiate the position with illustrations. In this section we will outline the process of change and continuity

[1] E. Lott, op. cit., p. 31.

and the dilemmas and tensions it has brought and the divisions it has created in the two major clusters of religious traditions – Semitic and Indian.

At this point we will not attempt to reflect on theological reasons for such change and its outcome. At the end of the outline we will come back to Lott with reference to his recent studies on the 'dangerous dynamics' of the modern world of religions in the context of an ongoing search for stable faith and distinctive identity. One may see this important contribution of his as a continuation of his original grasp of dynamic process as one of the dimensions of religion.

1. The Abrahamic Traditions

What was most unique in the Hebrew religious tradition was the perception and experience that their God Yahweh had liberated their ancestors from their slavery in Egypt. They were led through a hazardous journey through a wilderness and joined by other small groups who had been attracted by their social ethos and structure. On their arrival in the promised land they joined with a local group in fighting for their rights in a context of political oppression, and the whole community were called Israelites. They had their commandments from God with whom they made a solemn covenant that obliged them to establish a community on the basis of justice, love and peace. Internal and external impediments led them never to realise their original vision. In terms of being faithful to the covenant and obeying God's commandments they appeared to be exclusive. But at the same time they were open to adopting religious institutions such as a priesthood, rituals, festivals and a temple from the neighbouring religious communities, and to give them new meaning in the light of their root story of liberation from slavery.

The main struggle was with political and economic power. Internally, strong personalities clashed, and there was tension between the priesthood and laity. There was also tension in maintaining the monarch with limited powers, a development which itself had emerged in an ambiguous context of divided opinions. There were threats from powerful empires like Assyria. The prophets of the Israelite community played a key role in both strengthening the will of their people and challenging the moments of their deviation, as well as condemning the excessive behaviour of surrounding empires. Due to the atrocious rule of the popular king Solomon with the introduction of forced labour and the levy of heavy taxes, the country of the Israelites was divided into north and south, or Israel and Judah. The north was occupied by Assyria in the eighth century BCE and the south was invaded by Babylon in the sixth century. After the destruction of the Temple in Jerusalem and exile in Babylon, many of the exiles returned and rebuilt their community and Temple in the late sixth century. The following centuries saw the oppression of Jews by Persian and Greek rulers and in the first century by Rome. During this period beliefs concerning the soul, the last judgement, resurrection, heaven and hell crept into Judaism. There was, too, always a vision of the coming of an extraordinary ruler; according to one group he would be a military hero and political figure wielding absolute authority, and according to the other he would be a remarkable servant who through his identification with the oppressed and suffering would exert great influence on his own people as well as on other nations.

When Jesus came he encountered not only the above groups but also number of sub-groups with different political ideologies and religious theologies. People's perception of Jesus also changed, ranging from a prophet and teacher to Messiah and saviour. Those who accepted him as the Messiah were his disciples, most of whom followed him until his cruel death on a cross. On the third day they also experienced him alive after rising from the dead and continuing in fellowship with those close to him. The movement was further strengthened and consolidated when they had an extraordinary experience of being filled by the Spirit on the day of Pentecostal. Mainly through preaching tours the movement spread in the Middle East, Asia and Europe, and some of the members had to suffer persecution and harassment.

The Jesus movement, later called Christians, received all civic rights and political support when a Roman emperor became Christian and declared Christianity as the state religion in the fourth century. Subsequently, Christianity was allied with political power in Europe, and on a tiny doctrinal issue the Church fell victim of a schism in the eleventh century, with one side called the Western Roman Catholic Church and the other the Eastern Orthodox Church. In due course different orders and traditions emerged – especially in the Orthodox churches – depending on the geographical location, political structure and local culture.

Following voices against corruption and superstition in the Roman Catholic Church, the sixteenth century saw a decisive moment of Reformation in Europe. Consequently, there was a counter-reformation within Catholicism, and later a missionary movement to Asia, Africa and America was intensified. The Protestant Church, while bound by the mantras of Reformation – grace alone, scripture alone and faith alone for salvation – became divided on doctrinal issues, particularly on church structure. The personal and family issue of a king in England in the same century severed the relationship with Rome, and the effect was the formation of the Church of England, first as Catholic church there separated from Rome, and then incorporated a number of Protestant values and ideas, thus claiming to be a 'middle way.' Similar developments – politically determined – happened in Ireland too. Later churches established by the Anglican mission societies became members of what is known as Anglican Communion all over the world with the Archbishop of Canterbury as their loosely uniting chief Bishop, while continuing to be the head of the Church of England.

The Protestant Church includes major denominations such as Presbyterian, Congregational, Lutheran and Reformed. These were movements with a Protestant ethos, but which followed different internal order and took particular positions on socio-political issues. Some churches and groups represent a refinement within a Protestant branch. For example, the Methodist movement emerged within the Church of England in the eighteenth century and without any formal break developed into a new Church emphasising personal sanctification towards perfection, spreading holiness throughout the land, and social service. When the Methodist Church became established and subject to weaknesses of structure, the Salvation Army emerged within it and was established as a new organisation devoted to interdenominational evangelisation and social service. Methodism also represented a new beginning of pietistic revival, and in the following centuries there were several revivalist groups and charismatic churches developed all over the world of which the strongest is the Pentecostal Church, known by different names. They emphasise the personal experience of being filled by the Holy Spirit. Within its family it has the extreme wings, fundamentalist and radical.

Through the works of the several missionary movements representing the above bodies, churches of the same denominations were established in different parts of the world. The missionary movements were involved in not only spreading the Christian message with different emphases, but also in social services such as establishing educational and medical institutions. However, they enjoyed on the whole the economic and political power of the western churches of their denomination, and in most cases the churches they established followed their pattern in their home country in terms of church building, worship, specific vocabulary and music. When political and economic patronage started dwindling with the coincidence of the struggle for independence and self-hood, and with a view to being more effective in mission and Christian witness, united churches started to emerge in the twentieth century. For example, the Presbyterian and Congregationalist churches in South India came together in 1908 forming the South India United Church. Further negotiations with Anglican and Methodist Churches resulted in the formation of the Church of South India in 1947, the year of India's independence. Since then numerous united churches with varying combinations have emerged.

At an international level the World Council of Churches was formed in 1948, bringing together most of the Protestant Churches from all over the world. Today about four hundred churches are members of the WCC. On the basis of the fundamentals of Christian faith, they share several programmes organised with a view to initiating novel programmes for the member churches to follow. The Eastern Orthodox Churches maintain a peculiar and at times unsteady relationship with the WCC. Since the Second Vatican Council (1962-65) the Roman Catholic Church has been moving forward with new openness in the areas of mission and ministry. The WCC and RCC have mutual representation in their major gatherings, and joint programmes in the area of interfaith relations and social reconstruction. On the whole churches continue to deliver themselves from the chains of history and traditions, and theologically they share in common a considerable number of issues. The most serious sticking point is distinctive liturgical patterns and resources, church structures and, most of all, models of leadership. On the one hand Christians claim to celebrate a diversity of traditions within a common faith, and on the other hand, many of them are passionate about achieving the organic unity of the Christian Church all over the world which alone will be the most authentic mark of spiritual maturity, fuller self-understanding of faith and more perfect union with God who himself is constituted by an intimate divine unity among three aspects, 'persons' or modes, Father, Son and Holy Spirit.

Acknowledging dark and dividing moments in the past, both churches are striving individually and jointly to appropriate a holistic vision of salvation and multi-dimensional character of mission. While having to deal with the fundamentalist and conservative wings of their respective families, they work towards achieving greater credibility for their mission. Particularly they have considerably advanced in interfaith relations, understanding and dialogue. The most horrible anti-Semitism is openly given up with public apology. A considerable section of Christians regard such acts as well as giving up ignorance of other religions as liberating.

Islam was born in Arabia, combining the tradition of those who had been worshipping one God and the new revelation received by the Prophet Mohammed in the seventh century. Without belittling its originality it is not difficult to see the Judeo-Christian influence on the Holy Qur'ān, the tradition of the Prophet (Hadith) and the formulations of five duties (confession of faith in one God, five times daily prayer, fasting in the month of Ramadan, regulated alms giving or poor tax and pilgrimage to Mecca at least once in a life time) and six credal beliefs (one God, Angels, Books of God, Prophets of God, Resurrection and the Day of Judgement, and Predestination of Good and Evil). There have been theological discussions on reconciling divine predestination and human responsibility. Islam appears to be less complicated than the Judeo-Christian traditions. However, it too has encountered difficult moments. There have been times when the Qur'ān as the supreme authority has been found wanting to address particular issues. Then, the Hadith or tradition of the Prophet is taken as the second scriptural foundation for decision and judgement. When this fails to give clear guidance on certain matters, the principle of logical deduction or the practice of reasoning by analogy (*ijma*) is applied. When all these three sources are inadequate then the fourth foundation of the unanimous consent of the doctors of the law (*qiyas*) is evoked. Consequently, there are four schools of Islamic law, which differ only in trivial matters.

The inner dynamics and external connections make the situation quite complex. For example, the controversy over the succession to the Prophet after the fourth Caliph (Ali, the son-in-law of Mohammed) and the murder of his sons caused the separation of the Shī'as, which was originally a political party but then assumed the character of a sect, different from the Sunnis, the 'orthodox.' Instead of accepting any Caliphs after Ali, they looked to a series of Imāms or spiritual guides in his line. Apart from the Qur'ān they do not accept the other three sources but have their own. They broke up into many sub-sects which pinned their hopes in one or other of these spiritual guides, believing that he had not died but was hiding and would some day return as the Mahdī, or divinely directed leader, and this resembles the belief in the second coming of Jesus. Prominent sub-divisions of the Shī'as include Ismā'īlīs (who accepted Ismā'īl as the seventh Imām proper in a controversy), Bohras (a sub-division of the above, converts from Hinduism chiefly living in Mumbai and Baroda) and Khojas (another sub-division residing mainly outside India). Besides, Bābīs and Bahā'is are groups originally having affinity with the Shī'a doctrine of the Imām but later they, particularly the Bahā'is, were pushed into forming a separate religious tradition. Along with all such developments, Sufism developed a mystic path and orders that found favourable reception with Sunnis and Shī'as in different ways.

Judaism, Christianity and Islam are called the Abrahamic faiths as Abraham is accepted as their common ancestor. But there are differences between the Qur'ān and the Bible even in the narrative of Abraham. For instance, according to the Hebrew Scripture Abraham in obedience to God dared to offer to sacrifice his son Isaac on a high place in the land of Moriah, but according to the Qur'ān it was Ishmael on the mount where the Dome of the Rock stands today in Jerusalem. Moreover these three faiths believe in one God but the Qur'ān reacts quite strongly to the idea of Trinity, probably confused by the way Christians presented, seeing this belief as tritheism, comprised of Father God, mother Mary and son Jesus. This might reflect popular controversy among Christians over the explanation of Christ's divinity, Mary's significance and of the relationship between Father, Son and the Holy Spirit in the Prophet's time. Islam insists on the unity of God as one only without a second and understands literally the relational terms like Father and Son. Likewise Muslims are asked to respect Jews and Christians as the 'People of the Book' but the 'Book' is not exactly the Hebrew Scripture and New Testament that form the Bible, but it is something more authentic and pure but not extant for verification of what are seen as the twists and fabrications of the Bible. Again Muslims believe in a great number of prophets, starting from Adam, with Mohamed as the seal of all prophets including Jesus, though the latter is given very high regard.

Today there are important areas of tension between Jews, Christians and Muslims. Agreement on an independent homeland for Palestinians and public recognition of the state of Israel is yet to be achieved. Jerusalem as a holy city is contested by all three. The anti-Semitic attitude of Christians and their insensitive approach to the Hebrew scripture resulted in persecution of Jews at various levels and finally the holocaust, the killing of six million Jews in Europe during the Second World War, to which horror there are still living witnesses. The crusades ordered by the popes to recover the Holy Land from the Muslims during the 11th to 13th centuries are remembered as infamous milestones in Christian-Muslim relationships. Moreover, though military conquest was one of the means of spreading Islam along with immigration, trade and preaching, violent conquest only is highlighted by others. While *Jihad* is interpreted by moderates as striving morally in the way of God, extreme groups use it to denote holy war, and for this reason most of the terrorist groups today are identified with Islam. Some of them have spoken clearly that they are challenging the degraded western culture, but there are moderates and liberals who claim that Islam is not incompatible with the values of western culture.

2. The Indian Religious Traditions

These have a different story. Let us start with the Vedic religion, which was developing around 2000 BCE. As studies[1] show, sacrifice (*yajna*) is the most central element of this religion. Developments in understanding sacrifice provide a set of keys for understanding the dynamics of the Indian religious traditions. From a simple gift or food offering to gods, sacrifice developed into a complex ritual mechanism for generating the power to create and recreate the universe and all forms of its life. Dominant ideas of Indian religious thought such as *karma* (action), *Brahman* (holy power), *tapas*, (heat), *kāma* (desire), *artha* (wealth), *ahimsā* (non-violence) and *dharma* (ethical order) were developed in the context of ritual sacrifice.

Vedic ritual is unique in the sense that it was regarded as generating creative power, that is, it is not of merely instrumental but of intrinsic value. In any of a variety of ritual sacrifices, three power centres were identified: *karman* (ritual action), *Brahman* (holy power contained in recitations) and *tapas* (ritual heat produced by establishment of sacred fires and cooking the libations). The power generated in this way would sustain the regular functioning of the cosmos, nourish the gods, and give a new experience of intense feeling of the sacred for the patron of the sacrifice. The Vedic sacrifice was associated with the stratification of the society by four *varnas*, the prototype of the caste system, and *dharma* was the order connecting sacrifice, society and cosmos. There are clues in the Vedas to a group of wandering renouncers who questioned the extravagance of ritual sacrifice and exhibited extraordinary spiritual powers generated within. The first two parts of the Vedas (*samhītas* or hymns of praise and *brāhmanas* or ritual manuals) mention gods and ritual prescriptions in a clumsy way.

While the ritual sacrifice continues in the last parts of the Veda (āranyakas or forest books and *Upanishads* or discourse on metaphysics) we notice a further development in the search for meaning beyond ritual. An allegorical interpretation of the ritual items such as the whole universe as horse, its urine as rain and so forth was a further development. Alternative interpretations of the power centres were given: karman (ethical action), tapas (interior heat produced by controlling senses

[1] See I. Selvanayagam, *Vedic Sacrifice: Challenge and Response*, New Delhi: Manohar, 1996.

and actualising the interior power) and Brahman (cosmic holy power, one reality but manifest as many). The idea of *karma samsāra* (action-accumulated effect and chain of birth) was introduced, and liberation from its bondage to a state of freedom was sought through knowledge and meditation. The inward journey might end in self-sacrifice, which is variously interpreted. A few women appeared in participating discourses on ultimate reality, and, not caste and birth, but the desire to know qualified one to be a religious adept.

A greater challenge was from the renouncers of the two groups (Buddhists and Jains) established by their two founders, who were regarded as spiritual heroes of Enlightenment (Gautama Buddha and Mahavira) and who lived in the 7th to the 6th centuries BCE. Jains practised extreme austerity, whereas the Buddhists followed a middle path. They both challenged the notion of ritual power, and presented in its place an interior change or spiritual power created by ethical action and meditative discipline. They attacked caste rigidity and (after a short time) admitted women monks. Their influence on certain rulers, particularly that of Buddhism on the Maurian emperor Aśoka of the third century, was most remarkable. Following a period of bloody conflict, he renounced war, spread ethical ideals such as loving kindness and non-violence and propagated equal respect for different religious traditions.

The Maurian empire fell, and the Śunkan dynasty was established by a staunch Brahmin, Pushyamitra, at the turn of the second century. Sacrifice was revived with some modification. The six orthodox *Darshanas* (visions or metaphysical systems) made a strong response to the influence of the renouncers' traditions, basically reaffirming the authority of the Vedas. Particularly one of them (*Pūrvamīmāmsa*) presented a systematic defence of Vedic sacrifice answering the questions posed by the Buddhists and Jains. These systems continue to exist within Hinduism but there is no way of finding the number of people following each. One of them was *yoga*, which has become popular all over the world as a spiritual technique, though with little regard for its metaphysical foundation. Another response came in the form of law codes, which represent some level of synthesis. For example, when they extol non-violence as a virtue they exempt killing in sacrifice and war from its appeal. Along with injunctions to forms of high-minded morality, they regulated the caste rules, based on distinctions and gradations of purity/pollution, entailing the lowest and outcaste groups receiving rigorously oppressive treatment. The two epics *Rāmāyana* and *Mahābhārata* in their basic stories seem to represent the decline and revival of the Vedic sacrifice, while adding a large number of sub-stories and teachings.

A process of assimilation of indigenous local practice is evident in the above types of literature. Along with extravagant forms of sacrifice, simple forms of domestic ritual and rites of passage were introduced. Visiting holy waters, study of the Veda and feeding Brahmin priests were interpreted as equivalent to or a substitute for sacrifice. Renunciation was included in a new, largely ideal, scheme of four stages in life – student, householder, forest-dweller and renouncer. Likewise liberation was included in four-fold goals of life – earning wealth, fulfilling sensual and aesthetic desire, upholding the order of the cosmos through sacrifice and social stratification, and finally liberation.

The greatest assimilation was Brahmanism's incorporation of the Bhāgavata cult of which Krishna was a leader and divine hero. First his introduction as a black leader of a shepherd community into the Brahmanic fold was violently resisted. But when different traditions and schools of thought, with conflicting claims, threatened and Krishna grew in popularity, it was he who was taken as a rallying centre. The famous text, Bhagavad Gita – part of the great epic *Mahābhārata* – represents the outcome of the assimilation. It reaffirms the power and meaning of the Vedic sacrifice and the related worldview, mentions a variety of sacrifices such as godly sacrifice, material sacrifice, sacrifice of knowledge, sacrifice of prayer and self-sacrifice. It uses the categories of Sāmkhya, one of the orthodox metaphysical systems, for classifying different acts of sacrifice. The highest form of sacrifice is devotion to the Lord Krishna, now taken as an incarnation of the supreme Vishnu. In this sacrifice control of the senses and steady mindedness are taken to help unswerving devotion as well as fighting in the war, the immediate context. This means yogic steady-mindedness also helps being devoted to dharma, in particular caste duty, without being confused about its consequences. One can see Arjuna, the military captain, the devotee of Krishna, before being cleared of his confusion, reacting with the same attitude as Ashoka when faced with the same battle-field experience.

The Bhāgavata tradition, with Krishna as an incarnation of Vishnu, was the first developed devotional (*bhakti*) tradition, encouraging the emergence of a number of such traditions in the period from the third century CE. In time three major Gods were introduced in a kind of trinity or triad assigning each a particular work. Thus Brahma was the creator, Vishnu the protector and Śiva the destroyer. Subsequently Brahma receded to the background and Vishnu and Śiva were regarded as supreme, performing all the above activities and offering liberation to their devotees from the chain of births.

So, the process of assimilation continued. Vishnu incorporated a number of deities as his incarnations (*avatar*) and Buddha too was included. The incarnations had their consorts. Śiva does not take specific embodiments in avatar-form, but a kind of avataric theophany is evident in those stories that extol him. Śiva subjugated a number of regional and female deities through marriage and the extension of the divine family. Thus, Śakti (female 'power') became his consort in various names and forms and Ganesh and Subramanian became their sons. Books of stories and teachings of the major sects – Vaishnava, Saiva and Sakta – in Sanskrit and vernacular languages are numerous and voluminous. There are many forms of devotional literature too which have moving stories of the transforming experience of poet-saints attached to temples and images of their Gods, with poetry expressing heart-melting appeal for devotion. These powerfully emerging devotional traditions, along with a Vedic revival, caused a decline of the Jaina and Buddha movements. In particular, Buddhism lost its hold and was in effect eliminated from the country, with Hinduism, now as an umbrella of different traditions, claiming to have incorporated their core experiences and values into their system.

Though Buddhism was not able to establish itself as a major religion in India it was very successful in other Asian countries. Sri Lanka as a Buddhist country maintains the two major divisions of Theravada and Mahayana and the latter's different schools. Buddhism influenced considerably the cultures of countries like Cambodia, Thailand and South Korea. When it spread to China it found new allies like Shinto and Confucian traditions, and the combination of their elements resulted in the formation of distinctive traditions like the Pure Land Buddhism. Similarly it incorporated Tao elements in Japan and developed new forms of meditation such as Zen. Tibetan Buddhism has its special characteristics and through the Dalai Lama it has captured the attention of western countries. Buddhism is seen as a great resource to establish peace in a world of conflicts, and as a resource for a simple life-style in a consumerist world which faces life-threatening challenges such as the depletion of non-renewable resources and global warming.

The original converts to Buddhism and Jainism were Brahmins, followed by greater numbers of Kshatriyas and Vaishyas, and probably they introduced elements of the Vedic ritual. However, the rituals now began to be interpreted as instruments for obtaining full concentration in contemplation and meditation. At the same time elements of the sacrifice-centred Vedic religion continues with ramification and modification as evident in the ritual life of Hindu sects. In any case Buddhism includes both theistic and atheistic traditions as well as folk forms, and this could create problems for understanding Buddhism as one religion, unless it is seen within the framework of the poly-paradigmatic Hindu tradition, which includes in its elastic system a number of seemingly contradictory elements.

In broad terms it is reasonable to say that there are at least four strands that constitute what is known as Hinduism – Vedic ritual, Yogic meditation, Theistic traditions and diverse popular cults. Because of its incorporation of non-violence as a virtue and support of caste duty even if it involves killing in war there is tension between the universal imperative of non-violence and particular obligation to exert violence, and the seeds of this conflict are already found in the Gita.[1] Similarly, when the all-powerful ritual was associated with the supreme Gods Vishnu and Siva, in a Hindu temple worship, ritual and God seem to remain as parallel powers, and there are numerous stories to illustrate the tension involved.[2] Besides,

---

[1] See I. Selvanayagam, *The Dynamics of Hindu Traditions: Teape Lectures on Sacrifice, Gita and Dialogue*, Bangalore: Asian Trading Corporation, 1996, pp. 46-63.

[2] See Ibid., 64-83.

as the local temple myths reveal, when Śiva or Vishnu subjugated or assimilated the power of the hitherto independent deities, the process was not always smooth but conflict-bound to the extent of a female deity becoming a murderous bride on the first night. Of course Hinduism has the remarkable practice of covering all such conflicts and contradictions with the blanket of all-comprising Truth, or interpreting cosmic life as Divine Sport that transcends human reasoning and as all the fashions and fancies of the world.

Hindu tradition had to face external challenges as well. When Islam came to India the sub-continent with its composite culture and religious life had to face both a politically conquering power and the challenging theology of one God and universal brotherhood. The conflict developed into moments of violent confrontation. In such a context great figures like Kabir and Nanak of the 15-16th centuries developed a spirituality drinking from the wells of both Islam and Hinduism. Guru Nanak attracted a band of disciples (*sikshayas*), and they were the pioneers of the Sikh tradition which, after a period of suffering persecution, achieved stability by the efforts of the tenth cardinal Guru Gobind Singh (1666-1708). The fact that Sikhism is a synthetic religion is hotly contested by some Sikh teachers. In any case, apart from beliefs like *karma samsara* and practices such as funeral rites, their scripture Ādigranth is full of ideas and devotion reminiscent of Islam and Hinduism. Particularly, the idea of one God and one human race comes from Islam and the idea of human being with the central belief in the soul's transmigration comes from Hinduism. Many customs and cultural practice are shared in common with Hinduism, and that is one of the reasons that the Hindu community refuses to give the Sikhs independent status with their own personal law.

Although, the British presence in India in the 17th century began with a primary interest in commerce, soon political expansion of the empire along with the growing movement for Christian mission were equally part of the western presence. Western education brought to the sub-continent not only the English language but also knowledge of science and technology and liberal thinking. The Hindu response was not to surrender as expected but a new awakening that resulted in movements for reformation, renaissance and resurgence. In independent India the response took a more concrete and consolidated form in the 'Hindutva' movement, which is interpreted as cultural nationalism, the unification of Hindus, and claims to be the embodiment of true secularism. The debate continues as to who are the real proponents of the Hindutva movement and what is their true interest, including whether or not they have a vision for a healthy and peaceful nation of various religions within the control of a secular constitution.

Before we move on, two more developments need to be noted which have brought so much embarrassment to brahmanic Hinduism. One is the development of neo-Buddhism in the context of the struggle of the so-called untouchable community under the leadership of B. R. Ambedkar in the twentieth century. The members refuse to be called Hindus though they are counted among the Hindus in the census. Related to this, recent studies bring out the significance of subaltern religion and cultural traditions, which have not wholly been swallowed up by the all-devouring Hindu traditions. However, more studies are needed to determine their originality, or to what extent there is influence from the major Hindu religious traditions.

The dynamic process in the life-history of the two clusters of religions we have outlined shows a number of irreconcilable differences between them in their environment, sequence and ideas or beliefs. Therefore students of religion and religions need to be very cautious not to be carried away by sweeping generalisations either in the name of phenomenology or theology. Eric Lott, who suggested that dynamic process is a key dimension of religion, has recently done more extensive studies elaborating the social dimension of religion, taking into account corporate identities and personal identities that lead to a number of 'dangerous dynamics' in the modern world.[1] He takes *identity* as a key category for human self-understanding and evaluates the role of religions in its pursuit. In a fast changing modern world individuals and communities are seeking identity through the support of a distinctive narrative. Even if there are secular compulsions which push religious faith to a private arena, it bubbles within to relate to the wider world and community by means of different faith-persuasions and cultures. Political factors are inextricably part of the violent destruction of the twin towers on 11 September 2001. The powerful significance of religions in shaping human identities was revealed in this act that shocked the world though the powerful significance of religious faith is also revealed through this and the conflicts and invasions in the aftermath.

Slightly moving aside, and updating the fact of dynamic process, we have to acknowledge the upsurge of recent movements in different religious traditions. At least one study notes that they signify the continuing human research for truth and meaning with some amount of confusion on the way. It brings twelve case studies of rapidly growing religious movements around the world under the main title *Dynamic Religious Movements*.[2] The editor admits that the conclusions of the nature and growth of these movements remain tentative. The causes of their growth he observes: resurgence of cultural identity, charismatic leadership, reaction to threat of suppression, sense of clear belief and practice, all-encompassing teaching, lively worship-ritual-rites incorporating emotional elements from other traditions, a distinctive vision for the world, aggressive propagation of the faith, strategic use of media and establishment of charity institutions like schools. The editor in

[1] See E. Lott, *Religious Faith, Human Identity: Dangerous Dynamics in Global & Indian Life*, Bangalore: Asian Trading Corporation for the United Theological College, 2005.

[2] Ed. David J. Hesselgrave, *Dynamic Religious Movements*, Grand Rapids: Baker Book House, 1978.

conclusion mentions a definition of religion 'as to downgrade supernaturalism' and in the discussion which follows he mentions a few thinkers including Paul Tillich (religion as ultimate concern, and there is secular faith). Such studies today may have nuances and further dimensions.

Concluding Remarks

In this chapter we have shown how identification of aspects, modes or dimensions of religion and religious life have helped to gain a greater grasp of religion. We have demonstrated how the search continues, recognising new dimensions that add to the progress of understanding religion. We have not reproduced details and illustrations of dimensions, which are already popular for some time in the field of the study of religion. To avoid further complication, we have not given due consideration to important aspects of arts, symbols, music etc. but have included them in material dimensions. The political and economic dimensions identified by Ninian Smart towards the end of his long career of teaching and studying religion and world religions (or his preferred 'worldviews') need to be further explored as to how do they relate to other dimensions. One might argue that Smart was trying to avoid the notion of essentialism by introducing dimensional approach, but in the end did not quite escape falling into the trap of essentialism. We have, however, resisted any phenomenological reductionism by demonstrating the distinctive stages and experiences of the dynamic process taking place in the Semitic and Indian religious traditions. The process continues, giving ample scope and fascinating details for both the adherents of faiths and scholars of religious studies while, if they are truly committed, challenging them to do something in their own context by bringing out the salient features of religious life and warning against distortions and manipulations.

We have illustrated in some detail the aspect of dynamic process within each religious tradition thanks to responding challenges and making adjustments. We have pointed out some decisive moments in the development of the Semitic religious traditions and the major Indian religious traditions. Challenges, responses, assimilations etc. have not made the religious traditions less complex. Also, the complexity will be greater if the impact of great traditions on small ones is studied. For instance, the fact of 'hinduized' Christianity in India is clearly evident in popular terms like soul and moksha and Jesus-deity, forms/names such as temple and priest (with the suffix of a brahmin priest), and practices of caste and of dividing time as auspicious and inauspicious and so on while Christians try very hard to convert the Hindus! Moreover, to what extent there are elements of dynamic process due to the impact of modernity on the primal/tribal/popular cults in India as well as around the world merits a separate study.

Chapter 3

Implicit Religion and its Variety

A Variety of Religious Phenomena

The struggle to define religion continues and we have already given a summary of the inconclusive discussion. Likewise, recognition and classification of different dimensions of religion are growing. Also understanding a particular dimension in all its depth and breadth in relation to the core vision needs further clarification and work. In this context it is important to acknowledge efforts and suggestions on new types of religion. The term 'implicit' is taken to indicate the spirit and content of this pursuit. Folk religion, popular religion, invisible religion, para-religion and new age religion are related terms used by scholars and writers. In this chapter, we will mention first what is recognised as quasi-religion as a background and move to discuss on what is known as 'implicit religion' with illustrations.

Another popular term is spirituality. Again there is no single definition shared by all. Basically, spirituality stands for the non-material factors in life but inextricably relating to mood, spirit and attitude to the mundane life. Since spirituality suggests a dichotomy between spirit and matter, thus reaffirming some dualist notions, many take pains to explain it in particular ways suiting their own understanding or their particular religious tradition. Religiosity is yet another term, which is not beyond difference of opinion. With this preliminary consideration, we will explain in this chapter with some clarity these terms and their explanations, as they claim to gain a fuller understanding of religion. However, there is no guarantee of clarity without a certain ambiguity.

There are certain cultic forms, which cannot be brought under the existing categories of either explicit religion or implicit religion. Take, for example, ***Personality Cults***. Those who walk along the Marina beach in Chennai (Madras) would come across some tombs attracting crowds. C.N. Annadurai's tomb has an everlasting flame installed, and his triple principle is inscribed in the Tamil language around the tomb meaning: Duty, Dignity, and Discipline. Annadurai was a lieutenant, leader of the Dravidian Progressive Movement, called affectionately *Anna* (elder brother) revered as 'deity of our heart', and was a fascinating orator and vigorous writer. He was agnostic though he was open to rationalistic faith in the true God for social regeneration. In a context of multiplicity of gods and castes he declared 'One God, One Race' and this affirmation is depicted in his statues established all over Tamil Nadu. Struck down by throat cancer, Annandurai had a premature death in 1969 when he had hardly served two years as the first DMK Chief Minister of Madras State which he renamed Tamil Nadu. (The initials of the DMK party stand for Dravida Munnetra Kazhagam in Tamil (lit. 'Dravidian Progress Federation'.)

Annadurai's tomb is surrounded by a modernist monument pointing a slim spire to the sky. The tomb is of marble, and crowds visit it as they would visit a shrine in a pilgrim centre, removing sandals and paying homage. Similar reverence is made to the tomb of E.V.R. Periyar, the mentor of Annadurai, who split away from his mentor's Dravidian Movement, a social, rationalist and atheist movement. Periyar, a revolutionary to the extent of desecrating publicly the idols of Hindu gods and goddesses and of declaring God worshippers as fools and scoundrels, died in 1973. M.G. Ramachandran, a film actor-turned-political leader, broke away from DMK and formed All India DMK, captured power, and when he died in 1987 his tomb was situated close to Anna's with an everlasting flame. His mentee and political heir J. Jeyalalitha followed the same course and when she died in December 2016 she too was buried near him and she has already been acclaimed as mother and goddess. Similarly, there are a few popular figures in the cine world, who have attracted the reverence of people. A separate study is needed to ascertain the nature of this reverence in comparison with Hindu religiosity and implicit religion.

Quasi Religion is the term used in academic circles, mainly in the United States of America. As a caveat for misunderstanding there is no reason to take quasi-religion as meaning pseudo-religion. It presupposes that certain dimensions of religion such as ritual, mythical and experiential appear in a certain manner and degree in certain non-religious thought forms and organisations, or secular ideologies and their political structures. As early as 1961, Paul Tillich, a Protestant theologian and Existentialist philosopher, reflected not only on other religions but also 'different types of secular quasi-religions.'[1] Defining religion as 'the state of being grasped by ultimate concern', Tillich relates it to belief in God as far as the theistic religions are concerned. He acknowledges that there are non-theistic religions as well as Buddhist, Jaina and certain Vedantic traditions. 'In secular quasi-religions' he observes, 'the ultimate concern is directed towards objects like nation, science, a particular form or stage of society, or a highest ideal of humanity

[1] P. Tillich, *Christianity and the Encounter of the World Religions*, New York and London: Columbia University Press, 1963, 4.

which are then considered divine.'[1] Christianity's, or for that matter any religion's, encounter with this religion will influence each other. Sometimes what he calls quasi-religions are called pseudo-religions, but for Tillich, 'this is as imprecise as it is unfair. "Pseudo" indicates an intended but deceptive similarity; quasi indicates a genuine similarity, not intended, but based on points of identity, and this, certainly, is the situation in cases like Fascism and Communism, the most extreme examples of quasi-religions today.'[2] He continues to state:

> They are radicalizations and transformations of nationalism and socialism, respectively, both of which have a potential, though not always an actual religious character. In Fascism and Communism the national and social concerns are elevated to unlimited ultimacy. In themselves both the national and the social concerns are humanly great and worthy of a commitment even unto death, but neither is a matter of unconditional concern. For one may die for something which is conditional in being and meaning – as many Germans did who, for national reasons, fought under Hitler for Germany while hating National-Socialism and secretly hoping for its defeat. This conflict is avoided if the driving force in a national war is the defence of the vocational idea of the nation.[3]

For Tillich, it is not the nation as such, but the vocational idea like justice or freedom that is a matter of ultimate concern. 'Nations and social orders as such are transitory and ambiguous in their mixture of creativity and destructiveness' he observes. If they are taken as matters of ultimate concern in meaning and being, then, he would argue that their finitude must be denied. This has been done, and he illustrates with developments in his original country Germany by the use of the old eschatological symbol of a 'thousand-year period' for the future of Hitler's Reich, 'a symbol which originally signified the aim of all human history.' The same thing, he adds, has been done in Russia in terms of the Marxian type of eschatological thinking (classless society).

> In both cases it was necessary to deny the ambiguities of life and the distortions of existence within these systems, and to accept unambiguously and unconditionally their evil elements, e.g., by glorifying the suppression of individual criticism and by justifying and systematizing lie and wholesale murder – as happened in Italy and Germany and in Russia under Stalin. The quasi-religious character of any such 'rule of an ideology' (or 'ideocracy', as one might call it) makes these consequences unavoidable. But in such extremes

[1] Ibid., 5.

[2] Ibid., 5f.

[3] Ibid., 6.

> something becomes manifest that, in a moderate way, characterizes all ideologically conscious movements and social groups. It is the consecration of communal self-affirmation, whether this consecration happens in religious or secular symbols. It is an element in every nationalism, whether among the old Asiatic or the new African nations, whether in Communist or in democratic countries. This quasi-religious element in all nationalism gives it its passion and strength, but also produces the radicalized nationalism which we denote here by a generalized term: Fascism. The same dialectics is true of Socialism. In it the expectation of a 'new state of things' is the driving religious element, whether expressed in the Christian symbols of the end of history or in secular-utopian symbols like 'classless society' as the aim of history. This quasi-religious element in all Socialism was radicalized in the revolutionary period of Communism, and was, in its victorious period, reduced to an a-personal subjection under the demands of a neocollectivistic system. But even so the quasi-religious character persisted.[1]

Tillich also refers to a movement in which an early encounter of religion and quasi-religion took place, i.e. the religious-socialist movement in the 1920s in Central Europe. 'It was an attempt to liberate the socialist ideology from absolutism, utopianism, and the destructive implications of a self-righteous rejection of criticism from beyond itself. It was the prophetic criticism, or the "Protestant Principle", which judges all religious or quasi-religious absolutism.'

> This is not only a theoretical question, but may well be the question of the capability of the West to resist the onslaught of the quasi-religions in our present world. Liberal humanism and its democratic expressions are fragile forms of life, rare in history, and easily undermined from within and destroyed from without. In the periods of their heroic fight against the absolutisms of the past, their quasi-religious character was obvious, as was their religious background. In the periods of their victorious and mature development, their secular character became predominant, but whenever they had to defend themselves – as in matters of scientific autonomy, educational freedom, social equality or civil rights – they showed again their quasi-religious force. It was a struggle between faith and faith; and the quasi-religious faith could be radicalized to a degree where it undercut even its own roots, as, for example, in a scientism which deprives all non-scientific creative functions, such as the arts and religion, of their autonomy. If in the foreseeable future a total defence of liberal

[1] Ibid., 7f.

> humanism against Communism or Fascism should be necessary, a self-defying radicalization would take place and the loss of that very liberal humanism which is to be defended would be almost unavoidable.[1]

A power or movement that criticises the present and pushes forward to a new direction, Tillich calls 'religion of the Spirit.' He holds that both Protestantism and early Christianity can be called religions of the Spirit, free from oppressive laws and, consequently, often without law altogether. The real danger is not that they are overwhelmed by other less fragile forms of religion or quasi-religion, but that in defending themselves they are led to violate their very nature and shape themselves into the image of those who attack them. In such a critical moment we are living today.

Tillich's basic observation of and affirmations on quasi-religions found more substantial expression with analytical research in the US. For example, the volume *Between Sacred and Secular: Research and Theory on Quasi-Religion* (ed. by A.L. Greil and T. Robbins, 1994) contains discussions on the boundaries of the sacred, secular religions as the realm of 'para-religion', analysis of some religious and non-religious organisations transcending sacred and secular, and radical psychotherapy in a community context as quasi-religion. Some discussions centre around the ideas of sacred cosmology among the avant-garde, transcendence and identity in two twelve-step quasi-religions, gendered spirituality and quasi-religious ritual and a number of neo-religious movements reflecting an amalgamation of explicit, para- or quasi-religious elements.

Quasi-Religions: Humanism, Marxism and Nationalism (by John E. Smith, Palgrave, 1994) is a book that demonstrates religious dimensions at different degrees and levels occupying otherwise seemingly secular ideologies and movements. Ninian Smart also dealt with these issues in his book *Worldviews: Crosscultural Explorations of Human Beliefs* (1999). In the subsequent period there were no principles and guidelines employed by authors who used the term 'quasi-religion' for a variety of phenomena ranging from the tyrannical wars such as the second world war during which the holocaust took place, to health services. Following is one of the most recent examples.

'Reiki is a technique of Japanese origin on a Chinese, more ancient basis, in order to reduce stress, to relax and to increase just your own degree of physical and moral well-being. Broadly speaking, since a unitary organisation does not exist, the name "Reiki" is also used to indicate the movement of those who practise this technique and share a certain number of principles that support it. The technique is based on the idea that universal (*rei*) energy (*ki*, Japanese version of the Chinese "*qi*") flows inside all living beings. The flow of this energy can be improved or corrected, in case of deviation, through the gestures of a person initiated to Reiki

[1] Ibid., 9f.

that puts his/her hands on another person (or on him/herself), or simply raises his/her hands towards the other without touching him/her.

We would rather try to read the reality of Reiki, paying particular attention to the Italian scene, striving to understand it, on the basis of its phenomenology, Reiki can be simply considered a technique or, instead on the contrary, a religion.

On the basis of these elements, Reiki can simply appear as one of the alternative therapeutic practices, flowing into the immense network of alternative therapies. It can be framed, in its turn, in the large meta-network of the New Age. In particular, the historical evolution of the spreading of Reiki to the West and its present very remarkable international expansion, leads to think that such a practice has not suffered any damage but instead has drawn benefits from the evolution-decline of the New Age. It has taken place, starting from the second half of 1990s, in that phenomenon having a more individualistic character which is called New Age. The exact nature of Reiki continues to be explored, particularly in relation to religion, sacred etc. In this perspective the study of 'the reality of Reiki reveals to be a further contribution to the wide debate on the concept, the meaning, the role and the place that the religion occupies in our age.'[1] Yoga, massage and different practices of meditation can be brought under this category.

Implicit Religion – History of Development

In a conference on 'Spirituality of Secular Ideologies and Religions in the Contemporary Indian Scenario', held at the United Theological College, Bangalore, March 17-19, 2005, Edward Bailey (1935-2015), the Founder Director of the Centre for the Study of Implicit Religion and Contemporary Spirituality gave his key note address in the form of a paper entitled, 'Implicit Religion: A European Concept, with Wider Implications?' The original proposal for including the word 'implicit religion' in the theme of the conference was rejected by those from UTC who planned the conference for the obvious reason of its strangeness and ambiguity.

Bailey's paper set out the background of the continuing struggle to define and understand the nature of religion in the West. Drawing from his own journey in this connection, he gave three pointers 'towards a reality that needed to be studied before it could be described, and might, by definition, be incapable of definition.' The three pointers forming a cluster are commitment(s), integrating foci and intensive concerns with extensive effects. Actually when he originally introduced this in writing, he acknowledged as follows:

> They are three descriptions of the general reality that has been apprehended, and to which each expression tries to point. Their

[1] "The 'Quasi-Religion' of Reiki", by Andrea Menegotto, CESNUR, A paper presented at the CESNUR 2003 Conference, Vilnius, Lithuania. Preliminary version and quoted by the consent of the author. Ref. Website on Quasi-Religion, May 2006.

> plurality may suggest a lack of clarity or of decisiveness. Certainly all three have been worked with for over a quarter of a century without any preference emerging. However, it might therefore also be suggested, that far from indicating conceptual uncertainty, their plurality demonstrates phenomenal certitude. Their number, and hence relativity, witness to the absoluteness of that which is apprehended. It is a fact of experience, before it is a logical construct.[1]

Also, Bailey notes that a fourth definition, description, paraphrase or synonym came to his mind: 'human depths.' 'It has seemed appropriate and accurate,' he writes, 'but has not been worked with, perhaps because each of its terms is more difficult to explain, and potentially harder to agree upon, than those which have been used.'[2] If a list of synonyms or near synonyms is prepared, it should include 'inherent religion, innate religion, incipient religion, minimal religion, religion in general, civic religion, invisible religion, universal religion, secular religion and civil religion.' The two non-synonyms are *folk religion* and *popular religion.* 'Implicit religion directs our attention to expressions of commitment etc. that at present tend not to be seen in religious terms.' It asks whether there might be some aspect of a religious character in the returning procession of an Olympic gold medallist or in the emotional attraction of a shopping mall at Christmas. Similar or parallel activities would include the returning procession in a Corpus Christi fiesta and the ritual compulsion to go away on holiday, where the 'sacrifice' and 'devotion' are involved.

Bailey's own studies in the context of the Church of England raised new questions about the implications of 'being Christian' and 'believing' in modern society. When Bailey was a curate in a parish and chaplain in a school at Winterbourne in 1968, just outside Bristol, (until his retirement as Rector in 2006 Bailey was based in this place), he found no one who had done any study of human religiosity in the sense of what was later popularised as implicit religion. He began to read in the field of religious and secular studies, with a view to testing the viability of a new concept that was yet to settle with a satisfactory term and definition. He launched an empirical study. With different sets of questions he interviewed one hundred persons to find out their 'philosophy of life.' The outstanding impression left by the analysis of the answers was that each person had a Self, which was of supreme value. Many of the other themes seemed to be expressions of this core intuition. Another empirical study was based in a local pub talking to both those worked behind the bar and customers. The discovery was seven 'integrating foci.'

---

[1] E. Bailey, *Implicit Religion: An Introduction*, London: Middlesex University, CSIRCS, 1998, 22.

[2] Ibid., 24.

> The pub as an idea, and the pub as a building, are two inter-dependent foci. Another such pair are the doorway between the two sides, and the sides themselves. They, however, are so closely bound together, as to form a single focus … The fourth focus is also a duality (the bar on each of the sides), but in this case each of them, in parallel, independently integrates the life of its own side … The fifth focus is the 'busy time' … The sixth focus is the Manager … The last of the seven integrating foci is the 'transaction' of 'giving' the drink and 'giving' the money … These seven foci may provide, in miniature, a picture which is recognisable to those familiar with the life of pubs, and imaginable to any who are not.[1]

The full report discusses the place of 'Christianity' within the pub, the parallels between this local pub and the 'typical' local Church, and asks whether they are seen as rivals, or as complementary crucibles of celebratory spirituality. The inner meaning, it is suggested, and the dominant power within the pub, is the strength of its community feeling. This is never mentioned, except negatively: in complaints about the Manager, whose unitive function is therefore that of both presiding bishop and proverbial scapegoat.' 'Indeed', Bailey concludes his pub-study stating that it 'reflects human life generally. So, the implicit religion of the pub may … be described as possessing three facets. They are the ritual activity of "having a drink", the communal solidarity of the initiates, and the mental (mythical and ethical) rationale of "being a man". This is on the assumption that these three are common in religions as identified in studies. However, one may see the three-fold dimensions or foci very limiting as many more dimensions have been identified in a continuing process of a scholarly struggle to understand the height, depth and breadth of religious life.

Subsequently, since 1978 Bailey organised every year an annual conference at Denton Hall, near Ilkley in western Yorkshire, and since 1983 an annual short course in religious education. 'The charitable status of these activities was recognised by the formation of the Network for the Study of Implicit Religion, in 1985. The original wish to keep them professionally focussed, was advanced in 1997 when the recently formed Centre for the Study of Implicit Religion and Contemporary Spirituality was located at Middlesex University.'[2] One important result is that the 'secularisation thesis,' which experienced an Indian summer in the 1960s, has been relativised and shown to be 'an unproven hypothesis' for 'the process was not necessarily inevitable, global, or irreversible.' Further, there have been perceived reasons for challenging the stereotypical way of using the term 'secular' as anti-monastic and anti-church and thus maintaining a dichotomy between 'religious' and 'secular.' Bailey's Bangalore paper ends with

[1] Ibid., 52-58.

[2] Ibid., p. 44.

the observation of Raimundo Panikkar that 'it is possible that only the religious can fully understand the secularity,' which, it states further 'is now so prevalent, not only in our societies but also within our Churches and ourselves. If we ignore it, and its ultimate meaning(s), we may be missing God's left hand.'

Not unexpectedly, Bailey's paper provoked many questions. For example, what is the reaction to this stand from the church and academy? Can it be taken as close to the concerns of the writings on Transcendence? Is not the planetary consciousness devotionally expressed in Psalm 19:1 suggesting a transcendental consciousness and integrated spirituality? Most of the answers and comments from the group were in the affirmative. Calvin's dictum of 'divine sense' in every human consciousness and M.M. Thomas's observation that 'Marxism is a Christian heresy' were also referred to. While the transcendental awareness is common, human and universal, it was observed, in India secularism cannot be opposed to religion, as secular life and religious life are indivisible in the Indian society. But they do not settle down without tension as they involve communal identities and conflicting truth-claims and an exploration of this tension drew attention during major part of the rest of the conference.

From the lonely and strange query of a searching mind CSIRCS has developed a study network that attracts scholars from different parts of the world. It runs (since 1998) *The Journal of Implicit Religion* twice a year and publishes books, and these contain selected papers of the Denton Conference. Having moved from the Middlesex University, the CSIRCS operates as a network. There were once four centres at which research fellows/scholars were being supported to undertake contemporary issues relating to implicit religion: University of Leiden's Religious Studies Department, a similar institute in Bangor University of Wales, Cambridge Divinity School and United College of the Ascension, Birmingham. The Bangalore Conference mentioned above was the first attempt to take the idea of implicit religion outside the United Kingdom, and I was partly responsible for that. As a trustee of CSIRCS and principal of UCA I attended regularly since 2003 the Denton Conference and engaged in discussion with the research fellows and scholars. After the death of Bailey, changes have been made for the operation of CSIRCS and the venue of the annual conference has been shifted from Denton Hall to Sarum College, Salisbury. However, the conviction of the trustees about the importance of the study of implicit religion in its various forms is unchanging.

***Nationalism*:** According to Paul Tillich, 'Nationalism is ultimately rooted in the natural and necessary self-affirmation of every social group, analogous to that of every living being. This self-affirmation has nothing to do with selfishness (though it may be distorted into selfishness). It is the "love of oneself" in the sense of the words of Jesus about loving one's neighbour "as oneself." Such self-affirmation is, in pre-secular periods, consecrated and protected by sacramental rites and oaths; the group and its religion are indistinguishable. Nationalism in the modern sense of the word can appear only when secular criticisms have dissolved the identity of religious consecration and group self-affirmation, and the consecrating religion is pushed aside and the empty space filled by the national idea as a matter of ultimate concern. In the West this development continued after the Renaissance and the Enlightenment, symbolized in the names of Machiavelli and Hobbes and intensified by the rise of the secular state over the fighting Christian confessions and their destructive encounters.'[1]

For Tillich, a nation is determined by two elements: its natural self-affirmation as a living and growing power-structure, and, at the same time, the consciousness of having a vocation, namely, to represent and spread and defend a principle of ultimate significance. It is the unity of these two elements, he argues, which makes the quasi-religious character of nationalism possible. His examples include the Hellenic people who were conscious of representing culture as against the barbarians, Rome which represented the law, the Jews who had the tradition of the divine covenant with a community, and medieval Germany the festival of *corpus Christi* with its Eucharistic procession, which was both religious and political. He further connects the Italians with rebirth or renaissance, the British with a Christian humanism for all nations, especially the primitive ones, France with the highest contemporary culture, Russia with the saving power of the East against the West, China with the global centre, and America with the land of the new beginning and the defender of freedom. He sums up saying, 'now this national idea has reached almost all parts of the world and has shown both its creative and its destructive possibilities.'[2] The unity of its self-affirmation and the consciousness of having a vocation, he adds, makes the quasi-religious character of nationalism possible. There is of course the tension between the two which can lead to either realising a vision such as the kingdom of God or the destruction we have witnessed in the modern world. There were other contemporaries of Tillich who demonstrated that in their doctrine, their cult, and their devotion the secular ideologies as ways of salvation represent an alternative to religion in the twentieth century.[3]

Ninian Smart acknowledges Tillich's views of religion in its depth or as ultimate concern and then himself in his unique way finds the connection between nations and ideologies or religions in different variants around the world. For example, 'Marxism might represent itself as not a religion,' yet he states that, 'its role was very similar to that of the older established religions Orthodoxy and Lutheranism.' He illustrates its various expressions in the former Soviet Union, East Germany and Burma.[4] Smart illustrates his 'dimensions of religion' with different

---

[1] P. Tillich, op. cit., 14f.

[2] Ibid., 15.

[3] E.g. see Earnest B Koenker, *Secular Salvations: The Rites and Symbols of Political. Religions*, Philadelphia: Fortress Press, 1965.

[4] N. Smart, D*imensions of the Sacred*, 254ff; John Hick observes: '… the Communist ideology constitutes a mythic framework for life, providing both a motivation for idealism and a validation

aspects of the United States' nationalism.[1] Accordingly, the mythic dimension is contained in the received history – 'how the Union came into being, arising out of the rebellion against the British (pre-revolutionary history, including a slice of British history, to some extent serves as a sort of Old Testament). In subsequent history, certain items have a significant ritual role, especially the Civil War and its reflected depths as expressed on Memorial Day.' 'The doctrinal or philosophical dimension is expressed in the constitution as enshrining values of a democratic society, and loyalty to these values is an important mark of a genuine American citizen.' In this context, when communism came it was regarded as a doctrine of heresy.

> The ritual of the United States is seen in various activities: saluting the flag, singing the national anthem on important occasions such as baseball games, the ceremonial duties of the President, pilgrimage to celebrate national monuments and, more informally, the beauties of the American landscape, wearing uniforms where appropriate, the honouring of past heroes such as presidents, poets, musicians and writers.[2]

The emotional or experiential dimension may be found in 'reactions to moving national occasions, to celebrations of patriotism, to the singing of significant songs and so on.' The ethical dimension is evident in puritan ideals, democratic and patriotic values. Organisationally, Smart compares priests to schoolteachers who induct the young into the national myth, saints, heroes and heroines, and sacred people to military. There are tensions between being critical of the President and being loyal to the ceremonial head of the state, and the personal religion of some people may not allow them to bow to the ceremonial head of a state. Finally, Smart identifies the material dimension with beautiful landscapes, familiar marvels, memorials and buildings including battlefields of the Revolution and of the Civil War. Smart connects ritual with certain narratives and illustrates it with the 'historical account of President Lincoln's speech after the Battle of Gettysburg, and the same story can be used as the script during the Memorial Day ceremonies which form part of American national religion.'[3] There are few other connections made such as between tourism and pilgrimage. Such connections, identifications and comparisons can be made with reference to

---

of the existing social order; and the communist party is, sociologically, a Church with its own hierarchy, its sacred scriptures, its system of dogma, including doctrines of the fall (the development of capitalism) and eschatology (the eventual classless society), and having its exegetical disputes and heresies. The sociologist Robert Bellah speaks of the 'religio-political system of Marxism'; Hick, *An Interpretation of Religion – Human Responses to the Transcendent*, London: Macmillan, 1989, 22.

[1] Ibid., 13f.

[2] Ibid., 14.

[3] Ibid., 83.

the nationalism of several countries, particularly those which follow democratic principles and secular values.

Smart mentions India also for being in the strange position of a secular country with no actual anti-religious apparatus. The country has a secular constitution and is supposed to treat all religions fairly and equally. However, the majority being Hindus, the Hindutva movement identifies itself with cultural nationalism. Tactically, it is often very difficult to distinguish between the Mother Goddess and Mother India. One of the key resources for understanding the strange phenomenon of such nationalism, apart from saluting the tri-colour flag and saying the Pledge in school assemblies, are the nationalist songs. These songs in different Indian languages might well compare to hymns and psalms of the Christian tradition. Most of these songs pay homage to the Mother India, affirm unity in diversity and call for sacrificing to protect its values and uphold its glory. There is tension when some groups of minority religious communities refuse to comply with the practices such as calling the nation as their mother and saluting the flag.

What is often in conflict with religious nationalism is secular nationalism, which, at least in the Indian case exists side by side. While some argue secularism is different from religion, others demonstrate the certain characteristics of religion are inherited consciously or unconsciously by secular nationalism.

> Yet it seems clear in hindsight that to believe in the notion of secular nationalism required a great deal of faith, even though the idea was not couched in the rhetoric of religion. The terms in which it was presented were the grandly visionary ones associated with spiritual values. Secular nationalism, like religion, embraces what one scholar calls 'a doctrine of destiny.' One can take this way of looking at secular nationalism a step further and state flatly, as did one author writing in 1960, that secular nationalism *is* 'a religion.'[1]

In other words, secular nationalism seems to provide what a religion does, i.e. a collective identity, ultimate loyalty and moral authority though its sources and foundations are different.

At this juncture, it is in order to acknowledge different types of religious nationalism. We have already mentioned Hindu nationalism, on which there are detailed studies.[2] Basically, it is observed:

> Hindu nationalism is an attempt to make Hindus self conscious of their identity as Hindus. It seeks to create a Hindu identity that

---

[1] M. Juergensmeyer, *Religious Nationalism Confronts the Secular State*, New Delhi: Oxford University Press, 1994, 15.

[2] See, for example, John Zavos *et. al., Hindu Nationalism and Indian Politics*, New Delhi: Oxford University Press, 2004.

> can transcend the internal social, cultural, political and regional distinctions of people classified as Hindus. It attempts to make them self conscious of their own history and create a common identity, to mobilize this identity to protect and glorify the claims of Hindus, and most importantly to assert the cultural primacy of Hindus in the territorial entity called India, to define India primarily as the land belonging to Hindus.[1]

In a country united by the foreign rules, where majority of the population (more than eighty percent) is classified as Hindu despite several sects and traditions with their regional and local variations, but which has adopted a secular, democratic and republican polity, it is not easy to analyse the dynamics of different forces that have come together or that confront each other. What is most clear, however, is that the Hindu nationalists have taken advantage of their myths, rituals and doctrines for the political mobilization of Hindu masses, many of whom seem to have fallen a prey to manipulation.

An external study of one major component of Hindu nationalism is published with the title 'Political Hinduism.' The researcher has demonstrated 'that political claims are put forward in order to protect alleged Hindu interests. The introduction of a common civil code, the ban of cow-slaughter, the compulsory teaching of Sanskrit and Yoga in schools, the legal restraint on the conversion of Hindus and the liberation of *Rāma janmabhūmi* are examples of such claims.'[2] The violent face of Hindu nationalism was exposed when a 450 year old mosque was pulled down by Hindu extremists in December 1992 and several lives were lost in the riots before and after the event. It is still smouldering. The moderates are satisfied with an attempt to create a common civil code which cannot be done without the consent of minority religious communities including Muslims and Christians who, along with Hindus, enjoy Personal Law that governs issues such as family and inheritance. The extreme ones insist on the restoration of the traditional Hindu law codes which are not only archaic but discriminative. In this context, along with secular forces, the movements of Dalits, the worst victims of caste and untouchability, put a counterweight. To absorb all minority communities within Dharma, an undefined system which is the production of the Brahmanic Hinduism with its divisive and hierarchic caste at its centre, the outcome is that Sikhs, Buddhists and Jains have been covered by the Hindu Personal Law. The Sikh national movement for a separate Khalistan is partly due to this fact. Somehow, the Muslim and Christian communities which first challenged the Dharma, in spite of some continuing efforts, could not be

---

[1] P.B. Mehta, in his introduction to the Omnibus, Ibid., viii.

[2] E. Hellman, *Political Hinduism: The Challenge of the Viśva Hindu Pariṣad*, Uppsala: Department of the History of Religions, 1993, 20.

swallowed within its elastic belly. Hence, they are the main targets of Hindutva attack.

Apart from the mixing of Hindu cultural nationalism with secular nationalism, it is not difficult to see dimensions of religion in the thinking and practice of the Indian masses. In school assemblies children are asked not only to salute the tri-colour Indian flag, but also recite the pledge that starts with 'India is my country and all Indians are my brothers and sisters ...' This pledge has all the characteristics of a creed. And celebrations of Independence Day and Republic Day remind people of a spectacular religious festival. The ceremony starts with the Prime Minister, and his retinue places a wreath at the memorial of an 'unknown soldier'. The parades of decorated floats representing various states with cultural performances inbuilt have the power to drive the viewers ecstatic.

Also it is obvious to see people frantic at times of both tragedy and celebration while encountering the political leaders. Apart from the solemn singing of the national anthem, there are other singings of nationalist songs. The nationalist songs are in every vernacular. They have the rare combination of heroism and piety. When I think of the popular nationalist songs in Tamil there are too many for us to select and do an analytical study. It is hoped that scholars of religion will take them seriously and study them in depth.

Religious nationalism in the Muslim world has yet a different character. Some charismatic and thinking leaders in the Muslim world did not fail to notice the hidden force of Christian culture within the western secularism. However, they did not expose the 'Christian' source within it, perhaps with a view to not to jeopardise the inherent connections between the Semitic religious traditions. Their open slogan is westernisation. As Juergensmeyer observes, 'One of the things that most exercised the Ayatollah Khomeini in pre-revolutionary Iran was what he and others referred to as "West-toxification" or "Westomania." According to Khomeini, Islamic peoples have been stricken with Westomania since the eighth century, and partly for that reason they easily accepted the cultural and political postures of the Shah. More recent attempts to capitalize on Westomania, he maintained, have come from the insidious efforts of Western imperialists. The goal of the Islamic revolution in Iran, then, was not only to free Iranians politically from the Shah but also to liberate them conceptually from Western ways of thinking.'[1] Some other countries in the Middle East also perceive secularism to be their enemy because of its capacity as a mask to cover the Western agenda. For example, a leader of the religious right in Israel has declared, 'Secular government is illegitimate' and one of his rivals, a Muslim leader in Palestine, has echoed it by saying, 'a secular state is anti-Islamic' and that, 'no such thing exists in Islam.'[2] Many religious leaders attributed the failures in social, economic, moral and political arenas in their countries to the penetration and powerful influence of secularism. The ongoing

[1] Juergensmeyer, op. cit., 19.

[2] Ibid., 21.

struggle to re-establish a theocratic Muslim state throughout the Muslim world is based on this attribution.

Buddhism, a religion with its characteristic marks of non-violence and peace is not an exception in criticising secularism and trying to establish Buddhist states. 'The moral impact of Western secularism in Sri Lanka was devastating, according to the calculations of some leaders of Buddhist monastic organizations. One of them, in discussing this matter, carefully identified the evils of the society around him and then laid them fully at the feet of the secular government. "We live in an immoral world," the bhikkhu (monk) stated, giving as his examples of immorality, gambling, slaughtering animals for meat, and drinking *arrack* (a locally produced alcohol that is popular in the countryside). In each case the government was implicated: the state lottery promotes gambling, the state encourages animal husbandry, and it licenses liquor shops. The institutions of the government were all suspect, the bhikkhu implied: "People in public office are not to be trusted."'[1] Sri Lanka's unfinished religious revolt needs to be understood in this context. One can imagine the counter arguments from the secular side.

Studies on religion and violence, terrorism and religion, clash of civilizations or clash of fundamentalisms abound in today's research industry. In one way or other they deal with the questions and dynamics involved in grappling with the issues of secular and religious nationalisms. They are mentioned here just to point out the excessive developments from or associated with nationalism as a quasi- (in Tillich's sense) or implicit religion (in Bailey's sense). We do not need to divert and detail these developments here. Rather we will continue with examples of implicit religion.

Religion of Sports: 'Football is our religion' is the popular creed in England. There are studies in different contexts. In one such study done in the US in early 80s, the author, after stating that humans are extraordinary species, observes that 'Of all events in human history, the one to attract the largest audience was not a great political occasion, nor a special celebration of a complex achievement in the arts or sciences, but a simple ball-game – a soccer match. On a June day in 1978, it is claimed that more than a thousand million people tuned into the World Cup Final between Argentina and Holland. This means that something like one quarter of the entire world population stopped whatever they were doing and focused their attention on a small patch of grass in south America where twenty-two brightly clad figures were kicking a ball about in a frenzy of effort and concentration.'[2] Industrial organisation, emotional fulfilment and symbolic significance have been observed. Elements of a tribal solidarity with territorial aggression, aggressive outpour of valour and strength and heroes and fans with certain superstitious beliefs were obvious. Elements of animal hunting in Roman coliseums arranged for frustrated hunters could be reminisced.

[1] Ibid., 21.

[2] Desmond Morris, *The Soccer Tribe*, London: Jonathan Cape Ltd., 1981, 7.

The scale of the interest in soccer was evident in newspapers as if it was the most important thing in human life. It has many faces, both obvious and masked. The author of the above book compares soccer to a ritual hunt, stylized battle, status display and religious ceremony. The last point is significant for our study here.

> Many people – some jokingly, some seriously – have likened soccer to a religious order, and have caricatured soccer supporters as modern equivalents of religious fanatics. The grass that grows on the soccer pitch is often referred to as 'the sacred turf,' and the stadium is called 'the shrine.' Star players are 'worshipped' by their adoring fans and looked upon as 'young gods.' The directors' board room becomes 'the Holy of Holies.' Superstitions and magical practices are rife and on the terraces, the crowded ranks of the so-called hooligans sing songs in unison which, despite their often obscene words, sound for all the world like the hymns of massed choirboys. Indeed some of them *are* hymns, borrowed directly from the church hymnbook. Perhaps the comparisons that have been that have been made between a soccer match and church service are not so far-fetched after all.[1]

The massive gathering is more lively than many congregations! There are solemn movements and ecstatic moments with 'liturgical symbols and colours.' Repetition is unavoidable. The soccer match, the author points out, is a social drug, a big business and theatrical performance. There are taboos, moral rules and disciplinary actions. The 'central ritual' around which all other tribal activities are built, 'is the suspense-laden, strictly controlled, ninety minutes of play. Sliced into two halves by a brief interval, begun and ended by a shrill blast on the referee's whistle, this is the time when, for the devoted tribesmen, the rest of the world briefly ceases to exist. It is the time for non-stop concentration, for almost unbeatable tension and uncontrollable joy, for deep depression and wild elation.'[2] There are predictable and unpredictable moments of the rolling ball which with its optimum speed becomes the central focus of devotion. Its reach to the goal evokes the highest outpour of emotion. Songs of praise are balanced by hymns of hate!

There is a hero worship in soccer as the fans in a frenzy rush for the sports stars' autograph or catching what they would throw in the air. There is a difference of opinion between the traditionalists and modernists. 'The traditionalists believe that any softening of the ritual will inevitably rob it of its intensity and its significance; the modernists insist that without showbiz glamour and improved amenities the tribesmen will drift away and the sport will die. Soccer has been

---

[1] Ibid., 22f.

[2] Ibid., 94.

described as a pseudo-religion, and a similar conflict of opinion exists in the church itself, with those priests favouring high ritual clashing repeatedly with modernists who wish to bring religious practices up to date and more into line with twentieth-century attitudes and lifestyles. If their world is any guide and a parallel can be drawn, then the immense success of Papal pomp and ceremonial display in recent years would seem to favour the soccer traditionalists. Guitar-playing vicars who scorn difficult ritual have proved to be a signal failure. Perhaps if the soccer match becomes "fund for all the family" it will lose the very quality which has enabled it to spread around the world and attract larger, more devoted audiences than any other human pastime – the quality of a sternly fought contest.'[1] It is not difficult to decipher so many symbolic echoes from our primeval past.

It was Bill Shankley, a Manager of Liverpool Football Club who spoke famously that 'Some people say that football is a matter of life and death but they are wrong … it's more important than that.'[2] Football hymns follow some of the popular tunes of Christian hymns such as 'Guide me O thou great Jehovah' and 'Abide with me.' The way fans share stories of their favourite players with reference to their extraordinary performance suggests that they are not far from the style of religious myths of oral and written traditions. Managers of football clubs and captains of teams are sometimes called messiahs. Discipline in clubs appears to be more serious that it is practised in religious communities. The emotional outpouring at the time of a trophy being lifted excels the frenzy of massive religious groups. There have been several other studies on the 'religion of football.'[3]

The religion of sports is not only a western phenomenon but it has spread all over the world with varying intensity. In India cricket is the game that has attracted wide fans and audience. The experience and expressions we sense in the Indian cricket fans are not different from those in the English football fans. Moreover, kissing Gates of the stars and reverence before them or their portraits etc are very common.

---

[1] Ibid., 316f.

[2] Quoted, Nick Moxon, 'Religious Dimensions Seen in Football', paper presented to the course on Interfaith Studies, Wesley College, Bristol, 1997, 1.

[3] E.g. Scott Crawford, 'American Football as Religion: Some Theoretical Perspectives', *Physical Education Review*, 12/1 (1989), 12-20. The shred concepts include body, testimony, tradition, saints, domination by ruling patriarch, god-like figures, high councils, scribes, seekers of the kingdom, house of worship, symbols and faith and role of colour symbolism with illustrations; also see Hal W. French, 'Religion and Football: The Cult of the Fighting Gamecock' – paper presented in the 4th Denton Conference, 1981; this paper deals with war pattern, heroism and aggression. For a lively comparison between messianic visions in religion and football and between religious fundamentalism and footballmentalism, see Greg Watts, 'Face to Face: We are the Champions', *The Guardian,* Saturday October 21, 2000, 26; also see the Editorial of *Guardian*, Saturday August 16 1997, 3.

Princess Diana Cult

We have already mentioned certain personality cults in Tamilnadu India with special reference to Annadurai, M.G. Ramachandran and Jeyalalitha. There is enough reason for taking the Princess Diana syndrome for a detailed treatment, not least because of the magnitude of reactions and international and scholarly attention.

Princess Diana of England was killed in a road accident on 31 August 1997. The whole nation was shocked by the loss of a charming, down-to-earth and charitable member of the British royal family. Soon streets were filled with milling crowds with flowers and candles. Churches were unprecedentedly filled with people in tears and spontaneously praying. One pertinent question raised was: what made a nominally Christian but phenomenally secular behaviour of the British people instantly religious? More questions were raised: Was there a feeling in the subconscious which was pushed to burst out by this tragedy? Should a great princess die in such a tragic manner for people to become religious or spiritual for a while? A number of studies have been done on this phenomenon.

There have been critical perspectives on the Princess Diana phenomenon. For example, Paul Nathanson, in an insightful essay[1] has identified four viewpoints. First, it has provided millions of westerners with myths and rituals of various types of worldview. Second, 'this worldview can be described as emotionalism – that is, romanticism minus whatever intellectual substance.' Third, whether acknowledged as religious or secular, it remains implicit without any private or public acknowledgement. Fourth, it is closely related to or supported by one of the explicitly articulated worldviews such as feminism but in conflict with Marxism and traditional Christianity.[2] The phenomenon was not only unusual in historical terms but also revealing in cultural terms manifesting a link to their religious counterparts.

> Over and over again, for example, mourners referred to Diana as a 'saint' or a 'goddess' or an 'icon.' Some talked about 'praying' to Diana, even asking her to 'intercede in heaven for them.' When David Hasselhoff entertained the crowds at Althorp, Diana's ancestral Estate, he not only sang 'A Brand New Angel' (originally written for a dead character in his television show *Baywatch*), but 'prayed to the Princess to stop the rain. "And she did", he said. "It was the most amazing thing".' May be, as Simon Schama has suggested, this due partly to symbolic associations, no matter how remote or garbled, with royal thaumaturgy: just as Diana laid 'healing hands on the sick, kings

[1] Nathanson, "I feel, therefore I am: the Princess of Passion and the implicit religion of our time", *Implicit Religion, Journal of the Centre for the Study of Implicit Religion and Contemporary Spirituality*, 2/2 Nov., 1999, 59-88.

[2] This is a summary of the abstract given at the beginning, Ibid., 59.

> used to lay their hands on the sick ... Whether they called themselves 'pilgrims' or not, moreover Diana's mourners clearly came together from all over the country to makeshift shrines, and left behind personal offerings. No wonder some journalists referred to this phenomenon as a 'cult.'[1]

Though Diana was seen to be an ambivalent character in her lifetime, many people identified with her thinking of their own grief, loneliness and loss. However, for Nathanson, her death was just one expression, albeit the most dramatic one, of an implicit 'religion' which was unprecedented quite the same way.

Nathanson observes seven things associated with Diana's life: popularity, compassion, celebrity, maturity, fashion, victimization and triumph. After explaining each in an interesting and engaging way, he goes back to his thesis that the Diana phenomenon was 'an unacknowledged *variant* of religion' and explains further:

> I do not assume, in other words, that the phenomenon in question *is* religion. It is something that closely resembles religion, something that functions in many ways as if it were religion. Many ways, but not every way. Thus, unlike religion, it does not mediate the sacred. As I understand it, the sacred is not merely a characteristic feature of religion, but *the* characteristic feature, the defining feature, the *sine qua non*. Precisely what is the sacred? Definitions vary from one anthropologist or phenomenologist or another. But whatever it is, in my opinion, the sacred is irreducible to psychological, sociological, ethical, political, or any other terms. It is, as Mircea Eliade put it, *sui generis*.[2]

One implication he draws from this analysis is that, 'Diana's worldview – which is to say in a more significant sense, that of her followers – is best described as a "secular religion." And noting some other forms of secular religion such as nationalism and communism, he observes: '*Implicit* forms of secular religion, on the other hand, are not as clearly defined. Some, including various forms of feminism, are relatively easy to spot. But others are so elusive that their existence was not even suspected until very recently.'[3] He continues to observe that there is continuity between religion and secular religion, and the two overlap in many ways. Behind a popular cult, secular elements are discernible and likewise a film on secular myth may have elements close to a traditional religion: this Nathanson illustrates in his celebrated work *Over the Rainbow: The Wizard of Oz as a Secular Myth of America*, which for him resembles the religious epic *Ramayana* of India.

---

[1] Ibid., 59f.

[2] Ibid., 72.

[3] Ibid.

'Implicit religion' or what he calls 'implicit secular religion', for Nathanson, 'consists of whatever people truly believe about life in general and their own lives in particular.' He explains:

> As the term itself indicates, implicit religion does not coincide with explicitly religious beliefs (although it can coexist with them, and does so in many churches). It does not necessarily coincide even with explicitly political or other beliefs (although, presumably, it could coexist with them as well). It is, in short, whatever *actually* guides people in daily life, as distinct from whatever (if anything) theoretically guides them. It is an *unrecognized and unarticulated worldview*.[1]

Linking this to Diana, he observes, though she did not invent nor was aware of implicit religion, she presided over it and still does, 'as an image no longer bound by the reality of human mortality and finitude. The event of her death was like a volcano; what had long flowed placidly underground suddenly boiled upward to the surface and erupted with a colossal bang, sending metaphorical ash and lava cascading down into the public square.'[2] As recognized by words and actions, particularly at her funeral, with a multiple personality, Diana was Mother Nature, Goddess of victims and therapist surrounded by the scent of a million tearful roses.

What Nathanson sees in the Diana phenomenon is glorification of emotion at the cost of reason and a pervasive mentality of the implicit religion of many millions with Diana as their patron (matron!) saint. He identifies six aspects of this implicit religion of emotionalism: the origin of emotionalism, the dark side of emotion, emotional spontaneity, the feminization of emotion, the politicization of emotion and the Americanization of emotion. Then he explains each drawing historical, sociological, psychological and political insights. For example, he notes, the precursor of modern emotionalism was romanticism which was a reaction against the chain of Renaissance, medieval scholasticism, and Enlightenment. Evidently, for those who signed condolence books, 'it was not enough for them to *mourn* the loss of someone they admired. They had to *blame* someone for it.' And the soothing speeches of her adversaries in the royal family timely addressed the need of the crowd. 'Diana, of course, had come to present the new order: a class consisting of those who are emotionally open.' Emotional and sentimental, the mourners of Diana's loss were seen hysterical and media presented this in such a way that a debate can be initiated. The grip in the people was comparable to that of even a fascist ideology such as Nazism though the expression was different.

> They did not want to murder anyone. But they were intensely aware of themselves as a new kind of *community*, united by a common

[1] Ibid., 74.

[2] Ibid.

> *implicit religion*, and in possession of *collective power*. And they were equally aware of dissent from those who either could not or would not be part of this community. To be part of the crowd was to be part of a community; to be apart from it, therefore, was to be cut off from it – to be ostracized, humiliated, attacked in one way or another. Clive James explicitly *threatened* outsiders, declaring that 'although those who did not participate in the vigil might sit in judgment on us for our mass delusion, we will judge them, in our turn, for their inhuman detachment.' This mentality, though seldom expressed so openly, became pervasive.[1]

The 'dark side of emotion' found expression in condemning the royal family for not feeling the grief publicly. There was no system to criticize themselves!

From the perspective of 'the feminization of emotion, Diana, after being a wife and mother, soon became a feminist icon. Nathanson quotes Sarah Ban Breathnach writing, 'If Diana's death imparts only one lesson, it is that *passion is holy*, to be embraced, even as we tremble with fear that love will hurt us.' Nathanson comments by raising a question for the reason and suggests an answer: 'Presumably because our society has attached more importance to the supposedly male domain of thinking, than to the supposedly female domain of feeling.' After making 'supposed' comment on the nature of the 'superior reason' of women and the way feeling was expressed or restrained over the death of Diana, he comes to a conclusion: 'The fact is that feeling has *always* been much more popular than thinking. After all, thinking is *harder* than feeling. It requires effort, perseverance, discipline. And it often leads to 'inconvenient' conclusions. That is why the glorification of reason has never been the basis for a populist movement. That is also why intellectuals are usually among the first to be persecuted under ideological regimes ... It is not merely emotion that has been feminized, therefore, but men themselves. Men have emotions just as women do, after all, but they are allowed to express them only in ways approved by women. Poor Charles never understood that, but Diana did. This was her trump card.'[2]

As far as the 'the politization of emotion' is concerned, the starting point is that 'the fashion for apologies is surely a logical outgrowth of the fashion for feminism itself.' Coincidently, the newly elected Labour Prime Minister of Britain (Tony Blair) was projected as having the qualities of 'compassion, forgiveness, apology, understanding, and nurturing.' This was in contrast to his predecessor (John Major) who was committed to 'responsibility, self-discipline, the Protestant work ethic, stiff-upper-lippedness, the appeal to reason and intellect.' Nathanson notes:

---

[1] Ibid., 76f.

[2] Ibid., 78f.

> To put all this another way, the new order is defined in terms of stereotypically associated with women, and the old in terms stereotypically associated with men ... The old and new orders, apparently, are locked in mortal combat for supremacy in either the mind or heart, as the case might be, of every citizen. For the time being, one side has clearly one: Britain (and other Western countries) are rapidly being feminized. The rhetoric of choice for political leaders, in other words, is a 'female' idiom.[1]

One can see the return of the anti-intellectualism of many of the old Christian missionaries who went overseas. Curiously, in the modern or post-modern age it has become fashionable in much of the media, culture and even academia.

'The Americanization of emotion' could be seen in the emphasis on emotional caring, in all spheres, from the royal family to therapy. Diana personified the new status of emotion suggesting implicitly that monarchy, just like religion, should be 're-invented as a glamorized form of psychotherapy.' She was projected as the queen of passionate hearts that appealed to popular masses through talk shows.

In conclusion, Nathanson quoting various writers emphasizes the reigning of emotion that was evident at the death and funeral of Diana in strange forms of male tearfulness and weeping combined with public apology. 'Gone is the old dictum of René Descartes (the Public Enemy Number One of postmodernism): I think, therefore I am. This has been replaced with a new dictum: I *feel*, therefore I am.'[2] The concluding words of his conclusion suggest a convincing way of understanding implicit religion:

> ... it is fair to say that, even though some forms of implicit religion appear on the surface to be secular, but reveal religious paradigms just below the surface, other forms of implicit religion appear on the surface to be religious or quasi-religious, but reveal secular paradigms just below the surface. The former would be exemplified by some popular movies, such as the *Wizard of Oz*, which perpetuate very ancient ways of perceiving the world, but in the guise of secular entertainment. The latter would be exemplified by emotionalism, once associated specifically with romanticism and now with what has been called 'therapism:' it promotes a very modern (or post modern) way of perceiving the world, yet in the guise of a quasi-religious piety.[3]

Nathanson in his 'appendix' proposes a continuing programme of research on the many phenomena such as personal-official and private-public associated with Diana's death and cultural legacy. This would entail, at the very least, a

---

[1] Ibid., 80.

[2] Ibid., 81f.

[3] Ibid., 82.

systematic research into materials available – interviews with mourners, pilgrims to her tomb, notes and objects left there, entries in the condolence books, letters to editors of newspapers, articles on Diana's private and public problems, and critics of the whole phenomenon. Since this essay was published in 1999, two years after the death of Diana, several materials have been produced which deserve an elaborate analytical study.

Innumerable Variety

Those who read the papers presented in the Denton Conference (hereafter, Salisbury) many of which are published in the journal on Implicit Religion, may wonder if there is a limit to categorizing behaviours, movements etc. as implicit religion. The variety of themes and discourses seems to suggest an unregulated thinking market! And the addition of secular spirituality (later modified as 'contemporary spirituality') has opened the avenue wide open for free thinking. And there are few novel categories such as 'no religion.'[1] However, such categories are not self-evident. For example, here 'no religion' is put in negative term and it needs to be explored to find out what has replaced religion. In the case of implicit religion it is put in positive term although the variety of phenomenon of this category provides room for more research into subtleties and nuances.

It suffices to point out, apart from the above, church statistics in the UK, spirituality of theatres, faith and expression of teenagers, the charismatic and aggressive character of successful managers, spirituality behind the establishment of statues for some sports stars, the ethos of the Glastonbury festival, spirituality of the wild levels of happiness connected with buying a car, marrying and buying a house, internet hype with elements of messianic hope and so on. One of the research fellows did an analysis of the popular film *Bend it like Beckham*. Some of the dimensions of the explicit religion and discussion on classical theories of religion coalesce for making a case of implicit religion. Religious dimension is identified in compulsive buying.

Concluding Remarks

While 'religion' continues to evade a most convincing definition and dimensions of religion are yet to be neatly presented, new forms of religions add to the complexity. When Tillich used the word quasi-religion for nationalism and certain ideologies including fascism and communism he suggested that human beings have enormous spiritual capacity to direct lives and the course of history both positively and negatively. This is evident, for example, in American civil religion and nationalism of different types around the world. Religious nationalism is a unique type and it is neither implicit not overtly explicit. It is rather a movement within a religion with a view to project their nation as founded on the principles

[1] E.g., See Norval D. Glenn in "'No Religion' Respondents to U.S. National Surveys, Late 1950s to Early 1980s", *Public Opinion Quarterly* (1987) 51 (3): 293-314.

of a particular religion or to seek a national identity for their religion as it is challenged by new forces such as secularism and presence of people of other religions. However, in the ongoing interpretation and concerted action it is not easy to pinpoint its true nature. With this ambiguity it is included here.

The implicit religion proper, expounded by Bailey on the basis of three descriptions (commitment(s), integrating foci and intensive concerns with extensive effects), arrived at by research, provides a tool to discern aspects in ordinary life and extraordinary happenings. However, these three descriptions do not dovetail all phenomena of unusual type. Hence, the variety and open avenues to explore new forms of implicit religion. Two phenomena we have discussed with some detail: sports and the Diana syndrome. Some of the sports stars become respected out of their playing fields and their exhortation is heeded to by their fans about political and philosophical matters. The 'material dimension' (particularly economics) which we discussed in the last chapter could be connected with their possession and life style. The Diana syndrome reflects not only the religiosity of the British public but also the archetypal substratum of human life. Interestingly, all such issues suggest that study of explicit religion and study of implicit religion can help one another to find the depth and width of human life with its unfathomable religiosity.

Chapter 4

Dialogical Approaches to the Study of Religion

The Continuing Search for Comprehension

In the previous chapters we noticed that religion in its variety of form, practice and perceived meaning, is a reality too prominent in human life to be ignored. At the same time it is too complex for any claim to have achieved full comprehension. This is in spite of a plethora of definitions, approaches and analyses. Religion and those who pursue it aiming to grasp it fully may be compared to a game chased by a group of hunters. The game neither disappears nor appears close enough to catch. The hunters use all sorts of techniques ranging from enticing music to setting a trap. Their prey runs straight and then agile with instant turns and direction, takes a zigzag course, so that often the hunters find themselves back at their starting point.

We will illustrate the complexity of this unique pursuit by showing some of these changes, even changes in finding proper names. The different approaches will be referred to, as we have dealt with the definitions of religion. The main concern of this chapter is to identify *dialogical* approaches that have emerged from the study and analyses of other approaches and in the practice of interfaith dialogue.

The study of religion did not have the privilege of a precise date of christening with a permanent name. Max Müller (1823-1900), one of the pioneers of the study of religion, coined the term 'science of religion' towards the end of the nineteenth century. Since then it has been expanded as 'scientific study of religion'. The term 'comparative religion,' or 'comparative study of religion', or Ninian Smart's preference, 'comparative study of worldviews,' should not be taken to mean comparing and contrasting different religious traditions or concepts, but studying common features or dimensions of religion with reference to different religious traditions. 'History of religion' is yet another term, but this too should not be mistaken for a historical study of religion(s) which traces origins and development as well as defining key ideas and decisive moments. Since the 1960s the name 'religious studies' has become very popular. Smart established the first department of Religious Studies at Lancaster and then at Santa Barbara.

Again it is not easy to set boundaries to this. 'Phenomenology of religion', though, has a specific history and meaning as we will explain soon, sometimes being used to indicate in general the scientific study of religious phenomena.[1]

It may well be expected that in 'interfaith studies,' as well as in 'world religions,' there will be some discussion of methodology and different approaches to the study of religion. In particular, the study of religion's relationship with theology continues to be debated, and opinions differ. This difference finds expression in the way universities have structured departments of theology and religious studies. Often it is one department either having both the names ('theology and religious studies') or having only one name ('theology' or 'faculty of divinity') with the assumption that it includes the other. It would be a profitable study to bring together different institutional cases and study the presuppositions underlying their nomenclature and highlight the continuing struggle for greater comprehension.

The development of different approaches to the study of religion presents yet another example of the ongoing pursuit of grasping the nature and function of religion. Approaches normally include two aspects: attitudinal principles and methods of perspective and procedure. As we noted before, the word 'methodology' might frighten beginners in the field of the study of religion and they might be bewildered by the variety of ways scholars and writers use the term. One might try to exorcise the term by simply explaining that it stands for perspectives taken and procedures adopted. Sometimes discussions on methodology remain un-integrated into the main body of research and what is achieved in the end is a bundle of information of ideas and historical details. The problem lies not only in the term and its meaning(s) in English, but also in the different ways it is understood and applied.

Attitudes and Methodical Approaches to the Study of Religion

As far as the application of attitudinal principles to the study of religion is concerned, it is not true that the concern originated only when 'science of religion' took definite shape. To understand these changes of attitude a more balanced view of the western missionary era is needed. Normally that era is seen as dominated at worst by uncharitable, triumphalist attacks on other faiths and at best by comparison with a view to scoring points. Even Max Müller, while advocating

[1] E.g. See Mariasusai Dhavamony, *Phenomenology of Religion*, Rome: Gregorian University Press, 1973. The author discusses the method of 'historical phenomenology of religion' in which knowledge of history and phenomenology complement each other, but then he carefully distinguishes 'phenomenological method' from 'historical method' and 'comparative method.'

that missionaries make a serious study of the *Sacred Books of the East*, at least at the beginning of their translation and publication, betrayed his bias towards the missionaries by claiming this study to be 'as indispensable as the knowledge of the enemy's country is to a General.'[1] However, we should not lose sight of exceptional missionaries who called for an approach governed by reverence and respect. A detailed study of theologians and missionaries encountering world religions during 1846-1914 is given the title *Justice, Courtesy and Love*, and these words come from a missionary who worked in southern India.[2] Other missionaries who worked there (especially from the beginning of the twentieth century) can also be credited with a commitment to interfaith dialogue, a commitment that at times even aimed for empathy in their understanding of the religious feeling of those studied.[3] Therefore the connection between the missionary contribution to the development of a new approach to other religious traditions and the growing field of the 'scientific study of religion' needs due recognition.

The so-called scientific approaches to the study of religion did not emerge instantly. One can notice growth even in the understanding of such approaches. For example, a collection of essays on 'classical approaches to the study of religion' that appeared in 1973 has, apart from five chapters on a historical survey, forty one entries on major figures who contributed to the study of religion from different perspectives but without classifying them into methodological categories.[4] More than ten years later a collection of 'contemporary approaches' in two volumes carries, apart from a few essays about the nature and history of the study of religion, essays on the following approaches: historical and phenomenological, comparative, psychological, sociological, social anthropological and cultural-anthropological.[5] Subsequently, materials on one or a selection of these approaches have flooded the field. Even when two writers write about a particular approach, it is clear that they differ in scope, selection and conceptual framework.

More recently, a volume entitled *Approaches to the Study of Religion* (1999) includes essays on anthropological, feminist, phenomenological, philosophical, psychological, sociological and theological approaches.[6] One might question the suitability of two of the essays included in this volume. The last one on 'theological approaches' tries to analyse the connection between theology and religious studies, tracing the line of development in the western Christian tradition. Considerable

[1] Max Müller, *The Sacred Books of the East*, Oxford: At the Clarendon Press, 1879, xl.

[2] See Kenneth Cracknell, *Justice, Courtesy and Love*, London: Epworth Press, 1995.

[3] See Israel Selvanayagam, *A Second Call: Ministry and Mission in a Multifaith Milieu*, Madras: Christian Literature Society, 2000, 46ff, 175f.

[4] J. Waardenburg, *Classical Approaches to the Study of Religion: Aims, Methods, and Theories of Research*, Vol. I: *Introduction and Anthology*, The Hague: Mouton Publishers, 1973.

[5] F. Whaling (ed.), *Contemporary Approaches to the Study of Religion*, Berlin: Mouton Publishers, 1983 (Vol. I), 1985 (Vol. II).

[6] Peter Connolly (ed.), *Approaches to the Study of Religion*, New York: Cassell, 1999.

space is devoted to what is normally known as the 'theology of religious pluralism.' However, while it is almost impossible to separate theology from religious studies, and while there are distinctive *attitudes* evident in theological approaches, clearly it is not easy to establish theology as providing a particular *method* to the study of religions.

Secondly, it is interesting that feminist approaches have been given a due place in the above volume. However, it should be pointed out that its premises and concerns are common to feminist theology which has established a stable place in the field of theology. The basic premise is opposition in appropriate ways to different forms of oppression and discrimination, which women suffer because of their gender. It exposes the continuing power of patriarchy that dominates women and perpetuates a traditional notion of inferiority of women because of their distinctive biological structure as a gender, and the expectations and roles imposed on them by a particular cultural notion of gender. It is the special concern of the feminists to point out the power and function of patriarchy in religious traditions starting from Christianity. They also unearth myths and symbols that provide insights into ancient cases of feminine agitation to masculine power and domination. However, there is no reason to claim that feminist theologians provide a new 'scientific method' for the study of religion, nor that feminist scholars are incapable of contributing to other approaches to the same. It requires a separate study to highlight the recent contribution of women scholars to the study of religion although traditionally its pioneers and most popular figures are men.

Besides, a number of volumes presented the science or study of religion in different order and focus.[1] Particularly, a *Companion to the Study of Religion*[2] that appeared in 2005 has updated and proved much more comprehensive than the previous volumes. The two essays under 'introduction' explain the reason for the study of religions and its history. Under 'key approaches to the study of religions' the following titles are arranged: theories of religion, theology, philosophy of religion, religious studies, sociology of religion, anthropology of religion, psychology of religion, phenomenology of religion, and comparative religion. Part two deals with gender, postmodernism, orientalism, secularisation, mysticism, new religious movements, fundamentalism, myth and ritual, religious authority (scripture, tradition and charisma), hermeneutics, religious pluralism,

---

[1] E.g. see Peter Antes, Armin W. Geertz, Randi R. Warne, eds., *New Approaches to the Study of Religion*. Volume 1: Regional, Critical, and Historical Approaches, Verlag de Gruyter (Berlin & New York) in the Religion and Reason series 42, 2004; *The Future of the Study of Religion*, ed. by Slavica Jakelic and Lori Pearson, Leiden: Brill, 2004; *The Emergence of the Science of Religion in the Netherlands*, by Arie L. Molendijk, Leiden: Brill, 2005; *Comparing Religions: Possibilities and Perils?* Ed. by Thomas Athanasius Idinopulos, Brian C. Wilson, and James Constantine, Hanges: Brill, 2006; *Introducing Religion: Essays in Honour of Jonathan Z Smith,* ed. by Russell McCutcheon and Willi Braun, London: Equinox, 2008.

[2] John R. Hinnels (ed.), *The Routledge Companion to the Study of Religion*, New York: Routledge, 2005.

religion and politics, religion and geography, religion and science, religion and cognition, religion and culture, religion and the arts, and diaspora religion in the context of migration and transnationalism. As one can expect there is a great deal of overlap in these topics.

Similar to the feminist, political, geographical and diaspora concerns there are other concerns such as the subaltern traditions and identities, which have yet to find a place of recognition in religious studies, which otherwise is a western dominated field. But the concerns have been expressed elsewhere. For example, for the past twenty-five years Dalit concerns have attracted substantial studies. Dalits are the worst victims of the age-long caste system perpetuated by the Brahmanic Hindu tradition in India. Their awakening mainly in the twentieth century led to serious reconsideration of traditional theologies, methods of approaching religious traditions and secular ideologies in the Indian context. Particularly, the distinctiveness of the Dalit religion and their subaltern traditions as well as their connection with the Brahmanic tradition are hot topics in ongoing debates.[1] The unique experience and perceptions of Dalit women are recognised in such debates.

When particular community identities, with their distinctive problems, draw the attention of the study of religion, the field is not only growing but also becoming more complex. The tribal identities in India and the so-called primal societies of islands around the world have been taken seriously in the anthropological and sociological approaches. At the same time other group identities warrant recognition too. For example, the experience of children in their religious life can provide fresh insights into the nature of religion and into subtle ways of oppression on the basis of age or in the early stages of life. The exploration should be different from merely classifying them as 'infants' and 'adolescents' and should define their mental ability to receive appropriate religious education, which is done more than adequately at least in Christian circles and religious studies in the west. It requires a distinctive mindset and method to bring out the religious experience of children and to find out restrictions imposed upon their growth and broadening of vision by particular traditions. And some religious traditions, particularly Christianity, have important stories to emphasise the significance of children's experience and attitude for adults to shape their true consciousness and grow towards full personhood.

One more observation we want to make before we move to deal with main concern of this chapter, i.e. the dialogical approach to the study of religion. We need to be clear that a particular approach such as psychological and phenomenological is not monolithic. There are different methods applied in each and different conclusions arrived at. This is because of the background and aptitude of the researcher, the geographical and cultural location of the field or person and the analytical tools he/she handles. We would illustrate with an

[1] For different views on this matter, see the articles in a special issue devoted to Dalit concerns of *Religion and Society*, 49/2-3, June & September, 2004.

introduction of eleven key thinkers in the sociology of religion.[1] Historically they are from the classical period to the contemporary, and a quick glance will catch the eyes of the reader about the growth and variety of the most famous sociology of religion. Most intriguingly, Sigmund Freud of the psychological school is taken to be a sociologist. Justifiably, on the basis of his psychoanalysis he projects a tribal society in which the sons, being jealous of their father's domination over their mother and sisters killed him and being unbearable of his absence they marked a totem animal. Of course his theory and story have been criticised. This is not to challenge the interdisciplinary approach of Freud but to be aware of particular starting points, particular locations and particular conclusions. This will apply to almost all the 'key thinkers' presented in the said volume. This is acknowledged here and there. For instance, the author in his introduction mentions that 'Religion indeed does vary from one place to another in its ability not only to define, own, and circumscribe the sacred but to regulate and interpret the sacred.'[2] There is no doubt that we have the variety of experiences and expressions from studies but we must take the fruits as aspectual and perspectival, and only on their basis we cannot construct a comprehensive understanding of human religion.

Towards a Dialogical Approach

First of all it should be made clear that a dialogical approach is not anti-methodological. As Hinnels observes, there is no one 'right' way to study religions and the only 'wrong way' is dogmatism.[3] And dogmatic tendencies are discernible even within the 'scientific' approaches to the study of religion. Different approaches, however, provide important insights into not only the history of humanity but also the age-long quest for ultimate meaning and purpose of human life. For example, the *historical* approach in general provides the setting of the origin of a particular religious tradition, decisive moments of its development, forces of impact and changes and the present condition in its breadth and variety. *Anthropological* approaches deal with a variety of issues ranging from the study of fossil remains, to the evolutionary process, and to cultural behaviours. The findings of ethnographic studies too are of timeless value. *Psychological* approaches help us to understand different opinions about the states of consciousness, the structure and changes in the human brain that affect religious experiences and behaviours and even the contribution of myths and symbols to religiosity. *Sociological* approaches clarify the relationship and interaction between religious visions or the sense of the sacred and social structures and function at various levels. They emphasise the social function of myths, symbols and even the hierarchy of gods. *Philosophical*

[1] Richard Fenn, *Key Thinkers in the Sociology of Religion*, London: Continuum, 2009. Also See *The New Blackwell Companion to the Sociology of Religion*, ed. by Bryan Turner, Oxford: Blackwell Publishing Company, 2010.

[2] Ibid., 6.

[3] Hinnels, op. cit., p. 2f.

approaches appreciate and nurture the fundamental urge to ask questions about the nature of world and human life, the problem of evil and so on. We will soon point out the fundamental principles of *phenomenological* approaches as providing a leverage to get into a detailed discussion on a dialogical approach.

A *dialogical* approach, however, is critical of certain tendencies evident in the scientific approaches to the study of religion. First, it is critical of absolutising only one method, its presuppositions and challenges. We have already pointed out a development even in recognising approaches as well as certain dogmatic tendencies. We will notice how such tendencies have been countered by those scholars who advocate a poly-methodical approach.

Secondly, it is critical of the insistent tendency by scientific theory to diminish, even to ridicule, the significance of religion in human life, claiming to explain it away by bringing to light various non-transcendent dimensions. In particular, some psychological and sociological approaches appear to aim to exorcise religions of all irrational aspects, thereby posing some permanent explanation for all human experiences and behaviours.

Thirdly, a dialogical approach is critical of missing out a sense of mystery that surrounds all genuine religious experiences. If humanist and secular critics were willing to move away from their entrenched dogmatism, they could not ignore the fact that, belying all their predictions, religion persists in human history. If there is decline in one part of the globe there is revival in another part. The resurgence of religion in the former communist blocks and the emergence of new forms of religion and spirituality all over the world are too obvious to explain.

Fourthly, it is critical of the assumption that open expression of commitment to a particular religious tradition would obstruct objective enquiry and study of religious phenomena. We will argue that genuine commitment with openness would rather facilitate identifying some aspects of religious life and tradition, which have not been recognised by the application of mono-track methods.

Fifthly, a dialogical approach has the advantage of bringing together the fruits of different approaches and provides motivation for further investigation by asking fresh questions. We have already mentioned the significance of developing an approach to religion from the perspective of children.

At this juncture it is proper to acknowledge earlier links made between the comparative study of religion and dialogue. Eric Sharpe, in his most useful history of comparative religion devotes a chapter on 'Toward a Dialogue of Religions?'[1] He presents different views taken. Some have seen history of religions as a way to the unity of religions. This unity has been expressed in a variety of ways ranging from an affirmation of the Fatherhood (Parenthood) of God and Brotherhood (sisterhood) of Humankind, to a single essence or truth that unites all religions, and to the organisation of world conferences. At the other extreme, there have been those who have contributed to the study of religion but stayed faithful to

---

[1] Eric Sharpe, *Comparative Religion: A History*, London: Duckworth, 1975, pp. 251-266.

their particular religious traditions as they provide a centre of coherence and meaning. In between there have been those who have approached the study of religion with an open mind while finding it setting a background to positive approaches and friendly dialogue with others.

Against this background, what we are going to do is to present the contribution of three scholars and theologians. Unfortunately all of them are men. They represent three different continents–America, Europe and Asia. They represent both academic study and the practice of dialogue. Their original background, line of development and expertise are also different. After presenting the attempts of each we will raise questions about missing links, if any, and finally provide pointers to further development.

A New Perception on the Meaning and End of Religion

Wilfred Cantwell Smith (1916-2000), a North American scholar started his career as a missionary working in the Indian Subcontinent, and this experience brought him close to religious communities, particularly Muslims about whom he has written extensively. Then he entered the academic world and held positions including, most remarkably, Professor of Comparative Religion at Harvard University and Director for the Centre for the Study of World Religions at Harvard. His major book *The Meaning and End of Religion* (1962) has the sub-title *A Revolutionary Approach to the Great Religious Traditions*. It is not without reason that Eric Lott places him in the category of 'dialogical' following 'phenomenological' and 'comparative' as ways of investigating and interpreting religion.[1] As a recent *Reader* of his writings shows he was a historian, comparativist, critic, theorist, theologian, missiologist and prophet.[2] There have been several researches on his writings aiming to crystalise particular aspects of his unique approach.

Following a survey of different meanings attached to the word 'religion', Smith says that 'we, as heirs to the somewhat chaotic developments, commonly employ the term religion in four quite distinct senses.'

> First, there is a sense of personal piety ... Secondly and thirdly, there is the usage that refers to an overt system, whether of beliefs, practices, values, or whatever ... Finally, there is 'religion' in a generic summation, 'religion in general.' Its meaning is inevitably derived in part, for anyone using it, from his sense of the other three. In so far as it is historical, it is as complex as all 'the religions' taken together.

---

[1] See Eric Lott, *Vision, Tradition, Interpretation: Theology, Religion and the Study of Religion*, Berlin: Mouton de Gruyter, 1987, pp. 192ff.

[2] See Kenneth Cracknell (ed.), *Wilfred Cantwell Smith: A Reader*, Oxford: Oneworld Publications, 2001.

> In so far as it is personal, it is as diverse as the men whose piety it synthesizes.[1]

Then he suggests that the word 'religion' and its related concepts should be dropped because it 'is confusing, unnecessary and distorting' though the first sense of personal piety conveys some meaning. It was his conviction that the vitality of personal faith and progress in understanding of the traditions of other people throughout history and throughout the world, 'are both seriously blocked by our attempt to conceptualise what is involved in each case in terms of [a] religion.'[2] He illustrates from the academic study of religion to show how not only the term 'religion' but also the names of religious traditions as Hinduism, Buddhism and Islam have been western constructs with Christian presuppositions.

Smith proposes on the part of the participant in the process of understanding a penetrating insight into the vital and transcendental dimension which he calls 'faith' and which is focused on Something beyond, or God. This can happen only when the adherents of religious traditions are taken as persons, not defined by the systems or 'isms'. A person of religious faith living in a bewildering world and facing complex issues possesses the inherent capacity to have a sense of transcendence. There is disagreement among scholars and people of faith about the nature of this transcendence, a point we will deal with separately. The student of religion cannot aim at fully comprehending this transcendence. What is possible is to see it in the living human person.

Smith distinguishes 'faith' from what he calls 'cumulative tradition.' By faith he means personal faith and it stands for 'an inner religious experience or involvement of a particular person; the impingement on him of the transcendent, putative or real'. By 'cumulative tradition' he means

> the entire mass of overt objective data that constitute the historical deposit, as it were, of the past religious life of the community in question: temples, scriptures, theological systems, dance patterns, legal and other social institutions, conventions, moral codes, myths and so on; anything that can be and is transmitted from one person, one generation, to another, and that an historian can observe.[3]

The cumulative tradition changes but the faith of a person does not change. A person's faith is what his/her tradition means to him and what the universe means to him in the light of that tradition. The objective data of a cumulative tradition are available to a historian to observe and analyse, but no rigorous method can comprehend the human spirit, which is open to the transcendent. One needs to penetrate through to find 'faith' which gives expression to tradition,

---

[1] W.C. Smith, *The Meaning and End of Religion*, London: SPCK, 1978, 48f.

[2] Ibid., 50.

[3] Ibid., pp. 156f.

and is expressed by tradition in the forms of art, belief system, doctrine, theology etc., which is continuous yet modified. However, there is no communal faith such as Christian and Buddhist but only that of a person.

Without acknowledging openly that 'faith' is a Christian term emphasised by the Protestant tradition, and 'God' as a term is applicable only to the theistic traditions, Smith is comfortable expressing it in a way familiar to the Christian tradition and even with a Christian devotional fervour. For example, at the end of explaining what he means by faith, he declares:

> There is no ideal faith that I ought to have. There is God whom I ought to see, and a neighbour whom I ought to love. These must suffice me; and my faith is my ability to see that they abundantly more than suffice ... The traditions evolve. Men's faith varies. God endures.[1]

In the concluding words of the book Smith acknowledges that it is written within the discourse of the Christian Church, the university and humankind. The study is offered to fellow Christians 'in the hopes that it might contribute to our doing justice intellectually both to what we now know of the world in which we live and to what we know of God as Christ has revealed Him to us.' It is also offered to fellow scholars 'in the hopes that it might contribute to our ability to understand and to interpret to the world the long and rich religious history of man.' Similarly it is offered to fellow human beings throughout the world, including those whose religious faith is derived from other traditions and also whose faith is not religious, 'in the hopes that it might contribute to the intellectual aspect of our new task of together constructing a brotherhood on earth deserving the loyalty of all our groups.' This acknowledgement attests him as speaking primarily as a theologian both critiquing the claims of objective study made by applying scientific tools and appealing to the need to take seriously the human person, with the inner core perceived as faith.

On the basis of his understanding of faith, which for him 'differs in form, but not in kind,' Smith ventures into providing contours for a one world theology in his book *Towards a World Theology* (1981). The basic affirmation is: 'History is the domain of the specific, the multifarious; of recalcitrant fact; of the human. It is the domain of personal faith, in its depth and vitality and diversity. For the historian, then unity is not sameness, but is interrelatedness. It is not system but development; not uniformity but continuity.'[2] This is applied to religious diversity and construction of a world theology. This is not the place to elaborate the venture and vision of this understanding, and to evaluate its feasibility. Rather, we will point out affirmations and arguments as contributing to a dialogical

[1] Ibid., p. 192.

[2] W.C. Smith, *Towards a World Theology: Faith and the Comparative History of Religion*, London: Macmillan Press, 1981, 5.

approach to the study of religion. Smith recaptures with modification his earlier views on methodological approach to the study of religion.

Smith argues that, unlike the acclaimed mode of objective knowledge in the West, all human knowledge is self-consciousness, and approach to the study of human religiosity should be humane. As an alternative to polarising the objective and the subjective in our approach, he submits that

> in addition to the subjective, my individual and internalist awareness of something of someone, or of myself, and to the objective, the impersonal, externalist knowledge, there is a third position, which subsumes both of these and goes beyond them; and that it is this that we should posit as our goal – in the humane field, man's knowing of man. I call it corporate critical self-consciousness.[1]

Subjectivity is inadequate as we are ignorant of much of what goes into our actions, feelings, thinking and moral choices. We can distort what we know, and deceive or elude ourselves as well as others. Objectivity too is inadequate and it can be untrue, less than rational and alienating of persons. Unlike the case of natural science which is limited by objects and particular contexts, humane knowledge of other humans is expansive, critical, rational, inductive and corporate, 'ideally embracing us all both in our diversity and in our personalism.' It is possible only by self-consciousness of a community (minimum of two) of persons participating in a process of studying and being studied. Unlike the world of matter, no human situation is repeatable because each human experience is different from the inside and from without. 'No statement involving persons is valid,' Smith proposes, 'unless theoretically its validity can be verified both by the persons involved and by critical observers not involved.' Such way of knowing is more accurate, offering rich rewards. No theories, however scientific, are adequate to know the human qualities of self-transcendence and our immense capacity for good and bad. Participation of the knowing mind in our humanity seeks to know other dimensions of our humanness as an asset, not merely a fact. Those distinctive human qualities help us to know. It is then we have personal knowledge of life in all its dimensions.

From his visit to the magnificent temple of Meenakshi in Madurai, and reflective observation of what was going on, Smith found that beyond temples and symbols what matters most are the living persons who worship in them and with them. In Smith's words,

> The notion of temple, and that of symbol in general, are humane concepts, not objective. No building is objectively a temple. No space

[1] Ibid., 59.

> is objectively sacred. No object is objectively a symbol, in and of itself: the object becomes a symbol in the consciousness of certain persons.[1]

From this he reiterates his position that the only knowledge that is accurate of religion, culture and history is 'a knowledge that participates in the consciousness of those involved.' Treating other persons as ourselves in relationship in community is important for gaining this knowledge. To appreciate the significance of a temple or a symbol, without making judgements, we must get inside the consciousness of those for whom it is sacred and know how they feel, how they find those symbols meaningful, although we must also know the objective facts about them if we are to know the full truth.

This is true of studying religious traditions in general. To apprehend them we need, apart from collecting and analysing data with minute care, the human qualities of interpretation, imagination, insight, perceptivity, sympathy and humility. In short, a historian or rational student in any humane field, should 'stand imaginatively in the shoes of others.' Understanding and being understood are two fundamental qualities of humanity, and there is no person in the world that we cannot understand at all.

Smith criticises illustratively a tendency prevalent in the academic field. That is to go to an alien world, predict personal behaviour and even to manipulate it in order to arrive at a finding, which would serve either to corroborate or modify theories in one's discipline learned back home. Ultimately it is a contribution to western knowledge in terms of scientific generalisations and it would win the researcher a promotion or professional reputation. In other words, the researcher would explicitly make use of the people for purposes extraneous to them. Smith uses strong words to call this practice immoral, and universities that support such projects he condemns as immoral institutions.

In this connection his contention is that 'objective knowledge in the humane realm is an inherently immoral concept.' It does not render a knowledge that 'penetrates to the personal level of those,' the kind of knowledge 'on which to found friendship.' It is also idiosyncratic and sectarian because, just like missionaries, social scientists also write to those who share their presuppositions and who understand their jargon. There is an intellectual fallacy that human knowledge is 'the domain of a multitude of disparate idiosyncrasies.'[2] Smith welcomes the recent concept of 'interdisciplinary' but fears lest it but enlarge the group of those who know externally, 'without transcending the subjectivity principles of a closed group, of outside observers.'

Another important emphasis of Smith is being open to a new becoming in the process of learning. 'The process of knowing is a process of becoming. It is a

[1] Ibid., 63.

[2] See Ibid., 73ff.

matter not of using means, but of assimilating ends.'[1] It is moving beyond methods already calculated and prepared. Any methodology that implies 'that one knows ahead of time what one wants' collides with the principles of humane learning. At the same time, he admits, in principle one can learn techniques without necessarily becoming new and newer. In humane learning both the learner and the learned as two selves participate in the 'process of self-transcendence in which being human in part consists.' Such learning requires humility, which repays extravagantly. Humility, insight, compassion, respect for human dignity and integrity cannot be achieved by the application of techniques.

> Man cannot know man except in mutuality; in respect, trust, and equality, if not ultimately love. In this realm of knowing, accordingly, the attitude with which one approaches one's data proves to be at least as significant, as consequential, as the methods with which one handles them. One must be ready not only to receive the other but to give oneself. In humane knowledge, at stake is one's own humanity, as well as another person's or another community's. And at issue is humanity itself.[2]

Such an approach overcomes alienation, distancing itself from mere critique and irrational impersonalism. It is an alternative to false objectivity and inadequate subjectivity. It is 'a rational personalism in community.' This establishes Smith's thesis that 'the new mode of human knowledge is in terms of a disciplined corporate self-consciousness, critical, comprehensive, global.' By studying another, in fact, one studies oneself. 'Our solidarity precedes our particularity; and is part of our self-transcendence. The truth of all of us is part of the truth of each of us.'[3] It can be best realised in the knowledge of comparative religion, because 'inter-religious understanding is a form of intra-religious understanding' or one may simply say 'religious understanding.'

As religious life involves the whole person including will, emotion and intellect, Smith advocates taking the person or a religious community of persons seriously, focusing on meaning, purpose and coherence. We have to go beyond traditions and symbols, which help to transform, enliven, nurture and crystalise these essentials of life. The final criterion of the validity of the research, for Smith, is 'its verifiable contribution to such self-consciousness.' Even to deal with controversial matters, the sense should be not 'we-you-they' but 'us.' 'The goal is the corporate critical self-consciousness of a community of persons' who can say, feel, mean and grasp the situation. Similarly, what a student of religion concludes

---

[1] Ibid., 76.

[2] Ibid., 77f.

[3] Ibid., 79.

about Islam, for example, should be agreed to by an intelligent Muslim. The same applies in other contexts. Smith writes:

An academic statement about a religious community must be simultaneously intelligible to that community and to the academic community with its non-participant observers. In comparative religion, the intellectual task is to construct statements that will be simultaneously intelligible within two religious communities as well as in the academic world.[1]

Smith points out conclusions arrived at in the past in western universities about other religions, which bear the marks of arrogance. One antidote to this is the arrangement of representatives from other faith communities teaching and researching with Christians as done especially in some American universities. However, Smith does not give practical illustrations of concrete issues and does not take seriously the complex reality of sects and sub-sects in each religious tradition, which create tension within and without. Indeed, Smith's account of religion does not adequately help us understand its role in the 'dangerous dynamics' evident in the world scene today.

True knowledge, Smith contends, is something, which can be shared between observers and participants and verified by them if religious commitment is the common feature. Such knowledge requires 'erudition, critical acumen, imaginative sympathy and penetrating understanding; it takes time, effort and dedication; but is now possible, and therefore now requisite, to learn to say, and to mean, that we human beings on earth are diverse but not incongruous.' 'Our solidarity', he continues' ' precedes our particularity, and is part of our self-transcendence. The truth of all of us is part of the truth of each of us. It is self-consciously we who differ … yet we are not disparate. Indeed, yet we ultimately converge.'[2] This is the basis of Smith's Christian theology of comparative religion or religious pluralism, which, if it is true, becomes 'a Christian view from within all,' when as different groups we participate in world community. This leads to Smith's proposal for a world theology based on the common human feature of faith as self-transcendence. While this need not detain us here, it will require thorough treatment in the contexts of differing theologies of religious pluralism.

Although Smith, in passing, refers to the phenomenological principle of empathy (*Einfühlung*), with reference to Dilthey who like himself insisted long ago on understanding in the context of consciousness,[3] he admits that he never understands adequately what is loosely called 'phenomenology of religion.' He says:

> I get the impression that some, at least, among those who call themselves phenomenologists are inclined to hold that symbols somehow carry

[1] Ibid., 98.

[2] Ibid., 102f.

[3] Ibid., 69.

> their meaning in themselves. They might be seen almost as positing a Platonic idealism of symbolic forms. My own observations as an historian suggest rather that, as I have stated, no object is objectively a symbol: that things are symbols only in relation to certain persons, and not in relation to others.[1]

For Smith, this primacy of the personal subject makes 'the history of religion dynamic, complex and interesting.' This is not to study the 'historically changing to arrive at a vision of unchanging prototypes' but to observe how given symbols appear to some persons 'as participating in transcendence.' They can help them enlarge their vision of truth and transform their life. In this sense, whether it is a scripture and even God for some, these symbols function at the first level of meaning. For outsiders who study their history etc. they function only at the second level of meaning. This leads to the recognition of a new interpretation of not only 'symbol' but also 'revelation.' This is important when we have reached in religious evolution 'a stage where consciousness must be a universal self-consciousness: corporate; critical; both analytic and synthesising.'[2]

From the perspective of classical phenomenology, however, Smith seems to take a peculiar stand of both agreement and disagreement. He would agree on the attitudinal principle of empathy and solidarity, as well as on the possibility of penetrating into the core essence (which is for him faith as self-transcendence) but would disagree on the objective method of classifying data into different types and so on. On the question of value judgement he is silent. More significantly, his understanding of self-consciousness and symbol warrant greater clarification as to their connection with sign, narrative and language. This will be clear in the next section where we look at a discussion on the nature and limitations of phenomenology although, interestingly, Smith is not acknowledged at all.

Moving Away from Phenomenology

Gavin Flood, a senior lecturer in the Theology and Religious Studies Department at the University of Wales, Lampeter, has brought out his extensive study of different approaches to the study of religion in the western world through his book *Beyond Phenomenology*.[3] Beginners in the field might find it bewildering to be led at a canter through a thick forest of ideas, concepts and arguments by scholars both well known and not well known in the field. His point of departure is phenomenology both in its philosophical presuppositions and its application to the study of religion. The purpose of his study is to develop a dialogical approach. He calls it 'metatheory' and sometimes uses Russian philosopher of language

[1] Ibid., 86.

[2] Ibid., 97.

[3] Gavin Flood, *Beyond Phenomenology: Rethinking the Study of Religion*, London: Cassell, 1999.

and literature Mikhail Bakhtin's (1875-1975) term 'dialogism.' He illustrates his points with his acquaintance with and study of certain aspects of Hinduism. We do not dare to give even a summary of the full discussion but present the main line of argument and most important insights as contributing to the development of a dialogical approach.

Edmund Husserl (1859-1938), a German philosopher, introduced phenomenology as a pure epistemological science, which was later applied to law, psychology, values, aesthetics and religion. The word 'phenomenology of religion' was coined by the Dutch scholar P.D. Chantepie de la Saussaye, and it appeared in 1887 in one of his publications. Since then a number of scholars have expounded it as providing a right attitude and tool of study. Most notable are Nathan Söderblom, William Brede Kristensen, Gerardus van der Leeuw, Joachim Wach, Rudolf Otto, Friedrich Heiler, Mercia Eliade and Ninian Smart. Husserl provided two fundamental principles or concepts. One is *epoche*, meaning holding back, bracketing or suspending value judgements and being present impartially to what appears, thereby allowing the universal essence to appear to the consciousness. The other is *eidos* or eidetic vision, meaning an inner capacity or intuitive grasp to see the essence and implying a form of subjectivity. Others worked out procedures to organise facts and classify them so that there can be penetration into the real sense or pure essence without interruption. In general terms, phenomenology was taken to emphasise objectivity and impartiality to be achieved by acute attention and empathy to what the data or the testimony of the person of faith appeared to present to the observer.[1] Even in the earlier phase, phenomenology of religion did not achieve a full consensus as to its claims for pure comprehension, and different scholars identified the essence differently (sacred power, sense of holy, prayer etc.) and proved that a universal essence of religious life and experience could not be established.

Flood revisits these Husserlian principles of *epoche* and *eidos* and the presupposition that we can achieve pure objectivity, through empathy and inner communication and so pure consciousness. He claims:

> Metatheory provides a rigour at the level of discourse, interfaces with other disciplines and so integrates religious studies into the wider academy, and the only way a discipline can develop is through reflexive critique.[2]

He points out, for example, how theories of Vedic ritual are assumed without reflecting on them. He also points out how the textbooks of religious education reflect the bias of a common essence of religion, and how religion 'is presented as a *sui generis* phenomenon beyond other social and historical concerns.' He

---

[1] For a summary of key figures and their attempts using the phenomenological method, see Sharpe, *Comparative Religion*, 220-250.

[2] Flood, op. cit., 4.

refutes claims of pure objectivity and draws insights from Gadamar who has argued that 'prejudice is a precondition for understanding.' For Flood the kind of metatheory he wants to promote can be categorized as *dialogical*. He argues that phenomenology of religion 'contains implicit assumptions about an ahistorical subjectivity – it entails a philosophy of consciousness – that is inevitably imported into practice' whereas the dialogical model he wishes to support 'entails a philosophy of the sign.'

> This means that rather than subjectivity (belief, cognition, inner states and religious experience), language and culture, the observable realm of science, become the locus of inquiry. Phenomenological description contains hidden assumptions about subjectivity and transtemporal objects, but focusing on language emphasizes the dialogical and situated nature of inquiry, that fosters rigour in analysis, reflexivity, and critique.[1]

In a dialogical model the researcher and researched become co-partners in dialogue and share speech-genres. Difference and non-closure of research should be emphasized. 'Such a model moves away from a postulated universalism and objectivism towards the sharpening of difference and clarification of discourse.'[2] Metatheory, which argues for a dialogical approach provides the only possibility of shared discourse. It takes seriously the historical contingency that makes the discourse interactive, illuminative, contextual and reflexive.

The above is a summary of Flood's 'introduction,' which presents his basic position, with the rest of the book as elaboration. We will make a few observations and highlight some conclusions from the arguments, such as seem most relevant for our purpose of constructing a dialogical approach. Most important is to reiterate the dialogical nature of any encounter with religious texts and persons. Flood concludes a part of his argument with the following words:

> Dialogue therefore involves the recognition that all utterance is intertextual and all encounters intersubjective. Such an approach to the inquiry into religions, that might be called 'dialogical reflexivity,' becomes aware of the intertextual and intersubjective webs in which it is embedded, is sensitive to history, to language and to subjectivity. Furthermore dialogue is not agreement or consensus, but can be the clarification of difference; a clarification that will necessarily entail reflexivity in delineating the boundaries of a discourse against another's, which is also critique.[3]

---

[1] Ibid., 7.

[2] Ibid., 8.

[3] Ibid., 35.

Dialogue is concerned not only with what one perceives but also where one stands and for what reason. Such a concern leads to a dialogical reflexivity, which critically looks at the context and the method applied. The element of critique has direct bearing on the study of religion in many instances. Flood gives the example of the Hindu caste system and asks the questions: Do social actors create the system or are they powerlessly subjected to it? Or does it vary depending upon social actors within the hierarchical spectrum? His answer would be, in agreement with other studies, that both positions are true though he does not wish to argue 'but merely wish[es] to illustrate that modes of knowledge affect the result: the method to a large degree … determines the data.'[1] This does not mean that one cannot understand a system even if one does not agree with it.

Understanding the idea of religion remains inconclusive and we have already demonstrated this by bringing together a plethora of definitions. Recognising the difficulty, Flood gives his own definition:

> I broadly understand religions to be '*value-laden narratives and behaviours that bind people to their objectives, to each other, and to non-empirical claims and being.*' Such a definition, strongly influenced by Bowker, indicates a conviction that religions are less about truth claims and more about identity, less about structures and more about texts, less about abstraction and more about tradition or that which is passed on … The advantage of such a broad definition allows the incorporation of 'quasi-religious' dimensions of culture which might include crowd behaviour at a football match or New-Age managerial strategies, as well as secular ideologies and nationalism.[2]

After criticising theological universalism associated with an interpretation of religion by John Hick for its deluding nature, Flood agrees with John Clayton who has argued:

> what is ultimate is tradition-specific and it does not follow that what one tradition conceives as an ultimate reality is the same as an ultimate reality conceived by another. The goals of religions are specific, they are 'different paths to different goals'… The goal aimed at is as tradition specific as the path taken. The goal is constituted as goal by the path chosen. It is the tradition followed that allows the practitioner to recognize the goal as goal.[3]

The purpose of pointing out this, which is normally taken in theological discussion on religious pluralism, is to question the validity of 'a phenomenological

---

[1] Ibid., 39.

[2] Ibid., 47.

[3] Ibid., 56.

transcendentalism' on the one hand, 'a reduction to the biological organism' on the other, and to state the importance of taking seriously 'the intersubjective realm of the cultural sign.'

Flood moves on to 'locate three types of reductionism in the academic study of religions that claim that their theories are universally valid across cultures: naturalist or materialist reductionism (that itself can be subdivided into biological, sociological and psychological reductionism); phenomenological reductionism that claims to reduce phenomena to universal essences; and theological reductionism that ultimately denies difference and reduces diversity to a single, totalising, theological truth.'[1]

His main interest at this point is to analyse naturalist reductionism according to which religion should be studied at its own level without confusing it with other levels of understanding different subject areas. He joins those who criticise the outmoded scientific objectivism applied to the study of religion. This has resulted in taking a religious person as simply an object or thing that takes away the life of dialogue that would recognise personal complexity and interaction. And interpretation is needed to make sense and coherence but there can be no interpretation without foreknowledge, foremeaning, foreconception and relationship. Again Gadamar is invoked for hermeneutic work that is based on 'a polarity of familiarity and strangeness' and the '*true locus of hermeneutics is this in-between*.'[2] This is different from the idea of the detached self as subjective, intentional consciousness and of detached theory apprehending its object (religion) through a rational method as held by phenomenology.

> In this Husserlian understanding of subjectivity, there is a radical distinction between subjective consciousness (albeit intentional) and the world of other subjectivities: there is a gap between subjectivity and the other which needs to be bridged through the mechanisms of *epoche* and empathy. This isolated subjectivity leads to the focusing upon the *experience* of the flow of consciousness or the self's intentional structure, and an emphasis on experience as the focus of phenomenological inquiry. This view can be generally critiqued ... from a position which maintains that we are intersubjective prior to the *cogito*, a position which moves from consciousness to language and culture and which sees the observer as integrally bound up in the dialogical process of understanding.[3]

In this connection Flood consults Bakhtin for whom 'subjectivity or consciousness is non self-sufficient, for the subject only exists in dialogue with

[1] Ibid., 67.

[2] Ibid., 85.

[3] Ibid., 107.

others and is constructed out of contending voices; consciousness cannot exist alone but is multiple.' In Bakhtin's words,

> The consciousness of other people cannot be perceived, analysed, defined as objects or as things – one can only relate to them dialogically. To think about them means to talk with them; otherwise they immediately turn to us their objectivized side: they fall silent, close up, and congeal into finished, objectivized images.[1]

The redemption lies in taking seriously the sign and language in their contextual narrative forms because 'religions can be seen in terms of sign systems, as systems of signification and communication.' Narratives can either clash, overlap or compliment and there is no sacred narrative to supersede the local ones.

To establish the fact that there is no lived reality external to or unmediated by narrative, Flood discusses the importance of narrative, given the shift to the privileging of the sign with consideration of the 'text.' He identifies the emergence of three positions regarding narrative: 'narrative realism, that stories are lived; narrative constructivism, that stories are told; and narrativism, that stories are both lived and told.' He supports the third view, based largely on Ricoeur, 'that while narrative emerges from life (from history and geography) it is also constructed.' The implication of this for the study of religion is that 'insider and outsider discourses must be seen as competing – or perhaps complementing – narratives and that therefore there can be no epistemic privilege or distanciation provided by phenomenology, but only situated and contextual dialogue.'[2] He wishes to support the view 'that neither the method nor the object are free from narrative' and this is true of theories and descriptions proffered by phenomenology and social sciences.

Flood points out cases from different religious traditions to show how people 'live within religious narratives articulated as texts, which are subjectively appropriated in the context of a particular life.' The common pattern is the fusion between personal biographies and metanarratives of the respective religious traditions. Some traditions may claim a transnarrative privilege for *logos,* but word is not free from *mythos,* and one can easily see strong mythical dimensions even in the discourse of reason. 'Of course our narratives are always constructed by and within the cultures we inhabit and our identities given by those cultures, but this does not mean that narratives are not constrained by the temporal limits of birth, life and death, and of genetics and physics.'[3] Unlike the detached observer which phenomenology advocated, rather than 'the transcendental ego performing the acts of bracketing, eidetic reduction and empathy, in order to objectively

---

[1] Quoted, Ibid., 111.

[2] Ibid., 118.

[3] Ibid., 137.

understand the data presented to it, we have the observer within her own narratives engaging in a dialogical process with another narrative. In this dialogical process, the work of scholarship is produced and knowledge generated.'[1] What matters is not consciousness but sign or language, culture and intersubjectivity in a given context. Scholars of religion examine and critique other narratives from the perspective of their own. Their presuppositions can be reflexively revealed but they cannot claim epistemological privilege.

In a particular situation and concrete context the study of religion can be governed by a 'critical conversation' involving mutual interrogation. The knowledge and understanding achieved need not be claimed to be perfect and infallible but at the same time one should not drift into being sceptical. In a living situation there is always room for correction and improvement. Moving into relativism should be replaced by highlighting the particular. In the name of distancing and abstaining from making a value judgement even in the context of terrible practices like *sati* (immolation of widows on their husband's pyre), the student of religion fails to follow the dialogical principle of critical conversation.

After pointing this out, Flood summarizes the dialogical critique of the philosophy of consciousness by focusing on three themes: the relationship between 'I' and the 'other', the idea of utterance in dialogue, and in the idea of 'live-entering.' He examines each of these in turn in order to further contribute to the critique of the phenomenological method. Being open to oneself connecting yet distinguishing between what she knows and what she can know is central to the first theme. With regard to the idea of utterance, one realisation is that it is 'a link in a very complexly organized chain of other utterances' both preceding and succeeding and both of oneself and of others. Flood quotes Voloshinov who writes: 'Any true understanding is dialogic in nature. Understanding is to utterance as one line of dialogue is to the text. Understanding seeks to match the speaker's word with a counter-word.' Flood adds: 'While this brings to mind the hermeneutic circle that understanding of the whole entails an understanding of the part which in turn entails an understanding of the whole, for Bakhtin it is a hermeneutic spiral: understanding is gradually deepened and discourse illumined in the activity of dialogue.'[2]

He continues to quote Bakhtin repeatedly as to his view of the complex web of utterances in a dialogical encounter, the intersection of the process of centralization and decentralization, of unification and disunification and the rhythm of centrifugal and centripetal movements. Then he critiques Husserl's empathy or intuition of the *alter ego* on the following bases: 'first because it does not take account of communication and active understanding, secondly because it does not take into account the historicity of the understanding encounter, and

[1] Ibid., 137f.

[2] Ibid., 155.

thirdly it cannot deal with conflict, or the other's being closed to empathetic penetration.'[1] Then he explains these three problems.

To deal with the problem of communication, Flood again invokes Gadamar who says, Husserl's empathy is 'still oriented to the interiority of self-consciousness and fails to orient itself toward the full circle of life.' Then he contrasts Husserl's intersubjectivity with the many voices of Bakhtin's dialogism. 'For Bakhtin dialogical encounter makes empathy possible as the projection of myself into another. Such a projection and experiencing what the other experiences must always be constrained by limits, for I can never completely lose myself or become the other.' This projection 'Bakhtin contrasts with empathy (*Einfühlung*) in which there is a total merging and experiencing of the other from the other's place.' There is no losing of myself, no becoming pathological, but rather a live-entering, a 'creative understanding in which something new is produced through the dialogical interaction of self and other and so is a form of communication.'[2] This empathy is not a solitary, cognitive, imaginative act but a communicative and immediate experience involving both simultaneity and spatial distinction. It takes the historical context and process seriously and is able to re-imagine the past events that have affected individual consciousness and experience. The problem of conflict is tackled by openness and ongoing exploration in a dialogical conversation.

Then Flood takes up the question of truth and argues that instead of claiming to access some unmediated and pristine reality it should be reformulated in tradition-specific terms transmitted through generations. For him, dialogical religious study 'does not contain an implicit philosophy of consciousness, as does phenomenology of religion, but an implicit ontology of self-in-relation.' He points out the inadequacy of applying the criteria of scientific method to metaphysical truths proclaimed by a religious tradition, which 'are internal to the tradition and can be understood in terms of coherence within given frameworks.' For example, it is not possible to know about the truth of *nibbāna* outside the discourse of the Theravāda Buddhist tradition.

> Religious truth claims are … most importantly about religious, personal or community identity, perhaps perceived to be under threat, and form part of a framework, part of the rhetoric of a tradition, within which an individual or group formulates their life-objectives and organizes their time. Religious truths are part of the narratives, which inform and constrain the lives of religious people.[3]

---

[1] Ibid., 162.

[2] Ibid., 162f.

[3] Ibid., 174.

The implication of this argument is that a student of religion should bring in no external criteria to evaluate the truth-claims of a tradition, but try to understand them within the framework of the tradition as transmitted and lived. This, however, seems to contradict the earlier emphasis on critical conversation in which the researcher's own religious narrative can help to understand the narrative of the partner in a dialogical relationship. And also if a religious community has a fundamental obligation to communicate their truth to those outside the tradition, and if genuine conversion has taken place as the result of this communication, it is too restrictive to say that input and impact from 'outside' cannot help and understanding by outsiders cannot happen.

Without recognising this issue in the above way, Flood devotes a chapter to 'the ethics of practice.' Not only the problem of ethical judgment, he raises the deeper questions of 'whether any understanding or explanation of a human cultural practice or ideology is possible without some common basis of shared values, of the relation of ethics to politics, and other relation of ethics to jurisprudence.' He argues that a dialogical approach has the 'ethics of authenticity,' a dialogical ethic can draw on postmodern ethics articulated in postmodern ethnography, a reflexive understanding can 'both promote difference and offer cultural critique' while reiterating the view of the self in relation. He points out that even aesthetics, despite claims of transcendent manifestation, is not free from the 'pleasure principle' that leads to cultural commodification and is linked to capitalism.

Dialogical ethics, Flood argues, is based on awareness of distinctive self-identity, self in relation and interaction with a community of speakers. And for him, 'a dialogical ethics based upon the ethics of authenticity that does not assume the universality of people in communication, is an argument against total incommensurability.'[1] For example, dialogue as responsibility cannot condone the Nazi judgment that a Jew is a non-person. Then, how can understanding and explanation be achieved while respecting 'radical otherness' where there is no apparent common ground to justify liberal and pluralist ethic? 'One response to this question – that argues against the proclaimed "value-free" religious studies – is the postmodern response that genuinely recognizes difference, accepts the situated nature of inquiry, and that claims that a conflict of values is a conflict of power. This postmodern approach to religions rejects liberal notions of tolerance and empathy in favour of an analysis that highlights conflicting power in a world with no basis of common values.'[2] Judged from this orientation, pluralist religious studies based on phenomenology, would wish to replace dialogue with 'mutual suspicion.' In true dialogue any suspicion and related power-conflict is overcome by corporate commitment to investigate and understand the truth about power as operating in the social field.

---

[1] Ibid., 199.

[2] Ibid., 201.

The 'religious stranger' or the 'radical other' we encounter in religious studies, Flood observes, comes with a baggage of culture or sub-culture, class, history, needs and ideologies. It is a challenge for dialogical research to reveal and illumine the constraints at work within the life of an individual or group in relation to a wider body of community and the rational community of researchers. The hope of modernity to resolve ethical conflicts has not been forthcoming as 'there is little prospect of arriving at any non-ambivalent, non-aporetic ethical code.' In other words, the suggestions of post-modernity are far from any simple way out, which will be acceptable to all.

Flood asks the question: Is it possible to hold both a communitarian-oriented ethic that claims values to be relative to a particular community, and the Kantian claim that there are ethical universals? The answer for him

> will depend upon presuppositions and views of the self, but arguably both can be held together by dialogism which recognizes that social actors are ends in themselves, but also that we live in an ethically pluralist world without absolutes and that all positions towards the encounter between self and other must be worked in practice, dialogically. There can be no end to the question of ethics.[1]

It is indeed difficult to resist questions coming to our minds if we are aware of the perplexing issues arising within the concrete contexts of interfaith conflicts today. Flood remains abstract and for a dialogical approach he identifies the following four elements from what he calls dialogical ethnography: (1) focus of language as the location of evaluation and values; (2) an emphasis on an ethos of friendship; (3) the necessity of distance and outsidedness; and (4) the cognition of boundaries and unfinalizability or non-closure.[2] While being outside of each other with unavoidable boundaries, a friendship characterised by mutual interest, trust and responsibility with a recognition of language as the contested ground of meaning should be possible. The difficulties of holding such an ideal view, however, will become clear only when a variety of concrete cases are taken seriously in such discussion.

On the whole, despite technical and concise language, Flood helps us with a good summary of discussions on approaches to the study of religion in Europe covering a long period from Enlightenment to Postmodernity and including a wide range of thinkers. His argument for a dialogical approach taking the distinctive narratives in particular languages and traditions seriously and emphasising authentic selfhood and friendship with openness is very convincing. He presents clearly the views of others in support of his call to move away from the assumptions of phenomenology on objective and value free study, with its

[1] Ibid., 206ff.

[2] Ibid., 210.

emphasis on intuitive penetration into consciousness and recognition of universal essences. But at the same time he is not antagonistic to all who have taken these assumptions and acknowledges perceptions and sentiments that have emerged in the course of their work. For example, he endorses what Smart wrote as early as in 1973 that science of religion is 'aspectual, polymethodic, pluralist, and without clear boundaries' and what he wrote in 1993 saying, 'be clear about what you are doing, and then do what you like.'[1] However, he cannot agree with Smart that one's faith cannot be allowed in the academic study of religions.

In his 'epilogue' Flood discusses the questions of faith and theology and their connection with study of religion at some length. Though he has not mentioned it explicitly, from the way he constructs a dialogical approach there is no reason to believe that serious faith-commitment and acknowledged adherence to a religious community will hinder the process of an inquiry or distort insight. Qualifications for study of religion such as friendship, mutual trust, respect and responsibility are not the monopoly of any particular religious tradition or community. In fact in many cases faith commitment can nurture and enhance these qualifications. If, for instance, truthfulness or truthful living is regarded as equal to or even higher than the perception of the highest Truth by a person, s/he should be viewed as the most suitable candidate for the study of religion. And on the other hand, the 'methodological agnosticism' proclaimed by Smart, or even 'methodological atheism' by others, does not guarantee a more authentic and accurate mindset and behaviour in the inquiry into religious life.

Moreover, it is difficult to know whether methodological agnosticism or atheism could be distinguished from personal agnosticism or atheism. Then it becomes clear that the concealment of one's religious commitment is more due to the popular influence of a secular and anti-religious atmosphere rather than representing unique commitment to the pursuit of study of religion and search for truth. Moreover, students with open faith commitment can become passionate and create excitement. If they believe in God, for instance, their study can broaden their horizon and a realisation of the variety, richness and complexity of religious traditions can lead them to be 'lost in wonder, love and praise.' And their critique of demeaning beliefs and questionable practices on the basis of the criteria of their own religious traditions need not be less valuable than that of agnostics and atheists.

As we have already mentioned, Flood's discussion and arguments remain mostly abstract and concrete examples alone can test out if his ideas and suggestions are workable. A dialogical approach can work best only in the context of living with people of other faiths. This means, approaching a community or tradition as a visiting scholar with inadequate knowledge of the people of that community has its serious limitations. This is as true of the Orientalists who studied the Sanskrit traditions as of the westerners who study the Tamil traditions

[1] Ibid., 31, 235.

today. Their studies bear the marks of a kind of methodology with analytical tools extracted from cultural and ethnographic studies done elsewhere – not to mention their political influence and economic advantages. As such, our study of the following contribution is very significant.

Courage for Dialogue with Commitment and Openness

Following two major contributions, one by an American and the other by a European, in this section we will introduce the contribution of an Asian to the development of a dialogical approach to understanding religion and religions. Stanley Samartha (1920-2001) was a distinguished presbyter and theologian of the Church of South India who made a significant contribution to the ecumenical movement through being the founder director (1971) of the sub-unit on Dialogue with People of Other Faiths and Ideologies at the World Council of Churches. He lived 'between two cultures' focusing on 'ecumenical ministry in a pluralist world.' A doctoral study of him by a European scholar is aptly titled *Commitment and Openness*. As is acknowledged in the concluding evaluation of this study,

> Samartha has engaged himself in systematic theology; but his aim has not been system-building. The building up of relationships between people is the leading thread in all his contributions. Creating space for people, compassion for his neighbours, most of them of other faiths, are central concerns in his theology. No neat answers to vexed problems are given; because, ultimately, life itself is a mystery.[1]

In this sense, though Samartha's approach would share some concerns of the above two, it is more concrete, contextual, practical and reflexive. His contribution is not recognised by Smith and Flood in their rather abstract discussion although along with Smith and Hick Samartha contributed to the controversial volume *The Myth of Christian Uniqueness*. Perhaps it is true that the university-based western scholars are normally taken more seriously theologians of minority situations and committed practitioners of interfaith dialogue.

Though Samartha did not show much interest in methodology or in epistemological issues in the study of religion, as we will point out, the attitudinal principles mentioned in the foregoing sections found concrete expression in his work and writings. However, he was no stranger to discussions on religion and religions taking place in the West and even he was at great unease when those who worked and reflected in the West were unaware of what was going on in other parts of the world, particularly India. Let me illustrate this with a story from his life. After his initial years of study and teaching in a theological seminary in South India, Samartha had the opportunity to go abroad for graduate studies, first at Union Theological Seminary in New York and then at the Hartford Seminary

[1] Eeuwout Klootwijk, *Commitment and Openness: The Interreligious Dialogue and Theology of Religions in the Work of Stanley J. Samartha*, Zoetermeer: Uitgeverij Boekencentrum, 1992, 334.

Foundation in Hartford. At Union he worked for a master's degree in theology under Paul Tillich with the topic: 'The Hindu View of History According to Radhakrishnan.' Tillich gave him a copy of Niebuhr's book *Faith and History* which had just been published and it helped him a great deal to understand the inner relation between theology and history. He took several courses offered by Tillich and Niebuhr. As he listened to Tillich's lectures and read his books, it occurred to him that his thoughts on God as the Ultimate Concern were very close to the Upanishadic vision into the nature of Ultimate Reality, the Brahman, both in epistemology and ontology. But he did not have the courage even to suggest it. His first paper for Tillich was on 'The Metaphysical Basis of Radhakrishnan's Thought', making the point that this was deeply embedded in the Upanishads. Tillich read it and said to him, 'This is very much like my own thought.' He took the paper home, he said, because he wanted his wife to read it.[1] Those who read Tillich's view of the 'religion of the concrete Spirit' and Radhakrishnan's view of the 'religion of the Spirit' will find much in common though developed in two different contexts.

One of the best contributions of Samartha is the way he defines dialogue, which comes from his long experience of having personal encounter and conversation with friends from other faiths, and from organising bilateral and multilateral meetings of interfaith dialogue. The following is the most popular version of his definition:

> Dialogue is a mood, a spirit, an attitude of love and respect towards neighbours of other faiths. It regards partners as persons, not as statistics. Understood and practised as an intentional life-style, it goes far beyond a sterile coexistence or uncritical friendliness. It does not avoid controversies; it does not emphasize only points of general agreement; it recognizes difficulties in relationships as well. It is not a gathering of porcupines; neither is it a get-together of jellyfish. Sensitively understood, it helps people not to disfigure the image of their neighbours of other faiths.[2]

In multifaith communities, Samartha contends, dialogue is not an option but an imperative; not an activity of a few interested individuals, but of all living in community. It is not instrumental, but is intrinsic in terms of having value for building authentic relationship. It has its own integrity in celebrating life and sharing witness.

Avoiding false witness against neighbours of other faiths and distorting or disfiguring their images is a repeated plea of Samartha. This could happen in any

---

[1] S. J. Samartha, *Between Two Cultures: Ecumenical Ministry in a Pluralist World'*, Geneva: WCC Publications, 1996, 11f.

[2] Samartha, *Courage for Dialogue: Ecumenical Issues in Inter-religious Relationships*, Geneva: WCC Publications, 1981, 100.

religious group. One of his earliest attempts was to study and evaluate Hindu responses to Christ and Christianity. His analytical challenges could be very attractive if some Hindu scholars turned to his approach and conclusions. Even today while Christian students of the Hindu religious traditions try very hard to study and present them as objectively as possible, sadly, this is not reciprocated. While Samartha deplored any form of aggressive Christian militancy, he wanted to correct Hindu views of Christianity. But in a context of Christianised Hinduism and Hinduised Christianity authentic dialogue is yet to start. Probably this was the reason he was more creative in the western context than the Indian context.

Let us take one example of Samartha's study. Radhakrishnan, a former Spalding Professor of Comparative Religion at Oxford and President of India, was a formidable Hindu philosopher. Well exposed to and informed of Christianity, he challenged the exclusive claims of Christians and missionaries. He went further by interpreting Jesus in the non-dualist Vedantic category of a liberated self (*Jivan Mukta*), as the one who achieved oneness with God through his meditative discipline and ethical behaviour. Some other thinkers of his time and before him also did the same. Samartha started to study Radhakrishnan only and then expanded to include others. The fruit of this study was *The Hindu Response to the Unbound Christ* in which he states the purpose as 'to give a brief account of the views of Christ held by certain selected thinkers, to make a theological appraisal of them, and to indicate the preliminary lines of a Christology in India today.'[1] Though at such an early stage the criteria of the theological evaluation of the responses involved him deriving from a rather orthodox Christian standpoint, his intellectual acumen, engaging research and in this work, and his commitment to and concern for dialogue were noticeable. Being aware of his position as a descendent of converts only a few generations ago and as member of a minority church placed in a multifaith society with a Hindu majority, he regarded clarifying the distinctiveness of Christ and Christian faith as part of this commitment and concern without losing the mood and spirit of dialogue.

While being aware of the startlingly varied positions known in the field of the study of religion and dialogue between religions including methodological agnosticism and personal theism, Samartha was very open about his Christian commitment. For him the principal reason for dialogue is Jesus Christ, the Son of God, who has become man on behalf of all people of all ages and of all cultures. 'He is the true light that enlightens every man' (John 1:9); he is the Word become flesh 'full of grace and truth' (John 1:14); he is the one through whom God 'was reconciling the world to himself' (2 Corinthians 5:19); he is the one who became obedient unto death, 'even the death on a cross' (Philippians 2:8-9); and through him has God made known the mystery of his will 'to unite all things in him,

[1] Samartha, *The Hindu Response to the Unbound Christ*, Madras: Christian Literature Society, 1974, p. 1.

things in heaven and things on earth' (Ephesians 1:10).[1] Christ is God's dialogue with humankind and from him stemmed a community which in the freedom of the Spirit should be able to move on in relationship with people of other faiths. At the same time he hastens to add that since through incarnation 'God has relativized himself in history' we cannot absolutise this in doctrine. This obviously creates a tension, but a tension that Samartha never sought to resolve. One can hear the echoes of the dialogue of approach to the study of religion and of life which are elaborated by Flood as we have seen above.

In a dialogical approach we go with our own vision, experience, sign, and narrative as Flood has reminded us. And we go with openness to change as Smith and Flood imply. One of the vexed problems Samartha encountered was to provide a convincing revision of mission and evangelism. Without denying the fact that Christian faith is essentially kerygmatic, which means proclaiming Jesus as Lord in the midst of many 'lords', he denounces any form of aggressiveness. He calls for a radical shift:

> The search for new relations may lead us to risk the break up of cherished particularities of doctrine and structure, to break away from past captivities, and to develop new relationships in the *oikoumene* of God. Christians are not called upon to be advocates of the Lordship of Christ; they are not called upon to make declarations about the inadequacy of other lords; their responsibility is to be obedient to him and to live in such a way that their life is a clear manifestation of the lordship of Christ.[2]

Avoiding carefully the monarchical connotation of 'kingdom' and 'Lordship', Christians are called to witness to Christ as servant, redeemer and reconciler. They are called to testify to Christ as precious, as extraordinarily significant, and to rejoice in their experience with him, but without condemning the faith of other people. Such witness removes 'threat' from mission and offers an 'invitation' that 'seeks to enrich the life of our neighbours and be enriched by them.' What is needed, therefore, is not *missiology* but *witnessology*, which is a reflection on the content of the biblical term 'witness'. It is marked by humility, forgiveness, reconciliation, peace, justice and wholeness and it avoids aggressiveness and exclusiveness.[3] Of course this revision has been hardly convincing for those who have been carried away by the currents of triumphalist fundamentalism and stubborn conservatism.

Samartha never gave up his ministerial responsibility of educating Christians living in a multifaith milieu. He contributed to theological education and ministerial training at various levels in India, by being available as a resource person until the end

[1] Samartha, *Courage for Dialogue*, p. 12.

[2] Ibid., p. 98.

[3] See Samartha, "Christian Concern for Dialogue in India", *Current Dialogue*, No. 9 (December 1985), 6.

of his life. His 'Sermons, Poems and Bible Studies' reflects his creative imagination and reveals his pastoral heart and educating passion. They include reflections on otherwise insignificant biblical figures such as Lot's Wife, Pharaoh's Daughter, the Prodigal Son's Mother and Timothy's Father; reflections on commitment and tolerance in a pluralist society; and two sermons preached at a Hindu-Christian marriage and funeral. They are hung together on the thread of *The Pilgrim Christ.*[1] 'Pilgrimage' is Samartha's favourite image in which he finds a new departure following every arrival. This he applied to the journey of interfaith dialogue.

The most significant milestone in Samartha's journey of interfaith dialogue was when he worked out a revised Christology. Having in mind the Hindu responses to Christ, which he earlier evaluated, recognising the fact of one Jesus and many Christologies found in the New Testament, and the significance of the continuation of the Jewish tradition with a different understanding of Jesus, he moved towards a down-to-earth 'bullock cart Christology' suitable for Asian terrains as opposed to the noisy and dust-emitting helicopter Christology (brought from the west); of course it was a theocentric Christology.[2]

Another step forward was seeing the ultimate reality in terms of Mystery to which, he claims, there are different responses to be made, which are represented by different religions, as we have already noted. Seeing millions of people continuing to find inspiration and meaning in their own religious visions and traditions, can God's relationship in the world be confined to Christians? 'Can it be that plurality belongs to the very structure of reality? Or can it be that it is the will of God that many religions should continue in the world? 'These are', Samartha says, 'difficult questions indeed, and it may take a long time for the church to arrive at clear and unambiguous answers to them.' 'But, he continues, 'beginnings have to be made lest the church look like a fortress to be defended rather than the household of God where strangers and sojourners can become fellow citizens.'[3] It is a 'Mystery of Truth', 'Mysterious Centre' or 'the Truth of the Truth', something beyond yet influencing diverse perceptions and experiences. We leave this important issue for separate treatment in relation to theologies of religious pluralism.

What concerns us here is the influence of the above view on the process of knowing. Samartha contends that a vision of reality and experience are the most authentic ways of approach, seen as beyond debate in the Hindu classical tradition. Moreover, he identifies the distinctive way in which scriptural authority is interpreted in the Indian religious traditions. 'To the Hindu and Buddhist', he observes, 'the authority of the scripture does not depend on the *writtenness* of the

---

[1] Samartha, *The Pilgrim Christ: Sermons, Poems and Bible Studies*, Bangalore: Asian Trading Corporation, 1994.

[2] For a detailed and systematic treatment, see Samartha, *One Christ – Many Religions: Towards a Revised Christology*, Maryknoll: Orbis Books, 1991.

[3] Samartha, "The Cross and the Rainbow: Christ in a Multireligious Culture", in *The Myth of Christian Uniqueness*, ed. by John Hick and Paul Knitter, London: SCM Press, 1987, 72.

text, but on *hearing* and *seeing* the word (Śabda).' Simply by quoting and studying the texts one cannot arrive at the truth. 'Knowledge of God is not something to be *dis-covered* through the study of written texts. It is to be *re-covered* through *hearing*. The holiness of words is intrinsic. One participates in it not through understanding but through reciting and hearing it.'[1] Therefore, he points out, the 'Western notion of editing an *original text* is an intrusion into Eastern situation' where one is expected to go behind written texts to the sound of the word. We do not need to explain how such a view is upsetting in relation to western claims of studying other religions in general and Hinduism in particular, both in the past and in the present.

Samartha, on the whole, though not participating in the western discussions on proper methods of studying religion and religions like Smith and Flood, provides us with insights into the nature, function and fruits of dialogue that are unique. He shares with the other two the importance of corporate participation in understanding religious life with a spirit of openness, trust and love. However, his orientation and style are different. Commitment and openness, as two eyes of a dialogical mode, are clearly evident in the shifts he has taken in a long life-journey. And also his background of thinking and working – India and the ecumenical circle – has unique features requiring a distinctive combination of passion, a pastoral approach and intellectual acumen. However, in presenting the case of Indian religious traditions Samartha is too selective and generalising. He does not acknowledge the exclusive claims, the refutation of other claims and the outright rejection of them as evident within the dynamics of the Hindu religious traditions, although at an earlier phase he demonstrated how Hindu thinkers can distort the Christian position. Further, he does not acknowledge that his theistic framework cannot include the non-theistic traditions that flourished in India, which was mostly in protest against conflicting polytheism.

Concluding Remarks

We have brought together in this chapter the contributions of three scholars of different contexts and representing different ways to a dialogical approach to understanding religion and religions. It is worth noting that they do not acknowledge each other's contribution and this fact would illustrate how in the field of religious studies that often the left hand does not know what the right hand does! However, their contributions are significant. They are both complementary as well as different in approach and thrust.

A humane approach with love, respect and openness in relationship is emphasised by all the three of them and in this respect they, again without acknowledging, repeat what some earlier Christian missionaries did. They criticise the claims of 'objective study' made in the West either in general or using the principles of classical phenomenology. Smith is vigorous in his

[1] Ibid., 78.

criticism of this claim though he appreciates the need for competence to observe and analyse data. Flood has approached it from an epistemological perspective taking phenomenology as a starting point. Samartha, without referring to these claims has pointed out the importance of having living encounter with people of other faiths. Flood refutes the phenomenological claim of a single essence or essences but he does not try to explore the nature of ultimate reality in terms of a single totalising truth (as Radhakrishnan held) but stresses signs and how they are communicated in a specific tradition. Not agreement but clarification of difference is the fruit he sees of dialogue. For Smith the essential element of religious life is faith, or self-transcendence, while for Samartha, it is response to God understood as Mystery.

Most problematic is understanding consciousness and the question of going inside the consciousness of the other partner in a dialogical relationship. For Smith, penetrating through friendship, being self-conscious of sharing the essence of the other, and being open to a new becoming, are possible. For Flood, the philosophy of consciousness provided by phenomenology is untenable if we take dialogue seriously. In an isolated subjectivity, a flow of consciousness through intuition, for him, is impossible. What is possible is relationship and dialogical reflexivity, which is inter-textual and inter-subjective within limitations of individuals and their traditions and contexts. Samartha seems to have no interest in analysing the long-standing vexed philosophical problem of consciousness, but believes that understanding and change is possible in a dialogical relationship. He draws attention to the peculiar Hindu emphasis on vision and experience beyond what language can communicate in its written form.

Serious commitment, along with openness, is fundamental for Samartha in approaching and understanding the religious life of other people. He never concealed his identity as a presbyter of the Church of South India. Such commitment, for him, need not hinder the process of understanding but it can facilitate it, avoiding the temptation of distorting the image of others. Smith, originally a Canadian Presbyterian and missionary, at least in later phases of his life, is not too open about his own religious commitment and identity (though he is an Anglican turned to be Greek Orthodox in the UK), Flood is silent about the commitment of his own as well as that of others whom he quotes in support of his view. However, what all the three commonly emphasise is openness and non-closure, which makes change or a new becoming possible. Though they have not gone far enough and have not touched the sensitive issue of religious conversion in this context, they think the possibility of change guarantees the finding of solutions for problems that might arise in the course of disagreement in a critical conversation.

As points of such a critical perspective, though Smith is very general about misunderstandings Flood points out the cases of caste and widow self-immolation in India as examples, and Samartha would share these and other forms of injustice as well, especially when perpetrated in the name of religion.

As evident elsewhere, Samartha points out instances of religion being used as a cover for socio-economic injustice and his criticism in India of 'the politicisation of religion and communalisation of politics' point to deeper problems, which could be encountered in bilateral dialogues though the major partner (Hindus) need to initiate and sustain. Flood's observations that 'conflicts of values' are often 'conflicts of power', and that there should be corporate effort to understand the truth, need to be unpacked with concrete illustrations. All this is possible in a dialogical approach within what Samartha points out as an ecumenical affirmation, 'a civilization of love.'

One major challenge for formulating approaches and methods in the field of the study and understanding of religion and the faith experience of persons of other faiths is to get alongside partners in dialogue. While there is so much concern – especially emphasised by Smith – about having our statements about others verified, and even agreed to, by representatives of those faith communities, is it possible to have mutual participation in the continued pursuit of understanding the experience and tradition of each other? At the moment, methodological discussions both at academic level and at the level of interfaith relations are dominated by Euro-American-Christian attempts and viewpoints. That cooperation in the study of each other's religious tradition and scriptures is possible, as evident in few scattered attempts. Whether this cooperation could be extended to developing systematically a dialogical approach to religion and religions is an important question. And this begs yet another question: whether the motivation comes from an interest in the study of humanity as a science or from the committed pursuit of theology and spirituality from the perspective of a particular tradition.

Chapter 5

Naming the Transcendence

A Continuing Search

The word 'transcendence' is as vague in usage as it is abstract and ambiguous. It is often observed that humans are religious animals who are placed in a situation that forces them to transcend biological habits in order to survive and grow. But to some extent all creatures including animals are placed in such a situation. Is it a natural and inherent instinct of life as such or is it that humans are endowed with a special capacity? If so, is the distinction of human beings having the ability to imagine, articulate, and speak because of their higher level of mental and emotional status? Do their instinct and ability to transcend necessarily lead them to adopt religion? If it is the case at least for some humans, is not religious conversion or aversion to religion a stage in the transcendental process? What is the state of those who have secular vision of a utopia? What is the mental state of those who are nominally religious or secular?

The connection between religion and transcendence is not self-explanatory. There are different theories about the origin of religion such as magic, personification of terrifying natural phenomena and sacred power as we have already noted. It is true that many gods in Eastern religions betray this fact, e.g. the sky god Varuna (*ouranos*), and religious myths that expose the ingenious quality of imagination required on the part of their writers. This, along with ritual, doctrinal, experiential, social and ethical dimensions of religion which is yet to be defined conclusively has led to an identification of religion with transcendence. Sacred is often used as interchangeable to transcendence.

As early as 1981 Sabapathy Kulandran, a Sri Lankan scholar and bishop in the Church of South India, brought out his extensive research of western views on religion and transcendence with reference to the world's major religions in publication with the title *The Concept of Transcendence*.[1] What is clear from this study is that 'God' (defined as 'than that which nothing is greater') is not the ultimate as there are 'religions' who are atheistic or agnostic. To complicate the matter further, the Indian religious traditions hold side by side polytheism, henotheism, pantheism, pan-entheism, monotheism and monism. Also it is reasonable to say that thus religions have made 'transcendence' colourful, complex and attractive appealing to different human senses. Then the question is, what is in humans that corresponds to transcendence?

Whether the transcendence is the human imagination at work or the fantasy of subconscious neuroses, or the meaningless patter of language gone awry, or the ideological superstructure of a particular economic situation; or whether in a real world, or more real than this immediate one, is this immediate one perceived more truly; and whether, if it is real, it is personal, Jesus-like, rational, formless, moral, punitive, unknowable – all these are questions on which intelligent people have taken varying stands.[2] But those who casually avoid the God language and use abstract terms such as sacred dimension, the highest reality, the supreme, a sustaining and substantial power, ground of being, source and goal of life, and ultimate concern do not ask these questions nor do they have the instinct to engage in dialogue with others on these issues.

'Mystery' is another term used, sometimes escaping from dealing with issues as far as we can, other times expressing the 'beyondness' of human grasp. Stanley Samartha refers to two factors that have emerged out of India's long history of multireligious life; one is an acceptance of Mystery beyond all diversity and the other is rejection of any exclusive claim. He describes the Mystery using conceptual categories of knowledge known in the classical Hindu traditions. In his words:

> Mystery is not something to be used to fill the gaps in rational knowledge. Mystery provides the ontological basis for tolerance, which would otherwise run the risk of becoming uncritical friendliness. This Mystery, the Truth of the Truth (*Satyasya Satyam*), is the transcendent Centre that remains always beyond and greater than apprehensions of it or even the sum total of those apprehensions. It is beyond cognitive knowledge (*tarka*) but is open to vision (*drişti*) and intuition (*anubhava*). It is near yet far, knowable yet unknowable, intimate yet ultimate, and according to one particular Hindu view, cannot even be described as 'one.' It is 'not-two' (*advaita*), indicating thereby that diversity is within the heart of Being itself and therefore may be intrinsic to human nature as well.[3]

[1] S. Kulandran, *The Concept of Transcendence*, Madras: The Christian Literature Society, 1981.

[2] W.C. Smith, *The Meaning and End of Religion*, 155.

[3] Samartha, "The Cross and the Rainbow", 75.

Samartha continues to explain that this emphasis on Mystery is not an escape from the need of rational inquiry but to insist that it is not the only way to do theology and to recognise the contributions of mystical and the aesthetic. 'Mystery is an ontological status to be accepted, not an epistemological problem to be solved ... Without a sense of Mystery, *Theos* cannot remain *Theos*, nor *Sat* remain *Sat*, nor can Ultimate Reality remain ultimate.'[1] 'In religious life', Samartha continues, ' Mystery and meaning are related. Without a disclosure of meaning at particular points in history or in human consciousness, there can be no human response to Mystery. The history of religions shows that these responses are many and are different, sometimes even within a particular religious tradition. Quite often these differences are due to cultural and historical factors. Although, each response to mystery has a normative claim on the followers of that particular tradition, the criteria derived from one response cannot be made the norm to judge the response of other traditions.'[2] Brahman as *sat-cit-ānanda* (truth-consciousness-bliss) and God as Father-Son-Holy Spirit are two culturally conditioned responses and formulations, and they are symbolic pointers to the Mystery, 'affirming the meaning disclosed, but retaining the residual depth.' Therefore, while the divine significance of Jesus the Christ is normative for Christians everywhere, to claim Christ as the *only* way in which the meaning of Mystery is disclosed is to ignore one's neighbours of other faiths who have other points of reference. 'To make exclusive claims for our particular tradition is not the best way to love our neighbours as ourselves.'

Movement from abstract to naming and forming need not be unilinear, and the reversal with development of something entirely new is also possible. Thus, Raymundo Panikker observes:

> There have been many attempts to express the awareness of the Absolute. Two of the main attitudes could be summed in the expression *transcendent transcendence*, symbolizing the Semitic trend proper to the Jewish-Christian-Islamic and modern post-Christian tradition, and *immanent transcendence* proper to the bundle of religions we call Hinduism.
>
> The Buddhist approach is startling. It does not fit into this typology. It would rather say the true awareness of the Absolute is to have none.[3]

In the Buddhist case in the final analysis, language, word and speech have limited value and that can be realised only when one attains that which is unavoidably called Absolute. Further, after quoting a story of debate between

---

[1] Ibid., 75f.

[2] Ibid., 76.

[3] R. Panikkar, *Myth, Faith, Hermeneutics: Cross-Cultural Studies*, Bangalore: Asian Trading Corporation, 1983, 258.

Word and Spirit on their excellence, Panikkar concludes that India decided in favour of the Spirit while the West opted for the Word. This may not transpire as binary categories as our discussion progresses.

In this chapter we will make an attempt to delineate names and forms of transcendence as experienced and imagined, or revealed and received in two sets of religions – Eastern and Middle Eastern. This we will do from a dialogical perspective. It is important to recognise transcendence in its external and internal dimensions. The external dimensions include overwhelming forces of nature, intervention of gods or God or a stage which is beyond our definite expressions. The internal dimension is called in various names such as soul, self and, abstractly, that receiver of the signals of the supreme broadcast. We will note different ways the connection is described such as faith, knowledge, sacred action, intuition, devotion and enlightenment. To revert to the abstract one can easily see the transcendent transcendence and immanent transcendence as well as immanent immanence and transcendent immanence!

In interfaith contexts particular expressions confuse the right understanding of a term within the core vision and theological/metaphysical framework of religious traditions. This is not to deny common grounds and distinctive horizons. In this context, philosophers and historians of religion and religions do not always help; even worse, in fact they complicate further, either because of their power of language and expertise in vocabulary, overenthusiastic efforts to stress one's uniqueness or superiority, or passionate commitment to promote interfaith understanding and harmony in a religiously both ambiguous and explosive world of many religions and cultures. This will be clear during the course of our discussion.

Eastern Religions

Development of visions and counter visions, traditions and interpretations present a complex phenomenon. It has been approached from many perspectives, historical, anthropological, philosophical and so on. The visions, names and forms of transcendence are entangled and intertwined with endless manuals of ritual practice and myths of a perplexing variety. All we can do here is to point out the major standpoints, decisive moments and peculiar outcomes.

***Vedic Religion*:** Vedic religion is centred around sacrifice (*yajna*). From a simple gift or food offering to gods and ancestors, sacrifice developed into a complex ritual mechanism for generating the power to create and recreate the universe and all forms of life. This development in a complex way is evident in the first two parts of the four Vedas written in Sanskrit: hymns (*samhitas*) and ritual manuals (*brahmanas*). A highly sophisticated order of priesthood was part of this development. The generators of power were mainly three: ritual act with minute details and care (*karman*), ritual heat produced by establishment of fires and cooking the oblations (*tapas*) and the holy power of mantras recited in proper order and volume of sound (*brahman*).

The following verses are typical in demonstrating the belief in the efficacy and central reality of sacrifice in the Vedas:

The sacrifice is the navel of the world (*Rigveda* I. 164.35).

All power to our life through sacrifice
All power to our lungs through sacrifice
All power to our eyes through sacrifice
All power to our ears through sacrifice
All power to our backs through sacrifice
All power to sacrifice through sacrifice (*Yajur Veda* IX.21)

All this, whatever exists, is made to share in sacrifice (*Satapata Brahmana* III.6.2.16).

After quoting these, Panikkar observes: 'Although, the notion of sacrifice may have been modified, refined and interiorized down the ages, the underlying Vedic intuition remains vital. We might express the essence of sacrifice as that action which effectively creates, i.e. which is effective, potent, which attains the end it sets itself. Sacrifice is that action which directly links the activity and its result in the selfsame act. It is not a merely ephemeral action, which, once accomplished, would disappear as if no longer needed; it is rather an action that is an integral element in every activity. It is the act sustaining the action of whatever acts. The complicated procedures of drawing analogies between ritual and natural forces show an underlying belief in the supreme power of ritual sacrifice for creating and integrating the whole universe.'[1]

It is significant to note that sacrifice is affirmed as the ultimate truth. The most oft-quoted Vedic verse (*Rigveda* I.164.46) in connection with one truth-many names with its preceding note of context reads:

> Not understanding, and yet desirous to do so I ask the wise who know myself not knowing: Who may he be, one in the form of the unborn, who props in their place six Universal religions?
>
> They call him Indra, Mitra, Varuna, Agni or the heavenly sunbird Garutmat. The seers call in many ways that which is One; they speak of Agni, Yama, Matarisvan.

Most probably, the object that is described here is a bird-shaped fire altar and the context is presenting riddles in a ritual feast. Of course, Hindus, both scholars and masses today, repeat this verse as the solution for the problem of one and many in interfaith dialogue without any reference to its original context.

Further, Panikkar calls the essence of Vedic religion 'cosmotheandric vision' as there is a dynamic nexus operating between universe, humans and gods. It

[1] R. Panikkar, op. cit., 126.

is the sacrifice which nourishes the gods who in turn sustain the universe, and regular sacrifice by humans is indispensable. The relationship between gods and the sacrifice is described in a complex way and it is difficult to get an orderly sequence of development.[1] What is fairly clear is that gods such as Varuna and Indira take the reign one at the time and then recede to the background. Such picture is called henotheism and its further stage is belief in a Supreme Person or God and we will explain the names and forms of this Person later.

Renouncers and Counter-Visions: While sacrifice-gods-Supreme God identification in different forms continue, there are clues in the Vedas for the existence of a movement of renouncers (*sramanas*) which operated outside the Vedic fold but posed challenges to it. They were speculative too. They were prophetic and counter-cultural and challenged the belief in the intrinsic power of ritual sacrifice, and as an alternative they proposed interior sacrifice. There were several groups of this movement and they were often speculative and debating. For instance, when there are different accounts of creation involving sacrifice and gods are available, the following hymn of Rigveda (X.129.1-7) presents a different picture, which might be attributed to the renouncers.Then even nothingness was not, nor existence.

There was no air then, nor the heavens beyond it.
What covered it? Where was it? In whose keeping?

Was there then cosmic water, in depths unfathomed?
Then there were neither death nor immortality,

nor was there then the torch of night and day.
The One breathed windlessly and self-sustaining.

There was that One then, and there was no other.
At first there was only darkness wrapped in darkness.

All this was only unillumined water.
That One which came to be, enclosed in nothing.

Arose at last, born of the power of heat.
In the beginning desire descended on it—

that was the primal seed, born of the mind.
The sages who have searched their hearts with wisdom

know that which is, is kin to that which is not.

And they have stretched their cord across the void,

and know what was above, and what below.

Seminal powers made fertile mighty forces.

Below was strength, and over it was impulse,

[1] See J. Gonda, "Vedic Gods and the Sacrifice", *Numen*, XXX/1 (1983), 1-34.

> But, after all, who knows, and who can say
> whence it all came, and how creation happened?
> The gods themselves are later than creation,
> so who knows truly whence it has arisen?
> Whence all creation had its origin,
> he, whether he fashioned it or whether he did not,
> He, who surveys it all from highest heaven,
> he knows—or maybe even he does not know.

The Transition in the Upanishads: It is believed that in the Upanishads there is evidence for a paradigm shift although the sacrifice and the belief around it continued. The famous prayer of the *Bruhadaranya Upanishad* (I.3.28) – 'from the unreal lead me to the real, from darkness lead me to light and from death lead me to immortality' – is recited by a patron of sacrifice in the midst of the rituals and recitations of the priests with a desire for conquering the world. Though appearing to denote metaphysical benefits, in the context the words in this prayer indicate this-worldly aspirations.[1] Also the benefits of the ritual sacrifice mainly included prosperity, progeny, victory in war and a joyful life in heaven. But the heavenly life was not permanent. Therefore, rejection, criticism and a note on non-permanent benefit in heaven as one has to experience a re-death, constituted the background for raising questions for more ultimate meaning of purpose. For example, the *Aitareya Aranyaka* (II.3.3) states:

> This man is the sea; he is above all the world. Whatever he reaches he desires to go beyond it. If he gains the sky world he desires to go beyond it.

Such statements suggest that gradually there was dissatisfaction of the sacrifice, 'the unsafe boat', which could not guarantee permanent meaning and ultimate value.

In the process of this change there came new emphases and new meanings of old terms. Famous gurus appear to replace gods and teaching the truth of ritual actions. *Karman* was no more ritual action but moral action that carried effect, *tapas* no more ritual heat but interior heat actuated by the disciplining of senses and mobilising inner powers and *Brahman* no more holy power that rested on mantras but the all comprising and all compassing power that incorporates the whole universe and all life. The idea of soul provided a sense of permanence of individual life. And it was tied with *karma* and the idea of its lingering effect on the soul thus causing transmigration and cycle of life and death was introduced as

[1] For a useful exegesis see G. Gispert-Sauch, "An Inquiry into the Upanishadic Prayer: From the Unreal Lead me to the Real..." in *Dialogue in Action: Essays in Honour of Johannes Aagard*, ed. by Lars Thunberg et.al., New Delhi: Prajna Publications, 1988, 179-213.

a secret doctrine. Thus, Jaratkarava Artabaga questions the great guru Yajnavalkya: 'when a person dies what is it that does not leave him?' The guru answers 'name'. But when pressed further, the guru takes him aside and they discuss the issue in secret.

> The two went away and deliberated. What they said was *karma* and what they praised was *karma*. Verily one becomes good by good *karma* and bad by bad *karma*.[1]

Since then, except Brahman, the ultimate basis, principle or potency, all living beings including gods were subjected to *karma samsara* which became the greatest fact of human predicament from which liberation was sought in different ways as suggested by different Indian traditions. The Upanishads, while continuing with aspects and events of ritual sacrifice, extol the new vision of Brahman as the macrocosmic reality of which the microcosmic reality is individual soul (*atman*). The nature of relationship between them and the vision, tradition and interpretation of the ultimate goal and the means to achieve it have been the core subject of debate between different schools of Indian religious thought.

The Movements of Renouncers: Some of the *sramana* movements came to gain prominence and popularity. The *Ajivikas* (the men of livelihood) were strictly deterministic, ascetic and atheistic. Negating the sacrifice as the power centre and ultimate truth they regarded the principle of order as ultimate. In order to destroy the soul's embodiment they adopted austere measures to the extent of self-annihilation. Though they were one of the earliest movements they reached their zenith in the sixth century BCE when the Jaina and Buddhist movements were flourishing. Jainas and Buddhists regarded them as their opponents. The *Ajivikas* explained in detail the working of the *karma samsara* in an automatic way, and its final form is being born as *sramana*. In this life the action has no effect on the soul, and yet to act is because of the law which operates in a fatalistic order. For them the only way to liberate the soul from its embodiment is severe austerity that included lying on beds of thorns, self-inflicting wounds on their body etc.

The Jainas, the conquerors (of body and world) interfered in ritual sacrifices, preached to gods and priests and emphasised non-violence. They denied the sacrifice-centred world view, denied the existence of a creator, and propounded that the world is eternally self-existent and composed of constituent substances and automatic particles. This operation entangles the soul with the matter and going through the cycle of births in the forms of gods, sages, animals and humans, and by hard austere practices and non-killing life styles, the soul attains *moksha*, the supreme consciousness and bliss.

The Buddhist movement was more successful and later widespread. It is known as the middle path as it stood in between the worldly cult of ritual

[1] *Bruhadaranyaka Upanishad*, III.2.12.

sacrifice and the world denying position and austere practices of the Jainas. The movement got its basis from Buddha, the Enlightened One, who after trying all other ways to get rid of suffering in life, found craving and clinging desire as the fundamental problem and claimed that the remedy lied in the eightfold noble path that led to *nirvana* which was an ineffable experience the nature of which has been interpreted with the pivotal point of a supreme silence.

Connecting with the Hebrew commandment, 'You shall not utter the name of Yahweh your God in vain' and stressing the limitation of language, Panikkar gives a passionate interpretation of the 'double silence of the Buddha.' 'The Buddha ... does not answer questions on the ultimate nature of things. He refuses to be dragged into purely speculative discussions, for they do not lead to deliverance from suffering and so distracts us from the existential and concrete meaning of life. The famous parable is well known: when a Man is pierced by an arrow, to concern himself with conjectures on the direction whence it came, its nature, the possible motives for which it was shot, the identity of the guilty Man, whether he was right, etc., will cause the wounded Man's death long before that is time to answer the questions that were raised.'[1] Then he suggests a distinction of a double level in Buddha's silence.

The first degree of silence is the silence of the answer as manifested in Buddha's response of silence to questions about the nature of the ultimate end, i.e. *nirvana.* For Panikkar,

> The Buddha wishes to teach us to know silence, to love it and to grasp its message. He speaks of noble silence, to love it, to grasp its message. He speaks of noble silence and says the monk is a lover of silence. He thereby indicates that the reality of speech, the world of signs and expressions, can be surpassed. Concerning god total silence must be kept. Neither affirming not negating him can lead us to attain the threshold where divinity is found (or where it is also not found). His message invites us to go beyond the world of signs, words, speech, the realm of the *logos*. You will come to divinise the *logos*, he would have said, if you persist in trying to penetrate everything with the *logos* and go everywhere by the power of your discourse. This is what has happened in the West where, in reaction, Man has gone to the other extreme: antitheism. Without myth, the *logos* become absolute, it divinises itself, and a divinised *logos* destroys itself.[2]

The idea here is not that silence is simply Buddha's answer to human questions about God but a silent indication of its futility to try to find God's true

---

[1] Panikkar, op. cit., 261.

[2] Ibid., 262.

identity, name and form and characteristics, with selfish motives behind. This is the first degree of silence.

The second degree of silence is, 'the silence of the question.' Buddha refuses to give his opinion to controversial issues and questions. 'What the Buddha does is to silence the question, to pacify the questioner by showing him that his question has no meaning, rather that he does not have the power – hence the right – to put such a question. In a way he puts the question. In a way he puts the question, and thereby the questioner, in crisis. He puts the question in question, and thereby also the questioner who had unduly identifies himself with his question. The question becomes anguishing only when Man identifies himself with his reason and loses the global perspective of his human situation. The entire message of Gautama is to make Men understand that torturing oneself over the so-called major questions of life is the great human fallacy, the source of misery and the price paid for the utopia of believing one has the right, or worse yet the duty, to pierce the mystery of existence. An ideal like this is the fruit of human pride. What the Buddha requires is a realistic sense of acceptance of reality just as it presents itself, a total confidence in life, in what is given to us, without seeking to replace Reality with our own ideas. His faith is a cosmological faith, his hope is the elimination of any future, and his love is a compassion for Men of flesh and bone, our contemporaries, not an ideal entelechy that exists nowhere.'[1] This is one of the many 'interpretations of Buddha's silence', and later we will question speeches about silence which was not without its preceding judgements about other ways and preaching of noble ways. But Panikkar in his summing up mentions that: 'For the Buddha, to name the Absolute would be the greatest blasphemy. The Buddhist apophasis is at once ontic and ontological. Silence is taken seriously, not as another form of expression or speech.'[2] Connecting this with the question 'Is the principle of sufficient reason insufficient to name God?' asked by Castelli in his introduction to the French Colloquium on *The Name of God* (1969), Panikkar says that the above is the Buddha's genial answer according to the Buddhist tradition.

Pointing out the limitations of God-talk and God-imaging in different religious tradition, Panikkar observes that

> many religious traditions admit that to seek God implies having already found him, to ask about him means, in a way, to know him already. The questionable cannot be questioned, and if the Absolute is questionable it is no longer absolute. In other words, a real question about the nature of the Absolute cannot grasp its limits, can offer no criteria by which the answer might be verified, as modern parlance

[1] Ibid., 265.

[2] Ibid., 265.

> would put it. The question does not know what it is asking; it is not a question.[1]

As Panikkar puts it, this is part of the dialectical game about the name of God. He concludes the discussion on Buddha's silence with the words, 'The Buddha does not reduce the word to silence, nor does he speak of a word of silence; rather he helps us to discover the silence of the word: *The Buddha smiles!*' It is hardly convincing, however, that limited human beings cannot ask sensible questions about God and find answers within their limits which are meaningful for a limited life without denying that there is more to ask and more to know.

Buddha, the Highest God: In any case Panikkar's emphasis on the supreme silence of Gautama Buddha represents a minority strand of Buddhism as it spread far and wide. As Conze observes:

> The Buddha became a kind of God, the highest God of all. The adoration of the Buddha was rendered the more concrete by the representation of the Buddha in human form.[2]

This involved a process of perceptions and counter-perceptions. The debate on the original Theravada (Elders') Buddhism on the question whether it was a religion or metaphysics remains inconclusive. While accepting the belief in many gods as celestial beings with temporary existence in the cycle of *karma samsara*, Buddha denied the existence of a supernatural power, conceived as a supreme person, almighty being and creator. The origin of life (power of the process of dependent origination) is inconceivable, and life is automatic as a dynamic process in which craving desire causes suffering and 'stopping' that process leads to 'liberation'. *Anatta* (non-self or non-soul) is one of the three cardinal affirmations of Theravada, the others being *Anicca* (impermanence) and *Dukkha* (sorrowfulness).

Buddha did not overtly deny the existence of a supreme God nor did he argue against it. For him it was not a matter to understand human existence. What is called soul or self for him is a concurrent conglomerate of five elements: form or matter (*rupa*), sensation (*vedana*), perception (*sanna*), mental formations (*samkhara*) and consciousness (*vinnana*). No moment is repeated and permanent. The elements disappear as soon as they appear. The continuity of *karma samsara* was based on the moral law of cause and effect and the transfer from one birth to another through subtle elements. Nivana means cessation from craving and that is 'liberation'.

Accepting a law of dependent origination and the law of moral cause and effect, and continuity without identity was making sense to that class of Buddhists for whom Gautama Buddha was the most enlightened of Teachers. For some he

---

[1] Ibid., 271.

[2] Quoted, Kulandran, op. cit., 179.

was the greatest of gods while for others he was the one who attained Buddhahood and a source of inspiration. But the masses were not spiritually satisfied. Therefore an average Buddhist mainly in the popular tradition of *Mahayana* (great vehicle as different from Thervada which was called *Hinayana*, small vehicle) could visualise the Buddha as God. As Lynn de Silva of Sri Lanka observes:

> For the average Buddhist the Buddha is all the above and much more; in him they find the fulfilment of the human need to worship – and when they bow in worship before the Buddha image they give expression to the sense of awe and wonder before the ultimate mystery of life.[1]

The popular view here is affective as different from the orthodox view which is cognitive. According to the second, Buddha as a person is dead but to the first 'he is very much alive and potent over everything.' And the *Arhants* (worthy persons deserving worship) of Hinayana had to work out their own liberation without any external help. But the *Bodhisattvas* (those capable of enlightenment) of Mahayana could help others by transferring their merits, and they were viewed as saviours worthy of worship. Further, they were numerous, and in their name the gods returned to popular Buddhist worship and cults. When Buddhism spread to Japan and China it adopted various local elements that enhanced the worship of Buddha. For example, the worshippers of Amitabha Buddha in Japan seek his help for enjoyment in paradise. The new concept of three bodies of Buddha helped to connect it with original Buddhism. Accordingly the *Adi Buddha* (primal Buddha) has three bodies: *Dharma Kaya* (the fundamental body), *Sambhoga Kaya* (enjoyment body) by which he manifests himself to those in Paradise, and *Nirmana Kaya* (the body of transformation) by which he manifests himself in human form.'[2] Today, great emphasis on meditation having the statue of Buddha as a focal point and worship of him as the one worthy of worship or the great God happens side by side as well as simultaneously depending on the particular history and regional or local religious background.

The Development of Personal God: As we have noted earlier, in Vedic religion sacrifice was the supreme power and truth, and the existence of gods including the prominent ones such as Varuna and Indira depended on the boosting of sacrifice regularly performed. There are two gods who came to hold supremacy. One is the Primordial Man (*Adipurusha*) and the other is the Lord of People (*Prajapathi*). They were existent before creation and through self-evolution by the volition of love or desire they caused creation. But both of them were sacrificed and identified with sacrifice. Creation and recreation happened by the

---

[1] Quoted, Kulandran, op. cit., 75.

[2] Ibid., 87.

repeated sacrifice of Prajapati.[1] One popular term used for the parochial gods was *devas* (shining ones) and another was *Pati* (ruler or Lord).

When the concept of God as supreme and personal arose the term preferred was *Isvara* (highest Lord or God with supreme power, but in the Advaita scheme a penultimate reality). As all powerful, creator, universal Lord, and beyond perishable and imperishable, *Isvara* came close to the Vedic Prajapati and supreme Brahman of the Upanishads. Another name of the Supreme Person, mentioned specially in the *Svetesvatara Upanishad,* is Rudra-Siva. He rules the universe with supreme sovereignty as the macrocosmic power and is identified with the microcosmic soul. In this sense he is identical with Brahman who was identified with God as evident in the Vedantic discussion.

In the meantime, three Gods came to be prominent: Brahma, Vishnu and Siva. While they attracted their own devotees, as the Hindu mythic pantheon points out there were tensions and conflicts between them over supremacy. The outcome of a synthesis or divine ecumenism was the concept of the Indian Triad (*Tirumurti*). Accordingly, the three major activities – creation, preservation and destruction or absorption – were assigned respectively to Brahma, Vishnu and Siva. Though this idea gave a conceptual synthesis to thinkers in the face of several monotheistic religions, it did not have any appeal to the masses. In one sense it was conceived as the same God who manifested in these forms, thus fulfilling the supreme activities. However, this concept could not replace the individual existence of these three Gods and their various identifications. Also it was short lived and at a later stage while Brahma receded to the background having only a couple of temples in the whole of India, Siva and Vishnu, and their consort *Sakti* (power) in different names and forms came represent the One supreme God worthy of worship by their devotees. All other minor gods have been ruled by these supreme Lords and in spite of the popular interpretation that they are different forms of one God they could not be exempted from the sectarian character with specific texts, beliefs and theologies.

Siva (with many mythical names and epithets) is extolled by the Saiva community. Apart from sections in the epics of *Mahabharata* and *Ramayana*, there are Saiva *Puranas* (both in Sanskrit and in the vernacular) that describe the uncanny nature and divine sports of Siva. Along with them, Saiva *Agamas* (ritual manuals and doctrinal formulations in Sanskrit), the twelve devotional texts and fourteen philosophical manuals in Tamil constitute the Saiva canon. The philosophical system is called Saiva Siddhanta, the most influential system in South India.

The Saiva poet-saints with their outpouring devotion and heart-melting poetic embellishment have produced texts that continue to edify, guide and nurture millions of Saiva devotees. They praise both the supremacy and intimacy,

---

[1] See J. Gonda, "The Popular Prajapati", *History of Religion*, 23/2 (1982), 129-149.

and gracious acts of God. For example, Manikkavacakar, one of the cardinal poet-saints sings:

> To him who has neither name nor form
> A thousand sacred names do we sing (*Tiruvacakam* XI.1.2-3)
>
> Praise to Siva who owns the southern land
> Praise to God who is the Lord of every land (IV.164f)
>
> He is the ancient one who creates the creator of all
> He is the God who preserves the preserver of all that is created
> He is God who destroys the destroyer
> But thinking without thought he regards the things destroyed
> To the six sacred sects with their six diverse kinds of devotees
> He is the attainment of deliverance, and source of being to the celestial ones
> He is the possessor of all and identified with even insects
> He gave sun its lustre day by day
> He placed the coolness in the sacred moon
> He kindled in the mighty fire its heat
> He placed the pervasive power in the pure ether
> He endued the ambient wind with energy
> And sweetness to water of streams that gleam in the shade. (III.13-25)

Siva has embodied the paradoxical truth, and he is described in binaries such as erotic and ascetic, light and darkness, death and life and so on. Through his acts of theophany he performed miracles and transformed people who became their devotees. Siva is the cosmic dancer, and creation, preservation etc. are his sportive acts. His consort Parvati (and in many more names) is taken as the personification of power and grace as well as the paradigm of devotees. From a historical perspective, it is undeniable that the Goddess had been supreme in her own right but when she was married to Siva her malevolent power turned to benevolent. The same was true with regard to brothers, Murugan and Ganesh, with various names who were incorporated as the family of the Siva-Sakti couple. The epithets of these deities, together and separately, are sung with body movements and highest emotional fervour.

The same could be said about Vishnu who is extolled in the Vaishnava tradition. Vishnu was originally identified with sacrifice as the supreme power. Then he came to be identified with many names such as Narayana, and the concept of avatar helped to incorporate many popular figures. Most important were the divine heroes Rama and Krishna. Krishna, a black hero and leader of the Yadus and the kinsman of Satvatas, was introduced into the brahmanic fold as a guest in a sacrifice. First he was opposed, and after a fight Krishna became the spokesperson for a Brahmanic sacrifice but combined with the devotional tradition of the Bhagavatas. While several strands of Indian thought and heterodox sects appeared to be explosive, as Radhkarishnan observes, the popular divine-hero was readily available as a rallying centre.[1] Even Buddha was taken as an avatar!

The Gita presents Krishna as the creator and enjoyer of sacrifice and its corresponding social structure of four castes on the one hand, supreme Lord worthy of devotion from his devotees, on the other. In whichever way people approach, he claims, they ultimately come to him. He is attributed all the supreme qualities. For example, he is said to be unmanifest, immutable, unsurpassed, unborn, unchanging, knower of all yet being unknown (7:24-26; 9:13), pervading all the universe (9:4-10), the self of all beings (10:20), supporter of the whole universe (11:18), great soul, primal cause, primeval person, the embodiments of all the gods and elements and everything (11:37-45), the substance of the Vedas and the author of the Vedanta (15:13-15), the highest being (15:18), the Lord who dwells in the heart of all beings (18:61), the dear one and friend of his devotees. Through his 'I am' sayings Krishna identifies himself with the essence of all powers such as sapidity in water, radiance in moon and sun, the supreme mantra Om in all Vedas, sound in ether, manliness in every person, eternal seed of all beings, intelligence of the intelligent, splendour of the splendid, strength of the strong, desire of beings and so on (7:8-11; cf. 9:16-19).

Such a synthesis creates problems, e.g. Ritual and God appear to be parallel powers in Hindu worship.[2]

The soul is eternal. Human beings pass from one body to another like leaving the old garment and taking on new. The real self never ceases to be. The self or soul is indestructible, immutable, immeasurable, unborn, eternal and constant. Weapon, fire, wind etc. do not affect it. A constant cycle of birth and death is inevitable (2:12-27). Krishna presents this as one of the arguments in defence of doing one's duty even if evil such as killing in war is attended to.

In its synthesising of various strands and even conflicting ideas, the Gita talks about not only the ritual sacrifice but also the sacrifice of knowledge, action and devotion. The Buddha once said that sacrifice of knowledge in terms of interiorisation and interrogation was the best sacrifice. The Upanishads talk about sacrifice of knowledge as an inclusive term, meaning different stages in the process of interiorisation. But the Gita seems to be inconsistent. The reason is that it gives equal value to all kinds of sacrifice without acknowledging the primacy of one and conflict between them. In 18:70 Gita mentions that listening to the dialogue between Krishna and Arjuna in it itself is a sacrifice of knowledge.

It is interesting to note that the Gita uses sacrifice of knowledge in terms of undiscursive and undivided concentration as a tool for careful action, both ritual and moral, without attaching the actor to the results (fruits), as well as having fixed

[1] See I. Selvanayagam, *Vedic Sacrifice,* 188f.

[2] For a discussion see I. Selvanayagam, *The Dynamics of Hindu Traditions,* pp. 64-83.

one's mind on God in devotion. Thus, the pure and steady minded state without any confusion as extolled by the *sramanas* and their stress on renunciation is made subservient to acute concentration on God in devotion and non-attachment to the fruits of action in fulfilment of one's duty.[1] However, it was left to the Vedantins to argue and interpret the relevant texts of the Gita in defence of their respective metaphysical positions.

The Vedantins' primary resources – the Upanishads, the Gita and the Brahmasutra – contained different and even contradicting positions within because of transitions and attempts of synthesising. Also the other orthodox schools continue to assert their positions with apology but based on the Vedas which are the primary resources or testimonies for the Vedantins. Thus, the Purvamimamshas argue for the inherent power and efficacy of the Vedic ritual. Nyaya presents theories of proof for the existence of God and its ally Vaisesika identifies atomic ingredients of the universe and human soul. Samkhya works out in detail the dual principles of the Supreme Person and the Matter while its ally Yoga proposes a way out to get the supreme person or soul from its entanglement with the material world. The Vedantins try to respond to all these systems of thought either by refutation or by approval in accordance with their distinctive positions. The common name of transcendence or Supreme Being for all of them is Brahman, the Holy Power, which/who finally was taken to denote the ultimate reality.

Sankara of the early ninth century propounded non-dualism according to which one's Self is identical with Brahman. Ultimately there is 'only one Self, one Being, one pure Consciousness.'[2] Brahman is essentially self-luminous while illuminating all beings. Though Brahman is transcendent he is transcendently immanent and immanently transcendent. 'Transcendent Brahman is everywhere, within everything. It is quite impossible that such as Brahman should ever be the goal of going. For we do not go to what is already reached. Being "omnipresent and eternal like space", he is "the self that is within all". "Reaching the highest", therefore, must simply mean, "realising the Self."'[3] Brahman is one, and all the apparent phenomenal variety are names and forms such as clay and different pots, and iron and different instruments. Out of innate limiting condition and ignorance the self tends to superimpose features of non-self upon the Self. The ultimate Brahman is essentially unqualified, unconditioned, and without any attributes or qualifications that would require naming. However, in relation to the soul he or it might be seen as God or Lord (*Isvara*) and creator of the universe with glorious qualities, but when the leap of intuition occurs and self-realisation achieved, there is no distinction of I and you. Sankara himself is thought to have been an ardent devotee of Siva and has composed a poem portraying Siva as

---

[1] See for details, I. Selvanayagam, *Vedic Sacrifice*, 248ff.

[2] Eric Lott, *Vedantic Approaches to God*, London: Macmillan, 1979, 40.

[3] Ibid., 41.

a mother nursing her children. Nevertheless, finally all such imagination and naming cease, and an effable experience of oneness is achieved.

Ramanuja of the eleventh century developed a kind of monism determined by distinctions, and therefore his system is called qualified non-dualism. He interprets the Upanishadic statement 'thou art that' as that Brahman is the Self, supporter, inner controller and unaffected affecter of all embodied selves. There is distinction but inseparable relationship. The analogy he uses is the relationship between self and body. It is through worship with required ritual and intense devotion as evident in the experience of Tamil Vaishnava poet-saints that one comes to realise that she is part of the Brahman's body. As the Lord of all Brahman who is identified with Vishnu is attributed to more than fifty auspicious names indicating particular quality to the effect of realising Brahman's bipolar nature of supremacy and accessibility. The final act is absolute surrender, not out of slavish mentality but that of devotion to the loving Lord. It is the experience of iron being attracted to magnet, and as a result the self realising its true nature.

Madhva of the thirteenth century developed a radical dualism claiming that it is the truest representation of the scriptures. 'Undoubtedly it was his intention to establish and integrate monotheism. Like Sankara and Ramanuja, however, he had no intention of completely excluding the underlying polytheism of the Vedic tradition. Indeed … a functional hierarchy of deities became quite prominent in his system … However, the "dualism" by which his system is normally defined is at least in part a corollary of his doctrine of the incomparable greatness of the supreme Lord, from whom all other existents have to be distinguished.'[1] Like Ramanujua, Madhva also identified Brahman with Lord Vishnu who is all pervading and the greatest of the great. But for Madhva the Self does not rule over and control the non-self but as the original his reflection can be seen in the inner self of the individual. Through intense devotion by the help of mytho-poetic imagination and absolute surrender in love the illumined individual self enters into the overpoweringly effulgent sun at day.

At popular level the Hindu naming or de-naming, having form and formlessness in the same symbol such as the phallic stone taken by the Saiva tradition, the kaleidoscopic nature or poly-paradigmatic framework of the Hindu religious traditions is so evident. And categorising the oneness and plurality in terms of one truth and many forms and names (or formless and nameless) seems to be most convincing for Hindus of all levels ranging from a university professor to an illiterate villager.

Middle Eastern Traditions

Religious visions and traditions emerged in the Middle East in a different way. They are not always visions, counter-visions and amalgamations as in the case of the Eastern traditions. This does not mean that they have not interacted

---

[1] Ibid., 56f.

with each other. Again there are common roots and new horizons, core visions, perceived deviations and corrections. The names of the transcendence have the Semitic roots and their mythical traditions are less complex and less varied than the Eastern traditions.

God

The origin of the generic term God and its equivalents in other languages is unknown. God is taken as the supreme, creator and regulator of universe and society and one who hearkens to prayer. God is the ultimate judge too.

Zoroastrian God

The ancient Iranian religion Zoroastrianism, founded by Zarathushtra who lived probably around the beginning of the first millennium BCE, named the supreme God Ahura Mazda meaning 'Wise Lord.' The tradition held monotheism but also adopted dualism and they are seen not in conflict to each other as in the case of Hindu polytheism. Ahura Mazda is the creator of heaven and earth, day and night, and light and darkness and he could not be the source of evil, and therefore an opposite spirit was conceived to exist as the source of evil. In the *Gathas*, a section of the scripture Zend Avesta, we read:

> Two primordial spirits, who are twins, revealed themselves in a dream. They have two ways of thinking, of acting: the good and the bad. And, of the two, the one who acts well has made the right choice, not the one who does evil. And when these spirits met, they established at the beginning, life and non-life, and the consequence, in the end, of the Worst Existence for evil, and Best Thought for good. The evil one of the two Spirits chose to do bad things, and the Most Bounteous Spirit, clothed in the hardest stones, chose Truth, as is also true for all those who constantly strive to please the Wise Lord with honest actions. The *daiva* did not get to choose between the two, because the *Deceiver* approached them as they were making their decision. So, they chose the Worst Thought, and then ran to join Wrath, and together with it they have afflicted the world and humanity (*Yasna* 30:3-6).[1]

The ancient gods were dominated by the Ahura Mazda and they had no place in the new religion. However, those deities did not disappear completely but came back and they were regarded as worthy of veneration. And some gods such as Indra were not different from some Vedic gods. Of all the divine entities Anahita and Mithra were the most important, and they joined with Ahura Mazda and formed a triad. Everyone has a soul, and after death the soul can reach heaven or the infinite lights, passing through the stars, the moon and the sun. On the celestial journey the soul must undergo a dramatic trial, i.e. the crossing of the

[1] Quoted, Gherardo Gnoli, "Zoroastrianism", in ER, Vol. 15, 582.

Chinvat Bridge (the bridge of separation). Those good souls will easily cross but the evil ones being unable to cross will fall in hell. Those souls who do not possess majority good or bad remain in a sort of limbo, a mixed state, in a place of shadows where there is neither joy nor torment. On the whole the Zoroastrian tradition, known as Parsi in India, was influenced by the middle-eastern religious concepts and in turn influenced the Greek and Hellenistic religious world.

God in the Bible

It should be clarified that the Bible is the scripture of two related yet distinct religious communities, namely Judaism and Christianity. They both cohere and differ in the interpretation of key texts.

An important biblical designation of divinity is *el*, sometimes with the definite article: e.g. 'ha-el', the god. Unlike Elohim, *el* has clear antecedents to older Semitic languages. *El* was used in conjunction with a special characteristic. E.g. *El-elyon,* 'God Most High' and *El-shaddai*, 'God Almighty.' Whether they indicate different gods or attributes of the same God is debated. The Elohist source of the Pentateuch and some psalms prefer Elohim to other names. There are references to 'other gods' (Ex. 20:3; Deut. 5:7), 'new gods' (Jugs 5:8), and 'foreign gods' (Gen. 35:2; Jos. 24:20).

The disclosure of the name YHWH was decisive and most distinctive in the history of Israel. It happened as a pre-emptive act of liberation when the Hebrew slaves were groaning in slavery in Egypt (Ex. 3). It was mysterious and enigmatic, and Moses the original receiver of this name was perplexed by its meaning 'I am that I am' or 'being that to be.' The name should not be taken in vain and nobody can manipulate it. Yet the name can be invoked for an act of liberation. In other words, though the name YHWH was too mysterious and terrifying to pronounce, the presence of its referent was always assured in a liberative praxis and journey as experienced by the nomadic Hebrew community. The 'Lord' (Yahweh) was combined with God (Elohim) when two sources were connected as evident in Gen. 2:4. But curiously enough, people began to worship the 'Lord' only later (Gen. 4:26). Later, sensing the terrifying holiness of Yahweh he was called by the name *Adon* meaning Lord, master, husband etc.

Scholars are in agreement that Judaism was a monotheistic religion by the end of the Babylonian exile (sixth century BCE). Then there was monolatry, demanding to worship only Yahweh God to the exclusion of all other gods, though there is the affirmation that the Lord God is the God of all gods. Anthropomorphic and mytho-poetic language could not be avoided, hence we read of God's personality with hands, eyes and so on, his emotions such as loving and being jealous as well as his relationships such as father, husband and king.

Divine names in the Bible created a confusion when the Septuagint translated as *Kurios* ('lord, master, husband' etc.) which meant in usage both human masters and divine figures. Jesus was confessed as Lord, Christ and Saviour. Do these confessional titles warrant a belief that he was God? Was Jesus God or divine or human or a combination? In what sense was he both God's Son and Son of the Human One? The confusion reached its height when the divine-human natures and their combinations were hotly discussed in his dialogue with Jewish scholars and leaders as evident in the fourth Gospel and in the early councils of the Christian Church. The debate to some extent continues even today where in popular Christianity with a Jesus cult the confusion also continues![1] Yet another development was Trinity, conceiving, perceiving or experiencing God as a divine commune constituted by the Father, Son and the Holy Spirit. Biblical references to trinity are scanty (2 Cor. 13:14; Mt. 28:29; 1 Cor. 14:4-6). It is left to the Christian community either to articulate this reality or to take yet another name of God, enigmatic yet real in presence just as was Yahweh. Christian presentation of Jesus to people of other faiths is confusing if they do not take time to share the process of gradual perceptions of Jesus, the dilemmas and an enigmatic perception of him as part of the Trinity.

God in Islam

The following words succinctly and comprehensively present the pre-Islamic situation and basic witness to One God with Qur'anic reference:

> ... the Muslim faith defines itself ... both a renewal and explanation of the *mithaq*, the pact made by God with the human race in preeternity (surah 7:172), recalled by earlier prophets and validated and ratified by the pre-Islamic monotheistic believers acknowledged in the Qur'an. Abraham, the 'friend of God' (4:125), stands out in this context. He is described as being 'just and a prophet' (19:41), 'a true believer (*hanif*), having surrendered himself (*mulim*) to God' without compromise with the *mushrikun*, or polytheists, those who associate others with God (3:67).
>
> However, it is only the Qur'anic teaching that has given this basic faith its perfect expression and full value. This is not only true because the Prophet performed the obligations of religion as a *hanif*, giving to God the 'eternal worship' set out by the Creator from the beginning of time but partially corrupted by the 'peoples of the Book' (2:135); it is also true because Muhammed received the mandate to preach 'in the name of the Lord who created', in the name of the 'very generous one who instructed man by pen and taught him what he did not know.'[2]

---

[1] See Larry W. Hurtado, *How on Earth did Jesus become a God?: Historical Questions about Earliest Devotion to Jesus*, Cambridge (UK): William B Eerdmans, 2005.

[2] Louis Gardet, "God in Islam" in *Encyclopaedia of Religion*, ed. by Mircea Eliade, New York: Macmillan, 1987, Vol. 6, 26.

The 'peoples of the Book' are Jews and Christians, and then it is no wonder that the Qur'an echoes many of the affirmations and stories of the Bible. Their 'corruption' is exposed by the repeated insistence on God being the One without a second who has no wife and son and who has given the perfect teaching in plain language. The unity of God is central to Islamic theology. God is the unknowable, wholly other, yet he addresses humans who believe in the Mystery and are willing to surrender to his will as enshrined in the holy books.

The Arabic name for God *Allah* shares the same root of the Hebrew *Elohim*. God is all powerful, creator, supreme, king of all the ages and judge of all judges, on the one hand, and all merciful and most compassionate (*'al-Rahman al-Rahim*) on the other. God has given nothing greater than the proclamation of divine unity, ritual prayer, and commandments on all aspects of life. The transcendent awareness or sacred commitment of a Muslim is defined in terms of uncritical acceptance of them. The divine perfections are revealed in the 99 beautiful names of God which are revealed in the Qur'an, and they denote the supreme and compassionate qualities of God such as being holy and just. The Muslims are not allowed to add anything more and therefore there is no place for mytho-poetic imagination and creativity in the orthodox sects of Islam (*Sunni* and *Shiah*). In this sense the Sufi experience of God in most intimate ways even to the extent of claiming 'I am God or truth' is not only unorthodox but also heretical.

Soul in the Middle Eastern Traditions

No word can be more confusing than 'soul' and its associated words such as mind, spirit and self, in interfaith understanding.

The Hellenistic influence on the Judeo-Christian tradition seems quite natural but imperceptible. The typical view of the Hellenistic religions is expressed in a late oracle of Apollo at Claros:

> When someone asked Apollo whether the soul remained after death or was dissolved, he answered, 'The soul so long as it is subject to its bonds with the destructible body, while being immune to feelings, resembles the pains of (the body); but when it finds freedom after the mortal body dies, it is borne entire to the ether, being then forever ageless, and abides entirely untroubled; and this the First-born Divine Providence enjoined.[1]

Jewish-Christian Ideas

Though some of the Egyptian and Akkadian words are translated as 'soul' the Judeo-Christian view of the transcendental core of human personality is unique. Human is an unitary being or psycho-somatic unit, although it is blurred by

[1] Quoted, Jan Bremmer, "Soul: Greek and Hellenistic Concepts" in *Encyclopaedia of Religion*, ed. by Mircea Eliade, New York: Macmillan, 1987, Vol. 13, 437.

terminological complexity and confusion. Following are the most significant terms:

(a) *chayyim* (life or living) indicating life in general which is applicable to humans, animals and even plants (Gen. 1:20; 24:2:7).

(b) *neshama* (breath or breathing thing) is applied to God (Is. 30:33) and humans (Deu. 2 0:16; 1Kg.17:17). It is associated with blood which is everywhere in the body just like the breath (Gen. 9:6; Lev. 17:14).

(c) *nephesh* (living being); LXX translation *psyche* influenced the NT which can be misleading. Translations add to further confusion; e.g. of AV's 42 renderings the most common are soul and life. No notion of bipartite or tripartite structure of human personality is evident in the scriptures. The human person is soul in the sense of a living being by virtue of being a 'body' made alive by the 'breath' or the Spirit of God. Life is dependent on God (Gen. 6:3; Eccl. 12:7). There is no independent mortality. When living beings die they return to the dust (Ps. 104:29). On the whole the term *nephesh* is used to mean three things with little overlap:

   i. life, opposed to death (Ex. 4:19; Deut. 19:21; Job 2:4).
   ii. 'a man' or 'people' or 'the whole being' or 'living beings' (Gen. 46:27; Ps. 6:4).
   iii. that which experiences everything whether it belongs to the realm of feeling or knowing or willing; yet feeling is uppermost (Job 6:7); other popular rendering is 'self' (Deut. 12:20) and 'soul' meaning the whole being: 'Bless the Lord O my *nephesh*' (Ps. 103:1).

(d) *ruach* which describes, like *nephesh* and *neshama*, a universal element in human nature. There is a complex variety of rendering (e.g. in AV alone 17). Most common are spirit, wind and breath. Like *nephesh, ruach* is connected with *neshama.* A man or woman is a being in whose nostrils is the *neshama* of the *ruach* of life (Gen. 7:22). 'The *ruach* (breath) of God is in me' (Job 27:3); 'He gives breath to his people' (42:5). While *nephesh* denotes something that permeates the body with the breath of life, *ruach* is the word for the breath that comes and goes in breathing. With very few exceptions *nephesh* denotes an element in human beings and animals, but *ruach* in human beings and God. The *ruach* in human beings may be good or bad, new or old. Only once it denotes the spirit of the beast (Eccl. 3:21). In a few cases it means strength or power: 'War horses of Egypt are weak (flesh), not strong (*ruach*)' – Is. 31:3. The use of *ruach* in the common sense of 'the seat of life' (as often in Job, e.g. 34:14) is clearly distinguishable from its use to denote God's special gift given to people like the prophets. It is also related to creation and inspiration. In creation it operates as though God took a part of his perennial fund of air and gave to human beings, but withdrawing it at their death (Eccl. 12:7). In this sense God said, 'My *ruach* shall not always abide in humans' (Gen. 6:3). It is sharing part of his spirit, and the *ruach* of God is never identical with the *ruach* of the humans.

(e) *leb* or *lebab* demotes 'heart' which is rendered as inner human, mind, will and heart. It is often mentioned as one organ along with bones and bowels (e.g. Ps. 7:9; 22:14). Both the *leb* and *nephesh* are said to pant or throb (Ps. 38:30; 42:1). Along with flesh it denotes the whole being: e.g. 'my heart and flesh cry out with joy to the living God' (Ps. 84:2); so also with mind and soul (Deut. 6:5). It can be the seat of goodness or evil and a heart can be of stone or of flesh (Eze. 36:26).

Human beings are created in the image of God (Gen. 1:26). What does this mean? Of its 17 occurrences, 10 refer to various types of physical image: e.g. models of tumours and rats (1 Sam. 6:5); pictures of humans (Eze. 16:17); idols (Num. 33:52). In two places the Psalms liken human existence to an image or shadow (39:7, 73:20). The other 5 are in Genesis (1:26, 27; 5:3; 9:6) indicating 'resemblance' between God and humans as well as between humans and humans. The word likeness (*demuth*) paralleled with image (*tselem*) is transparent in its meaning as 'to be like' or 'resemble' as evident in most of its 25 occurrences in Ezekiel (e.g. 1:5).

There are various interpretations of the word 'image'.

(a) Traditional Christian exegesis (from Irenaeus of the 2nd century): image indicates natural qualities in humans like reason and personality that makes them resemble God, and likeness indicates supernatural graces with ethical implications just like the redeemed becoming god-like. This interpretation is untenable because of the interchangeability of these terms as in Gen. 5:3.

(b) Image denotes the mental and spiritual faculties that humans share with their creator. There is no clue for this meaning in the scriptures.

(c) Image consists of physical resemblance of God as Seth bore Adam's image (Gen. 5:3). This goes against the commandment that God cannot be compared to any image and likeness.

(d) The image makes humans as God's representatives on earth as claimed by the Oriental kings. Some Assyrian texts describe the king as the image of God. But there is no indication of it denoting a collective form of people.

(e) Humanity's dominion over the creation on the basis of Gen. 1:26; 2:19; 9:2; this includes authority to name, control and rule (Ps. 8:6; Gen. 9:2, 3). It is a delegated authority with limits as there are restrictions: e.g. 'not to eat the blood' (Deut. 12:16; Gen. 9:4) and against unclean beasts (Levi. 9). There is always temptation to transgress the limits and to become all powerful and all knowing like God as the 'story of fall' points out.

(f) The image indicates a capacity to relate to God with a consciousness to respond to God's love in freedom and to cooperate with God's continuing creation and recreation. Limitation is overcome by enjoying the relationship of God and fellow humans.

'The creation of man is introduced more impressively than any preceding work by the announcement of divine resolution: "Let us make man." God participates more intimately and intensively in this than in the earlier works of creation. The use of the verb *bara* in v.27 receives its fullest significance for that divine creativity which is absolutely without analogy. It occurs three times in the one verse to make clear that here the high point and goal has been reached toward which all God's creativity from v.1 was directed.'[1]

With regard to the meanings of image and likeness von Rad, after consulting ancient Oriental myths and ideas, observes:

> The marvel of man's bodily appearance is not at all to be expected from the realm of God's image. This was the original notion, and we have no reason to suppose that it completely gave way, in P's theological reflection, to a spiritualizing and intellectualizing tendency. Therefore, one will do well to split the physical from the spiritual as little as possible: the whole man is created in God's image. Even later times did not exclude corporeality, as is clear from a tradition referred to by Ezekiel, according to which the first man was perfect in beauty.[2]
>
> It is necessary, however, to be careful not to see something additional in this image of God in man. It is not limited to any part of man. Man is like God in the way in which he is called into existence, in the totality of his being. And here, finally, in the supreme mystery of the whole work of creation, the language of P takes on a solemn tone (v.27). Of course even here P limits itself to fixing the matter. It refrains from any reflection of this "gracious act of God who, in his sovereign freedom, has willed out of all creation to have man alone as his counterpart with whom he will speak and have communion."[3]

Just like erected images of powerful kings in areas of their domination, humans are placed on earth as God's representatives to rule over animals, and 'summoned to maintain and enforce God's claim to dominion over the earth. The decisive thing about man's similarity to God, therefore, is his function in the

[1] Gerhard von Rad, *Genesis*, London: SCM Press, 1972, 57.

[2] Ref. Ez. 28:12; Ps. 8; Ibid., 58.

[3] Ibid., 59.

non-human world'. Humans have to remind the world and all creatures that they belong to God. They are created as male and female.

Islamic Belief

Arabic terms *ruh* and *nafs* are of the same as the Hebrew *ruah* and *nephesh*. In Qur'an the *nephesh* is human soul while the *ruah* is from God – nothing beyond the grave. The atomist, changeable and materialist natures of the soul are debated in Islamic theology.[1] And the celebrated image of a bird to signify soul in the ancient Near Eastern tradition seems to have survived in Islam. Accordingly, *haamah*, a bird-like apparition resembling a small bird, departs from the dead and remain as bird until the day of judgment. In the case of a slaughtered man as an owl it perches by his grave and continues to shriek as if asking for a drink until the death is avenged.

"And when the Lord said to the angels: 'I am about to place a vicegerent in the earth', they said, 'Will you place therein such as will cause disorder in it, and shed blood? and we glorify you with your praise and extol your holiness.' He answered, 'I know what you know not' (2:31)." The word used for vicegerent (*khalifa*) means one who came after and stands in the place of someone; an Imam or supreme religious head; and a sovereign king or ruler. The human mission was to look after God's creation.

"And he taught Adam all the names, then he put the objects of these names before the angels and said, 'Tell me the names of these if you are right' (2:31). They declared: 'Allah only as the All-knowing one, Wise' (2:33). And He said, 'Adam, tell them their names.' He said, 'Did I not say to you, I know the secrets of the heavens and of the earth, and I know what you reveal and what you conceal?' (2:34). The angels were asked to submit to Adam and they did except Iblis, the Satan; he was proud and of the disbelievers."

The human soul relates to the divine spirit since God brings life to humans by breathing into them of his spirit. With death, the soul leaves the body, to rejoin it on the Day of Judgment. The dominant Hindu idea is that the soul takes on another body in the cycle of death and birth, however, Islam as well as the Judeo-Christian tradition do not accept this view.

Interreligious Interaction and Synthesis

We have already noticed interaction between different traditions. But there are greater developments in terms of new religious traditions reflecting a strange kind of synthesis, individuals with uncommon religious experience drinking from different wells simultaneously and different suggestions made from long periods of study and dialogue with people of other religious traditions.

---

[1] See M. E. Marmura's essay on soul in Islam in *Encyclopaedia of Religion*, ed. by Mircea Eliade, New York: Macmillan, 1987, Vol. 13, 460-465.

Interfaith synthesis – Sikhism: Combination of the Vaishnava devotion and Islamic ideas that influenced poet-saints such as Ramananda (1360-1470) and Kabir (1398-1518) who accepted Muslim disciples. In the 15th and 16th centuries bhakti (devotional) movements were popular everywhere and the guidance of a guru was needed. Gurunanak (1469-1539) appeared to be such a guru. His disappearance for 3 days during which he received a commission to serve and teach charity and prayer signify his vocation. The opening pronouncement of his mission was 'There is no Hindu; there is no Muslim.' He accepted the basic teachings of Hinduism including *karma samsara* and the Muslim idea of one God. Placed in a polytheistic context with many names and forms he established a name for God which was in a way de-naming.

The opening lines of the *Japji* part of the Sikh scripture *Guru Grandh Sahib*, the Sikhs' morning prayer, clearly states Nanak's concept of God.

There is one God.
He is the supreme truth.
He, the creator,
Is without fear and without hatred.
He the omnipresent,
Pervades the universe.
He is not born,
Nor does he die to be born again.
By his grace shalt thou worship him.

Before time itself
There was truth.
When time began to run its course
He was the truth.
Even now, he is the truth,
And evermore shall truth prevail.[1]

God was One, omnipotent and omniscient. Both epithets and names that come from both the Hindu and Muslim traditions are used *Pita* (Father), *Pritam* (Lover) *Malik* (master) *Rahim*, Ram and Govinda. He insisted on the role of guru to guide the community. He said 'I have no miracles except the name of God.' Of the three ways (*margas*) of liberation – work, knowledge and devotion – as described in the Gita, he took the way of devotion (*bhakti-marga*). Praising the name of God is the major event in Sikh worship which is done through lyrics with devotional fervour.

The fifth guru Arjun (1563-1606) freed the Sikhs from the tutelage of the parent communities: the Hindus and the Muslims, and launched them on their

[1] Quoted, Khushwant Singh, "Sikhism" in *Encyclopaedia of Religion*, ed. by Mircea Eliade, New York: Macmillan, 1987, Vol. 13, 316.

own. One passage of the GGS reflects the separate identity Sikhs had acquired in their hundred years of existence:

> I do not keep the Hindu fast nor the Muslim Ramadan.
> I serve Him alone who is my refuge.
> I serve the one Master, who is also Allah.
> I have broken with the Hindu and the Muslim,
> I will not worship with the Hindu, nor the like the Muslim go to Mecca;
> I shall serve Him and no other.
> I will not pray to idols nor heed the Muslim's *azān*;
> I shall put my heart at the feet of the one supreme being,
> For we are neither Hindus nor Muslims.[1]

It was the tenth guru Gobind Singh (1666-1708) who organised the Sikhs as a community with self-dignity and the right of self-defence. The eruption of a somewhat militant force alarmed the neighbouring Hindu chieftains and the Muslim Mughals. After his time, as he prescribed, the scripture Guru Granth Sahib took the place of a guru.

Conceptual and Visionary Fusion: There are proposals and visions that while relating to other religions with openness, 'we than I have. Dialogue in the real sense arises precisely where I (or we) discover the same currents and problems within the religion of the 'other' as I (or we) find in my (or our) religious world.'[2] Here Panikker's main theme in this connection for discussion is religious experience, Hindu-Christian, non-dual and devotional. This is not the place to discuss the nature and varieties of religious experience. However, Panikkar's drawing of insight from the non-dual position for understanding the Christian Trinity is worth noting.

> If God, the Father, is the ultimate I who calls – generates – the Son as His thou, manifesting and reflecting Him, then the Spirit is not only the personified Love of the Father and the reciprocal self-gift of the Son, but the nonduality (*advaita*) of the Father and Son. In other words, *advaita* applied to the Trinity would mean that there are not three distinct beings (as if this would ever possible ultimately!) but that the only I loves himself and discovers his nonduality (which is the Spirit) in the (him) self which is the thou (the Son). The Trinity on the other hand, applied to *advaita*, would show that non-dualism can have room for Love – understood precisely as the inner movement of this 'One without a second (*ekam eva advityam*).[3]

---

[1] Quoted, Ibid., 319.

[2] Panikkar, Op. cit., 278.

[3] Ibid., 287.

Of course there are other thinkers who have proposed a similar understanding of the Trinity within the framework of a dynamic relationship, but this way of naming the Ultimate Reality or God may dry up the relational vitality of God-experience and God-talk.

Faith and New Interpretations: The Evangelical Alliance of UK in October 2006 'contributed to the discussion on the future of multiculturalism in Britain by calling for any attempts by Prince Charles to belittle the sovereign as "Defender of Faith" rather than "Defender of the Faith" – meaning the Christian faith – to be resisted. Concerned that such a belittling would be seen to endorse syncretism – the merging of the worship of different faiths – the Alliance's report "Faith and Nations" argues that the coronation should remain an act of Christian worship at which representatives of other faiths might be guests.'[1] Also there is apprehension about superficial notions of other religions in Religious Education. Faith schools which lead to a kind of syncretism and thereby to non-commitment to any religious vision and tradition. There can be no common faith as such, the committed ones warn, and needed is seriousness and in-depth study.

Panikkar, quoting Is. 7:9 ('Without faith you cannot exist' cf. 'Have firm faith, or you will fail to stand firm'-REB) out of context, interprets faith as that which makes humans as unique creatures. But the word 'faith' is a unique Judeo-Christian concept. He mentions the Gita which uses the word *sraddha*, which, he admits, 'originally signified the theandric condition essential to the efficacy of the sacrifice.' Actually in fact it was the sacrificer's confidence in the efficacy of the ritual. And the Gita uses it in a particular sense of classifying human characteristics. Yet Panikkar claims that his thesis is 'in harmony with the spirit of the Indian religions, and in general with every religion.'[2] He continues to elaborate faith as a fundamental quality and condition of a human being.

Following is a bare summary of Panikkar's elaborate interpretation of faith.[3] Faith is necessary to reach full humanity; it is a constitutive human dimension; it unites humankind; it is another term for the human's ontolological relation to the absolute. If religion is what binds humans to their foundation, faith is what frees them from mere cosmic existence and relates them to the Trinity. It may also serve to free religion from its exclusivistic aspects. It is the foundation and guarantee of human relations. It is also a condition for love and guarantees its creativity. Faith can be recovered because it was never lost. Faith can be expressed in several formulae, leaving room for a certain doctrinal pluralism. One cannot deny the intellectual character of faith without denying faith itself. However, though it needs an intellectual vehicle or a conceptual system, doctrinal affirmations do not correctly express the ever-transcendent mystery of faith. 'When a single light beam of faith is refracted in the prism of our consciousness, it is decomposed

[1] *Methodist Recorder*, 26 Oct 06, 1.

[2] Panikkar, op. cit., 189.

[3] Ibid., 190-218.

into as many conceptual beams as there are intellectual structures by which the pure act of faith is expressed.' Faith contains a practical, sentimental and volatile element that leads to truth and good. In Christianity, faith is axiomatic of a theistic transcendence. Faith helps an atheist to discover himself without a theistic orientation. It should be something common to all, guaranteeing salvation to all. Faith is a universal gift from God, and it implies freedom and possibility of either refusal or acceptance. Faith is fundamentally dynamic, functional and that which one hopes. Human dignity resides precisely in the anthropological dimension of faith and therefore human being is an ever open, infinite being. The essence of faith lies in the question rather than in the answer, in the inquisitive stance, in the desire rather than the concrete response one gives. Good faith is self-evident without needing defence and interpretation. Good faith is pure, unique, innocent, spontaneous and singular. Faith is the presupposition of understanding, but the latter seems to offer no support to the former. Faith is mythic and being unsatisfied with answers faith asks more questions without knowing if there is an answer.

W.C. Smith, in the way of suggesting a world theology of religions, was unique in making a distinction between belief and faith. Belief, according to him, is part of the cumulative tradition, which is complex and changing. The unchanging core, however, is faith, which is the fundamental personal quality, potentiality and transcendental dimension, common to all. He further explains:

> Faith, then, is a quality of human living. At its best it has taken the form of serenity and courage, and loyalty and service: a quiet confidence and joy, which enables one to feel at home in the universe, and to find meaning in the world and in one's own life, a meaning that is profound and ultimate, and is stable no matter what may happen to oneself at the level of immediate event. Men and women of this kind of faith face catastrophe and confusion, affluence and sorrow, unperturbed; face opportunity with conviction and drive; and face others with a cheerful charity.[1]

If faith is engendered and sustained by a particular religious tradition, as Smith claims, it may be problematic to establish that the meaning of 'faith' is the same for all and the term is especially Judeo-Christian. Even in the Bible the term faith is used in many senses of which most important is the ability to transcend and move 'mounts'. Then one needs to study the motivating force for the faith to act as opposed to faith which is regarded as a state of mind or an experience with the ultimate. Today the term 'secular faith' is commonly used. It should be a fascinating study of and discussion on the meaning and dimensions of faith in

[1] W.C. Smith, *Faith and Belief: The Difference Between Them*, Oxford: Oneworld Publications, 1998, p. 12.

today's life as perceived and experienced by people of different religious traditions and ideologies.

Jesus' extraordinary understanding of faith is not adequately acknowledged by Jews and Christians. He appears to have lived in the presence of God, participating in God's continued work of liberation. He did what he perceived his heavenly Father doing. He was not at all interested in expounding fixed doctrines of faith. For him faith is the ability to move on, go beyond and change. It was like a mustard seed which can grow into a great tree. Those who have the faith can move mountains. He found this faith in certain individuals within his tradition who dared to make new possibilities and alternatives. He appreciated the same in some people of other faiths. While his disciples came to their sense and asked Jesus 'increase our faith' he lamented about his religious community lacking faith.

Transcendence of Favoured Names: In matured spirituality it is appreciated that one can use names of God that come from other traditions. Thus, for instance, a reformed Jew, apart from using names and epithets of God from the Bible such as Dodi (my Beloved) and Rachmana (feminine form of Compassionate One) in prayer, is able to use Al'lah, Brahman and Om.[1] But what about epithets with reference to mythological portrayals of sectarian gods such as Krishna and Ganesh? If we extend the discussion we may very well come to a limit to names and epithets with a clear distinction of what is common, abstract and absolute and what is particular and parochial although the latter might be taken by their devotees as signifying the former. On the whole unlimited and uncritical plurality of names ascribed to the ultimate may be seen as a generous position but where particular traditions and commitments are attached to favoured names with mythological or historical references it is improper to judge them lower or pre-matured. Social critics will say that such 'hybridization' should find expression in joint work of service in the context of poverty and social degradation.

Concluding Remarks

Whereas implicit religions and secular ideologies use abstract terms for signifying the ultimate, explicit religions use a variety of names. These names are evoked and celebrated in colourful ways, and the stories behind them are commemorated or re-enacted. Admittedly, we have not covered popular diverse cults all over the world. We have consulted the major theistic traditions such as the Zoroastrian tradition, Hindu devotional traditions, Judeo-Christian tradition, Islam and Sikhism. We have identified the naming of the absolute or the sacred both in its transcendent and immanent dimensions. But there is no way that all these traditions have the same meanings as some of the common names, although in the case of the Eastern traditions – Vedic religion, Buddha and Jaina traditions, Upanishadic thought, Hindu devotional traditions – and that of the Middle Eastern traditions

---

[1] Charles Burack, "Embracing the Many Names of the One: A Multifaith Journey to Wholeness", *Interreligious Insight,* 5/1 January 2007, pp. 19-25.

– Judaism, Christianity and Islam – there are common terms such as God and soul. As we have pointed out, however, the development of meanings around these terms is different between these two blocks of religious traditions. The Sikh tradition has its own origin and development, but in terms of using divine names in worship it is directly indebted to the Hindu and Islamic traditions. On the whole the naming of the transcendence in both theistic and non-theistic terms in the religious traditions is not problem-free. The bewildering variety of names and even terminological confusions as in the case of the name 'Lord' and 'Soul' present a complex picture that requires patient and persistent pursuit.

Although, a plurality of names and diversity of traditions are positively looked at in today's interfaith movement and although there is a call for celebration and respect of them, there is reason to see in them a kind of superficiality. They may well be seen as lacking depth and serious commitment. Buddha, for example, a serious adept of search after reality, after being puzzled with a conflicting variety, finally found meaning and serenity in a remarkable way. He found the ultimate solution for all suffering and religious bewilderment. But the nature of the 'final release' could not be explained, and Buddha remained silent. Religious scholars such as Panikkar have taken this as profound, providing a new key in the midst of conflicting forms and names of reality. Nevertheless, what is undeniable is that the Buddhist tradition has not remained silent nor is satisfied with one name and form. Hence the growth of Buddhism with elaborate visions, symbols and names. And even if 'silence' is ultimate in that the followers of the Buddha have found a transcendent immanence or immanent transcendence. It is a position-less position as some of them have described.

The foregoing discussion also has shown that absorbing all the variety and undermining irreconcilable differences into one reality with a defining name such as Brahman or God betrays one particular position. Vedantic interpretations of Brahman are the best example for this. Particular names based on particular disclosures need to be only those culturally conditioned because there is a claim for their universal appeal. Therefore, in a multifaith context, one needs to move forward from stereotypes such as one truth and many names and forms, with a view to see with openness the distinctive ways in which particular persons and communities find particular names and their associated traditions to be uncompromisable.

Chapter 6

Meaning and Meanings in Religious Life

Evocative Yet Elusive

'Meaning' is like a particular slippery fish, which is close to the boat but when caught, even before we have the feeling of having caught it, it slips into the water. 'Everywhere humans seek meaning in life.' This and similar statements have been made by a number of people ranging from religious enthusiasts to practitioners of interfaith dialogue. While we are not inclined to dispute their observation, it is not inappropriate to ask the questions: What do they mean? Is it something based on one's own experience and observation of others' behaviour? Are there many people who themselves say, 'I seek meaning in life'? While 'religion' continues to be evasive of a single and convincing definition, can the meaning of religion or religious life be defined? Is it possible to argue that 'meaning' is an English word, taken onto the discourse on religious life from the philological and philosophical world? The conclusion of this chapter might well be an answer in the positive. However, before that we have to recognise the difficulty of catching the real meaning of religious life, and for this exercise we will consult the areas of philosophy, theology, study of religion and interfaith dialogue.

Classical discussions on 'the meaning of meaning' in philology and philosophy with support from psychology remain inconclusive.[1] However, they provide several insights that can be applied to exploring the meaning of religious life. The influence of language upon thought and vice versa, for example, helps us to analyse the claims of unanimity of experience and of silence as the ultimate expression of the experience of meaning; so does the realisation that meaning of words and ideas are relational and personal. Meaning does not simply depend

---

[1] E.g. see C.K. Ogden & I.A. Richards, *The Meaning of Meaning*, first published in 1923 and the ARK edition 1985, London: Ark Paperbacks, 1985.

on a subjective feeling and self-assessment but on consequences and openness to newer, higher, richer and finer meanings. Meaning, furthermore, is not the present mental state in response to an evocative force, but it connects with interpreting the past, analysing the present and anticipating the future. At popular level, it is claimed that seeing the Monty Python's award winning film 'The Meaning of Life' (1983) with entertaining stories of fun and some food for thought is claimed to be a substitute for reading Bertrand Russell's *A History of Western Civilization*! It is fair to say that no one wants to remain or be perceived as meaningless!

The English word 'meaning' is ambiguous enough not to be able to help in our attempt to get a clear idea. Without an adjective such as 'religious' it can add confusion as in usage it is attached to a variety of areas: linguistic, cognitive, emotive and descriptive, focal and picture theory. Meaning of life in general and religious life in particular relates to the ideas of truth and value, but again we have to guard carefully the discussion of meaning from the various dimensions of truth and value which could be treated separately. Perhaps what is common in the various areas and shades of the meaning of 'meaning' is that it cannot remain in isolation without reference to or in relation to something 'other' or significance of a metaphysical entity. Moreover, as some thinkers have observed, belief and meaning, meaning and communication, meaning and mind, are interdependent. Any idea of meaning as a self-referral experience is senseless, at least for others.

With the above recognition of the vagueness and complexity of the topic and warning against side-tracking, my intention in this chapter is to present issues that relate to religious life, both explicit and implicit. After considering an observation of current discussion on modernity or post-modernity, we will move on to identify pointers in the study of religion, philosophical theology, mission and interfaith dialogue. The aim is to find a public language to communicate meaning which will make sense to common people as individuals and communities.

When life-threatening problems of poverty, war, oppression and injustice challenge the modern world, is a discussion on the abstract idea of meaning credible? Should it not be the priority to solve these problems using common sense? Raymundo Panikkar, in his introduction to the cross-cultural study of myth, faith and hermeneutics states: 'I feel that these questions cannot in any way be dismissed as unscholarly or nonpertinent. If intellectual activity divorces itself from life, it becomes not only barren and alienating, but also harmful and perhaps eventually criminal.'[1] Though the urgency of these problems cannot be minimised, he argues, they should not obscure the importance of analysing the human problems. The reason for restraining from making connections with action and proposal for programmes, he says, 'is because the nature of radical reflections is that they do not impose just one line of conduct. They leave room for tensions and polarities; they nurture branches and leaves, even fruit and flowers, without reducing everything to a single manifestation. An authentic idea inspires, but does

[1] R. Panikkar, *Myth, Faith and Hermeneutics*, 2.

not dictate. Commitment, responsibility and active involvement are not logical conclusions of syllogisms, nor do they abolish the constitutive polarities of the human condition.'[1] Panikkar is optimistic about the effect of such inspiration in causing repentance towards maintaining the God-world-human nexus through the perfect balance of word and deed.

Search for meaning is not necessarily an unscientific pursuit. There is no doubt that science has made the universe and human life more comprehensible than ever before. But those scientists who are conscious of the limitations of science will agree that such comprehension has not produced any point or meaning. Other than simply believing, we have yet to be convinced that human being is nothing but a physical mechanism, mental states are nothing but physical states of the central nervous system and volition, and feeling and instincts are nothing but the result of physio-chemical changes. If moral consciousness, love, freedom and engaging interpersonal communication cannot be simply accounted for by scientific analysis, artists, poets and theologians can never be made redundant.

Not only the conditions of finitude but also feelings of weariness about mechanical routines, boredom of repetitive words and acts etc. also challenge 'meaning of life.' This is true of not only routine duties and works but also of unchanged liturgies, rituals and postures. This is true of the new forms of religion or expressions of religiosity such as sports. For example, research might well show that the vocabulary in hymn singing and commentary preaching in a football match is less than the same in a church. However, because of basic prejudices, group interest and identity-guarding, people may not come in the open acknowledging the limitation of whatever they do in pursuit of happiness, satisfaction or fulfilment. Admittedly, this chapter collects the views and expressed feelings not of those who participate in overt religious life, one way or other, but that of those in observing, analyzing and theory-making.

Setting the Scene: Modernity and the Myth of Progress

From an interfaith perspective labels such as pre-modern, modern and post-modern remain within a circle of intellectual elite in Europe and North America. Because of the claims of civilization, economic development, technological monopoly, and the power of political bargaining with a threatening measure of weaponry, these labels acquire some respect among the educated people even though all of them do not understand the complexity and ramification entailed in these labels.

Philosophical theologians have something to say about meaning. For example, Paul Tillich, used the basic presuppositions of existentialism for his philosophical theology. For him, 'Religion opens up the depth of man's spiritual life which is usually covered by the dust of our daily life and noise of our secular work. It gives us the experience of the Holy, of something which is untouchable,

[1] Ibid., 3.

awe-inspiring, an ultimate meaning, the source of ultimate courage. This is the glory of what we call religion. But beside its glory lies its shame. It makes itself the ultimate and despises the secular realm. It makes its myths and doctrines, its rites and laws into ultimate and persecutes those who do not subject themselves to it. It forgets that its own existence is a result of man's estrangement from his true being. It forgets its own emergency character.'[1]

Religion as ultimate concern is the meaning-giving substance of culture, and culture is the totality of forms in which the basic concern of religion expresses itself. In abbreviation: religion is the substance of culture, culture is the form of religion. Such a consideration definitely prevents the establishment of a dualism of religion and culture. Every religious act, not only in organised religion, but also in the most intimate movement of the soul, is culturally formed.[2]

But Tillich does not fail to recognise the human failure in the process of realising one's creative potentials but then created a bondage of will thus resulting in destructive structures that alienate them. Hence, the need for existentialism.

> Existentialism, in the largest sense, is the protest against the spirit of industrial society within the framework of industrial society. The protest is directed against the position of man in the system of production and consumption of our society. Man is supposed to be the master of his world and of himself. But actually he has become a part of the reality he has created, an object among objects, a thing among things, a cog within a universal machine to which he must adapt himself in order not to be smashed by it. But this adaptation makes him a means for ends which are means themselves, and in which an ultimate end is lacking. Out of this predicament of man in the industrial society the experiences of emptiness and meaninglessness, of dehumanization and estrangement have resulted. Man has ceased to encounter reality as meaningful. Reality in its ordinary forms and structures does not speak to him any longer.
>
> One way out is that man restricts himself to a limited section of reality and defends it against the intrusion of the world into his castle. This is the neurotic way out which becomes psychotic if reality disappears completely. It involves subjection to the demands of culture and repression of the question of meaning. Or some may have the strength to take anxiety and meaninglessness courageously upon themselves and live creatively, expressing the predicament of the most sensitive people in our time in cultural production. It is the latter way to which

---

[1] P. Tillich, *Theology of Culture*, New York: Oxford University Press, 1964, 9.

[2] Ibid., 42.

> we owe the artistic and philosophical works of culture in the first half of the 20th century.'[1]

As early as the middle of the twentieth century, particularly after the two World Wars, Christian theologians started to recognize the failure of the secular modernism and suggested a return to religion, not to its orthodox form but to its pure core with the tool of a protestant critique. For example, recognizing fear, anxiety and the alienation of modern life, as a Christian theologian Tillich claims that more than other gods and idols, Jesus presents a new reality in which there is a way to overcome anxiety and finitude, law and tragedy, unity with God and fellow humans, which the church is supposed to maintain.[2] But Tillich does not make an attempt to consult parallel realities and figures in other religious traditions.

Hindu thinkers like Radhakrishnan proposed spirituality by using the yogic techniques to actualize and mobilize the inner forces of human life and unity of all religions on the basis of Reality or Brahman as the basic substratum of life and achieving oneness with it [him] the ultimate goal. Muslim thinkers emphasized the need of submitting to the will of God by following the minute prescriptions of worship and life found in the Islamic law. Minor differences could be easily adjusted if one takes the paradigm of 'one essence and manifestation of religions' or 'a variety of religious experiences.'

Has the situation changed since these claims? Do the discourses on modernity and post-modernity make things clearer and more promising? While introducing the historical and conceptual background to post-modernism, and its effect on the self-understanding of the modern culture and individuals Lawrence Cahoone observes:

> But because minds and cultures are harder to understand and specify than airplanes, this recognition makes the specification of what makes modernity modern endlessly controversial.
>
> The positive self-image modern Western culture has often given to itself, a picture born in the eighteenth-century Enlightenment, is of a civilization founded on scientific knowledge of the world and rational knowledge of value, which places the highest premium on individual human life and freedom, and believes that such freedom and rationality will lead to social progress through virtuous, self-controlled work, creating a better material, political, and intellectual life for all. This combination of science, reason, individuality, freedom, truth, and social progress has, however, been questioned and criticized by many. Some critics see modernity instead as a

[1] Tillich, 4.

[2] Ibid., 40f.

> movement of ethnic and class domination, European imperialism, anthropocentrism, the destruction of nature, the dissolution of community and tradition, the rise of alienation, the death of individuality in bureaucracy. More benign critics have argued sceptically that modernity cannot achieve what it hopes, i.e. that objective truth or freedom is unavailable, or that modernity's gains are balanced by losses, and that there is no alternative either to modernity or to its discontents. This is not the place to debate the relative truth of these claims; nevertheless, it can at least be said that while there is some truth in each of them, the whole truth is more complex ... The debate is complicated by the question of the historical parameters of modernity. The reason is that the location of the historical starting point of modernity depends on what one regards as modernity's essential feature.[1]

It is not difficult to infer from this that for the majority of the 'religious community' around the world such labels (modernity, post-modernity and so on) do not mean anything. Either they live in the primitive world or pre-modern world or, if considerably influenced by outside currents, orthodoxy, modernity and post-modernity roll around as a big bundle of knots, growing bigger and bigger.

One trend, however, which has been prevalent at different degrees in different societies is that meaning is measured by the individual's sense of happiness. The Stoics, as early as the third century BCE stated publicly that the primary purpose of human life is seeking happiness within themselves. The negative side of it as some recognised was that any excess and dependence on others or uncontrollable forces could create anxiety and frustration. Chrysippus, a Stoic of the beginning of the third century BCE is said to have died from laughing at his own joke! In the place of jokes one can put other bliss-inducing drugs, drinks and casual sex to make it contextual. It seems there is no material corollary to enduring happiness. We will come to this issue of individual and community later.

Worship of the goddess of reason following Enlightenment seems to be declining. However, its product of individual freedom is still notionally honoured, but in practice it is increasingly recognised that every individual act affects the society and vice versa. Smoking is an individual freedom for some kind of fulfilment, but now it was estimated that when the ban on public smoking came into effect in England in July 2007 the NHS would save about 15 million pounds a year. This is applicable to other areas of human engagement such as teenage pregnancy and gang-crime. When such restrictions are proposed with a view to bring order and health in the society the usual criticism is that there

[1] L. Cahoone (ed.), *From Modernism to Postmodernism: An Anthology*, Malden: Blackwell Publishers, 2000, 12.

becomes a nanny state or police state. Therefore unlimited individual freedom is proved disastrous for any society.

When people from the developing world come to the developed world, most striking in their first sight is road traffic control. Time passes on, and they notice, compared to life in their society, how complex and complicated life is in general. Market and morality are not regulated as much as traffic. Chaos on the road can obstruct movement, but the same in the market is falsely accepted as the standard with increasing choice that brings much stress on the customers, apart from a vast amount of wastage, and massive profit for the investors. From healthy eating to stable parenting, family values are being reinforced, and responsible sex emphasized, with a constant tension between sensitivity and sensibility.

Without respecting the fact that the universe and its resources are not unlimited, people particularly in the developed countries have consumed or encouraged to consume non-renewable resources of the earth far beyond any proportion. But a realisation of this fact creates anxiety and fear. Meerton ter Borg observes:

> In an anomic situation, we are confronted with the limits of the symbolic universe, and thus with its finiteness, its vulnerability and frailty, which is frailty of our own existence as well. We are in danger. Philosophers and psychologists point out that the awareness of the finiteness of existence causes anxiety, that is to say, fear without an object ... It is fear, not concerning any object we may meet in our life, but fear concerning existence itself.[1]

He further points out that the main alternatives are: to flee, to defend yourself, or to accommodate yourself to it. 'But in the case of anxiety', he continues, 'people have nothing to flee from, nothing to defend themselves against, and nothing to accommodate themselves to. To overcome this *anomie*, people have to choose or construct, to create it themselves. This creativity is the correlate of anxiety. But what is created? In principle, there are two possibilities: either an enemy, to escape from or to defend yourself against, or a refuge to flee to. And of course, it can be a combination of these two. The relationship between these two is very interesting indeed. Jesus was both a scapegoat and a saviour; Oedipus began and ended as a saviour, and in between he was a scapegoat.'[2] If the *anomie* is overcome, that is a relief, almost a miracle, which creates trust and gratitude. Borg moves on with the discussion taking sociological categories, and connects it with modern day personifications of the charisma, ranging from popular politicians to pop musicians.

[1] Meerton ter Borg, "Charisma Today" in *The Secular Quest for Meaning in Life: Denton Papers in Implicit Religion*, ed. by E. Bailey, Lewiston: The Edwin Mellen Press, 2002, 106.

[2] Ibid., 107.

The fear and anxiety of the future of the universe is ever increasing, and scientists are warning against natural catastrophe as there are signs in the environment such as climatic change. But the reaction from the public is not encouraging: the majority either go on in the habitual way or remain callous about the danger. It is a minority who plays the role of a theologian or prophet as they tirelessly highlight the issue. In this context, meaning of life in general and religious life in particular is important not only for analysing the situation with observable data but also motivating with the three complementary ways in which 'implicit religion' is defined – commitment, integrating foci and intensive concerns with extensive effects. In the study of explicit religion more dimensions are identified as we have already seen, but our concern here is to point out meanings of meaning that have been derived from interfaith studies and dialogue.

Challenges from Missions

One-sided views and imbalanced histories of the Christian mission in the colonial period have created guilt among western Christians. Whereas they sent missionaries and spent considerably for mission work, they are nervous to face the neighbours of people of other faiths who were once targets of Christian mission when they lived in the 'mission field.' Does it show a generation gap or betray a mentality that was part of the colonial mission? Was the confidence of the people during this period in the power of the Christian message or more consciously in the empire which reported back along with the missionaries that all the participants in the empire and mission were engaged in the costly pursuit of civilizing communities of the pagan world? The continuing decline of Church life in Europe has also seemed to contribute to the above nervousness. In this context, those mission societies who want to continue their operation in the 'world church' do not talk about their faith but are satisfied with their charity and development work. Some societies appear to be glaringly agnostic and follow the methods of the non-missionary Charities! It appears that the third world poverty and under-development is the only justification for their existence as mission bodies.

Nevertheless there are a few voices which try to restore the credibility of the good work of the missionaries with reference to their contribution to social transformation and cultural renaissance. Then they dared to criticize their own culture. For example, Lesslie Newbigin (1909-1998) who spent more than thirty years in India and several years in the ecumenical movement returned to the UK in 1974. He was shocked by the way the culture of his country has changed, a culture which achieved a respectable civilization due to the combined impact of Enlightenment and Christianity. He realised that certain hope and sense of meaning found among the young generation in south India to be missing in this country. He pioneered a movement called Gospel and the Contemporary Culture, the programmes of which include a critique of modern secular and philosophical thinking and restoration of confidence in the power and meaning of the Christian message. About the secular society that he saw he writes:

> We have learned, I think, that what has come into being is not a secular society but a pagan society, not a society devoid of public images but a society which worships gods which are not God. But the myth of the secular society remains powerful. Let me remind you again of the definition of myth ... 'an unproved collective belief that is accepted uncritically to justify a social institution.' The idea of the secular society has been accepted by many Christians uncritically because it seemed to offer the Church the possibility of a peaceful coexistence with false gods, a comfortable concordat between Yahweh and the Baalim. But the promise is illusory.[1]

With this observation Newbigin calls Christians to discard the moods of timidity and anxiety and to inculcate confidence in the sufficiency of God. He welcomes some measure of plurality but rejects dogmatic pluralism. For him the quest for truth is search for meaning. His conclusion is: 'We must reject the invitation to live in a society where everything is subjective and relative, a society which has abandoned the belief that truth can be known and has settled for a purely subjective view of truth – "truth for you" but not truth for all. For one thing, I doubt whether such a society can long sustain its integrity in the face of the claims of those who have a firm commitment to some vision of truth.'[2] One hopes that mission boards and missiological circles move beyond analyzing what has happened in history, leaving aside charitable work, and create opportunities to initiate and engage in discussions on the meaning of life in a confused society.

Mission is no longer a Christian enterprise. Other religious communities are also involved in mission work. Gurus from the East come to the West and teach the art of living. Their yogic techniques of mind-calming or heart-warming have great appeal to a society which is maddened by excessive consumerism. For shoppers of spirituality there are many choices of techniques and schools of thought in the spiritual superstores. Such consumers in the West are too polite to ask the question to their spirituality providers, why in their home countries there continue the social evils such as poverty, illiteracy, untouchability, bonded labour and child labour, and corruption in spite of the long traditions of spirituality which have flourished there. More recently, there are Islamic missions in the West working with a view to introducing Islam as a cure to a degraded culture that has lost its soul. The Islamic Mission in the UK, for example, promotes the Muslim community's welfare and honour so that they will influence the wider community in this country.

---

[1] L. Newbigin, *The Gospel in a Pluralist Society*, London: SPCK, 1994, 220.

[2] Ibid., 244.

Discovering Meaning: Insights from the Study of Religion

It may be surprising for us to realise that no dictionary or encyclopaedia of religion has meaning as an entry. Even the Bible does not have a topic called meaning. That means, meaning is something either realised or interpreted. Where philosophy of religion is discussed there the word meaning occurs, but again meaning does not occur in isolation but always in connection with other dimensions of religious life such as culture and experience as well as their corollaries. We have room here only to point out those aspects as identified by the study of religion that help us to understand the meaning or near-meaning of religious life.

Comparative Study: As we noted earlier, Max Müller encouraged the Christian missionaries working in the East, explaining that the study of the religions of the East was as important as the study of a General about the enemy's camp. Also perhaps he and his colleagues had a hidden agenda of mastering the knowledge about the non-western world, its history, culture and religion. This is not to question his desire to explain 'the intricate relations he believed to exist between religion, mythology, language and the human mind'. He suggested that 'in perceiving the finite we always perceive the infinite also.'[1] For him the origin of religion lies in the perception of the infinite through the perception of the uncontrollable natural forces such as storm, sky, sun and moon, as evident in the Vedic religion of India, and a kind of moral sense was its corollary. Religion, therefore, is 'the perception of the infinite under such manifestations as are able to influence the moral character of man.'[2] As Eric Sharpe observes, 'In this and so much else, Max Müller was a true son of the Enlightenment, and genuine disciple of Kant.'[3] And by accepting the theory of the interdependence of language and human thought he refused to take on board Darwinian evolution of humanity from the depths of an animal brutality. For him intellect belonged to humans from the beginning.

But at the same time, in the so called mytho-poetic period the human intellect experienced 'a period of temporary insanity' which produced a disease of language the outcome of which was personification of natural forces attributing personal characters such as gender. Of course this sequence in a process has been refuted by other nature-mythologists but yet it has stimulated more theories of mythology. For our purpose what is significant is as to how Müller led the process to have a ground for a humanist-theological affirmation:

> However imperfect, however childish a religion may be, it always places the human soul in the presence of God; and however imperfect and however childish the conception of God may be, it always represents

---

[1] Quoted, E.J. Sharpe, *Comparative Religion,* 38.

[2] Quoted, Ibid., 39.

[3] Ibid.

> the highest ideal of perfection which the human soul, for the time being, can reach and grasp.[1]

Finally, it is left to universities and study centres to place study of religion in a particular department in combination.

A Critique of Objective Study with Analytical Tools: For example, W.C. Smith whose particular definition of religion we have dealt with, says that in so far as it is historical, it is as complex as all 'the religions' taken together. In so far as it is personal, it is as diverse as the men whose piety it synthesizes.'[2] Then he suggests that the word 'religion' and its related concepts should be dropped because it 'is confusing, unnecessary and distorting' though in the sense of personal piety conveys some meaning. It was his conviction that the vitality of personal faith and progress in understanding of the traditions of other people throughout history and throughout the world, 'are both seriously blocked by our attempt to conceptualise what is involved in each case in terms of [a] religion.'[3] He illustrates from the academic study of religion to show how not only the term 'religion' but also the names of religious traditions as Hinduism, Buddhism and Islam have been western constructs with Christian presuppositions.

Smith proposes on the part of the participant in the process of understanding a penetrating insight into the vital and transcendental dimension which he calls 'faith' and which is focused on Something beyond, or God. This can happen only when the adherents of religious traditions are taken as persons, not defined by the systems or 'isms'. A person of religious faith living in a bewildering world and facing complex issues possesses the inherent capacity to have a sense of transcendence. Though there is disagreement among scholars and people of faith about the nature of this transcendence, students of religion cannot aim at fully comprehending this transcendence. What is possible is to see it in the living human person.

Smith distinguishes 'faith' from what he calls 'cumulative tradition.' For him, belief is part of the cumulative tradition and thus different from faith. By faith he means personal faith and it stands for 'an inner religious experience or involvement of a particular person; the impingement on him of the transcendent, putative or real.' By 'cumulative tradition' he means observable historical data of institutions, scriptures etc. The cumulative tradition changes but the faith of a person does not change. A person's faith is what his/her tradition means to him and what the universe means to him in the light of that tradition. The objective data of a cumulative tradition are available to a historian to observe and analyse, but no rigorous method can comprehend the human spirit, which is open to the transcendent. One needs to penetrate through to find 'faith' which gives

[1] Quoted, Ibid., 44.

[2] W.C. Smith, *The Meaning and End of Religion*, 48f.

[3] Ibid., 50.

expression to tradition, and is expressed by tradition in the forms of art, doctrine, theology etc., which is continuous yet modified. However, there is no communal faith such as Christian and Buddhist but only that of a person.

Without acknowledging openly that 'faith' is a Christian term emphasised by the Protestant tradition, and 'God' as a term is applicable only to the theistic traditions, Smith is comfortable expressing it in a way familiar to the Christian tradition and even with a Christian devotional fervour. For example, at the end of explaining what he means by faith, he declares:

> There is no ideal faith that I ought to have. There is God whom I ought to see, and a neighbour whom I ought to love. These must suffice me; and my faith is my ability to see that they abundantly more than suffice ... The traditions evolve. Men's faith varies. God endures.[1]

In the concluding words of the book Smith acknowledges that it is written within the discourse of the Christian Church, the university and humankind. The study is offered to fellow Christians 'in the hopes that it might contribute to our doing justice intellectually both to what we now know of the world in which we live and to what we know of God as Christ has revealed Him to us.'

Approach to the study of another person's faith should be humane. Subjectivity is inadequate as we are ignorant of much of what goes into our actions, feelings, thinking and moral choices. We can distort what we know, deceive or elude ourselves as well as others. Objectivity too is inadequate and it can be untrue, less than rational and alienating of persons. Knowing is becoming and with such openness what is possible is a dialogical approach at a personal level with mutual respect, trust and penetrating discernment. Nevertheless, as many have pointed out, Smith could not guarantee that the faith dimension in every human produces the same kind of 'meaning' comparable to the personal and communal experience of all believers.

Smith's identification of the transcendental core of human being as faith is not far from reductionism. His recommendation to participate in the religious life of the other, or almost relive it, is impossible in the face of the immense variety of the forms of religious life. Western scholars have shown more interest in studying the performance of extravagant Vedic rituals, the devotional postures in worship places, and practices of meditation. But the majority of Hindu India, for instance, hold diverse popular cults and some include practices like blood sacrifice, hook-swinging and rolling on a scorching rock in order to fulfil a vow. Recently scholarly attention has turned to the popular cults, but what is not clear is the required qualification to participate in such expressions if they can be called that of 'faith'.

---

[1] Ibid., 192.

Interdisciplinary Approach: Reductionism can happen when scholars take one aspect or one tradition within a family of religions such as that of what is known as Hinduism. For many western scholars, Indian religious tradition means Hinduism, Hinduism means Vedanta, Vedanta means advaita Vedanta and advaita Vedanta means Śankara's advaita Vedanta! In his unique treatment of theology, religion and the study of religion together, Eric Lott refers to 'the ritual/ mythic imagery in which religious traditions are grounded, and in which our doctrinal and ethical articulation is deeply embedded, as such a "primal matrix of meaning".' While reaffirming the multi-dimensional character of religious life, Lott asks, 'Without some more integrating centre, some more inclusively creative focal point, however, can we think of the phenomena found in myth/ritual/ symbolism as in themselves providing this primal role?'[1] However, in his answer to highlight the 'visionary centre of religious life' he demonstrates how strikingly different are the perceptions of the one Transcendent (with many names), highest self, ultimate Brahman or the Great One of Vedanta with special reference to the three cardinal exponents, namely Sankara, Ramanuja and Madhva. However, Lott's discussion does not cover the other equally important devotional traditions within Hinduism with reference to regional and local deities, community and family deities, and communal and personal deities. Such an undertaking would have yielded far more relevant and contemporary insights into Hindu practice.

Similarly, different types are true of the trans-theistic traditions also, as Lott points out with illustrations. For example, tradition holds that when Gautama Buddha was asked to explain the nature of *Nirvana*, the final state of enlightenment, he remained silent, and the derived assumption was that it could not be explained by finite human language. But if it remained as an ineffable experience as some mystics claimed, for others it may appear meaningless. Therefore, it is not surprising that within the tradition there were attempts to put in words with inevitable figurative language. Lott quotes the following:

> Whoever wishes to be free from age and death … set free from passion, hatred, dullness, from pride and from false views, he crosses the ocean of rebirth, dams the torrent of his cravings, is washed to be clean of the three-fold stain, and destroys all evil within him. So, he enters the glorious city of Nirvana, stainless and undefiled, pure and white, unaging, deathless, serene and calm and happy, and his mind is emancipated as a perfected being.[2]

Similarly, in the Jaina and Yoga traditions the ultimate goal of religious life is 'the isolation of the soul in its essential purity, tranquillity, consciousness, bliss, infinitude and freedom. Indeed the purification of this transcendent inner life,

[1] E.J. Lott, *Vision, Tradition*, 39.

[2] Ibid., 44.

its release from all karmic and finite fetters, and thus its emergence into a state of omniscient, blissful tranquillity, is what is aimed for in a discipline either of rigorous ethical and ascetic practice, or of yogic meditation and posturing.'[1] What will be observable is the ethical and ascetic life, and particularly the ethical life guided by the moral principles of non-stealing and non-lying and so on relate to others who share in the meaning of the religious adept. Those who are on the journey towards the ultimate goal will experience different measures of meaning within and demonstrate different levels of meaning without. The ultimate experience of oneness with the supreme Brahman in the advaita Vedanta is similar to the above. But in devotional traditions with the names of Siva, Vishnu and so on the goal will be perfect intimacy with God involving the whole being, a foretaste of which is available in this life. The level of intimacy differs from devotee to devotee depending on the maturity of his/her life, and also the experience as individual is different from the experience as group or community. Lott illustrates such differences within Islam and Sikhism as well.

Further, Lott identifies 'certain common features in the ways in which religious traditions, especially literate traditions, articulate the meaning-patterns' while not failing to note the various types in this theological process. For him, 'Probably the most basic and invariable characteristic of faith-articulation is its *grounding in and commitment to a particular sacred tradition*, with its rituals, symbols, myths, scriptures, spiritual discipline, community life, and of course its doctrines … In this interlinked religious life there is, no doubt, the sense of a primal matrix of meaning, and it will be recognised that it is from this primal source that any theological articulation is to derive its directions.'[2] Further features include some degree of 'distancing' from the immediacy of vision-experience, 'the dialectic between continuity and discontinuity in the theologian's relationship to the community', loss of grounding and commitment due to external influence, religious language that is drawn from a variety of secular and empirical contexts, and communication of meaning at diverse levels. It is the last one, namely, the communication of meaning concerns us most here.

Lott recognises that 'there are numerous levels at which there is communication of meaning within the community.' He explores these diverse levels by looking at some of the different dimensions of religious life with reference to different religious traditions. Thus, myths are interpreted, mytho-poetic forms have been transposed to more doctrinally systematic conceptualised forms, certain artistic forms are made with theological potency, scriptures are exegeted and interpreted, dialectic approaches adopted, and moral guidelines provided.[3] He also demonstrates how 'contrary trends' find both in religious traditions. For example, sexual symbols and imageries from the *tantrika* cult are taken into

[1] Ibid., 46.

[2] Ibid., 63.

[3] Ibid., 74ff.

the Siva and Vishnu cults, and female potency (Sakti) is personified as consorts of the male deities with different names and forms. Even Buddhism is not free from such amalgamation. *Vajrayana* (Thunderbolt Vehicle) represents the third type of Buddhism, a result of amalgamation of the Buddha's noble path and its opposite, particularly in the case of sexual practices.[1] The history of such a process of amalgamation might reveal complex yet fascinating developments within particular cultural and religious contexts. Even where compulsory adjustments are quickly made an attempt to find meaning of the hybrid form even though it might appear arbitrary.

While Lott points out cases of different interpretations of the same phenomenon or idea within a particular community, he does not deal with the contradictions and refutations evident in the pursuit of making meaning and communicating with others. For instance, the Saiva vision and experience is never taken to complement the Vaishnava vision and experience. Each has clues to ridicule or degrade the other. The conflict between these traditions and the Buddha and Jaina movements resulted in not only antagonism but also persecution. Each of the cardinal Vedantins refuted the claims of the others and interpreted the scripture according to their overall position. Such elements are not absent between different denominations of the Christian Church as amply evident in history and to some extent even today. That means that what is meaningful to one is meaningless for the other within.

I want to emphasise the conflict and contradiction entailed in the process of interpretation with a view to communicate publicly some meaning which is understandable. In some cases it is to do with the contextual appeal of an ancient vision and experience. For example, in the advaita Vedanta the ultimate goal is to join with the supreme Brahman with all the duality and multiplicity having been overcome. Swami Vivekananda (1863-1902), the most famous neo-Vedantin who was exposed to western education and life and Christian teaching emphasised the horizontal dimension of the experience of oneness. That means we have to see Brahman in every human being, and of all the forms of this supreme person, he found the clearest one in the form of the poor. With a view to redeeming millions of the masses in India from grinding poverty and disabling illiteracy he founded the Ramakrishna Mission. Today even those who are not bothered about the ultimate experience of oneness appreciate what he derived from that vision which has great appeal and relevance to the common people. Similarly, there are those who come in the line of the Vedic ritual school (*Purvamimamsa*) who interpret the ritual corpus as meaningful and the performance of it as inherently powerful to sustain the life and balance of the universe. Today there are occasions where certain Vedic ritual sacrifices are performed involving hundreds of priests and expensive oblations in the name of world peace and prosperity. But there are

[1] Ibid., 58.

Hindus who ridicule this performance and belief in its power and who advocate actual working for world peace and prosperity.

It is common knowledge today that the same scripture inspires both saints and suicide bombers. In the case of the scriptures of the Semitic traditions including the Bible this fact (e.g. 'terror in the mind of God') has been demonstrated considerably. The famous text Bhagavad Gita, celebrated as the Hindu Bible even outsiders in ambiguous ways. [1] Though the Gita belongs to the Vaishnava tradition, M.K. Gandhi projected it as the most basic Hindu scripture. It inspired him to stand for non-violence while his assassin M. Godse too was inspired by the same Gita. An objective study of the central message of the Gita with the support of the interpretation of Hindutva leaders such as B.G. Tilak may justify Godse's stand. There is even a proposal to build a temple for him among sections of the Hindu community today.

Similar glaring examples can be cited from Christian circles also. There are fundamentalists who give literal interpretation of certain texts of their favourite selection. Thus, there are right wing fascists trying to apply the invasion theory of the Hebrew scripture to their approach to people of other faiths; there are those who test with snakes and other poisonous reptiles as fulfilling a scriptural text and get bitten and even killed. In the Qur'an the word *jihad* is understood by some as fighting against the disbelievers or non-Muslims, but interpreted today as 'striving in the way of God' meaning to fight corruption and injustice wherever they are found. What is clear from these examples is that criteria of meaning and articulation of meaning and appeal to public life may be different from certain interpretations within the tradition. Sometimes violence is justified when with great examination certain individuals decide to finish off a powerful serial mass murderer with a right view to save the life of millions. Those who dare to do may be fully or partially inspired by their faith or scripture.

Without realising this fact there is another reductionism in the study of religion, that either overemphasises the ethical dimension or defines ethics in terms of moving from self-centredness to other-orientedness as John Hick put it. Then religious acts of extravagant ritual performance, mechanical routine, belief in *karma, samsara* or, belief in a multiplicity of gods and idol worship which have been criticised by voices within remain untouched in the name of abstaining from value judgements. Sometimes, the golden rule (do to others what you want them to do to you) is claimed to be the core of religions. But how it is interpreted and applied is different. For instance, one can take it as 'I want to give others coffee with sugar because I want them to do the same for me'! But others can see the meaning as 'I always ask others in what form they want the coffee as I will expect them to ask me.' All these suggest that we cannot take the meaning at its face value but it requires exploration, i.e., corporate exploration and common appeal.

---

[1] E.g. The text of the Gita also inspired Robert Oppenheimer, the chief scientist who constructed the Atomic bomb that destroyed two cities in Japan during the WW2.

Experience is another aspect pointed out by scholars in religious studies. Rudolf Otto's celebrated book *The Idea of the Holy* best represents this act. In passing it is worth mentioning that the 'approaches to the study of religion' in India are overloaded with the repeated emphasis on experience as the core of religious life but without any analysis.[1] Otto suggests the nature of the numinous with reference to the way in which it is reflected in the mind in terms of feeling. 'Its nature is such that it grips or stirs the human mind with this and that determinate affective state.' Over and above the elements of faith, trust and love, through sympathy and imaginative intuition, he found the lives of people around him in the early decades of the twentieth century, 'in sudden, strong ebullitions of personal piety and the frames of mind such ebullitions evince, in the fixed and ordered solemnities of rites and liturgies, and again in the atmosphere that clings to old religious monuments and buildings, to temples and churches.'[2] The most appropriate expression he found for this phenomenon was *mysterium tremendum et fascinans*.

The feeling of it may at times come sweeping like a gentle tide, pervading the mind with a tranquil mood of deepest worship. It may pass over into a more set and lasting attitude of the soul, continuing, as it were, thrillingly vibrant and resonant, until at last it dies away and the soul resumes its 'profane', non-religious mood of everyday experience. It may burst in sudden eruption up from the depths of the soul with spasms and convulsions, or lead to the strangest excitements, to intoxicated frenzy, to transport, and an almost grisly horror and shuddering. It has its crude, barbaric antecedents and early manifestations, and again it may be developed into something beautiful and pure and glorious. It may become the hushed, trembling, and speechless humility of the creature in the presence of - whom or what. In the presence of that which is a *Mystery* inexpressible and above all creatures.[3]

Without further asking questions about the background of those who are caught up by the tremendous fascination of the mystery, one might be led to conclude that such experience occurs abruptly in a *tabula rasa*. Otto refers to the narratives of the Hebrew Bible more, but he fails to recognise the fundamental story of that bible, God's choice of a community of slaves to liberate them and to make them instruments of God's purpose in the world. The meaning and inspiration that story conveyed caught the imagination, not only of Jesus and the early Christian community, but also of several communities around the world and the waves of its effect have not stopped.

For understanding the most authentic expressions of such experience with extraordinary poetic embellishments one should read the basic devotional texts of the Tamil Saiva and Vaishnava traditions of South India. Again their meaning-

[1] See Harbans Singh (ed.), *Approaches to the Study of Religion*.

[2] R. Otto, *The Idea of the Holy*, Oxford: Oxford University Press, 1928, 12.

[3] Ibid., 12f.

making experience with creative imagination and interpretation of mythic symbols are different.[1] For instance, the ugly appearance of Siva wearing a necklace of human skulls wandering in a cremation ground is interpreted by the poets as marking his transcendence, beyond the fashions and fancies of this world. The divine couple in the Vaishnava tradition provides, on the other hand, a model for human couples. Though there is a commonality sharing the experience of Otto's description, and personal transformation through devotional fervour is evident, that does not mean that its value and effect in the particular tradition's community is the same.

Such a mysterious experience which Otto mentions as the core of religious life is comparable to the mystics of different religious traditions. There was a time when it was guarded against any claim of intellectual grasp and analytical studies. But recent studies of mysticism show how before the experience and after the experience their particular religious traditions are inevitable to provide the preparatory ground and language to express the experience respectively. And those traditions have different myths, symbols and concepts.

The claim of ineffability is hardly helpful to understand the meaning of religious and mystical experience. It has adversely affected the practice of interfaith dialogue. Those who have praised 'dialogue in the cave of heart' (Swami Abishiktananda) and 'dialogue in silence' (Panikkar) or those who have claimed that 'all mystics speak the same language' (Radhakrishnan) can stimulate thinking. But if the actual experience and meaning is ineffable we are not wrong in dismissing them from any discourse on meaning. Of course they mean the depth or the ultimate stage of dialogue and they would not undermine the pursuit of knowledge and method to meet the challenges humanity is facing.

Another limitation of the scientific study of religion is that it does not distinguish between those nominal and committed in the religious communities they study. They might consult the scriptures, observe behaviour and talk to experts. But they may fall into the trap of taking the nominal ones along with the committed ones. Further, at the next level there may be people for whom adhering to a religion and attending worship is habitual with the side effects of meeting in a safe place and meeting familiar people. Uncritical conservatives are not far away from this category. Such people cannot help in our understanding of meaning of religious life.

Before we leave this section mention needs to be made about the limitation of western studies of eastern religious traditions. Subjective study of religion (Smith and Lott) and the objective study of religion (Muller and Gonda). This is a debate that has consumed much time and generated a lot of heat in the last few decades of scholarship. It might be better you make some comment on the relationship between the two. But we cannot generalise. For example, Wilfred Cantwell Smith

---

[1] See Israel S., "The Role and Meaning of Saiva Symbols in Manikkavacakar's Tiruvācakam" in *Bangalore Theological Forum*, XV/1, Jan-April 1983, 21-38.

and Eric Lott started their career as missionaries in South Asia and from their study and encounter with people of the regional traditions in actual dialogue they developed scholarship. No one has pointed out their distortion of facts about other religions. On the other hand, Max Müller, in spite of his being the chief-editor of the 50 volumes *Sacred Books of the East* and had the honour of Max Müller Bhavans established in India, never visited the country. Jan Gonda (1905-1991), the greatest Dutch Indologist, despite the Indian government's invitation for a public act of acknowledgement and honour, refused to go to India and discouraged his students as well because he was fixed in his mind that if one went to India one would have been bitten by snakes and tigers! This raises the question about the real qualification of someone who is engaged in finding the meaning of religious life, though no one can out rightly undermine scholarship.

Study of Implicit Religion: Implicit religion is not freer than explicit religion and meaning in definition, parameters and boundaries. It touches on the borders of and even overlaps with philosophy, sociology and psychology of religion, theology and empirical studies. Its scope is unlimited and the freedom it gives is generous. However, one might still wonder how different aspects of human religiosity studied under the auspice of implicit religion cohere around the triple dominions that define it – commitment, integrating foci and intensive concerns with extensive effects. Nevertheless this fact does not weaken its credibility in a fast changing world of complex realities. If the meaning of meaning is elusive, no wonder proper definition of implicit religion too is elusive but not without compelling fascination.

It is important to recognise that a major publication of the network of the study of implicit religion is titled *The Secular Quest for Meaning in Life*. Meaning is not defined but issues related to it. We have already referred to Meerten ter Borg's article on 'charisma' which contributed to setting the background for an exploration of meaning(s) today. He has proved the usefulness of both his concept of charisma in modern times and of the concept of implicit religion. As his 'conclusion' notes, 'Modern man is as much concerned about the ultimate condition of his existence, as traditional man was. Living a meaningful life in a coherent world is for him as important as ever. The social mechanisms to keep his world coherent have not changed in essence. What has changed are the modes in which these mechanisms operate, not the mechanisms themselves.'[1] However, such mechanisms have cultural implications around the world.

There are many aspects that have been studied are helpful for grasping meaning in religious life. Kevin Sharpe's study of the pursuit of happiness, for example, clarifies an important aspect of meaning. He and Rebecca Bryant first reflected on happiness from an interfaith and scientific perspective. They demonstrate how philosophers and theologians emphasised the achievement of happiness as the goal of religious and intellectual life. They also show how several

[1] Borg, op. cit., p. 114.

spiritual traditions emphasise the promise of happiness in after life. Then they move on stating the scientific conceptions of happiness with reference to results of empirical studies and of scientific analysis of the genetic predisposition and chemistry of the human brain. They identify a clash looming between religious and scientific accounts of the nature of happiness, a clash within the implicit religion of the pursuit of happiness.

> Scientists define happiness as physical well-being, while theologians define it as spiritual or intellectual satisfaction. Religious thinkers seek to understand happiness in the future as well as the present, while scientists concentrate firmly on the here and now. Even more important, these two disciplines differ in their methodology: science is an empirical venture which constructs and tests hypotheses, while, traditionally, the only empirical aspect of theology has been its consistency with scriptures, tradition, and religious experience. With regard to the study of the physical universe, the traditional approach to theology construes it as non-personal.[1]

Of course Sharpe and Bryant point out how both the camps ignore each other in their claims, limitations and questions. They also point out other critics who hold that geneticists 'try to reduce the holistic human experience of happiness to nothing but the actions of genes, electrical activity, and chemicals' but ignoring 'the real subjective realm.' Three other voices they quote: 'Joy comes with activities that we share with people who have learned to trust, and that enable us to share meaning across the existential barrier that separates each of us from all others. So happiness is not made by a chemical.' 'True happiness is the ability to receive pleasure without grasping and displeasure without condemning, confident in the knowledge that pain and disappointment can be tolerated.' 'It's worse to wake up in the morning without having a larger purpose in life than to wake up unhappy. Just feeling good is a poor measure of the quality of a person's life.'[2] Their suggestion to resolve the issue include the following points:

- Any complete explanation of the nature of happiness is likely to involve spiritual as well as physical aspects because all human traits involve environment, circumstances, and individual wilfulness, as well as genes.
- Theology is therefore initially justified in claiming that happiness must involve more than an account of the action of genes, electrical activity, and chemicals. However, it must couch such claims in a form that science may evaluate.

[1] K. Sharpe & R. Bryant, "Implicit Religion and Inter-faith Dialogue: A Scientific Perspective", *Implicit Religion*, 2/1, May 1999, 9f.

[2] Ibid., 11.

- Both scientists and theologians should adopt an open, interdisciplinary approach to concepts of mutual interest, such as happiness, and be prepared to accept that spiritual and physical explanations are not mutually exclusive.[1]

They conclude with an emphasis on the importance of a joint approach of religious people and scientists to explore the issue of happiness by asking the right questions for a more comprehensive and holistic understanding and mutual recognition of limitations and willingness to enrich the understanding by the witness of the other.

Kevin Sharpe more recently elaborated the pursuit of happiness with reference to evolutionary origins and psychological research, pointing out implications for implicit religion. Given the limited space, I find no better way than stating the summary of the essay given by himself at the beginning.

> Scientific studies of happiness (as subjective well-being) provide a lot of information about it: thus, a person's level of happiness usually stays within a certain genetically determined range despite life's ups and downs, happiness relates to activity in specific parts of the brain and to the presence or absence of serotonin and dopamine, and we have evolved to pursue happiness. Raising happiness within the set range can involve high self-esteem, a sense of control over life, and an outgoing, optimistic personality. In addition, the person's view of the world influences his or her level of happiness. Flow, personal relationships, and having values and goals can also contribute.
>
> Pursuing happiness and seeking to remove unhappiness appear to be primary human motivations, biologically based. The study of implicit religion, therefore, ought at least to look at happiness and ask about the relationship between it and implicit religion.[2]

It should be noted that the above studies have taken the happiness of only an individual or what the individual may experience in the company of a group. But there is a social dimension of happiness when, for example, communities celebrate a festival, frenzy fans shout in a playground and communion of saints enjoy a fellowship.

Acknowledgement of one more contribution will enrich the discussion on meaning in relation to implicit religion. William Swatos in an essay entitled 'Meaning and Contradiction' explores the contradictions that are inherent in the joint problematics of 'the meaning of meaning'. He argues for taking the

---

[1] Ibid., 12.

[2] K. Sharpe, "The Pursuit of Happiness: Evolutionary Origins, Psychological Research, and Implications for Implicit Religion", *Implicit Religion*, 8/2, July 2005, 118.

participant actor as the primary locus for meaning giving yet allowing an outside observer to analyse the situation from another perspective. Taking insights from Max Weber's sociology of religion with particular reference to meaning, Swatos argues that meaning giving should not be limited to the intellectual pursuit of scholars of religions who may not be sensitive to issues like warrior ethics in a religious tradition. He observes: '"Meaning" is the core myth of the academic study of religion in the presumption of both meaning construction and the need for meaning construction as universals within people's biographies. This should not, furthermore, be taken as an assertion that these people's lives "have no meaning", but that the category of "meaning" is a meaningless category to them for articulating the meaning of their lives, which lives, ironically, may indeed appear to the observer as "meaningless" ... It is a mistake for the study of implicit religion to assume that everyone's life must "have meaning", hence have a religion or a religiousness. This remains something to be tested. An important question to be clarified here is whether "meaning" and "pleasure" may be understood as equivalents – or the cases in which they may or may not.'[1]

What we call 'meaning', Swatos argues, is for some ordinary people who 'achieve a modicum of life satisfaction' while for others it is 'pleasure.' He illustrates with an advertisement which appeared to be religious, but it was for a music store, and he advocates for taking music seriously by the study of religion. For him specificity and context do matter. Taking the view of implicit religion as involving 'transcendence of the middle range' he says that certain experiences of 'getting outside our self' in everyday life might be called religious or spiritual experiences, but they do not constitute a religion. 'Perhaps we need a skilful addition of the lucid and religion to such components of Weber's discussion of the social psychology of world religions as the aesthetic and the erotic, rather than an attempt to view sports or games as religions.'[2] In any case, he suggests, to watch the process of religiosity or middle range transcendence getting constituted, involving things like dogmaticisation, ritualisation, hierarchicalisation and mystification. On the whole his main concern is that 'we need to be attentive to a variety of important definitional, methodological, and ethical considerations'. Of course this concern is not new because in the study of 'explicit religion' these and other related considerations have been amply evident. However, it is good to be reminded again that religious life is immeasurably complex and defining meaning of religious life cannot be less complex.

Interfaith Diaogue: Prospects and Problems

We have already noted voices for interfaith attempts to explore the meaning and meanings of religious life. Here we will consult three examples for representing the major concerns and approaches.

---

[1] W.H. Swatos, "Meaning and Contradiction", *Implicit Religion*, 4/2, Nov. 2001, 100.

[2] Ibid., 103.

From Critical Dialogue to Centering on Liberation: The question of truth and meaning is often raised in interfaith dialogue. We will have a chapter on Truth and truths in which we will consult the positions. Here we will briefly mention direct references to the 'meaning of meaning.' Concluding an explosive critical survey of 'Christian Attitudes Toward the World Religions', Paul Knitter, a Catholic lay theologian of the USA earlier suggested three guidelines to evaluate the value and meaning of a religion: 1) *Personally,* does the revelation of the religion or religious figure—the story, the myth, the message—move the human heart? Does it stir one's feelings, the depths of one's unconscious? 2) *Intellectually,* does the revelation also satisfy and expand the mind? Is it intellectually coherent? Does it broaden one's horizons of understanding? 3) *Practically,* does the message promote the psychological health of individuals, their sense of value, purpose, freedom? Especially, does it promote the welfare, the liberation, of all peoples, integrating individual persons and nations into a larger community?[1]

But later Knitter shifted his focus on interfaith dialogue with a view to developing interfaith cooperation for liberating people from all forms of oppression and suffering.

Knitter's above emphasis acquired a centre stage position in the arena of interfaith relations and dialogue with the efforts of his one-time mentor Hans Küng, a famous German Catholic theologian, who studied Chinese religion and a promoter of interfaith dialogue. Those who are familiar with Küng's earlier works *Christianity and the World Religions* (1986), *Christianity and Chinese Religions* (1988) – both with shared authorship – *Global Responsibility – A Search for World Ethic* (1993), and *A Global Ethics for Global Politics and Economics* (1997) will see his book *Tracing the Way*[2] *as* representing a more distilled presentation with sharpened focus. His 'creed' which has gained worldwide popularity occurs at least three times in this book, once in a slightly changed version:

No peace among the nations without peace among the religions.
No peace among the religions without dialogue between the religions.
No dialogue between the religions without global ethical criteria.
No survival of our globe without a global ethic. (xv, 266, 232)

Though the book on the whole provides a good introduction to most of the world religions, obviously the focus is on each one's contribution to a world ethic. In the field of science or history of religions, ethics is regarded as one of the many dimensions of religious life, the other dimensions being such as ritual, mythical, social and mystical. It is interesting to note that the sub-title of this book has the words 'spiritual dimensions' and it may be confusing unless the world 'spiritual' is taken in a holistic sense. For our purpose, we will focus on the possibility of developing an interreligious global ethic for a corporate meaning of life.

---

[1] P.F. Knitter, *No Other Name?* London: SCM Press, 1985, 231.

[2] Küng, *Tracing the Way: Spiritual Dimensions of the World Religions,* New York: Continuum, 2002.

Küng points out the commonality and difference between world religions with the help of scholarly studies of religions. All that contribute to human dignity, just relationships, environmental health and world peace, he claims, are available in one degree or other in each religion. But how to activate and mobilize them is a question which has been asked in discussions on inter-faith dialogue for a long time. Küng has given a new focus using the term 'global ethic'. However, it is beyond the scope of this book to provide a concrete solution in terms of political-economic-social structures that guarantee achieving it for universal meaning which will be agreeable for all religious traditions. Moreover, it is important to identify activating forces within each religious tradition moving towards a world ethic as well as obstructing forces that operate using religion for selfish interests. Knitter of late has written extensively about the 'suffering other' as the focus of dialogue, and liberating them is not only giving a new meaning to their life but also gaining a new meaning for ourselves. What is desirable is not dictating an ethic from outside but being together as practitioners of dialogue alongside the victims of many-sided oppression. Actual experiments need to be known and one can expect interesting counter-perceptions of meaning from the opposite sides irrespective of religious adherents.

When such abstract solutions flood into the academic market from the famous scholars, those who work with commitment to save the present world, with and without any reference to a particular religion, calls the world community including politicians for using their common sense. It is estimated that as tiny as one-eighth of the defence budget of all the countries would be enough to eradicate poverty and illiteracy. Because of the mistrust or ongoing construction of enemy-images, countries, particularly the super powers, go on increasing their budgets for piling up more and more sophisticated weapons with systems of intelligence. Even when such intelligence misleads governments to wage illegal and immoral wars, thus increasing destruction and tension, there is no repentance or restoration. An awesomeness and wonder is created about safety and security with incredible structures of personnel and weapons. If a world with equal opportunities to realise the full potential of every human person can create a condition for better realisation of meaning in life in whatever way one defines it, it shows the utter foolishness of a so called progressing humanity. How unfortunate that this is pointed out more by theologians, artists and poets than by those who go on studying the meaning of meaning!

Meaning, a Continuing Quest in the Modern World: An Example

We will bring to a close our discussion on religion and meaning by acknowledging a revealing study.[1] It is admitted that 'the study of meaning has always been

---

[1] *The Human Quest for Meaning: Theories, Research and Applications*, ed. Paul T. P. Wong, New York: Routledge, 2012. Twenty eight chapters (divided into three parts: Theories, Research and Applications) by forty-four researchers/authors, most of whom based at universities in USA,

plagued by the subjective and objective controversy' and the need for both. The editor notes that according to his own implicit theory, research which has been replicated in Asian cultures– 'there are eight (though seven actually noted!) sources of meaning: happiness, achievement, intimacy, relationship, self-transcendence, self-acceptance and fairness.' He identifies six different stages – inertia, exploratory, discovery, completion, emergency, stagnation – in the process of the search for meaning. Then the question is turned to levels of meaning including ultimate meaning. Steger's definition of meaning seems to be comprehensive, to which some other authors turn:

> Meaning is the web of connections, understandings, and interpretations that help us comprehend our experience and formulate plans directing our energies to the achievement of our desired future. Meaning provides us with the sense that our lives matter, that they make sense, and that they are more than the sum of our seconds, days, and years. Comprehending our experience in this way builds the cognitive component of meaning in life. The cognitive component of meaning in life thus refers to the misunderstandings that we develop of who we are, what the world is like, and how we fit in with and relate to the grand scheme of things.[1]

The following discussion seems to be an elaboration of this definition. What makes life worth living? Wong's answers include money, fame, a stress and anxiety-free life. Based on numerous studies, he has found that 'the worthy life consisted of the following components: happiness, achievement, relationship, intimacy, religion, altruism, self-acceptance, and fair treatment.'[2] From the conclusions of other scholars he quotes, we read statements such as, 'purpose, efficacy, value and self-worth', 'discovering the meaning of suffering', 'fulfilling God's calling', 'excellent conditions of having what one wants in life', 'commitment to a higher purpose', 'being shaped by cultural norms', 'states of satisfaction, success, personal growth, and meaning fulfilment.' All others are more or less combinations and permutations of these. The place of emotion in having a sense of meaning is treated by connecting with the structure of the brain.

We limit to note the points that deal with religious life. Foremost, the Buddhist mindfulness is shown as the way.

> Loving kindness, empathic compassion, and shared joy practiced in meditative equanimity form the alpha and omega of Buddhist action ... The Nirvana emptiness and the extinction of unwholesome craving

with an inviting Foreword by Shane J. Lopez, try to answer the important question, 'What is the meaning of life?' The immediate second question raised is, 'what is the meaning of meaning?'

[1] xxxv.

[2] Ibid., 4.

> are not sufficient in themselves. Meaning is derived from the daily practice of the social meditations. Thus, awakening – the experience that Duhkha has ceased – is just the beginning to be better able to help others.[1]

From that of the Greek philosophers Aristotle and Plato to the modern youth of different backgrounds a variety of perceptions and experiences of meaning is covered in this important study. Apart from social locations, psychic conditions etc. an alternative view to craving for enjoyment of fleeting things is observed as growing in the average American life. Alternatives are pointed out. For example, meaning in many persons' lives, seems to lie not in self-satisfaction but in fulfilling the obligations of a vocation in which success or failure is unpredictable and emotion is directed in a prophetic way. This is mentioned in passing with reference to Gandhi and a few others, and one may argue that their way may provide an antidote to the growing global problem of meaninglessness if properly applied. The place of religion is confined to providing a mindset of hope. But religion in its variety has more dimensions than only the experiential. What is most important to observe in such studies is that the quest for meaning of meaning continues just as for the meaning of religion does.

Concluding Remarks

This chapter deals mainly with the nature of its topic. It started with a recognition of the vagueness and ambiguity of the term meaning, and set the modern background to the discourse on or pursuit of meaning in life, especially the meaning(s) of religious life. It has pointed out the challenges of religious missions. It has identified the primary issues related to theories of meaning in the study of religion including in the implicit religion as well as in different perspectives of interfaith dialogue. To update the discussion, the summary of a recent study has been given. Perhaps what this chapter has achieved is not so much clarity as pointing out the enormity of its dimensions and complexity. What comes from this achievement are not blue prints for solutions but insights that might motivate serious and sustained dialogue at different levels, interfaith, intra-faith, faith and science and so on.

It may be suggested that meaning of life is what one gives to it, and there may be number of conditions that help what one gives. Meaning is not handed to one on a plate unless one is in a desperate mental and physical condition that requires the help of others. Even if the meaning of life depends on happiness individually and collectively, when those moments of happiness and fresh experience of possessions flee, meaning is also lost. At the same time happiness can be something that is not confined to one's state of mind but something is sustained in interactive and interdependent relationships.

---

[1] Ibid., 268f.

In the name of objectivity and abstaining from value judgement, those involved in the study of religion stop with interpretation of texts and symbols. Theories and categorisations with reference to orthodoxy and tradition must be tested against what people experience in today's life. Also, if there is enough confidence and courage, people of faith need to come forward with honesty to share their faith and perception of meaning with people of others faiths, scientists of all types including those who study religion in its explicit and implicit manifestation.

The meaning of religious life can also drift to momentary excitements induced by manipulative techniques. But at the same time, beliefs, assumptions, feelings, values and cultural practices that constitute meaning with a cohering whole shared collectively seem to promise more permanent sense of meaning. If there is cooperation in the study and pursuit of meaning with openness and mutual trust, it may be expected that the slippery fish will become less slippery. In the process of the catch we may be excited, seeing it as part of a cluster or company. How to handle them with care, enjoy without endangering and sharing with others with fairness is a matter of corporate exploration. It might be fascinating without falsifying, compelling without controlling and leading without a map, for those who care to turn and listen and see.

Chapter 7

The Process of Secularization

Defining Secularism: Yet Another Struggle

Having unpacked some of the issues in defining the word 'meaning' and extended meanings in the previous chapter, this chapter aims to recognize the challenge of secularism for religion and the process of its impact. Liberation, individual rights, democracy etc. were noted as the cardinal principles. Since the 15th century Renaissance it has been a much debated concept and became complex when it was experimented in different countries with different 'creeds'. Secularized religion and secular spirituality have been the main interest of the study of implicit religion. In the case of Indian secularism which travelled from Europe through the British Empire, there are peculiar characteristics. We point out the tension between the secular polity and religious commitment which raises many practical questions and exposes the fact of multi-religious India with many religious superstitions and of struggles to realize the positive fruits of secularism. This begs the question about the meaning of secularism and its relationship with religious commitments and communications. Just as defining religion conclusively is not possible, so also defining secularism is not possible. Unbelief or irreligion is not the durable option. The basic reason is that human life and history have dimensions beyond easy grasp.

The English word 'secular' comes from the Latin word *saeculum* meaning an age, world and time from which is derived the meaning 'this age', 'this generation' and 'this world'. In other words it may imply 'this worldly' and 'here and now'. The negative connotations are: no sacred, no transcendental, no control from above, and no religious authority. 'The word "secularization" was first used in 1648, at the end of the Thirty Years' War in Europe, to refer to the transfer of church properties to the exclusive control of the princes. What was a matter-of-fact statement then became later, after the French Revolution, a value statement as well:

on November 2, 1789, Talleyrand announced to the French National Assembly that all ecclesiastical goods were at the disposal of the nation, as indeed they should have been.'[1] It was George J. Holyoake (1817-1906), a thinker in England whose religious upbringing was transcended when he came to be an outstanding secular politician and led a rationalist movement of protest, who coined the term 'secularism' which took the shape of an ideology of progress. For him and others secularism is non-religion, non-God and non-eschatology. Hence, the popular pairs of opposites such as sacred-profane, sacred-secular, metaphysical-empirical, ecclesiastical-individual and eschatological-historical. In terms of power and its location the gradual process of secularization is catastrophic for the religious as it was essentially 'freedom of society and culture from the domination of religious institutions and symbols.' Don Cupitt, a British philosopher of religion observes:

> The secular something means to transfer from the sacred to the secular realm ... However, that implies that the sacred is being methodically stripped and in the end completely swallowed by a confident, well-organized and self-conscious secular power ... The shift, then, is from myths to maths, from animism to mechanism, and from explanation down from above to explanation up from below.[2]

It is not too difficult to argue that in history that the transfer from sacred to the secular is not complete; the sacred is not stripped or swallowed by the secular power. And what we see at least in India is the coexistence of myths and maths, animism and mechanism and upward looking and downward looking. Religions have reacted to the secularization process in novel and creative ways. The response has included adaptation, resistance, complimenting, refusing to be ideologies, more critical self-examination and developing the confidence to dialogue with secularists on the most fundamental issues of human life beyond institutional ties. We have already seen the upsurge of new dynamic religious movements and noted the revival of religion in the Eastern Bloc. And it is not without reason that there are those who call secularization a myth.

René Descartes (1596-1650), known as the father of western philosophy, famously declared, 'I think, therefore I exist' and this affirmation gave him a sense of the self and the meaning of the world. It is to be questioned if this will apply to every individual experience. When we discussed the implicit religion of the Princess Diana syndrome we came across the assertion, 'I feel, therefore I exist' and it is not impossible to construct an integrated spirituality combining thinking, feeling and action as has already been done.

---

[1] T.N. Madan, "Secularism in its Place" in *Religion in India*, ed. T.N. Madan, New Delhi: Oxford University Press, 1991, 394.

[2] Quoted, *The Oxford Dictionary of World Religions*, ed. J. Bowker, BCA-Oxford University Press, 2002, 871.

The Western Background

The process of secularization — along with its allies such as scientific and technological development and urbanization — appeared to be an unparalleled challenge to religion in western society. However, the response from religious thinkers came almost immediately. Obviously, since secularism swept the so called Christian countries, Christianity was the first to make a concrete and extensive response. Apart from moments of confrontation there have been continual dialogue, and this dialogue is continuing.

Theological responses reached a peak in the 1960s, by which time there were interesting new developments in understanding and working out the secular vision. Harvey Cox, an American theologian, made penetrating observations and published them through his famous book *The Secular City* (1965). To start with, Cox distinguishes secularization from secular*ism*. He explains this in the following words:

> Secularization implies a historical process, almost certainly irreversible, in which society and culture are derived from tutelage to religious control and closed metaphysical world-views ... Secularism, on the other hand, is the name for an ideology, a new closed world-view which functions very much like a new religion. While secularization finds its roots in the biblical faith itself and is to some extent an authentic outcome of the impact of biblical faith on Western history, this is not the case with secularism.[1]

It was then the responsibility of theologians and church leaders to purge Christianity of all unbiblical baggage that had accompanied it over the years, although they themselves differed in the approaches and degrees of change they allowed. Cox provides a good survey in this regard. Words like 'religionless Christianity', 'secular meaning of the gospel' and 'non-theistic God' or the Supreme Reality represented different proposals which quickly spread all over the Christian world.

Nineteen years later, in continuation of the above, Cox published another book entitled *Religion in the Secular City: Towards a Postmodern Theology* (1984). It portrays further developments in the process of secularization and religion's changes, which presented a much more complex situation. At the one extreme, there developed Christian Fundamentalism in America,[2] a pioneer of different

---

[1] Harvey Cox, *The Secular City: Secularization and Urbanization in Theological Perspective*, New York: Macmillan, 1965, 20f.

[2] 'The name comes from a series of booklets called *The Fundamentals*, issued from 1910 to 1915, which delineated what their writers believed were the irreducible doctrines of the faith, the beliefs without which Christianity could no longer be called Christianity. These fundamentals of the faith included belief in the deity of Christ, the Virgin Birth, the bodily Resurrection of Christ, the imminent Second Coming, the substitutionary atonement, and – very emphatically – the

religious fundamentalisms. On the other extreme, with a new realization of religious plurality, there emerged a new form of conversation called interfaith dialogue. Cox observes:

> Interfaith dialogue becomes neither an end in itself nor a strictly religious quest but a step in anticipation of God's justice. It becomes praxis. Similarities and differences — between those whose sacred stories are used to perpetuate domination and those whose religion strengthens them for the fight against such domination — emerge more clearly.[1]

Justice here means the new scale (primacy of the poor) provided by Jesus in his teaching on the inclusive framework of the Kingdom of God.

What Cox does not acknowledge, however, is the comparative study of religion, the forerunner of the modern movement of interfaith dialogue. Comparative study has taken in not only attempts to define religion, methodological approaches to the study of religion and comparative analysis of belief systems, but also new forms and dimensions of religion evident in some secular systems. Eric Sharpe, one of the best known historians of comparative religion, while sharing the views of Cox, observes:

> At least the secular ideologies which take the place of religious traditions contain a surprisingly large range of traditional religious ritual expressions — prophets, priests and kings, temples and shrines, pilgrimages and processions, holy scriptures, orthodoxies and heresies: the ultimate point of reference in the new secular ideology lies within the world, and not beyond it.[2]

He also points out that the secularization process was not necessarily accompanied by 'unbelief' because 'often belief in intellectual terms simply shifts sideways into another area, no less committed, no less social, no less ethical' than religion. As an example Eric Sharpe refers to Marxism for which heaven is to be a classless society on earth controlled by natural forces. There is no reason, he points out, 'to absolutely deny transcendence' even when people prefer a secular ideology to religious faith. Today the idea of transcendence and the experience of ultimate meaning in secular ideologies like Marxism is pursued far more seriously as we will point out later. Further, there are studies on nationalism, political parties etc., which in their outworking betray religious dimensions. In this connection, the study of implicit religion and secular forms of experiencing the sacred is very

---

verbal inspiration and inerrancy of the whole Bible.' H. Cox, *Religion in the Secular City: Towards a Postmodern Theology*, New York: Simon & Schuster, 1984, 44.

[1] Ibid., 238.

[2] Eric Sharpe, *Understanding Religion*, 117.

significant. As we earlier saw, on the one hand it builds on the western discussions on religion by raising new questions and making observations, and on the other, points out dimensions of religion in sports, administrative structures and new aspirations of the electronic world. It is to be welcomed that it takes peculiar situations of the non-western world for understanding distinctive expressions of spirituality and belief with and without connection with explicit forms of religion. We will soon see the peculiar situation of India.

Before we leave this section, it might be helpful to point out some recent developments in the western world. Sharpe may be right in rejecting Cox's conclusion that 'the process of secularization is irreversible.' The failure of the Soviet experiment and the resurgence of religious life in the countries of the former Soviet Union is a case in point. Moreover, the expected death of religion in western society is either getting considerably delayed or showing in some areas signs of resurrection! Critics of uncritical secularism point out that consumerism has increased the thirst for more choices, rather than quenching it. Increasing number of broken families, teenage pregnancies and crimes raise new questions about the civilizing effect of secularism. And individuals don't seem to be free from the forces of commercial sports and unregulated market with the overwhelming support of the highly manipulative mass media. As case studies show, those militants involved in horrific acts of destruction such as 9/11 are good and well-informed individuals, who see western culture as having lost its soul. One analogy shared in an interview is that even if it is made of gold, if a pen has no ink it has no value.[1] Nevertheless opportunities have not been sought, nor created, to discuss about the soul of a person and the tools of assessing a culture. And also, there is an identity crisis all over the world, which results in either the resurgence of fundamentalist and conservative forces or the development of terrorist movements. State terrorism in different forms is too obvious to deny. In the name of freedom and democracy, war has been waged unilaterally by one country as we continue to worry about the tinderboxes of war around the world. The fast development of right wing nationalism with fascist tendencies in different countries poses a great threat to the world community. God's name is not spared in arguments.

The Distinctive Situation of India

Though Vedic religion of the pre-Christian era combines this-worldly and other-worldly happiness maintained mainly by the priestly class (through ritual sacrifice and teaching the tradition) and princely class (through fighting in war and ruling), for centuries new movements challenged the excesses. A comprehensive order (dharma) covering all aspects of order from ritual to social and cosmic, was maintained by the collaboration of the ritualists and rulers. Around the sixth

[1] See Mark Juergensmeyer, *Terror in the Mind of God: The Global Rise of Religious Violence*, New Delhi: Oxford University Press, 2002, 69.

century BCE there emerged new movements that challenged this order and its maintenance. The Buddhist influence was greater than others, particularly through the policies of the great Mauryan emperor Ashoka of the third century BCE. In a context of conflicting claims by different movements his principle of 'equality of all religions' (*sarva dharma samabhava*) opened the avenue for concerned adherents to reassert their religious traditions which had been ridiculed and brought low for obscure practices, along with the new movements to emerge. From the fifth century CE the Vaishnava and Saiva traditions of devotion checked the influence of particularly the Jaina and Buddhist traditions, and they flourished with royal patronage. Centuries later, in the context of Hindu-Muslim conflicts, as an offshoot of the bhakti tradition, charismatic personalities such as Kabir (1440-1518) and Guru Nanak (1469-1539) preached a strange teaching, transcending particular names of God and their traditions and the spiritual equality of all humans. They practised meditation on the one hand and sang poetic and lyrical songs, on the other. To coincide this new trend, the Mughal Emperor Akbar the Great (1542-1605) experimented with *Din-I Ilahi* (religion of the unity based on the oneness of God) but met with a discouraging response. But he established the Mughal Empire, propagated tolerance, abolished the poll tax for non-Muslims and appreciated and used talents found among non-Muslims as well. Therefore Muslim scholars hold that Akbar laid foundations for a united and secular India.[1]

On the whole, one may say that India has had the effect of both the traditional Buddhist enlightenment of inner freedom as well as the modern European thinking on culture and education and, consequently, the situation is much more complex. Few will deny that secular ideas were rooted in Indian soil by the 300 years of direct British rule and that they found a clear shape when the Indian National Congress was founded in 1885. The INC was in the forefront of struggle for independence and was made the first ruling party when the country achieved independence in 1947. Nevertheless the INC could not control fully the fascist forces which sowed suspicion in the minds of Muslims. There were voices such as 'India for Hindus' and 'Gandhi is Mahatma.' The costly and painful partition could not be avoided and influential sections of Muslims opted out for Pakistan, a separate Muslim country. Ironically, Muslims who decided to remain in India were more than those who went to Pakistan. Fortunately, both for internal and external compulsions, India could not become a Hindu theocratic state though there have been voices to that effect. Thus, in terms of secularism the Indian case is distinctive.

Even before seeing the sweeping effect of globalization, both Cox and Sharpe have not failed to point out the distinctive kind of secularism operating in India. In 1965 Cox saw that 'the future of India depends on continuing secularization. Tribal, caste, and religious interests must be subsumed by broader policy needs.

[1] See Asghar Ali Engineer, "Secularism in India: Theory and Practice", *Social Action*, 44/1 1994.

They must be relativized – not discarded, but subordinated to the more crucial and more inclusive objective of achieving a balance between productivity and population.'[1] He praises Jawaharlal Nehru, the first Prime Minister of the independent India, who exemplified the critical difference between secularism and secularization because Nehru 'was never a dogmatic secular*ist*.' Sharpe quotes the following famous words from Nehru's *The Discovery of India*:

> We have got to get rid of that narrowing religious outlook, that obsession with supernatural and metaphysical speculations, that loosening of the mind's discipline in religious ceremonial and mystic emotionalism, which come in the way of our understanding ourselves and the world.[2]

Nehru, of course, with his background of western education, was one of the exceptional leaders of the Indian National Congress who could not tolerate the secular party being tainted by religious-communal interests. As an avowed agnostic he stoutly refused to have any dealing with the Hindu and Muslim movements. For him systems like water reservoirs and hydro-electrical power plants were the new temples of the developing India.

At the same time M.K. Gandhi, the venerated leader and respected colleague of Nehru, was different. He mobilized masses for standing with the Congress in the fight for national independence, but projected himself as the true representative of Hindu ideal. He openly declared himself as a *Sanatani* Hindu, which means he believed in the Hindu scriptures, *varnashrama dharma* (the prototype of caste system), protection of the cow and idol worship, with slight modifications to make sense for the modern world. As a practising Vaishnava with Ram as his favourite deity, he appeared to be more conservative than many educated Hindus of his time. Even the reactionary leader of the Arya Samaj Swami Dayananda Saraswati, who was out rightly anti-Christian and anti-Muslim, but who had denounced idol worship as a perversion and regarded most of the scriptures (including the Upanishads and the Gita) that emerged after the first hymnal part of the Vedas as a distortion. Gandhi had only a one-sided view of the consequences of conversion from Hinduism to Christianity (creating disharmony and leading to beef-eating and drinking liquour). There are those who invoke the ghost of Gandhi with reference to his position on the highly sensitive issues of idol worship, cow-protection and conversion. Those who do this, even in scholarly fashion, point out only the negative side of the early Christian missionary approaches to Hindus. For example, they call for presenting Christianity as one of the many religious paths (*sampradaya*) and advocate raising the icons to the level of idols as some

---

[1] Cox, *The Secular City*, 8.

[2] Sharpe, op. cit., 117.

Roman Catholics have done.[1] Although, Gandhi was the epitome of religious tolerance, it should be pointed out that his legacies on the above issues have been tinder-boxes of communal riots which continue to threaten the strange secular fabric of the Indian polity.

The different, even quite contradictory, positions of Nehru and Gandhi, would explain the strange kind of secularism that India is struggling to maintain. As the Preamble to the Indian Constitution states, India is a socialist, democratic and secular republic, although the term 'secular' was inserted by the 44th Amendment of the Constitution in 1976 during the time of Emergency. Even before this addition there was no doubt in the minds of those who framed the Constitution that India was indispensably a secular state not least for consolidation and unity. But what kind of secularism they were envisioning and promoting? Right from the earliest discussions in the Constituent Assemblies it has been a hot issue still waiting for clarity. Early attempts to clarify in the midst of heated debates repeat the following: in a country of many religions we cannot think of secularism in the western sense of the term: the state would not favour one religion over the other and would maintain neutrality; however, at the same time it should not be indifferent or opposed to religion; it would respect individual choice and promote equal respect for all religions. As D.E. Smith observed as early as 1963:

> The secular state is a state which guarantees the individual as a citizen irrespective of his religion, is not constitutionally connected to a particular religion nor does it seek either to promote or interfere with religion.[2]

But since then the Indian experiment of secularism has gone beyond a clear shape. For example, the law of the nation could not be secularized as there have been persistent voices for the continuation of the Personal Laws.[3] And creation of a uniform civil code is still the desire of many but is opposed by a considerable portion of the population cutting across religious boundaries.[4] There is constitutional provision for the freedom of religion for every individual to profess, practise and propagate his or her religion (within public order, morality and health); there is no special tax for promoting one's religion but there is no

---

[1] See J.K. Bajaj and M.D. Srinivas, "Core Issues of Hindu-Christian Dialogue: Idol Worship, Cow-Protection and Conversion", *Journal of Hindu-Christian Studies*, Vol. 17, 2004, 3-11.

[2] Donald Eugene Smith, *India as a Secular State*, New Jersey: Princeton University Press, 1963, 4.

[3] In India while all communities have a common criminal law, in matters of inheritance of property, family (marriage and divorce) etc. what is known as Personal Law is applied. Hence there are Hindu Law, Muslim Law and Christian Law. Buddhists and Sikhs are included in the purview of Hindu Law. To complicate the matter, there are regional variety and exemptions! See Robert D. Baird, "Uniform Civil Code and the Secularization of Law" in *Religion in Modern India*, ed. R.D. Baird, New Delhi: Manohar, 1981, 417-446.

[4] For a detail of debates, see Ibid., 389-446.

support for religious education. This would explain certain religious acts of public nuisance and how complicated and complex the question of identity for which every religious community is striving.

In the centre of the white band of the tri-coloured Indian flag there appears in navy blue the Ashokan wheel with 24 spokes, signifying equal respect to all religions. The State is committed to be impartial to religious communities and is equally committed to equal respect to all religions and all practices in the name of religion. However, in the absence of guidelines on what are the most acceptable public religious practices in a secular nation, one is pushed to a difficult position of having to respect certain ambiguous practices and even claims of improbable experiences which might reinforce a particular religious tradition's claim in relation to others. Consequently, what seemed to have happened is an upsurge of one religious tradition as exactly happened in the post-Ashokan era, i.e. the revival of Brahminic religion with some modifications.

The main question one has to ask is whether it is possible to achieve secularism in a country where one religious community is the majority. About 82 per cent of Indians are registered as Hindus although recently the Dalit community (untouchables) has been claiming that they are not part of the caste-ridden Hindu community. Nevertheless, it shows the extraordinary generosity and tolerance of the Hindu community that accepted a secular polity. But given the long process of assimilation even of contradictory elements and traditions within, the pan-mythic Hindu religious tradition has the capacity of accommodating the secular principle. But the question is whether all Hindus understand the responsibility laid on their shoulders in terms of having to make extra efforts to make the minority religious communities to feel at home in India.

To compound the above complexity, the Kashmir issue continues to be a running sore in the neck. Soon after the Partition, a group of Pakistanis occupied part of the princely state of Kashmir claiming that it belonged to them. In a shock, the prince ceded Kashmir to the Indian Union with certain conditions pertaining to the State's protection and special privilege. This may be a simplistic view and elaborate research has been done. The general view that prevails is that Nehru never wanted to let go of Kashmir for strategic reasons and persuaded the Raja to cede it to India. The other real problem was, there was a demand for referendum and if the Raja went for it, he was sure to lose as Kashmir was predominantly Muslim population with a Hindu minority kind unlike Hyderabad which was predominantly Hindu populated but with a Muslim Nawab. Both avoided referendum for fear of losing the popular vote. In the end, Kashmir decided to join India and Hyderabad was forced by the Indian army to join. There was no actual battle of sorts but a symbolic descending of Indian army into Hyderabad compelled the Nawab to relinquish the princely state. These were the two last states that joined India after independence.

Conflicts continue, and the attitude of Indian Muslims towards Kashmir and through it to Pakistan is different from that of the political Hindus. Another issue is discrepancy in giving privileges to religious minorities. The constitutional provision stipulated that religions of Indian origin will be given the privilege of claiming SC status alongside the tribal communities with ST status. The argument against Christianity and Islam were both based on the idea that they were from outside and hence the converts were given choice to either remain Hindus or lose the special status. The real problem was that while Muslims made a general claim that caste does not apply to them, the Christians were represented by the then Kerala Christian leadership [in the absence of a strong Christian leadership from other parts of India] who claimed that they were from the upper castes and therefore they did not want to be classified as SCs. The unfortunate situation at the time, notwithstanding the fact that majority Christians in the India at that time and even today are in the South, they were led by the privileged classes from Kerala who did not understand the other parts of India. Despite the fact that the constitution committee was chaired by a Dalit (Ambedkar), he lost against the pressures of the dominant Hindu leadership, especially Nehru who did not want the Dalits to leave Hinduism for fear of losing the elections. For as long as they remained in Hindu fold and under the caste system, then the caste leadership in the villages could compel them to vote in favour of their choice rather than allowing the people to vote as they chose. So, there were a number of complex issues that led to the constitution making the type of provision it did to distinguish Dalits of Hindu background and those of Christian and Muslim backgrounds. In any case, by a Presidential Order of 1950, non-Hindu Dalit converts to Islam, Christianity, Buddhism and Sikhism were exempted from those privileges and reservations meant for Scheduled Castes and Scheduled Tribes. Later, Buddhist and Sikh converts were included as eligible for the concessions. The other parties' struggle continues.[1] At the same time, from time to time the debate on the relevance of concessions in secular India on the basis of caste is resumed. In the following decades after independence, many agrarian based dominant castes have claimed OBC (Other Backward Classes) status on the basis of economic arguments both in the South and in the North. The demands of different communities for this status seems to be unending. One reasonable voice is that that special status and concession must be granted not on the basis of religion and caste but on economic condition. A consensus has yet to be reached.

Whatever way one defines the nature of political Hinduism, the Hindutva movement represents a small minority who want to retain the age-long Brahmanic hegemony which includes the system of a complex and extravagant ritual and caste. They would tolerate new ideas and even reformation in certain areas but

[1] In response to the long struggle of the gypsy community the Government of India recently gave them Scheduled Caste and Scheduled Tribe status. Using this occasion, the Tamil veteran leader "Karunanidhi seeks SC status for Dalit Christians", *The Hindu*, 30 May 2016, 4.

not any challenge to this basic system. They would betray this fact if they attempt to give clear definitions of what is claimed to be cultural nationalism or Hindu way of life or 'Indian-ness' or eternal order (*sanatana dharma*). But they have the capacity to give a picture that they represent all Hindus including even those who claim that they are not part of the Brahmanic tradition. In many cases their age long companionship with the rulers seems to remain intact.

One advantage of the Hindutva proponents is to communalize politics and bureaucracy. They have a rich variety of symbols that can be used for distorting the secular image of the country and for mass mobilization. For example, the national song *Vande Mataram* depicts India as a mother clothed beautifully with her rich resources, but even when she appears holding the national flag she is a woman of fair complexion wearing a silk sari with features of a wealthy Brahmin. More significantly, she is identified with the Mother Goddess, one of the goddesses of the Hindu pantheon. For this reason some religious communities refuse to sing *Vande Mataram*, and this act is construed as anti-national.

Political leaders who are supposed to be the guardians of the secular ethos of the nation are co-opted into the process of what Samartha calls 'politicization of religion and communalization of politics.' Ministers including Prime Ministers have gone to the extent of stooping down before Hindu Mutt *(matha)* leaders and sadhus to receive blessing and counsel. Those who know the history will understand in this act the reinforcement of the age-long bond between the princely class and priestly class, or rulers and ritualists.

Theologically, the Hindu weapon is the repeated position of 'One Truth-Many religions.' We have already noted the inappropriate reference to a Vedic verse.[1] At the same time one can understand with sympathy that this position was taken in response to the apparent onslaught of the Muslim and Christian claims of 'One Truth-One religion.' It gave strength to the Hindu community to get over the feeling of minority in the face of challenging claims of these foreign religious traditions. In the above verse the Hindutva proponents find the foundation of true secularism while they call their secular critics 'psuedo-secularists.' Further, presentation of the *advaita* (non-dualist) experience as the crown of all other experiences including those of other religious traditions, as done by influential figures such as Swami Vivekananda and S. Radhakrishnam, indirectly supports the Hindutva position. Again this was in response to certain Christian claims that Christ or Christianity is the crown of Hinduism and other religions. In any case, the above Hindu position does not leave any room or motivation for Hindus or Christians to understand the distinctive core visions of other religious traditions.

When the 'majority' religious community became culturally dominant, politically manipulative and theologically absorbing, understandably the religious minorities were both nervous and agitating as porcupines. This is not to condone the fundamentalist outpouring of the minority religious communities

[1] I. Selvanayagam, *The Dynamics of Hindu Religious Traditions*, 98ff.

in order to establish their identity and make their voices heard by any means including seeking separate treatment or nationhood. The Indian Muslims, the largest minority in India (about 12 per cent), with different camps within, have been motivated by certain fundamentalist groups.[1] This is also true of the Sikh community who form about 2 per cent of the population.[2] The moderates and reformers of these communities try to remind them of the moments of history in which their forebears contributed to religious tolerance and communal harmony. They also point out that secularism in principle need not be a threat for their identity and function.

Christians stand numerically in between the above two (2.3 per cent), and although they have not taken part in any militant struggle to achieve separate socio-political identity, they have demonstrated a kind of verbal militancy in the name of mission. A church leader, well known for exceptional commitment to programmes of social regeneration and nation building, observes that ninety per cent of the Christian population in India could be called fundamentalist in the sense of the Protestant fundamentalism in USA.[3] It is the greatest irony in the history of Christian thought that Christian fundamentalists and conservatives have hijacked the beautiful label 'evangelical' and unashamedly call their programmes 'crusades' in India. There are of course individuals and institutions who call for a new reformation in the church.

'Communal rage in secular India' continues to keep up old hostility and manifests from time to time in disastrous ways. The wounds caused by communal riots that took more than a million lives at the time of partition in 1947 are yet to be healed. The Hindu rage unleashed on the Sikhs following the assassination of the then Prime Minister Indira Gandhi in 1984 is yet to be fully assessed and the grievances of the victims settled. The destruction of the Babri Mosque in Ayodhya in 1992 and various riots before and after have taken hundreds of lives and the issue continues to be a tinder box of communal unrest. In connection with this, what happened in Gujarat in 2002 represents an epoch of credulity, the outburst of an accumulated beastliness and heinous genocide. Studies with balanced views show the combination of fascist trends, old grievances, historical distortions, religious misconceptions and twisted projections of past heroes.[4] Most striking in almost all these communal riots is that almost all victims are the poor and the illiterate who form one third of the Indian population. While the minority communities

[1] For details of major movements see Mumtaz Ahmad, "Islamic Fundamentalism in South Asia: The Jamaat-i-Islami and Tablighi Jamaat of South Asia" in *Fundamentalisms Observed.* ed. by Martin E. Marty and R. Scott Appleby, Chicago: University of Chicago Press, 1991, 457-530.

[2] See T.N. Madan, "Double-edged Sword: Fundamentalism and the Sikh Religious Tradition" in Ibid., 594-627.

[3] R.K. Sail and A. Sail (ed.), op. cit., 218.

[4] For a recent study with passion and valuable information, with a foreword by Amartya Sen, see Rafiq Zakaria, *Communal Rage in Secular India*, Mumbai: Popular Prakashan, 2002.

remain speechless and numb, along with the cries of the survivors and outcries of moderates and thinkers, one can hear in louder voices, from the religious wing of the majority, the slogans of equal respect for religions and one truth-many religions. This seems to betray the nexus of communal interest combined with sweeping theological positions, which have great appeal to the masses but which have no concern about the real truth of the matter.

What do all these mean for understanding the process of secularization in India? It is fascinating to watch ongoing discussions about the real nature of secularism in the multi-religious context of India. For example, in one of the recent studies, it is held that though ethical dimensions of secularism can be enhanced by a 'transfusion of the principle of tolerance to be found in all religious traditions' one cannot assume 'a transference of values between the religious and the political domains of life without the appropriate mediations and interventions at the levels of concept and practice.' The reason is that 'religion as faith and religion as ideology ... are neither synonymous nor mutually exclusive.' They impinge on each other's priorities and orientations, 'which is what makes the question of faith such a complex one to decipher and negotiate in today's world.'[1] But an open exploration of such faith is hampered by not only religious fanatics but secular fanatics also. Holding religious as diametrically opposed to secular, just like darkness and light, betrays 'hegemonic interests of the liberal elite' and leads to what is called 'secular bigotry.'[2]

There are secular conservatives who are stuck in old positions such as the Nehruvian legacy of secularism without willing to move on in the light of the development of differing positions in the process of secularization that India has been experiencing. On the other hand, there are those who have shaped themselves to be both religious and secular without allowing one to set the criteria for their identity. They distinguish between toleration and respect. One of them identifies at least five categories of secularists in India, which conceal 'layers of complicated history and multiple archaeologies of the self which have yet to be researched adequately at psychological levels' and points out the possible 'shifts between and within different secular positions,' before observing:

> The sheer *instability* of the secular as a cultural and political category needs to be acknowledged as the new point of departure for interpreting secularism(s) in India today.[3]

This acknowledgment is indispensable because just like religion, secularism is also dynamic transcending normative definitions suiting personal interests and

---

[1] Rustom Bharucha, *In the Name of the Secular: Contemporary Cultural Activism in India*, Delhi: Oxford University Press, 1998, 3.

[2] This is with a particular reference to Salman Rushdie's controversial novel *The Satanic Verses*, see Ibid., 4.

[3] Ibid., 19.

ideological positions. On the whole, the emergence of secularism and the process of secularization created ripples of different forces causing different effects. As we saw earlier, Paul Tillich called the secular movements as quasi-religious and some of them developed into fascist organizations such as the Nazi party in Germany. But the case of 'Hindu India' presents peculiarly unique situation and distinctive issues. It will be a rewarding study to compare the effects of secularism in different parts of the world.

Interfaith Attempts to Assess and Respond to Secularization

It is hard to deny that there was an impact of secular trends in Europe and America behind the monumental World Parliament of Religions in Chicago (1893) and the first World Missionary Conference in Edinburgh (1910). The former called for a new relationship between different religious communities based on goodwill and proper understanding; the latter called for a new approach to people of other faiths guided by a sense of justice, courtesy and love. In due course, the effects of secularization drew the attention of those committed to interfaith dialogue and those involved in world mission. Then it was not a surprise that in the second World Missionary Conference in Jerusalem (1928) one major session was devoted to the challenge of secular civilization. A Quaker leader, who wrote a report on the theme, mentioned:

> The civilization which we have been building is inadequate for man's life and for his complete spiritual health. The world of business and industry and secular aims starves and dries up the soul, even where it does not corrupt and defile. It is not possible to live up to the full height of man's potential being without drawing upon the deeper resources of the spirit. No civilization is 'safe' or adequate for the needs of the soul which does not draw upon the spiritual forces of the universe and weave them into its inmost warp and woof. Inventive skill, nimble cleverness and enthusiastic passion will not take the place in the social structure of faith in God and consecration to the spiritual ends of life.[1]

He found the antidote in Christianity if churches were engaged in reformulating their faith, socializing the gospel and evaluating the effects of secularism in their context. He invited other religious communities to become allies of Christians in making a corporate response to questions about the ultimate meaning and purpose of human life.

Certain individual theologians made radical observations about the secular meaning of the Christian message. For example, Dietrich Bonhoeffer (1906-1945), a pastor cum theologian, the leader of the Confessing Church in

[1] Rufus Jones, "Secular Civilization and the Christian Task", in *The Christian Life and Message to Non-Christian Systems – Report of the Jerusalem Meeting of the International Missionary Council, March 24th.-April 8th., 1928,* Humphrey Milford: Oxford University Press, 1928, 312.

Germany which was formed in protest against the Nazis, died a martyr of Hitler's murderous fascism. He was a pioneer of the theology of secularity. He took history seriously and stressed that humans had to play a creative role in directing it towards a better future. For him humans have come of age and a religion-less Christianity is possible. There can be a bold, positive and autonomous living within the framework of 'holy or sacred worldliness.' Some seminal ideas of these themes can be found in his best known book *The Cost of Discipleship.*[1] He influenced considerably the subsequent liberation movement and theology with the watchword 'Let My People Go', and the influence continues.

This engagement with the process of secularization continued even after the formation of the World Council of Churches in 1948. For example, in the Report of the third General Assembly of the WCC held in Uppsala (1968) the concern was expressed about the effect of secularization in connection with the discussion on worship. The crisis of worship experienced in the decline of church attendance in the West was attributed to this effect. Although, it was felt that 'the concept of secularism and secularization was extremely difficult to define in a way which would be acceptable to all participants', the adopted report states that it has both positive and negative possibilities. 'In its positive sense, it is an affirmation of the true potentialities of man and of the world. In its negative sense, it becomes an ideology of a closed world and can destroy man's true freedom and dignity.'[2] This ideology, the report warned, could lead to a 'secular idolatry'.

When formed in 1971 as one of the programme units of the WCC, the name of the Sub-Unit was 'Dialogue with People of Other Faiths and Ideologies'. But in due course, to avoid any misunderstanding, the word 'ideologies' was omitted. Nevertheless, the concern was never dismissed. There have been both indirect and direct references to the process of secularization. In a discussion on Christian-Marxist dialogue, for instance, after pointing out parallel and shared concern with Marxism and referring to Marx's saying that 'as long as humankind reflects, it reflects religiously,' Hans Ucko, one of the Executive Secretaries of the then 'Office on Interreligious Relations' of the WCC, writes:

> And even if we set all prisoners free, fed all the hungry, clothed all the naked, healed all the wounds, and banned all the wars, we would still always hear the voice within us: 'Who am I? From where do I come and where do I go?' This voice is a voice of spirituality, which keeps on asking us if we are not more than ashes. Someone has rightly called it (*in German*) an ocean-like feeling.[3]

---

[1] London: SCM Press, 1959. The titles include costly grace, discipleship and individual, truthfulness, hidden righteousness- prayer- devout life, and simplicity of the carefree life.

[2] Norman Goodall (ed.), *The Uppsala Assembly Report*, Geneva: WCC, 1968, 76, 79.

[3] Hans Ucko, "Christian-Marxist Dialogue: Crisis or Kairos?", *Current Dialogue*, No. 18, 1990, 25.

The intention of the author of course is not to underplay the importance of struggling for equal human rights and socio-economic equality, but to move the discussion on to touch upon the deeper dimensions of human life. This will be certainly shared by most people of other religions.

In parallel to discussions both in ecumenical circles as well as in India, there have been contributions from the field of comparative study of religion and the theology of religious pluralism. W.C. Smith, as we have already referred, suggests a world theology of religions, making a distinction between belief and faith. Belief, according to him, is part of the cumulative tradition, which is complex and changing. The unchanging core, however, is faith, which is the fundamental personal quality, potentiality and transcendental dimension, common to all. He further explains:

> Faith, then, is a quality of human living. At its best it has taken the form of serenity and courage, and loyalty and service: a quiet confidence and joy, which enables one to feel at home in the universe, and to find meaning in the world and in one's own life, a meaning that is profound and ultimate, and is stable no matter what may happen to oneself at the level of immediate event. Men and women of this kind of faith face catastrophe and confusion, affluence and sorrow, unperturbed; face opportunity with conviction and drive; and face others with a cheerful charity.[1]

If faith is engendered and sustained by a particular religious tradition, as Smith claims, it may be problematic to establish that the meaning of 'faith' is the same for all and the term is especially Judeo-Christian. In any case, at least for Christians, it is an occasion to reread the Bible to understand the different senses in which this term is used. It is very significant to point out here that Jesus understood faith primarily as an ability to transcend, to move on and to cross boundaries. Jesus found this faith not only in some exceptional individuals of his own tradition but also outside.[2] Today the term 'secular faith' is commonly used. It should be a fascinating study of and discussion on the meaning and dimensions of faith in today's life as perceived and experienced by people of different religious traditions and ideologies. Whatever may be the specific outcome of a particular study or dialogue, if done with openness, surely it will help the participants to grow in 'faith' and deepen their 'spirituality.'

There are a few platforms in India where dialogue on the 'secular faith' in relation to the Christian faith has been promoted. The most obvious example is the Christian Institute for the Study of Religion and Society at Bangalore in India. Since its inception in 1957 it has been engaged in conversations on the nature of

---

[1] W.C. Smith, *Faith and Belief*, Princeton: Princeton University Press, 1979, 12.

[2] For a detailed Bible study, see I. Selvanayagam, *Relating to People of Other Faiths: Insights from the Bible*, Thiruvalla: Christian Sahitya Samithi – BTTBPSA, 2004, 124-134.

secularism and nation-building in India and the role of the secular movements and religious communities, particularly Christians. P.D. Devanandan (1901-1962), the founder-director of CISRS studied the re-interpretation of the Hindu idea of *maya* (false appearance), its impact on Hindu thinkers taking history seriously, and the importance of interreligious co-operation for nation-building. He found resurgence, renaissance and reforms within the Hindu religious traditions as providing a new *kairos* for creative dialogue between adherents of religions and ideologies.

His successor M.M. Thomas (1916-1996), who, because of his involvement in politics, was made the Governor of Nagaland, one of the North East Indian States) engaged in an in-depth analysis of the question of the nature of the human persona as evident in major ideologies – Liberal Nationalism, Socialist Humanism, Marxism-Leninism, and the synthetic frameworks such as Communism and Fascism, Radical Humanism. He shows how secular anthropology seeks to connect inner strength and bold social involvement with questions of enduring values and ultimate goals. If proponents of these positions do not absolutise their claims, Thomas points out, there are possibilities of creative dialogue in the future. From a Christian theological viewpoint, consulting some Christian theologians of the West, he mentions the following realities as significant: human beings as created in the image of God, human beings as a fallen creature, 'the Crucified and Risen Jesus Christ as the true man and as the source of renewal of human nature and through it of all things', and the Kingdom of God as the consummation of the absolute future of human beings and society.[1] For Thomas, salvation is humanization in the process of which secular ideologies and religious visions could creatively inter-play. Even after Thomas, there have been attempts to explore dimensions of transcendence in secular ideologies, particularly Marxism, and connect them with the Christian position.[2] If faith is understood in Jesus' sense that self-transcendence and ability to move on alone qualifies someone a person of faith or a group community of faith, there is scope to continue this kind of dialogue involving people other faiths too.

It is not without reason that the ironical connection between fundamentalism and secularism is called the 'Indian predicament' in a group effort elsewhere to assess the situation.[3] However, what seems to be achieved in such individual and group reflections is only a set of monologues, and the partners in dialogue have been taken for granted. In a situation where religion is politicized and misused

[1] M.M. Thomas, *The Secular Ideologies of India and the Secular Meaning of Christ*, Bangalore-Madras: CISRS-CLS, 1976, 195ff.

[2] See Paulose Mar Paulose, "Marx's Concept of Transcendence: Some Implications for the Life of the Church" in *Essays in Celebration of the CISRS Silver Jubilee*, ed. by S.K. Chatterji, Bangalore-Madras: CISRS-CLS, 1983, 194-210.

[3] For papers presented in the Gurukkul Summer Institute 1994, see Andreas Nehring (ed.), op. cit.

by vested interests, opportunities for honest and open conversations between responsible persons who affect the course of the political process and who lead the life of religious communities are hardly available. This is the greatest challenge for thinkers, both religious and secular, who are committed to a vision for life and a tryst to move on with openness.

For obvious reasons, we have taken the Christian position in the main which in general has made a response to the challenges of secularism. We have mentioned in passing the stern position of Nehru and the ambiguous position of Gandhi. There are Hindu thinkers who claim that secularism is not a threat to their religion. For example, Swami Vivekananda claimed that with the Vedantic emphasis on divinity and dignity of every individual there is a foundation for true secularism. If one watches the current debate in India, the largest secular democracy in the world, even the religious fanatics claim fashionably that their religion is compatible with secularism. Both in India and in the world scene Islam is often caricatured to be anti-secular. But there are Muslim thinkers and leaders who point out that Islam is amenable to the secular values of equality, justice and freedom. It is often suggested that avoiding generalization one has to study each situation separately taking into account the history, decisive moments and legal expressions.

The most important question being raised in India is about religious behaviour in a multi-religious and secular context. It is intriguing that the so called Christian countries of the West (e.g. the United Kingdom) is much more secular in public life than in India! We have already mentioned the absence of a uniform civil code in a secular democracy. Also we mentioned the global ethics suggested by Hans Küng which overlaps with the UN (and Commonwealth) Charter of Human Rights etc. And there are Codes of Conduct (published by the UK Interfaith Network) and so on. In India people do not know nor do they search for a theoretical framework of secularism and its practical outworking. It may look too 'this worldly' (the meaning of the original Latin word *saeculum*). For example, can political leaders worship publicly in a spectacular manner? Can portraits of deities or religious symbols be allowed in public offices and transports? When in the name of a deity having erupted in a particular spot demanding worship can that public spot be given up? If shrines are built encroaching part of a road and public path can it be tolerated because it is a sensitive issue? When religious festivals or daily worship become noisy and irritating, thus being a nuisance and hazard to health, what should be the response of the public? And what sort of control is in place when the state media are used for the display of a religious event including the display of rituals? In such a context what does equal respect for all religious acts and toleration mean? Genuine voices are stifled in the name of sensitivity by religiously communalized bureaucracy and political platforms with the repeated mantra of tolerance and harmony.

Debate on Indian secularism continues in far more comprehensive way in connection with the bold experiments here than anywhere else. Apart from the continued broadcast from high political galleries, one may read with great interest what is written by sociologists, cultural anthropologists and social thinkers who are well informed of secularization process or thesis of the West. We will note a few positions of those who are more or less based in academic campuses in New Delhi.

Ashis Nandi thinks that the imported idea of secularism along with modernity is unsuitable for the South Asian culture. He calls himself anti-secularist because he feels that 'the ideology and politics of secularism have more or less exhausted their possibilities. And we may have to work with a different conceptual frame which is already vaguely visible at the borders of Indian political culture.'[1] The process of the major religious traditions becoming ideologies thus reinforcing the oppressive side of modernity was the backdrop of this observation. Secularism was forced to compromise with religio-social ideologies with the justification of domination and violence in order 'to sustain these ideologies as the new opiates of the masses.'[2] Instead of trying to build up tolerance on the good faith or conscience of a small group of de-ethicized, middle-class politicians, bureaucrats and intellectuals, a far better and serious venture would be to explore the philosophy, the symbolism and the theology of tolerance in the faith of the citizens who can teach us tolerance from every day living of their faith.[3] Further, he draws insights from Gandhi whose 'religious tolerance came from his anti-secularism which in turn came from his unconditional rejection of modernity.'[4] Nandi's alternative has yet to take a definite and detailed shape.

T.N. Madan goes a long way with Nandi but does not reject secularism totally. Basically, he takes the positive side of being modern, which 'means larger and deeper things: for example, 'the enlargement of human freedom and the enhancement of the range of choices open to a people in respect of things that matter, including their present and future life-styles. This means being in charge of oneself. And this is one of the connotations of the process of secularization.'[5] Then he submits that 'in the prevailing circumstances secularism in South Asia as a generally shared credo of life is impossible, as a basis for state action impracticable, and as a blueprint for the foreseeable future impotent.' He explains:

> It is impossible as a credo of life because the great majority of the people of South Asia are in their own eyes active adherents of some

---

[1] Ashis Nandy, "The Politics of Secularism and the Recovery of Religious Tolerance" in *Secularism and its Critics*, ed. Rajeev Bhargava, Delhi: Oxford University Press, 1998, 326.

[2] Ibid., 343.

[3] Ibid., 338.

[4] Ibid., 344.

[5] T.N. Madan, "Secularism in its Place", 394.

> religious faith. It is impracticable as a basis for state action either because Buddhism and Islam have been declared state or state-protected religions or because of the stance of religious neutrality or equidistance is difficult to maintain since religious minorities do not share the majority's view of what this entails for the state. And it is impotent as a blueprint for the future because, by its very nature, it is incapable of countering religious fundamentalism and fanaticism.
>
> Secularism is the dream of a minority which wants to shape the majority in its own image, which wants to impose its will upon history but lacks the power to do so under the democratically organized polity...Secularism therefore is a social myth which draws a cover over the failure of this minority to separate politics from religion in the society in which its members live. From the point of view of the majority, 'secularism' is a vacuous word, a phantom concept, for such people do not know whether it is desirable to privatize religion and if it is, how this may be done ... For the secularist minority to stigmatize the majority as primordially oriented and preach secularism to the latter as the law of human existence is moral arrogance and worse ... political folly.[1]

Since Madan's categories of majority and minority are abstract and anonymous it is difficult to visualize them with their core visions and variety of traditions within.

Madan thinks that 'despite ongoing processes of secularization and deliberate efforts to promote it, secularism as a widely shared worldview has failed to make headway in India. Obviously what exists empirically but not also ideologically exists only weakly.'[2] The power structures and power relations in religions, for him, pose serious problems. He is critical of developments in the West as well. For him the reformer Martin Luther also was a man of his times. Therefore simple transferability of secularism to South Asia is beset with many difficulties. Then, in the end, 'Secularism must be put in its place: which does not mean rejecting it but of finding the proper means for its expression. In multi-religious societies, such as those of South Asia, it should be realized that secularism may not be restricted to rationalism, that it is compatible with faith, and that rationalism (as understood in the West) is not the sole motive force of a modern state. What the institutional implications of such a position are is an important question and needs to be worked out.'[3] For him, secularism in India is a gift of Christianity, and Islam and Buddhism also have elements to construct a healthy secularism. Earlier

---

[1] Ibid., 395.

[2] Ibid., 396.

[3] Ibid., 404.

we pointed out the process of 'politicization of religion and communalization of politics' and raised questions about religious expressions and behaviour in India, a multi-religious and secular country. Nandi's division of religion as faith and religion as ideology is found to be helpful to analyse this process.

The right attitude and guidance of the religiously neutral state through a committed bureaucracy and conscientised citizens are vital for the working of true secularism even if it is imperfect. We have noted earlier Gandhi's and Nehru's positions on the relationship between state and religion. Madan points out 'while Gandhi put his faith in the reformed, ethically refined individual, in creating a better if not ideal society, Nehru considered the shaping of suitable institutions as the best means to achieve the same goal. And of all the modern institutions it was the state which he believed would be the principal engine of social change.'[1] Nehru, having been defeated in his struggle to win the confidence of the proponents of Partition into remaining in a united secular India, Madan recognizes, clarified until the end of his life that the state was not opposed to religion but honoured all faiths and gave them equal opportunities. He acknowledged the limitation of the so called secular humanism and the difficulty of generalizing the scientific temper. For him secular minded persons could confront fundamentalism and revivalism as much they could empathize with religion.

The success of secularism depends not only on checking religious zealots and misguided masses but also corruption and violence. Madan quotes Nandi who has put it thus: 'There is now a peculiar double-bind in Indian politics: the ills of religion have found political expression but the strength of it have not been available for checking corruption and violence in public life.'[2] The question is whether everything is lost irretrievably. Admitting his inability to give a conclusive answer, he asks to take both religion and secularism seriously. 'Secularism would have to imply that those who profess no religion have a place in society equal to that of others, not higher or lower.' He ends his stimulating paper with a quote from Karl Marx: 'Ideas which have conquered our minds ... to which reason has welded our conscience, are chains from which we cannot break away without breaking our hearts; they are demons which man can vanquish only by submitting to them.'[3] There is much to ponder in this statement for those who arc truly religious or secular!

Rajeev Bhargava observes that in South Asia culture is inseparable from religion, and argues for the separation of some religious and non-religious institutions. The secularism he envisages 'does not deny the difficulty of disentangling religious and non-religious practices. What distinguishes it is its advocacy of the value separating *some* of these actions in their institutionalized forms, largely because it finds the alternative action less satisfactory. It follows that

[1] Ibid.

[2] Ibid., 408.

[3] Ibid., 409.

secularism is compatible with the view that the complete secularization of society is neither possible nor desirable.'[1] He is of the opinion that contextual secularism cannot hysterically avoid traditional or modern religious institutions. Those who stick on to their identity with traditional names and practices or modern institutions are automatically debarred from the public sphere. Even after the painful partition, Hindu-Muslim relationships could not be made healthy and stable. In this context what kind of secularism is best? He answers that which is based on

> (1) A strong defence of minority rights, to be supplemented on the one hand by, (2) deploying the resources of religious tolerance to isolate bigotry and encourage internal reform and on the other hand by, (3) consolidating whatever space of the common good already exists.[2]

In a recent seminar,[3] in his presentation on 'Religion and the Promise of Indian Contextual Secularism', Bhargava pointed out that one conception of tolerance in a secular polity is that even if the other is morally reprehensible and one has the power to intervene one should restrain even if there is violence in frenzy is unworkable. On the other hand, the idea of political secularism based on the separation between religion and state presupposes a comprehensive secularism held by atheists, humanists and some religious. In countries predominantly secular, separation is not exclusion. Obscurantist religious practices may be there but religions should not be excluded because it has not lost all its significance and it contributes to self-cultivation, self-perfection etc. True secularism cannot be anti-religious but pro-interreligious. For Nehru, not only the issue of religion but also that of caste and women which are important for realising and safeguarding secularism. The state must step into addressing all sorts of discrimination. It can only do so, if it is able to remain neutral and secular stance provides it that unique status that religious affiliation does not.

Similarly, Partha Chatterjee argues for reconfiguration of secularism for tolerance, neutrality, equidistance, safeguarding religious freedom, protection of the religious minorities, challenging Hindu fundamentalism, respecting 'the right not to offer a reason for being different' and the formulation of a political concept of toleration through its liberal democratic roots.[4] Amartya Sen is of the opinion that 'the state must steer clear of any association with any religious matter whatsoever', but what is needed is a symmetric treatment of all religious

[1] "What is Secularism for?', in *Secularism and its Critics*, ed. Rajeev Bhargava, Delhi: Oxford University Press, 1998, 489.

[2] Ibid., 542.

[3] Organized by the Dept. of Christian Studies at the University of Madras, 22nd February 2016.

[4] See M.T. Cherian, *Hindutva Agenda and Minority Rights: A Christian Response,* Bangalore: Centre for Contemporary Christianity, 2007, 45f.

communities. This is not violation of the principle of secularism as it presupposes preservation of religious freedom.[1] Defending Nehru's stand on secularism he stresses that even if there is some dissatisfaction, abandoning secularism does not guarantee a better condition.

Debates and dilemmas continue with regard to gaining clarity of secularism and its manifestation in religiously vigorous India. I want to close by noting four recent events. First, the Minister of External Affairs supported by the Hindutva spokespersons declared the Bhagavad Gita to be the national scripture of India.[2] It was presented by the Prime Minister as the greatest gift of India when he visited foreign countries. Gita is part of the epic Mahabharata, and when it was translated into English by a British civil servant it reached the Vaishnava thinkers such as Gandhi who projected it as the one Hindu scripture. It was to counter the single scriptures of Christianity, Islam and Sikhism. But nobody expected that the central ministers of a secular country would promote its reading for the people of all religions. Naturally, they provoked strong reactions.

Second, in January 2015 Shiv Sena, a Hindu movement based in Mumbai, a member of the Hindu political confederation known as the Bharatiya Janata Party (ruling at the Centre) called for dropping the words 'socialist and secular' from the Preamble to the Constitution. The Union Telecommunications Minister indicated that the Government wanted to debate on whether the words should be in the Preamble, opining that we do not need these words to be a secular country. The issue became controversial (not for the first time) and hit the headlines. Some Hindu parties continued to stress their position that 'if Pakistan was carved out after Partition for Muslims, then the rest of the country is a Hindu Rashtra.'[3]

Third, in September 2015, in the most populous and most Hindutva-influenced State of Uttar Pradesh, a Muslim was lynched for allegedly keeping beef in his house. His son survived a heinous attack. This provoked several academics and thinkers to return their national awards and to condemn intolerance. Further investigations and legal actions continue.[4] In actual fact, in a country like India, multi-religious and secular, there should be a sustained dialogue on what we tolerate and what we can't, and guidelines on appropriate behaviour.

Fourth, the Supreme Court's judgment in May 2016 on defamation has been seen as a blow to free speech and freedom of the press. One writer has commented critically:

> The Supreme Court has always had an ambivalent relationship with the freedom of speech and expression, treating free speech more as

---

[1] Amartya Sen, "Secularism and its Discontents", in *Secularism and its Critics*, ed. Rajeev Bhargava, Delhi: Oxford University Press, 1998, 456.

[2] See *The Hindu*, 8 December 2014, 12.

[3] *The Hindu*, 29 January 2015, 1.

[4] See the update report, *The Hindu*, 1 June 2016, 12.

> an annoyance than a right. Its defamation law judgment continues that long, unfortunate history … The judgment creates a bizarre legal situation where criminal liability for defamation is attracted to a lower threshold than civil liability … It is journalists and newspapers, fighting frivolous cases in court, who have to deal with the very real consequences.[1]

Earlier, foreign journalists' movements were either curtailed or limited so that the real situation of poverty, violation of rights, inadequate protection of environment etc. of the 'Hindu Rashtra' may not be known to the outside world. Also the communalized historiography by the Hindutva exponents that has twisted history and distorted facts in the school text books has been alarmingly criticized by well-respected secular historians. The fundamental question is whether those seriously committed, religious or secular, are mature enough to dialogue with openness and find ways of influencing politics and bureaucracy. In other words it is being seriously open to the ever unfolding of Truth and truths.

Concluding Remarks

Following the Enlightenment, the process of secularization appeared to be an unparalleled challenge to religion in western society. Anything connected with the supernatural was questioned, and that which appealed to empirical experience alone commanded any respect. Individual freedom, without any collective control like the ecclesiastical authority and traditional culture, was extolled as the only way to achieve fulfilment. This remarkable development evoked different kinds of responses from Christianity, the religion which governed the thinking of western society for centuries. However, the process of secularization was not sailing smoothly as its perceived conclusion was upset by two major world wars. Some Christian theologians assessed the situation, challenged the moral bankruptcy and offered new interpretations of the Christian faith, but at the other extreme there was the eruption of fundamentalism. In some measure the same happened in all religious traditions.

Secularism in India is quite distinctive. A secular Constitution was a necessity to govern people of different religions, traditions and cultures. When secularism triumphs in certain cases, every religious community claims that they have resources to contribute to the sustenance of secularism. When the minority religious communities become noisy and self-serving, the majority Hindu community trumpets that India belongs to them and only a Hindu Rashtra can provide unity, cultural nationalism and uniform law. What they do not realize is that they have a responsibility to make the minorities feel comfortable and safe. And fundamentally, uncritical religious practices and caste which is a hierarchical and discriminative system make things so complex that a reasonable and creative

[1] Gautam Bhatia, "A blow against free speech", *The Hindu*, 16 May 2016.

dialogue looks almost impossible. Hence the dilemmas and tensions in the current debates on secularism in India. Is a corporate search for meaningful and fulfilling spirituality for all people possible? What level of maturity is required of adherents of religious traditions and secular ideologies? These are some of the questions that need further deliberation.

Chapter 8

Truth and Truths of Religions

Is Truth Untouchable in the Study of Religion?

Normally, questions about truth and value are avoided in discussions and books on the study of religion with only a few exceptions.[1] The reason is that the study should be objective without being tainted or conditioned by particular perceptions or experiences of truth mediated by the religion or religious tradition of the student. Especially since the phenomenology of religion and its presuppositions came to dominate the field, scholars have been reverently aware that they should not pass any value judgments on the data they observe and interpret. However, this situation has been changing. We have already discussed Gavin Flood's *Beyond Phenomenology: Rethinking the Study of Religion* which is quoted by others also, particularly in support of the critics of phenomenology.[2] Further, in his outstanding study, J.S. Jensen questions the traditional assumptions of the scientific study of religion. He recalls the works of such classical phenomenologists as Chantepie, Tiele and Kristensen, and points out their attitudinal principles of objectivity or abstaining from judgment, classification of the data and interpretation of the 'essence' of religion. He observes: 'the unholy alliances between "transcendentalists" and "objectivist realists" have in many ways counteracted the development of productive comparative theories and methods in the study of religion.' He quotes Talcott Parsons's words that 'Almost everything from the sublime to the ridiculous

[1] See the chapter on "The Question of Truth" by Ron Geeves in *The Study of Religion: An Introduction to Key Ideas and Methods*, London: Bloomsbury, 2014, 303-336. The issues of religious pluralism and the philosophy of knowledge and truth are given prominence.

[2] See Ibid., 157-182.

has in some society been treated as sacred', which may be amply demonstrated by a quick glance at almost any bibliographical classification.[1]

But without wanting to restrict and limit their number, Jensen permits students who are dissatisfied to come up with new definitions and theories. 'Definitions, generalizations, and taxonomies should be inter-subjectively sharable and theoretically informed so that they can assist in the production of rational evidence.'[2] Recognising the possibility of exaggeration, and the danger in straight applications of modes of knowledge from scientific and secular fields, the author states and explains three modes of comparison: the evolutionist, the universalist and the relativist. He does not seem to expect them to be free of defect and exaggeration. Then he turns to some programmatic considerations in the reformulation of the comparative and general study of religion. Among the issues are: normativity, reductionism, a non-speculative-particularistic-descriptive method, and the tension between the normative and general studies. He hopes for inspiration from the model sciences for increased level-headedness.

What is Truth?

Truth as a theological, philosophical, epistemological and scientific category is as hard to define as religion and everything associated with it. The question is, who and for what purpose this question is asked. Perhaps the following New Testament instance is a good starting point. Pilate, the Roman governor based in Jerusalem, posed this question to Jesus who was on trial before him. This was in response to Jesus' saying in an interesting conversation that 'My task is to bear witness to the truth.' Jesus had earlier said 'I am the truth.' Pilate asked this not out of curiosity to know how philosophers dealt with the questions of ontology and epistemology. Nor did he have a spiritual quest after the ultimate goal of human life. He was a bureaucrat without backbone or any independent view of politics, but simply a functionary of the Roman emperor. He exposed a high degree of cynicism that had no regard for the 'criminal' standing before him. He never tried to find out the truth behind this trial. Pilate typifies all those who ask questions about Truth but without any commitment to finding out truths in terms of actual, ordinary facts that affect the lives of innocent people. Pilate's example may shed a light to help clarify the use of the term 'truth' in religion and interreligious dialogue.

The word 'truth' is used in different senses, and the exact sense will become clear only when the concerned context and conceptual framework is taken seriously. For example, notice the following Rigvedic verse:

Truth is One; the wise call it by different names.

---

[1] Jeppe S. Jensen. *The Study of Religion in a New Key: Theoretical and Philosophical Soundings in the Comparative and General Study of Religion*, Aarhus, Denmark: Aarhus University Press, 2003, 100.

[2] Ibid., 108.

But in the context of the text Truth signifies a bird-shaped altar. As we have already noted ritual sacrifice is central to Vedic religion. Arguably, in Brahminic worship, either public or in the sanctum sanctorum of temples, the key of the sacred power is handled by the priests. No worshipper can ask for the meaning of the minute actions and muttering recitations of the priest but must accept the efficacy of the priest's actions which is in continuation of an ancient tradition. At the same time, as we have noted many times, the above Vedic verse is presented in order to reinforce the pluralist framework on one truth-many religions.

Another example gives entirely a different meaning. When Vedic ritual was challenged and a new search for truth became popular there was an interesting dialogue about the supreme truth beyond the ritual power. After a series of experiments, the father declares to his son who has just completed the Vedic studies (The *Chandogya Upanishad*, 6th chapter):

> That Being which is this subtle essence, even That all this world has for its Self. That is the True. That is the Soul. That you are.

Similar verses were the basic texts of the Vedantic philosophy. However, different interpretations could not be avoided. Hence, different schools of Vedanta.

At the time of his enlightenment, knowledge and insight arose in Gautama Buddha. He claimed that he had discovered the Four Noble Truths: the fact of suffering, the cause, the possibility of its cessation and the way to do it. For Sikhs, the God is the True Name. For Gandhi Truth is God. The Theosophists hold that 'Truth is higher than all religions.' There are historical truths, scientific truths and religious truths. How do we distinguish one from the other? Is there something which can be called 'the truth, the whole truth and nothing but the truth'?

In this chapter we cannot give a clear answer to such questions, but can only hope to clarify the questions themselves. Its scope is rather limited. It tries to consult some of the discussions and studies on the subject and to suggest care and sensitivity in using the word 'truth' in connection with religion and interreligious dialogue. The most challenging moments in dialogue are when representatives of particular religious traditions come with claims of 'absolute truth' or slogans of 'one truth and many religions.' In my opinion such positions do not help but rather hinder the process of interfaith understanding.

The Species of Religious Truth

David Gnanaprakasam Moses, a Tamil Christian scholar of southern India, made a searching study of the question of religious truth based in Columbia University which was published in 1950. He starts by looking into the nature of philosophical, artistic and scientific truths and distinguishes them from religious truth. For him 'religion stands or falls by what it affirms to be theoretically significant or cognitively true.' He points out how revelation, experience, faith and imagination relate to religious truth. These form the first part of his study. In the second part, he refers to three thinkers who were very influential in his time: Radhakrishnan, a former Spalding Professor of Comparative Religion at Oxford and President of India, William Ernest Hocking, an American philosopher of religion, and Hendric Kraemer, one of the greatest Christian missionary theologians of the twentieth century.

D.G. Moses' first major task was to demonstrate that there are different species of truth, thereby challenging any claim for an all-encompassing absolute truth dealing in a single stroke with all aspects of life in the universe. The reality, he notes, 'is infinitely complex and endlessly diverse'. He writes:

> Truth will not mean the same identical thing in the different realms. In other words, if reality is not a static homogeneity expressing itself in a monotonous identity in every one of its parts, but a dynamic heterogeneity manifesting itself in different ways in different orders, then it will follow that the truth about reality will be different accordingly as it refers to one or other aspect of it. What is true in one level or aspect or department of reality need not be true in another level or aspect, and the fact that it is different will arise as a natural consequence of its different relevance. So that we seem to be justified in our assumption that there can be different species of truth.[1]

He warns against all attempts 'to squeeze truth into one mould' and calls for a recognition of 'different kinds of truth and different kinds of explanations.' Subsequently, he examines the different kinds of truth and shows how they differ from religious truth.

Philosophical truth is animated by intellectual curiosity. It is:

> an intellectual comprehension of the universe, the result of an attempt to think things through. In a sense religion also begins in wonder, but it is wonder which is more akin to mystery. The religious individual is not primarily interested in understanding the mystery that surrounds him, but his chief concern is to enter into a practical relation with it. Religious truth is therefore not an intellectual formulation of the mystery but a statement of the practical significance which it has for one's life.[2]

'Truth in philosophy is the logical, conceptual exploration of meaning throughout the whole of reality.' And truth in religion is rather 'the discovery of a significance in reality which demands worship.' Philosophy takes into account of 'the notion of significance and its various kinds and weaves them into its picture

[1] D.G. Moses, *Religious Truth and the Relation between Religions*, Mysore: The Christian Literature Society of India, 1950, 20.

[2] Ibid., 24f.

of the universe' from the viewpoint of 'the objective observer, the impartial spectator.' 'Religious truth, on the other hand, is the statement of a significance that demands commitment and a complete reorientation of one's life. It is discovered in an attitude of participation and not of contemplation.' Correspondingly, philosophical truth is 'logical, conceptual, abstract and general.' 'Religious truth is concrete and metaphorical. The language of poetry with its suggestive analogies and overtone of hidden meanings is what is most conducive to the expression of religious truth.' Further, philosophical truth is an understanding of the universe in impersonal or non-personal terms; the religious truth tends to interpret the universe in personal categories; it is in terms of 'I and Thou' relationship. Both cannot exclude other modes of experience in ordinary life like ethics and art, but their starting points and purpose are different.

Religious truth relates to artistic truth in a different way. Art is 'expressive and communicative, and the artist in all his efforts is deeply concerned to reveal something real as he has seen is with his heightened power of perception.' Art may include 'propositions of various kinds, some historical and some scientific, and these may be true or false.' But the art may have a truth value as experienced by great figures such as Rabindranath Tagore in India who was simultaneously interested in religion and spirituality.[1] Moses' perception that just as art is interested in the individual so is religion, and just as art is especially concerned with the world of values and appreciations so is religion, may not convince the followers of Tagore. However, Moses tries to make up when he says that they are similar also in that both refer to '... something metaphysical, something in the eternal nature of things.' They have something to say about the inner reality and the significance of things. It is also true that religion has invariably used the artistic media for the expression of its insights. Religious language is always that of poetry and poetic imagery.[2]

It may be even said that art springs from religion. But, argues Moses, 'in spite of all this affinity which religion has had with art, it is fundamentally different in one important respect. Artistic truth, we have seen, is the result of imaginative contemplation, but religious truth is the result of active commitment. It is the consequence of the religious individual committing or surrendering his individual will to the universal will.'[3] Art may stop with aesthetic concern, but religion places great demands on the individual which can be matters of life and death.

According to Moses, religion is far more related to art than to other realms such as science. Science deals with natural laws, observable data and verifiable truth. 'The aim of science in every study is to arrive at ever wider generalizations so as to include an ever-increasing number of facts observed.' Compared with

---

[1] See Harsha V. Dehejia and Makarand Paranjape (eds.), *Soundarya: The Perception and Practice of Beauty in India*, New Delhi: Samvad India Foundation, 2003, 240ff.

[2] Moses, op. cit., 37.

[3] Ibid.

religion, there are a number of sharp contrasts. Scientific truth is concerned about being quantitatively precise; religious truth with being qualitative. Scientific truth is selective in character referring to well-defined aspects of reality; religious truth is concerned about the whole of reality, the meaning and purpose of life. Verification in science is a process which is undertaken with regard to a particular hypothesis; religious truth has its own system of verification in relation to the significance of an individual's life for whom acceptance of the truth is prior to verification.[1] Religious experience is based on faith which never passes into demonstration as in science.

Moses moves on, examining scholarly views on religious truth and religious experience. Concerning the distinction sometimes made between religious consciousness and religious experience, he seems to agree with the view that religious experience is a modification of the normal consciousness of a human being. Even mysticism is not a separate and distinct type of religious experience but is constituted by different ingredients of religious life and expressed in various forms and intensities. Even in the Bible one can see the tension between the claim of 'testing God' and 'putting God to the test.' He concludes by saying:

> It is clear that we cannot say that religious truth is the result of religious experience. Religious experience ... already implies religious truth. Its identification as religious is itself the outcome of an interpretation by means of the religious conviction present in the mind of the believer. This conviction is born of religious faith, which is inherent in religious experience.[2]

Religious experience is 'the vivid realization in personal experience of truths held in the mind.' An awakening is necessary to bring to mind what is already hidden within it.

As far as revelation and religious truth is concerned, Moses refers to the traditional distinction in Catholic Christian theology between general revelation, through nature and reason, and special revelation in certain specific events of history. In addition, Christian faith is based on a unique revelation in Jesus Christ which theologians like Barth have held to be the only real revelation. Moses tries to balance both the universal revelation of God and his decisive disclosure in Christ. In his words,

> If God is a Righteous Will and a creator God, then the world he has created will reveal to some extent his hidden characteristics. Its order and beauty, its adjustments of parts to the whole, the adjustment of the mind of man to his environing world and the suitability of the natural order for the development of character, all these will show forth his

[1] Ibid., 44ff.

[2] Ibid., 55.

> power and intelligence. More of him will be revealed in the human world, in the world of self-conscious personalities with moral sense and reason. In the categorical imperative of morality which demands of man unconditional obedience, he will be revealed as the ultimate good and righteous will. In the world of history, the world which is the scene of the conflict of individual and collective will, he will be seen as the ultimate principles that govern history. And since none of these revelations could be complete because nature is impersonal, and morality is less than personal in that it is only a law that faces man here, and personality is never revealed completely except in a person, it might be urged that there must be a final incarnation in the form of a Son of Man, on the plane of history, in one indivisible whole of truth and life.[1]

According to Moses, the 'experience of revelation is an act of faith' which is 'a mixture of an awareness and an obedience.' This is consummated in the life of the individual when the apprehension of it takes place through the self-certifying and self-authenticating inner testimony of the Spirit. The rational powers help clarification and communication of revelational experience. 'Since it is the result of the exercise of reason on the content of revelation, it will both bring out unexplored depths in the original experience and correct formulations that are incorrect. This what justifies the idea of a progressive revelation. Even a final revelation does not exclude infinite progress *within* the revelation, an endless reaching forward to newer and newer truths contained in the original and explicated with the growth of ordinary knowledge and spiritual experience.'[2] This is a statement that calls for both conviction and openness for continuing exploration into our own faith and it can be well extended to others' faith too.

In a chapter entitled 'Religious Truth, Faith and Religious imagination' D.G. Moses tries to find a valid reason for perceiving the absolute reality as God. 'The Absolute is a cold abstraction, whereas the God of religion is a rich, palpitating reality.' God alone can satisfy the longing of our hearts and the searching of our reason. And imagination is a 'co-operating power in the expression of religious truth.' 'God is both organic to the world and above the world. This does not mean that ultimate reality is self-contradictory. The law of non-contradiction is not merely a logical law, it is also a law of things.' No single image is adequate to express this reality. The term 'faith' has a 'cognitive, a volitional and an imaginative element in it.' Faith as a source of religious truth is 'a positive response of the whole nature of man, involving all the elements of his conscious nature, and an act of self-commitment.'

---

[1] Ibid., 61.

[2] Ibid., 64.

Moses acknowledges that religious truth is not easily communicable. Language is inadequate. Religious utterance has always a mythic, poetic and emotive character. It is not a truth to possess and sell but to live and do. Demonstration or verification is not possible yet, he argues, there might be justification for its reasonableness. Then what in his view is the criterion of religious truth? He insists that 'one cannot decide the validity of a religious truth on the basis of its conformity or congruence with a philosophic system.' Even the conservation of values cannot define the validity of religion. 'On the contrary', Moses writes, 'the very discovery of values is very often the result of the religious attitude, and historically we can point to a number of our cherished values as having their origin in it.' 'The criterion of a religious truth will be the extent to which it satisfies these universal and insistent needs of religion.' Another test is the degree of success with which it is able to solve the problem of the power and guilt of sin.

The above summary of D.G. Moses' study, done nearly seven decades ago, sets a historical background to the discussion on religious truth from an Indian context. Those who are aware of different strands of thought on this subject, prevalent in his own time and after, have valid reasons to criticise his approach. The connections or differences he makes between religion, philosophy, art and science may be found to be somewhat superficial. His concentration on European and Christian philosophers and theologians without taking the fruits of the comparative studies of religion into consideration is limiting. Even many Christian theologians would find his definition of faith reductionist, as he does not recognise the different definitions of faith found within the New Testament itself.

At the same time, it is fair to say that studies of religions and religious ideas with a high degree of specialisation – historical, sociological, anthropological, psychological and phenomenological – have not helped to gain a clearer and simpler understanding of truth. One tends to go back to D.G. Moses, affirming the 'infinitely complex and endlessly diverse' nature of reality. As we have pointed out, a single definition of religion acceptable to all is elusive; it may not be surprising to see a single definition of 'truth' is also elusive. Studies of religion point to the immense complexity of truth and there is no sign of a definition of truth and religion equally acceptable to all philosophers, scholars and believers. For instance, recently, from a phenomenological perspective, the following observation is made:

> The concept of religious truth expresses various aspects of human experience: reality that is permanent, immeasurable, unconcealed, effective, powerful; personal character that is sincere, good, genuine, valuable; and knowledge that is certain, accurate, pure, clear, and convincing. Truth emerges out of the basic human experience of valuation (both as assessment and appreciation) as a necessity for

> human survival and well-being. Human life is characterized by the need to distinguish between what is real and unreal, powerful and powerless, genuine and deceptive, pure and contaminated, clear and confused, as well as relative degrees of one extreme to the other. In an attempt to understand the character and variation of the existential engagement with truth in different religious traditions, we recognize three aspects of truth: (1) the character of accurate knowing, (2) the nature of the reality known, and (3) the formation of value as the power to actualize this reality in authentic living. As a general concept, religious truth can be defined as the knowledge and expression of what-is for the purpose of achieving the greatest well-being possible (i.e., salvation, absolute freedom, or total harmony) ... Religious truth entails the continuing development of a valid relationship between self-consciousness and one's most extended and most profound environment (reality) ... five different approaches or ways of knowing the truth ... are: (1) intimate experience of spiritual presence(s), (2) symbolic duplication of sacred reality through myth and ritual, (3) cultivation of appropriate relationships, (4) awakening transcendent consciousness, and (5) cognition of necessary and eternal realities.[1]

It is not surprising that most scholars of religion prefer to ignore the debate on truth in favour of a descriptive analysis of the observable data available to them. However, Christian theologians, particularly those who are interested in understanding the mystery and complexity of religious pluralism, are not willing to dismiss the question of truth both in its absolute and multifarious senses.

Truth and Interfaith Dialogue

Radhakrishnan was emphatic about the advaita view of Brahman, the supreme reality, which includes the variety of the phenomenal world, and which is refracted as it passes through the distorting medium of human nature. Symbols and language are inadequate to comprehend this reality and one should strive for the dawn of the liberating knowledge which makes one realise that the microcosmic one is identical with the macrocosmic One. For Radhakrishnan 'Truth is always greater than man's reach; there is more in God than we know.' Different religious visions represent in his view imperfect perceptions of this Truth at various levels and degrees. 'The bewildering polytheism of the masses and the uncompromising monotheism of the classes are for the Hindu the same expression of one and the same force at different levels.' In this light religions need to move further in interpenetration and co-operation to achieve the ideal of one world religion. In Radhakrishnan's words,

[1] F.J. Streng, "TRUTH" in *The Encyclopedia of Religion*, ed. by M. Eliade, vol. 15, 63ff.

> The political ideal of the world is not so much a single empire with a homogeneous civilisation and a single communal will, but a brotherhood of free nations differing profoundly in life and mind, habits and institutions, existing side by side in peace and order, harmony and co-operation, and each contributing to the world its own unique and specific best, which is irreducible to the terms of the others ... I see no hope for the religious future of the world, if this ideal is not extended to the religious sphere also.[1]

In this view any exclusive religious claim will lead to conflict. D.G. Moses makes a response to Radhakrishnan point by point. He points out how this advaita view, which is claimed to be the universal Hindu view, tries to cover up the inner contradictions within Hindu religious traditions and the irreconcilable differences between religions. For him, 'it is not surprising that Prof. Radhakrishnan should fall into the pit of agnosticism while trying to avoid the pit of anthropomorphism.' He concludes his response by saying that 'If religions can reform themselves it can only be by the acceptance of some new truth, something greater than what they already contain.'[2] The possibility of religious reform and growth implies for him that all religions are not equally true.

William Earnest Hocking (1873-1966), an American philosopher of religion and critic of Christian mission, defines religion as 'a passion for righteousness, and for the spread of righteousness, conceived as a cosmic demand.' He proposes three ways to a world faith: the way of radical displacement, the way of synthesis and the way of reconception. D.G. Moses points out that the Christian missionary movement was not always for radical displacement of other religions and in many cases it was for fulfilment. On the way of synthesis, he says that there is the danger of compromise, of purely romantic appreciation, of moral and mental idleness and of sacrificing one's own central convictions for breadth of understanding. This is not to deny the growth of a religion by appropriating to itself whatever is valid in another religion.[3] According to Hocking the most promising and healthy way is the way of reconception, which will ultimately to a world faith. It promises an ever new discernment of the essence of religions and a new grasp of the eternal identity of faith. For Moses this assumption is 'both a historical and logical error' because there is no support for it from the comparative study of religion. He writes:

> The logical defect of this position consists in a failure to hold fast to the idea that religion claims truth and that therefore different degrees of it may be possessed by different forms of it. To say that

[1] Quoted, Moses, op. cit., 118.

[2] Ibid., 122.

[3] See Ibid., 136f.

> all that a particular religion needs to do in order to adjust itself to another religion is to reconceive its essence in the light of the new facts revealed by the other is to imply that all religions contain the truth inherently and essentially. This is the reverse of the fallacy of modernism, according to which all religions are only relatively true.[1]

He points out further that the way of reconception implies that there is no real growth in religious perception and new discovery of facts and meanings in an evolutionary process. And also it distorts concepts and personalities which have distinctive significance in their original setting. It is difficult too to apply criterion to the position of religions in an ascending order leading to one world faith.

Finally, D.G. Moses takes up the Dutch missionary and scholar of comparative religion Hendrik Kraemer (1888-1965)'s position of radical discontinuity between the *sui generis* revelation of Christ and other religious perceptions and experiences for a response. Kraemer's book *The Christian message in a Non-Christian World* influenced not only the third World Missionary Conference held in Tambaram (Chennai) in 1938 but also a generation of missionary theologians. Kraemer's 'Biblical Realism' presents the Christian message as something different from any philosophical ideas, religious experiences and ethical ideals. The revelation in Christ has nothing to do with the ultimate reality or the nature of the divine essence but with God's redemptive will towards humankind. The incarnation in a given moment of history still remains a mystery, 'an adorable mystery.' All other religions represent various human efforts to apprehend the totality of existence. Kramer admits God's shining through in a broken and trouble way which alone can account for the human urge for 'truth, beauty, goodness and holiness stirring in science, philosophy, art, religion' and the revelation in Christ challenges all subjectively-motivated perceptions and experiences and demands a response from all in faith.

D.G. Moses is not fully satisfied with Kraemer's understanding of faith. 'It is because all the emphasis is put on the *act* of revelation, without any attempt at an elaboration of its significance for life and thought.' The Christian faith is 'more than the mere occurrence of a historical revelation.' Moses affirms with A.G. Hogg, a Scottish educational missionary in Chennai, that Christianity is unique because of the unique content of the revelation to which it is called to bear witness. 'And that content must win conviction by its own direct appeal, by its illuminating and renovating power' (Hogg). It is not merely a conception of reality but a communication from God. If the content is taken seriously, similar content can be discovered in other religions also, 'and yet room can be left for their supplementation by the greater or fuller truth of the Christian faith.' Moses insists the continuing work of the Spirit enlightening hearts and minds will bring to understanding the hidden truths. He does not agree with Kramer's sharp

[1] Ibid., 140.

distinction between non-Christian religions and Christian faith. Those religions are not simply products of human effort to apprehend the totality of existence. 'The awareness of the Divine, in every religion, is not simply a soothing, comforting feeling, assuring the satisfaction of one's heart's desires, but also the experience of an objective claim for surrender.' The view of utter discontinuity leaves no room for recognising 'intuitions of mankind embodied in the non-Christian revelations as finding their fulfilment in the Christian faith.' And even with reference to the difference between the Old Testament and the New Testament, fulfilment does not mean natural development but a modification also. 'In other words, it is not contradictory to speak of a fulfilment by repudiation.' For Moses, while Kraemer's thesis states the problem of religious truth seriously, 'it answers it in too dogmatic a fashion. A reaction from extreme pragmatism and relativism makes him swing to the equally untenable extreme of anti-rational dogmatism.' The final words of Moses reflect his own position:

> We have not ... raised any question as to the possibility of a final or a unique faith. If the claim of religion to truth is taken seriously, one cannot but admit that religions can at least be evaluated in terms of more true and less true. But it does not fit the facts of the case to say that the relation between religions is one of utter 'discontinuity.'[1]

It is beyond the scope of Moses' study to suggest ways in which the 'continuity' exists and operates between religious traditions, to suggest criteria to evaluate the relative degree of truth and to deal with claims of particular religious traditions for finality, perfection and fulfilment. And in any event one may question whether it is possible to do this in the religious market place of competing and even contradicting truth-claims.

The product of a conference on the philosophy of religion held in Birmingham in 1970 was a book entitled *Truth and Dialogue: The Relationship between World Religions*. A group of distinguished scholars, philosophers and theologians of religion participated in the conference. One would expect that they would have answered the knotty question of competing and even contradicting truth-claims. But the truth is quite different. The papers suggest how varied and complicated a discussion on truth and religions can be. Every participant, in the absence of an agreed understanding of the boundaries of truth in relation to religions, presented their own convictions. For example, R.C. Zaehner, after illustrating many insights from Vedantic Hinduism, declared that the Holy Spirit who is building us all in secret into a 'spiritual house' 'is the inspiration of all religions and peculiar to none.'[2] Wilfred Cantwell Smith received particular attention from participants, as his novel ideas about religion, theology and faith were referred to either in

[1] Ibid., 159.

[2] R.C. Zaehner, "Religious Truth", in *Truth and Dialogue: The Relationship Between World Religions*, ed. by John Hick, London: Sheldon Press, 1974, 18.

agreement or disagreement. For Smith, truth is a humane, not an objective, concept. It does not lie in propositions. It is apprehended by persons, within history; yet insofar as it is true, it transcends history. It is therefore inherently a transcendent as well as human concept. It is this fact that allows a student of history to combine a basic respect for, and acceptance of others – persons, eras, cultures, groups – rather than an arrogant sitting in judgement on them, with a basic critical stance for oneself (for ourselves).[1] No religion, not even Christianity, is true absolutely, impersonally, statistically; rather it can *become true* if it is appropriated, internalised and lived out. Faith, for Smith, stands for the inherent human transcendence which is different from belief. However, his *Questions of Religious Truth,* the book which was repeatedly referred to at this conference, does not give an answer convincing to all. The dynamic and complex ways in which religious traditions develop, the different ways they ignite and nurture the 'faith' and the striking differences in their understanding of the term 'truth' call for more thorough study and discussion than is available in his book or in the conference papers. Interestingly, in his own presentation to the conference, which was on 'A Human View of Truth', after affirming his view that the locus or central locus of truth is human persons, Smith explains the three Arabic terms for truth popular in Islam. They stand for 'the truth of things', 'the truth of persons' and 'the truth of statements.' The first one 'is a term par excellence of God. In fact it refers absolutely to Him, and indeed *al-Haqq* is a name of God not merely in the sense of an attribute but of a denotation. *Huwa al-Haqq*: He is reality as such. Yet every other thing that is genuine is also *haqq* – and some of the mystics went on to say – is therefore divine. Yet the word means reality first, and then God, for those who equate him with reality.'[2] The other terms stand for an honest living and correct knowledge of things. However, what is missing from this discussion is the mention of the source of truth or knowing, which is for Muslims the decisive divine revelation through Mohammed, and the question of how Muslims perceive their truth and the truths in other religions.

Kenneth Cragg, in his article on 'Islam on Incarnation' points out how what is a fundamental truth for Christians can be an unforgivable sin for Muslims. This is said with reference to associating Jesus with God as the Son of God or the incarnation of God, which is 'Islamically impossible.' However, he shows that Muslims and Christians have much in common to explore, particularly regarding divinity in relation to the greatness of God and the greatness of humanity.

Ninian Smart's contribution criticises Cantwell Smith's appeal to faith and God as a 'simplistic attempt to resolve the question of truth.' For him religion should be taken in all its dimensions – ritual, mythical, social, ethical, doctrinal and experiential. If the meaning and end of religion is faith and God then, he argues, Buddhism is excluded from the list of religions. He concludes his paper

---

[1] See W. C. Smith, *Towards a World Theology*, 190.

[2] Ibid., 22.

on 'Truth and Religions' by stating: 'It seems that there is still unclarity about the threefold distinction between Christian theology, philosophy, and the scientific study of religion. This is one reason why there is not a sharp view of the problems about the criteria of religious truth.'[1] Since the other presentations deal with different aspects of religion or one aspect of a particular religion, a clarity in this regard could not be achieved.

John Hick, the organiser of the conference, evaluated the outcome of the conference in his own terms and reinforced his own position. As we have acknowledged in the first chapter, he defines religion as a historical-cultural phenomenon. The intersections of 'divine grace, divine initiative, divine truth, with human faith, human response, human enlightenment' in different moments and places resulted in the emergence of religions which have contributed to the development different cultures around the world. He writes:

> But now that the world has become a communicational unity we are moving into a new situation in which it becomes proper for religious thinking to transcend these cultural-historical boundaries. Instead of asking, which religion is true … we can see these religions as historic streams of human life, each of which may be built partly upon truth and partly upon error. Instead then of asking whether a religion, as such, is true in some absolute sense, we are free to recognize religious truth, wherever it is evident, within all man's cultures and civilization.[2]

Hick does not here provide a criterion to distinguish between truth and error, a means whereby 'to recognise religious truth, wherever it is evident', and as we have already noted, what is truth for one religion is error for another. And also in his thinking Christianity is associated with European culture. Is the fact of 25 million Christians living in 'Hindu India', being part of the culture yet trying to transform it, then an aberration or an accident? Many such questions can be asked from the perspective of the 'Third Church', which is numerically bigger than the First and Second Churches of Europe and America.

Hick gives no room for questions as how to identify religious truth in his scheme of religious pluralism. He takes a great leap to proclaim the Hindu slogan of 'One Truth – Many Religions' to which we will return. Like Hocking and Radhakrishnan he envisages the coming closer of religions through co-operation and interpenetration which may lead to one faith just like one world. He tries to minimise the difference between the Hindu belief in the transmigration of souls and one particular Christian view about the transforming stages of the soul after death. And despite different forms of cultic life and theological frameworks, he says that 'we may expect the different world faiths to continue as religious-

---

[1] Ibid., 58.

[2] Ibid., 142.

cultural phenomena, though phenomena that are increasingly interpenetrating one another. The relation between them will then be somewhat like that now obtaining between the different denominations of Christianity in this country.'[1] Hick held this position until the end of his life and elaborated it in his writings since the 1970 conference. Those who take the concrete reality very seriously in their pursuit of truth may have sufficient reason to view such vision as exposing a wishful thinking which is as superficial as shallow.

One Truth – Many Religions?

We have already noted more than once the Rigvedic verse 'Truth is One and the wise call in different names.' This verse is taken as a basis for the most popular slogan with regard to religious pluralism in India from where it has spread abroad. Ordinary people, politicians and philosophers thrive on this verse when they have to speak about the fact of religious plurality. Very often, rural masses worshipping in Hindu shrines and temples are interviewed by journalists for radio and television programmes. To the question about worshipping different gods and goddesses of their choice, the most usual answer is 'one God or truth and many forms or names.' And there is no other scriptural verse with which politicians are more familiar with than the above Vedic verse. They use it as a foundation for the secular principle of Hinduism. One famous example is the Congress president quoting it in the face of criticism that she is a Christian and a foreigner and therefore is not eligible to become the prime minister of India.[2] Almost all Hindu speakers in a meeting about interreligious dialogue would quote this verse. Outside India, John Hick stands out as the one who is never tired of quoting this verse in support of his 'Copernican revolution in the theology of religions.' He also quotes from the Bhagavad Gita, where one verse has Krishna saying that 'In whatever way people identify with me, in the same way do I carry out their desires. People pursue my path in all ways' (4.11). These verses have inspired Hick to declare the following:

> Now the possibility, indeed the probability, that we have to seriously consider is that many different accounts of the divine reality may be true, though all expressed in imperfect human analogies, but that none is 'the truth, the whole truth, and nothing but the truth.' May it be that the different concepts of God, as Jahweh, Allah, Krishna, Param Atma, Holy Trinity, and so on; and likewise the different concepts of the hidden structure of reality, as the eternal emanation of Brahman or as an immense cosmic process culminating in nirvana, are all images of the divine, each expressing some aspect or range of all aspects and

---

[1] Ibid., 152.

[2] "Sonia's Conversion" which is defined as "By stressing Hindu values the Congress president is enhancing both personal acceptability and party appeal", *India Today International*, 1 Feb., 1999.

yet none by itself fully and exhaustively corresponding to the infinite nature of the ultimate reality?[1]

We have already clarified that the textual context of the above Rigvedic verse is a bird-shaped altar of a ritual ceremony. Western scholars often fall into shortcomings when they rely on interpretations of the religious community concerned but not being able to read the original texts.

The Vedic association of truth with power-engendering sacrifice continues in the Upanishads. For example, the famous prayer starting with the words 'Lead me from untruth to truth' (*Bruhad-aranyaka Upanishad* I.3.28) is said in the context of sacrifice by the one on whose behalf the sacrifice is made. Studies on the context and meaning of this prayer show that there is no reason to take it beyond what the sacrifice was believed to bring to the sacrificer.[2] This is not to deny that some Upanishadic texts speak of Brahman as the one, All-inclusive Supreme Self. While the Gita reduces Brahman to a mental state of equanimity, it tries to synthesise different 'religious paths' which were competing with each other. Radhakrishnan unusually makes a reference to history. He points out that the editors of the epic *Mahabharata,* of which the Gita is a section, 'felt that some popular hero must be made the rallying centre to counteract the mighty influence of the heretical sects. The figure of Krishna was ready to hand.'[3] Hence, Krishna claims all different approaches (without naming them) finally lead to him.

Focusing on one rallying centre as contextual necessity may cover up the dynamic dialogical process that has been taking place within the Indian religious traditions. For example, those belonging to the Saiva tradition are not able to appreciate Krishna as the ultimate point of all religious paths. Although one can argue that Krishna here represents the Supreme God, the Saivas have difficulty accepting this because according to their position God cannot take a human form for this would involve undergoing life controlled by the effect of actions in a previous birth. More illustrations can be given from other Indian traditions. The Buddhists and Jains rejected the Vedic worldview centred around sacrifice. At a time of revival and amalgamation, the brahmanic tradition incorporated some of their values and even went to the extent of taking their worst critic, the Buddha, as one of the *avatars* (descents) of the Lord Vishnu. When the six orthodox schools of Hindu philosophy were developed they all claimed to be based on Vedic authority. But they differed amongst themselves over identifying the constituent elements of the universe and the process of creation, recreation and liberation. Within the school of Vedanta there emerged different sub-schools holding different views

---

[1] John Hick, *God and the Universe of Faiths*, London: Macmillan, 1973, 140.

[2] E.g. See G. Gispert-Sauch, "An Inquiry into the Upanishadic Prayer: From the Unreal Lead Me to the Real…", in *Dialogue in Action*, ed. by Thunberg and others, 213.

[3] S. Radhakrishnan, *The Philosophy of the Upanishads*, London: George Allen & Unwin, 1924, 494f.

about God or the Reality and his relationship to the world and human beings. While they rejected the Buddhist and other views from outside the tradition, they also rejected or corrected certain views within. And indeed there is much scope for continuing such dialogue, though preferably without the polemics. But the Rigvedic slogan discussed above is the greatest hindrance to such a creative dialogue. It discourages rigorous thinking, discussing and comparing, and instead what is perpetuated is intra-Hindu and interfaith ignorance. For example, J.A.T. Robinson's *Truth is Two-Eyed* takes only the debate on the personal and absolute nature of God or Reality within the Vedantic and neo-Vedantic traditions, thereby ignoring the experiences and perceptions of the majority of Hindus. While the Saivas would point to the Three-Eyed Siva as the Supreme, those who repeat the slogan of 'one truth – many religions' would go for a many-eyed truth. Outsiders can ask if all eyes have their equal vision and clear focus!

Being Open to the Unfolding of Truth

As the above discussion indicates, the question of Truth is a complex one. It is not a question for people like Pilate. It requires serious engagement, commitment and openness. D.G. Moses is mistaken in his view that unlike in science, philosophy and art there is commitment in religion, for in any field the sincere desire for knowledge requires serious engagement and commitment. And it is a striking fact that religion has more nominal adherents or misguided ones than any other field. At the same time religion represents an important dimension in human life which has enduring value despite several challenges raised against it in history. Further, religion relates to other areas of life at different levels and degrees depending on the case of a particular religious tradition, its environment and development. For example, in India philosophy from the beginning philosophy is based on religion whereas in the West philosophy and theology are separate and distinct. The challenge of science, history and the use of art is almost the same for both contexts. As newer challenges continue to appear, perhaps it is time for launching an integrative approach to understanding and realising the Truth involving different areas of inquiry.

Where there is openness there is humility and the recognition of limitations. We will illustrate this from the field of science. In his study of the nature and structure of scientific revolutions in which he recognises paradigm shifts requiring a conversion on the part of scientists, Thomas Kuhn mentions 'truth' in passing. With reference to the effectiveness and efficiency of electrical research he quotes Francis Bacon's methodological dictum: 'Truth emerges more readily from error than from confusion.'[1] In paradigm shifts, however, as he points out, truth need not necessarily emerge from confusion at all. Much depends on the 'the manner in which a particular set of shared values interacts with the particular experiences

[1] Thomas Kuhn, *The Structure of Scientific Revolutions*, Chicago: The University of Chicago Press, 1970, 18.

shared by a community of specialists to ensure that most members of the group will ultimately find one set of arguments rather than another decisive.' Those who embrace a new paradigm do so, notes Kuhn, in defiance of the evidence provided by problem-solving. They must have 'faith that the new paradigm will succeed with the many large problems that confront it, knowing only the older paradigm has failed with a few. A decision of that kind can only be made on faith.' Nevertheless, on the whole, Kuhn observes:

> In the sciences there need not be progress of another sort. We may, to be more precise, have to relinquish the notion, explicit or implicit, that changes of paradigm carry scientists and those who learn from them closer and closer to the truth.[1]

This is of course not ultimate truth but scientific truth which primarily saves scientists from having to work with incompatible rules for a while. However tedious and frustrating the process, when problem-solving rules are presented before them they take a leap in faith and relish on the excitement.

Unfortunately, this kind of exploratory risk taking does not easily happen in the world of religions in which often stubbornness and arrogance dominate. It is absurd to claim that religion has the answer for all the problems facing the nature, history and human life. From the primitive beginnings to the post-modern stage changes and developments in every field are incredible whether we call them evolution or revolution. It is true that religion has a unique role to play in the area of the real structure and nature and the ultimate meaning and goal of human life. At the same time honesty requires every religious person to admit that there are many problems which remain unsolved, not the least those related to the relationship between God or Reality and nature, history and human life. There is no single meaning for 'meaning' either as we have already demonstrated. Such acknowledgement need not lead to a permanent state of scepticism and speculation, but it can help to understand faith and religious commitment in a new way.

Those who are concerned about the startling 'truths' of the world around rightly refuse to allow the question of Truth to be hijacked by philosophers and scholars. They wish to make a distinction between plurality and downright contradiction. Different colours, tastes and cultural practices are matters of plurality. But socio-economic discrimination and struggles against unjust powers are matters of contradiction. Likewise, there are overlapping beliefs and practices in different religions or different traditions, sects and denominations which signify plurality. But there are also irreconcilable differences and incompatible elements among them. For example, it is not easy to reconcile the belief in the transmigration of souls and the allied idea of the chain of births and deaths

---

[1] Ibid., 170.

which is fundamental to the Indian religious traditions. Those with a sense of urgency try to transform Indian society which is marred by massive poverty, illiteracy and corruption find notions of karma and fate as great hindrance. Ideas of predestination and divine will in Islam and Christianity are not far from them. It is therefore proper to ask the question about the relationship between some of the most ancient traditions of spirituality that flourished in India and the fact of nearly half of one and quarter billion Indian people today are illiterates living below the poverty line. It is often the case that in the name of plurality such contradictions are covered up in the name of plurality, rainbow, different streams to the sea, different paths to the hilltop and different photographs of the sun. Those in other religious traditions who strictly hold the sovereign will or predetermination of God yet speaking of change and judgement face the same challenge. No religion or religious truth is credible if it does not try to tackle the contradictions in society. Perhaps there must develop a healthy competition between religious communities in their proportionate efforts to transform their socio-economic situation which can be an authentic test for the validity of what they call 'truth.'

Truth is not simply a subjective category or a personal quest, and it demands a right approach to history and society too. To give one more example from the Indian scene, the 'Great Soul' (*Mahatma*) Gandhi is well known for his 'truth force' (*satyagraha*) which influenced numerous people all over the world. He is acclaimed as an incarnation of God by many Indians; as a modern saint not only in India but also abroad.[1] Gandhi calls his own life and career 'experiments with Truth.' He was committed always to speaking with conviction and yet being open to the unfolding of Truth which for him was God. His 'rock-like integrity' and courageous actions for setting oppressed people and his country free are well known. He did not separate his 'experiments with Truth' from his religious convictions, and the last word on his lips was the name of Ram, one of the incarnations of Vishnu. But at the same time Gandhi's perception of the history and society of India, which was decisively shaped by brahmanic Hinduism, is found to be defective. While he denounced untouchability as a crime against God and humanity, he justified the caste system which is inseparable from the idea of untouchability and which continues even today. The Dalits (outcast, untouchable and downtrodden) who fight for their rights and for redressal view Gandhi as not genuine in this matter. They have many stories to point this out, particularly about his controversy and conflict with great Dalit leader B.R. Ambedkar who later with more that 35,000 of his followers publicly denounced brahmanic-caste-ridden Hinduism and joined the Buddhist movement as part of a 'pursuit of Truth.' And it is not surprising that the Dalits point out other 'Great Souls' whose pursuit ran counter to that which Gandhi defended. For instance, Mahatma Phule organised in 1873 the *Satyashodhak Samaj* (Society for the Search for Truth) with a view

---

[1] See John Hick, *The Fifth Dimension*, Oxford: Oneworld Publications, 1999, 18.

to save 'the lower castes from the hypocritical Brahmans and their opportunistic scriptures.'[1] Some may find this example not relevant to the quest for Truth, but for those who take the actual reality around them seriously, such 'truths' are inseparable from the 'Truth.'

Finally, for Christians it is important to know that Truth for them is not simple and abstract but it is a 'Truth of many truths' which provide insights into a particular vision, tradition and commitment. They should share the Hebrew wisdom that 'There are things hidden, and they belong to the Lord our God, but what is revealed belongs to us and our children for ever; it is for us to observe all that is prescribed in this law' (Deut. 29:29). It is significant to note that in the whole of the Hebrew scripture God's truth is revealed in the covenant and law of justice, and what is expected of his people is truthfulness, steadfastness and stability. In the New Testament, the term 'truth' occurs very rarely in the Synoptic Gospels and only in the sense of actual fact and telling the truth. It is in John's Gospel that it occurs more times and carries theological meaning. Presumably, John's readers were familiar with the term and its various meanings. And again the dialogical context and different senses in which the term is used should not be forgotten. Ultimately, grace and truth were revealed by the incarnation of the eternal Word (1: 14, 17). But while this truth signifies a new dimension in the history of salvation, it never makes the Hebrew truth obsolete or an error. We hear the Hebrew tone clearly when Jesus says to the Jews that 'If you stand by my teaching, you are truly my disciples; you will know the truth, and the truth will set you free' (8:31f). Knowing the truth in this way will continue and when the Spirit of Truth comes he will guide them into all truth (16:13). In a context of dialogue in the midst of many claims for truth Jesus said 'I am the truth' (14:6). In his reply to Pilate his language changed slightly: 'My task is to bear witness to the truth' (18:37). Here truth does not seem to be a capsule of an abstract but openness to the unfolding of what God is doing in individual lives and history. For Christians, not only Jesus' words themselves are significant, but also what his disciples and, through them, further disciples perceived in his death and resurrection. For apostles like Paul the whole truth of God and his purpose for humanity was revealed in this act which is historically decisive and universally significant.

Christian truth is located not in a proposition but in a story, and in interfaith dialogue it is important to tell the story, the whole story, and nothing but the story. Given the history of Christian thought, this story has been often buried under the rubble of endless debates on the formulations of faith and doctrines which appear confusing the insiders (hence denominations and sectarianism) and mystifying to outsiders. The scientific and critical studies of the Bible with hyper-criticism often miss the kernel of this story. 'Truth is stranger than it used to be' is the title

[1] Quoted, John Webster, *The Dalit Christians: A History*, Delhi: ISPCK, 1994, 32.

of a recent book.[1] The authors try to recover the narrative of the biblical story and its appeal to the crises of the modern age. However, the story is not presented so dynamically with all its profound insights as to challenge the different claims of truth and make it relevant to those who struggle with the truths of life. Seen in an interfaith light one can miss those profound insights which are obscured by the myths, tales, ritual prescriptions and devotional expressions which are comparable to such materials in other scriptures. The primary insight of the story is about a God with an enigmatic name (Yahweh) and a liberating presence choosing a tiny nomadic community to be the instrument for revealing his nature and will for the whole world. After redeeming them from social slavery he became their intimate partner, journeying with them, guiding them and criticising them when they went wrong. He balanced judgement and condemnation with hope and mercy, and awesome transcendence with a meek human figure who expressed his heart. Jesus Christ was the historical embodiment of this figure whose life, death and resurrection created a new community and new moral force. This community projected Jesus not only as Lord, Christ and Saviour through confession, but also became the rallying point of all humans and the whole world. Just like God his Father, Jesus the human one was giving solidarity with the victims of all sorts of injustice. As the last book of the Bible describes him, he is a vulnerable Lamb with the perfect authority characterised by love, knocking on every one's door but never breaking in. Christians are committed to telling this story not only by words, but more effectively by creating a community of collective charisma which can move on in solidarity with the victims and vulnerable in society. The stories that people of other faiths have may coincide with these insights at different levels and degrees or even contradict them. There is no place for arrogance in this communication because Christians are supposed to speak 'the truth in love.' The Church which is not open to the unfolding truth and change finds its worship, prayers and missionary outreach become hypocritical and deceptive. Moreover, where there is no love there is no truth and that is true of interfaith dialogue also.

Concluding Remarks

Traditionally, study of religion has carefully avoided the question of truth, particularly the ultimate nature and value of human life and history. When phenomenology stressed a value-free perception and interpretation of the empirical data the question of truth was further avoided. But in due course there was difference of opinion about ascertaining factual truth and assessing religious visions of ultimate truth. The question, 'what is truth?' cannot be given a simple and straightforward answer as it is complex with many dimensions just as religion is. It is spoken in terms of 'different species of religious truth' with recognition of different meanings in distinctive realms. While philosophical truth is animated by

[1] J. Richard Middleton & Brian Walsh, *Truth is Stranger Than it Used to Be: Biblical Faith in a Postmodern Age*, London: SPCK, 1995.

intellectual curiosity, religious truth extends its concern to areas such as art and experience. There have been figures like Tagore who could integrate philosophy, art, religion and spirituality. The religions which celebrate certain revelations gain additional insights to gain comprehensive meaning in life although the ways in which meaning is articulated and lived out are different.

The idea of self-authentication with the help of some inner testimony (e.g. Spirit) assists in the process of choosing from different images or visions of God or supreme reality. Further, religious truth expresses various aspects of human experience: inner stability and purity, personal character with ethical values, valuation and evaluation of real and unreal, genuine and deceptive, and so on. Across the religious traditions, three aspects of religious truth are commonly accepted: the character of accurate knowing, the nature of reality known and the formation of value as the power to actualise this reality in authentic living. The final achievement is the greatest wellbeing possible which is named as salvation, liberation etc. Truth is often used in interfaith dialogue as well, but different terms and definitions used, including God and Reality, present a complex picture. Thus in Hinduism, for example, a ritual altar, supreme Brahman, incarnation of a particular God (Vishnu) or the God himself (Siva) is called truth. Again there was fierce debate within the Vedantic tradition about the nature of Brahman or God. Sometimes even before assessing what is obvious or revealed recourse is made to a mysterious Mystery. What is desired is being clear about what is known and open to the unfolding truth in future, though such position may contradict that in which what is known is absolute and unchangeable truth.

Chapter 9

Religious Pluralism and Dialogue

Is Study of Religion only Academic?

Normally those who are engaged in the scientific study of religion with different labels and methods of approach do not bother about the concept of religious pluralism and the practical side of dialogue. In the same way many theologians of religious pluralism and practitioners of interreligious dialogue do not dare to appropriate the fruits of the comparative study of religion. And those who resorted to the mystic path of religious experience do not think that study of religion and practice of dialogue have anything to with their pursuit. Of course there are exceptions. In any case, Eric Sharpe, one of the early writers on comparative religion, has devoted three chapters: 'Religion, Comparative and Absolute', 'Toward a Dialogue of Religions?' and 'Twenty Years of International Debate.'[1]

Recognizing the western Church's preoccupation with the challenges of science (e.g. theory of evolution), secularization and world events like the World Parliament of Religions, Sharpe gives a useful outline of missionary encounters with other religions and a group of European theologians who reflected on other religions from the Christian theological perspective. To compliment Sharpe, forty years later Kenneth Cracknell brought out his resourceful book *Justice, Courtesy and Love: Theologians and Missionaries Encountering World Religions, 1846-1914.*[2] Put together, these and a few other studies, made an epoch about the Christian attitude to people of other religions. The five theologians and eight missionaries introduced by Cracknell overlap with those treated by Sharpe, but there are many more.

---

[1] E.J. Sharpe, *Comparative Religion,* 144-171, 251-293.

[2] London: Epworth Press, 1995.

The account of missionary encounters suggests a kind of intellectual and theological conversion. They went with a definite mandate to take the gospel of light to heathenish darkness. But those who 'dared to know' and who were open to change on the basis of what they saw were bold enough to change their opinion about other religions and some of their studies and views irritated their patrons at home. The words 'Justice, Courtesy and Love' was suggested by a missionary as marks of Christian approach to people of other religions. He and others used words like broken lights, scattered seeds, fruits of the Holy Spirit, Christ as the crown or fulfillment of other religions or remains hidden or unknown in them. These and more ideas were elaborated by the theologians. The missionary and theological thinking influenced the first World Missionary Conference, Edinburgh, 1910. Although, the empire mentality was betrayed in their renewed agenda of 'evangelizing the whole world within this generation' The *Missionary Message to Non-Christian Religions* implied a radical change in missionary attitude and the attitude of the younger churches toward their neighbours of other religions.

Soon, taken from the World Parliament of Religions, the fascinating slogan of 'One God and One Humanity' was spread through countrywide conference. It was interrupted by the World War II and resumed subsequently. Sharpe quotes Jabez T. Sunderland who had the responsibility of arranging the conferences in Asia:

> Believing that there is one God over all the world, and that all religions contain truths that are of vital and prominent importance to men, representatives of all faiths were invited to come together to confer with one another as brothers, on the broad basis of the Universal Fatherhood of God and the Universal Brotherhood of Man.[1]

More specifically, the conferences were expected to promote acquaintance between adherents of different religious traditions, to stress the universal elements of all religions and try to create in all the religions 'the conviction that they have a great work to do together for the moral uplift of the world.'[2] Sunderland's appeal had a positive response in India where, for example, the two disciples of the great sage Ramakrishna, Keshab Chandrasen and Swami Vivekananda, preached the unity of the divine and humankind, and later S. Radhakrishnan developed the idea of one World Culture. But whether these ideas were experimented in caste ridden and poverty-stricken India is a different question. Moreover, we should mention that though suggested, there was no sign of scholars of the scientific study of religion with their organs such as the 'International Association of the History of Religions' promoting interreligious dialogue. There are voices for an

[1] Sharpe, op. cit., 253.

[2] Ibid.

integrated approach. For example, E.O. James, a British anthropologist, wrote in the first issue of *Numen*, the journal of IAHR in 1954:

> The study of religion, be it for academic purposes, as a way of life, or in the interests of inter-religious understanding and international peace, demands both a historical and scientific approach and a theological and philosophical evaluation, it is to be understood in its essential nature and ever-developing content, and its foundations are to be well and truly laid.[1]

W.E. Hocking came with the idea of a 'Rethinking Mission' and since 1971 there has been a programme on interreligious relations at the World Council of Churches. Again it is to be asked if it takes seriously the current trends and fruits of the academic study of religion.

It is important to note that in the process of the above developments the word 'Faith' came to be used as interchangeable to religion. For example, a 'Fellowship of Faiths' was formed in 1918 with a view to promote spiritual unity and it was reconfigured as the 'World Fellowship of Faiths' in 1923. Eric Sharpe's book of 1977 on Christian attitudes to Hinduism in the nineteenth and twentieth centuries was titled *Faith Meets Faith.*[2] Since then Orbis, Maryknoll has been publishing a series on this general title. In the fifth assembly of the WCC Nairobi 1975 dialogue was presented in the general assembly for the first time. It fired a controversy as mainly the Scandinavian delegates threatened the continuation of dialogue as it appeared to compromise on Christian truth and betray the mission. Following recommendations, a consultation was held in Chiang Mai in 1977. The intense reflections on dialogue in community by a group over eighty five delegates from all over the ecumenical movement was published with the titles *Faith in the Midst of Faiths*[3] and it was taken from the presentation of an Indian Evangelist (Paul Sudhakar). The word 'faith' became so popular that guide books such as *A Global Guide to Interfaith: Reflections from around the World* appeared.[4] Does 'faith', which has a strong Christian connotation, clarify the matter better than 'religion'? Knowing the difficulties of defining these two terms it seems to be proper to leave them for sharing and expounding in an actual context of dialogue.

Paradigms of Religious Pluralism – An Outline[5]

Recognizing a Fact: Plurality as a matter of fact or pluralism as a concept is both fascinating and puzzling. Whether we like it or not we live in a pluralistic

---

[1] James, "The History, Science and Comparative Study of Religion", *Numen,* No. 1, 1954, 105.

[2] London: SCM Press, 1977.

[3] Ed. by S.J Samartha, Geneva: WCC, 1977.

[4] Ed. by Sandy & Jael Bharat, Winchester: O Books, 2007.

[5] This is slightly the modified version of the following: I. Selvanayagam, "Paradigms of Religious Pluralism: A Clarification", *Ariopagus: Journal of the Association of Faculty for*

world. Most fundamentally there is plurality or diversity in nature with different landscapes, waterways, fauna and flora and so on. All these constitute an integrated whole called the universe. Human beings are part of it. Then take a human person who carries within her a bundle of diversity with different limbs, joints, tissues, vessels, nerves, pipelines, liquids etc. There are also non-material factors endowed in human personality such as soul or spirit or life-force, feelings, emotions, conscience, volitions, aptitudes, attitudes and characteristics. Naming each of them and defining the inter-connections and connections with the body are far more difficult than analyzing the human anatomy. The fundamental and necessary question is if there can be plurality with integration and integrity. Without this question, the tense and seemingly unsolvable questions about the nature of unity we seek and the contradictions that can mar it will continue.

We live in a religiously pluralistic world. Some of us may wish there had been only one religion, one culture and one language! Though things would have been simple and straight forward, others would imagine that then life would have been unbearably boring and un-motivating. Though the human body is understood variously in different religious traditions it is the non-material or 'spiritual' factors that concern us most in thinking about and understanding religion and religions. If there is one supreme power or intelligent designer behind all religions what sort of purpose did s/he have in mind? Was there a divine intention to test people's ability to choose the best?

The Shaky Triple Model: A Christian approach to religions or religious communities has not been simple and straightforward. The reason is that, as has been amply clear, religious life is 'immensely complex and immeasurably varied' (Lott), and one approach is not adequate. While there is commonality and mutual resemblance, there are irreconcilable differences and even contradictions between religions. Traditionally, the triple model of exclusivism, inclusivism and pluralism has been suggested and repeated. I contend that this is simplistic, misleading and even confusing. Different strands within each of these models are not adequately recognized. For example, exclusivism is based on either having chosen the best or the only one as valid. But in Christian terms, condemning others as heathens and consigning them to hell fire is one form of exclusivism. To claim that there is no continuity between God's revelation in Jesus Christ and other religions, is entirely different. There is a sense in believing that Christian faith is distinctive with its own visions, traditions, values, even though it has common roots with Judaism and later Islam and maintained a special relationship with both. One may raise the question whether in the context of religious plurality there can be a committed adherence to one particular religion or sect within that religion without having some kind of exclusivism.

Inclusivism also has many strands. Positioning itself in one framework, it incorporates or absorbs into this different religious visions and experiences.

Religion, Philosophy and Culture, Vol. 1, 2011, 75-84.

It may assign different rungs on a spiritual ladder to other traditions while claiming one's own as the top rung or crown. It may incorporate other positions by including them within the canvas of cosmic and eternal Word or Christ as present yet unknown in other traditions or as touching the lives of others who remain anonymous Christians; or as the Holy Spirit inspiring and guiding all those genuinely religious, there being a special focus on Christ in her work; or as the reign of God whose trajectory draws all the noble and good values and experiences of others; and so on.

Arguably, inclusivism is also a form of exclusivism as long as it holds one's own religious category as the base, core or cover and inclusive framework of all religious experiences and ethical values. At this juncture it is important to realize that Hindus and Muslims, for example, also have exclusive and inclusive positions. In Hindu tradition, for instance, there is ritual and cognitive purity exclusively maintained by a particular caste. There are also poet-saints of the bhakti traditions who openly affirm that theirs (Siva, Krishna etc.) is the only Supreme and they would not dare to pronounce the name of another deity. Then there is the Vedantic category of Brahman, the source and substratum of all religious experiences, and attaining oneness with whom represents the top rung in the spiritual ladder or crown of all religious experiences. In a different way Islam is also inclusive in the sense that it is open to all those religious who surrender to one God, but exclusive when it affirms Prophet Mohammed as the seal of all prophets and the Holy Qur'an the only infallible scripture.

Pluralism too has different strands or paradigms. To enumerate and explain these is the main purpose of this section. Before I do so, an explanatory note is in order. We tend to recognize those paradigms which are spoken or written. Yet, there is in religious experience that which is ineffable Mystery and which some say should be the starting point in the journey of spiritual life. Relatedly, dialogue should take place in the 'cave of heart' (Abhishiktananda). To speak is to spoil. The Buddha's famous moment of silence in response to a question about the nature of nirvana also comes close to this. One may argue that only those who are not confident about the validity of their religious path and those who are unwilling to recognize the distinctive visions and experience of others take refuge in the mysterious. At the same time we have to acknowledge that there are a few who hold the view that we start with Mystery and end in Mystery and in between we do speak and do listen. In any case, in the following section we identify ***eight*** strands of pluralism which we can call paradigms. They include not only the pluralistic positions with different names taken by Christian scholars/theologians to solve the problem of 'One and many' but also those suggested in the phenomenological study of religion as well as recent affirmations of Hindus and others that different gods, goddesses and spirits exist simultaneously. As in the case of paradigms in other disciplines there are overlaps in the paradigms of religious pluralism as well. And we have space here only to mention each one with a short explanation giving the name(s) of its major proponents.

1. ***Essentialist Pluralism*:** The early phenomenological school, as we have seen, identified what appeared to them as the essence of religion behind and beneath its various manifestations. However, they were not unanimous about the true essence and in naming it. For example, Van der Leew saw sacred power (*mana*) as the essence. For Frederick Heiler it was prayer, and for Rudolf Otto the sense of holy which he called *mysterium tremendum et fascinans*. It is typical of Hindu thinkers to use the word 'essence' without explaining. Probably assertion of one essence or one truth is to counter the onslaught of the Christian and Muslim claim that there is only one God, one faith and one scripture. In any case this truth was either relativised within the Hindu tradition or denied by Buddhist, Jaina and other renouncer traditions. Such perceptions and counter perceptions would challenge those who declare without much thought that 'essentially all religions are the same.'

2. ***Monotheistic Pluralism*:** John Hick's book *God and the Universe of Faiths* (1973) expounded the relationship between one God and many religions in terms of equality and familial resemblance. Moving away from the Christ-centre towards God-centre he called it the 'Copernican Revolution in theology of religions.' Of course he was not aware that in Hindu India this was an old story. The slogan 'one truth-many religions' has been repeated by Hindus of all kinds, from university professors to illiterate persons. Julius Lipner, in his thorough study of *Hindus* (2010), suggests 'polycentric monotheism', illustrating this with the image of a banyan tree. Going back to the position of Hick, his God-language was contested as it was not applicable to non-theistic traditions such as Buddhism and Jainism. Consequently, he and his American colleague Wilfred Cantwell Smith modified and used terms such as Truth and Faith to indicate religions' centre or commonality. The fact of fierce debates in the past, not only on God in relation to the universe and humans but also on Truth, between Hindu and Buddhist schools of thought as well as between different Hindu devotional traditions, between orthodox philosophical systems, and between Vedantic schools, would render their position naïve and superficial.

3. ***Relativist Pluralism*:** This is often confused with the above. According to this position every religion is partial and incomplete possessing one or two aspects of the whole. All such partial perceptions must be put together to get the whole. The usual example that comes from the Buddhist (some say Jaina) folklore is that a king asked six blind men to feel an elephant and each, feeling just one part of the animal, came up with different answers: that the elephant was a pillar, a wall and so on. Though an example has a limited meaning and particular focus, it has been challenged by the following questions: who is the king today who is able to see the whole? What is the guarantee that all religious 'blindness' will feel the same reality? If the different perceptions do not match each other, what would be

the overarching vision able to contain them? More problematic in this position is that it denies reality to the vision of devotees who are convinced that their vision of God or Truth is whole and for which they would sacrifice anything, even their life. They have not only searched but perhaps have also found, and what they have found seems to them quite complete. Why should we think there is some Olympian height from which we can have a condescending view of all religions?

4. ***Teleological Pluralism*:** Krishna in the Gita says that whichever way people follow they finally come to him. From a historical perspective such an all-embracing position was greatly needed in a context of explosive religious contests. As we discussed earlier, when many traditions were in conflict the new figure Krishna, a hero and leader coming from the Bhagavata tradition, from a shepherd community, was readily available at hand as a rallying centre. Not without some tension he was now incorporated into the Brahmanic fold, and became the goal of different religious pathways. Those who hold this view do not bother about starting points or spiritual means to attain the goal. Just like different pathways go to the same hilltop and streams join the sea different religious persons go to the same goal. Though the goal is here Krishna, made into one of the avatars of Vishnu, he has to be taken as the supreme Lord of all. This is difficult not only for non-Hindus but also for sects within the Hindu fold. For example, a Saiva devotee will never stomach the idea that she will go to someone other than her beloved Siva.

5. ***Parallel Pluralism*:** Mark Heim, an American theologian, after studying religious traditions as to their different starting points and goals, has suggested this model. He finds views of salvation and truth to be plural and they do not match. Therefore what is to be affirmed is that different religions represent different paradigms and parallel pathways that lead to different goals. Perhaps there is divine generosity evident. However, there are at least two problems in this model. One is that it does not give due weight to the historical connections between religious traditions. Thus, Judaism, Christianity, Islam have integral connections as well as new or distinctive horizons. The connections between the Indian religious traditions are very obvious; so also the connection of Sikhism with both Islam and Hinduism. The other is that it hardly gives any motivation for interfaith dialogue unless those travelling on these parallel paths find talking to others indispensable and even at some point feel their path has become drudgery and convert to other paths.

6. ***Ethical Pluralism*:** Hans Küng popularized the idea of global ethics in the early nineties. As noted earlier, his starting point is that there is no peace in the world without peace between religions, and no peace between religions without interfaith dialogue. While the emphasis is valid and noble, he has been criticized from different perspectives. First, he has not analysed concrete situations of interreligious conflicts to ascertain whether religion has been causative or instrumental. There are studies which suggest that religion is often taken merely

as a cover to achieve vested interests. Also, compared to documents such as the Magna Carta or the Universal Declaration of Human Rights by the UN, the articles of which have been subsequently elaborated and modified and used in international treatises, regional human rights instruments, national constitutions and legal systems, apart from ethical resources in forms of communal systems and massive ancient literature at least in the case of the South Indian context, Küng does not suggest anything radically new. The question is, in what way religious traditions, with their ethical appeals integrally related to their beliefs, will be motivated to respond to yet another prescription! What are the spiritual resources that can be mobilized to equip people of different religions and cultures to comply with a global ethic? Paul Knitter, while sharing the concerns of Küng, concentrates on liberation from suffering through interfaith dialogue and cooperation. Again, the suggestion is not as simple as it appears to be. For example, a Buddhist will teach the profound truth of craving as the root cause of all suffering. As is repeated again and again, the greed of a minority of persons and super powers causes untold suffering for the majority of poor nations and their people. And such a minority needs to be challenged; any implicit siding with them while talking about the suffering of others will be tantamount to pinching the baby and rocking the cradle.

7. ***Polytheistic Pluralism*:** Jordan Paper's book *The Deities are Many: A Polytheistic Theology* (2005) represents yet another challenging position. It collects experiences of people about the simultaneous existence of various gods, goddesses and ancestral spirits. It coincides with the recent Hindutva affirmation of the existence of many gods and goddesses. As we mentioned earlier, there was a time when Hindu thinkers had to respond to the challenge of Muslims and Christians' claim about one God by presenting different gods as different manifestations of the same essence, reality or one God. Now the situation has changed. The Hindu revivalists argue that belief in one God was the political weapon used by Muslims and Christians to subjugate the people, mainly the Hindus of the sub-continent. Now they call them to fully identify with the nation by accepting the plurality of gods and goddesses. This has given a new credibility to the diverse and popular cults which celebrate the presence of, and ask for protection, health and prosperity from minor deities as well as various spirits found in their community. There are two concerns in this connection. One is that as the Hindu pantheon in texts like the Puranas is described and bhakti literature refers to, there are conflicts between gods for attaining supremacy. Even the great gods Siva and Vishnu are presented in such conflicts. The other is that among Hindus those belonging to the Saiva and Vaishnava traditions and their movements hold a strong belief in one God, although some of them do not deny the existence of minor deities who depend on Siva or Vishnu. It would be an interesting empirical study to assess the situation on the ground.

8. ***Nationalist Pluralism*:** Around the time of Indian independence in 1947 there was debate at the national level about the position of religion(s) in politics. Jawaharlal Nehru argued that there should be total separation between religion and the state as their combination would lead to communal politics which would be harmful. But Gandhi argued for due place for religion which has shaped and sustained communities for generations. He also emphasized the Indian ethics of tolerance and promoted the idea of equal respect for all religions (*sarva dharma samabhava*). Since there was no discussion about the sensitive question of what is 'true religion' some argued that without discriminating between good belief and bad belief, lower form and higher form and so on, equal respect for all religions would mean equal respect for every superstitious belief and meaningless, harmful practice. Today the public ethos expects not to talk about such matters openly, although some atheistic movements have been vociferous against such beliefs and practices. While the Indian Constitution provides freedom of religion and the practice of Personal Law for different religious communities, the rights and responsibilities of the religious communities in the multifaith context of India with a secular-democratic polity continue to be discussed.

***Closing Notes*:** Just as there is no one form of exclusivism or of inclusivism, there is no one form of pluralism. We have identified eight paradigms of pluralism with unavoidable overlaps. Each one of them needs to be elaborated. And there are suggestions with new labels such as inclusivistic pluralism (K.P. Aleaz) which actually bring in no greater clarity. Also it is important to acknowledge the observation that indiscriminate and uncritical pluralism without some criteria for evaluation in fact is another form of exclusivism (Gavin D'Costa).

Let me offer four concluding remarks: first, pluralism can be a superficial slogan of those who are nominally religious without any commitment. For some, religion or spirituality is a commodity in the consumerist spiritual market within which we can pick and mix. Second, in the name of plurality and diversity, innate contradictions may be tolerated. This has socio-economic implications as well. For example, can poverty, illiteracy and untouchability ever be part of a healthy diversity and plurality in a nation or society? In the case of beliefs, does karma, fate or predestination provide impetus for changing one's existing condition? Third, Christians cannot be boxed into any of the above paradigms. With commitment and openness, in one sense they need to be 'pluralistic' in their approach to different religious traditions and peoples. This is because historically different traditions are related to Christianity differently. For instance, its relationship with Judaism and Islam is different from its relationship with Indian religious traditions. Also, a Christian's position depends on the particular person(s) she meets with a particular spiritual maturity and understanding of his/her religion. Fourth, Christians are called to be both committed and open. They may not have clear answers for all the questions concerning religious pluralism. They should trust that God can bring about the necessary balance and synthesis of varying experiences and values while exposing humanity's evil and wrongdoing. They need to re-conceive and explain new ways that Trinity provides a vision for profound relational intimacy between three 'persons' and to maintain a healthy and dynamic balance. It is their responsibility to define and refine the distinctive Christian uniqueness and witness to it by continually reforming the church so that it will present a collective charisma in a bewildering world of conflicting truth claims and yet a common humanity.

Approaches to Religious Pluralism

1. ***An Opening* Observation:** Greater awareness of the multi-faith reality of the religious world through studies and encounters has led to serious considerations of the theological or philosophical worth of other religions. Those religions who have a missionary obligation and commitment to change the world have been in the forefront of studying other religions casually, academically and theologically. There is no doubt, with the support of the so called scientific study of religion, Christianity has excelled in ensuring study of other religions in it educational and training programmes. It has been the pioneer of interfaith dialogue in the formal sense too. Christian theologies of religious pluralism are elaborate without claiming to be exhaustive and absolute. Also it is true to say that it is through the Christian forums do we come to know what people of other faiths think about their appeal to other religions and explore the possibility of interfaith dialogue. However, in many cases there is a long journey to go beyond positions of defense, justification and absorption. The above mentioned paradigms of religious pluralism are general and each religious tradition may or may not identify with some or all of these paradigms. Now we turn to see the specific points of emphasis in each major religious tradition in relation to people of other faiths.

2. ***An Introduction to the Views of Major Religious Traditions***

We have a few materials which bring together 'pluralism in the world religions.'[1] To start with, ***Judaism*** is based on the story of liberation from Egypt and the covenantal relationship with God with a view to establish a model community based on the law of love, justice and peace, thus a light to the world. In the Hebrew scripture one reads of the alternatives of exclusivism, inclusivism and pluralism.[2] Most remarkably the vision of keeping harmony and tolerance of other worships (Mic. 4:3-5), reconciliation between Assyria, Egypt and Israel (Is. 19:23-25), and common human justice and humility (Mic. 6:8) is most stunning. But over the years the Jews had to face dilemmas, hostility and persecution mainly from Christians. However, some of their leaders, have maintained a view of

---

[1] E.g. Harold Coward, *A Short Introduction: Pluralism in the World Religions*, Oxford: Oneworld Publications, 2000; D.E. Singh & R.E. Schick (eds.), *Approaches, Foundations and Models of Interfaith Relations*, New Delhi: ISPCK-HMI, 2001.

[2] I. Selvanayagam, *Relating to People of other Faiths: Insights from the Bible*, Thiruvalla: CSS-BTTBPSA, 2004, 196-201.

salvation on the basis of meditation on one God, purity of soul and morality of personal and social life.[1]

Today Jewish Rabbis and scholars contribute enormously to ecumenical dialogues. For example, in one such event of Jews and Asian Christians in sharing fellowship and engaging in dialogue, a Rabbi pointed out how his tradition celebrates diversity in creation and human personality (not two in the same form!). The Rabbis, with some differing interpretation, insist on the seven commandments given to the children of Noah, as a basis on accepting people of other faiths: having laws of justice and prohibition of idolatry, blasphemy, sexual immorality, blood-shed, theft and the limb from a living animal (and any form of cruelty).[2] Belief in one God in connection with the prohibition of idols has been debated. Moreover, more than any other community, the Jews have worked out the most comprehensive procedure of establishing peace that will lead to reconciliation. It is clearly demonstrated the aim is shalom, and the guiding principle is justice.[3] Unfortunately most Christians continue to be of the supersessionist attitude towards Judaism, forgetting the common roots they share with them and its continued existence as an influential living community.

Being non-theistic, non-dogmatic and focused on right living, ***Buddhism*** seems to maintain a critical tolerance. As a preaching religion it has a goal of mission for the whole world. The history of Buddhism shows a degree of flexibility leading to different formations and emphases thus creating a pluralism within. The Buddha with his experiential vision of dependent origination and perpetual becoming taught a 'provisional faith' and therefore there is no room for hostility towards other visions although dialogue and even debate is encouraged. The following verse of Buddha is illustrative:

> If anyone were to speak ill of me, my doctrine or my Order, do not bear any ill-will towards him, be upset or perturbed at heart; for if you were to be so, it will only cause you harm. If, on the other hand, if anyone were to speak well of me, my doctrine or my Order, do not be overjoyed, thrilled or elated at heart; for if so it will only be an obstacle in the way of forming a realistic judgment as to whether the qualities praised in us are real and actually found in us.[4]

---

[1] See Coward, op. cit., 5ff.

[2] Norman Solomon, "Faith in the Midst of Faiths: Traditional Jewish Attitudes" in *People of God, Peoples of God: A Jewish-Christian Conversation in Asia*, ed. by Hans Ucko, Geneva: WCC Publications, 1996, 84-98.

[3] See Lavinia Cohn-Sherbok, "Judaism – Reconciled to Difference" in *Conflict and Reconciliation: The Contribution of Religions*, ed. by John W. Bowker, Toronto: Key Publishing House, 2008, 208-240.

[4] *Digha Nikaya* 1: 3; quoted, Coward, op. cit., 128.

At the same time an evaluation of religions was proposed by one of the cardinal disciples of Buddha. Ananda, for example, says that there are four false religions and four religions that are unsatisfactory but necessarily false.[1] But, on the whole, there is no compromise on the fact that the central Buddhist view of life and the eight-fold right way are applicable to all humans though some of their religions may appropriate them in their systems or find them overlapping with theirs. On the whole, in the words of Masao Abe, a well-known exponent of Buddhism and participant in interfaith dialogue, Buddhism stands for a dynamic unity in religious pluralism with boundless openness.[2] Also, today Buddhist mission for world peace and healing emotions, to a considerable extent, readily seeks cooperation of all religious traditions.

Hinduism itself is a conglomeration of numerous religious traditions, sub-traditions and diverse popular cults. We have already come across the claims for universal dharma and the challenges such as the caste and untouchability. Elsewhere I have applied the triple model of exclusivism, inclusivism and pluralism to Hindu positions on religious traditions.[3] The Vedic ritual with belief in its intrinsic power which sustains all life and the attached notion of purity-pollution divide is most exclusive; so also is belief in Vishnu, Siva and the Goddess, together and separately. And shades of exclusivism can be found in the interpretation of Brahman either as personal with characteristics or impersonal without characteristics as interpreted in the Vedantic and bhakti traditions. Speculations in the Vedas, the amalgamation between the Brahmanic-Bhagavata traditions, the affirmation that all paths reach one deity or avatar of Vishnu (as in the case of Krishna in the Gita), the ladder scheme assigning lower rungs to other religions and asserting the highest rung being the advaita oneness (as interpreted by Vivekananda and Radhakrishna) and popular slogans such as different streams joining the same sea and different pathways leading to the same hill top are examples of inclusivism. The paradigm of one Truth-many religions or one essence-many manifestations, the analogy of one sun and many photographs, and the relativist view of partial views of a whole (the story of six blind men sensing parts of an elephant) point out the pluralist view.

---

[1] 'The false religions are: 1. materialism, which asserts the reality of the material world alone and denies life after death; 2. any religious philosophy which recommends an immoral ethic; 3. any religion that denies free will and moral responsibility and asserts that persons are either miraculously saved or doomed; and 4. any religion that asserts the inevitability of eventual salvation or release for all.

The four unsatisfactory but necessarily false religions are those which in some sense maintain a concept of life after death, moral values, freedom and responsibility. Religions in this category include those based on: 1. the conscience of the founder while in both conscious and unconscious periods of existence. 2. revelation of tradition. 3. logical and metaphysical. 4. pragmatic skepticism or agnosticism.' Ibid., 130.

[2] M. Abe, *Buddhism and Interfaith Dialogue*, London: Macmillan, 1995, 17-39.

[3] See I. Selvanayagam, *The Dynamics of Hindu Religious Traditions*, 84-93.

Islam originated in a context marked by polytheism, idol worship and many other superstitious practices. When the prophet received the divine revelation, it came to take the form of the Qur'an, the infallible scripture. Mohammed's mission was carried out in the context of a struggle. It is said in many stories that at varying degrees the Jews and Christians in Medina supported him. They are recognised in the Qur'an as the People of the Book although their present books are regarded as distorted. That means the Bible is good as far as it subscribes to the views of Islam. Consequently, some Christian doctrines are indirectly refuted. For example, Trinity, probably influenced by certain Christian groups, is taken as a kind of tritheism (Father, mother Mary and Son). Jesus Christ was no more than a prophet, but next to Mohammed, who will come again at the end of the world. There are many references to the Word of God and Spirit but they are not given equal status to one God.

Jihad was first waged against idol worshippers and then those who opposed the Prophet's movement. But when it became a political force wars were unavoidable. The enemies were agents of jin, the devil. Who are those enemies today? Primarily those who subscribe to the western style of secular life including many Muslims. But in due course jihad was interpreted as spiritual striving in the way of God. Then, what is the nature of this striving? As we pointed out, one section of Muslims feels obliged to annihilate those who are not only corrupt but also who have lost their soul just as a fountain pen without ink. The problem is as to what group we should take as the authentic representatives of Islam. Not without reason that many Muslims repeat that Islam means peace and any element of terrorism is against the spirit of Islam. They point out from the Qur'an that God is most merciful and incomparably compassionate who wills pluralism and that there is no compulsion in religion. If God willed, he could create one religion and by allowing many religions to emerge and thrive he wants to test his faithful.

Pointing out positions and counter-positions, particularly peace lovers and militants, Coward hopes that:

> In the future, with Islam increasingly having to experience itself as a minority with a foreign host culture, these traditional views of other religions undoubtedly will be modified. Modern education will offer Muslims an opportunity to understand each religion in terms of its own culture, history, worldview and claims to truth. This will have an effect on Islamic self-perception. The religious pluralism of the modern world will force Islam, finding itself in much the same position as the other traditions, to come to grips with the rather provincial character of some of its past views of other religions.[1]

---

[1] Coward, op. cit., 83f.

He does not fail to recognise some of the modern revolutionary movements of militant Islamic fundamentalism which are diametrically opposite to religious pluralism.

Since Coward said the above, the destruction of the twin towers in New York on 11 September 2001 by the so called Muslim terrorists spread shock waves throughout the world, causing a war and creating what is known as Islamophobia. As a response ecumenical discussions on the relationship between the Semitic religions stressed the fact that the three religions – Judaism, Christianity and Islam – are Abrahamic faiths. And a group of Muslim scholars came public with the idea of 'a common word' of love as a basis of dialogue, particularly with Christians. No other religion has attracted the attention of the world community as Islam as evident in consultations and publications.[1] It may not be wrong to suggest that for an improved situation for Muslim attitude to religious pluralism the starting point is not peace in troubled times but serious and committed engagement in the study of religion.

Because of the peculiar process of formation as a 'synthetic' religious movement ***Sikhism's*** self-identity in relation to Islam and Hinduism has always been in question and the answers are varied. However, the elements of Sufi experience, Vaishnava devotion and yogic meditation are easily observable in its history, scripture and social life. In the writings of the proponents of the movement, then a religion, Kabir and Guru Nanak, one can read sections of a will and purpose with the support of experience and empirical observation, to move beyond the existing religions of conflict and dead ceremonies. In spite of political conflicts within and without there is a strong sense of being open to apprehend the Truth, the only name of God. Sikhs are non-dogmatic and laity-based, and open to use Hindu methods for the construction of theology. Above all, the ethical implications of this construction is supremely challenging. John Parry in an informative essay on the recent theological researches by Sikh scholars, gives a quotation from the Guru Granth: 'Truth is highest, but higher still is truthful living.'[2] Is this not the surest foundation for a world ethic?

The ***Baha'i Faith***, though small in the number of adherents, which originated in Iran and spread to North America and other parts including India, seems significant in a discourse on religious pluralism. It arose in the 1860s from Babism which had been founded by the Bab (1819-1850), founder of a messianic sect of Shi'a Islam, which was led to expect a new prophet of God and a saviour who would teach about the coming age. Baha'ullah (1817-1892) claimed he was the expected messiah and founded the Baha'i Faith. He was a threat to orthodox Muslims who believed that Mohammed was the seal of the line of prophets. Therefore persecution and exile were unavoidable. 'Bah'ullah

[1] See 23 papers by Christian scholars of Islam, in Singh & Schick (eds.), op. cit.

[2] *Moving Forms of Theology: Faith Talk's Changing Contexts*, ed. by I. Selvanayagam, Delhi: ISPCK, 2002, 91-97.

spent the last twenty-four years of his life creating the principles and institutions of the new religion, which included the unity of God, the unity of the world religions, the unity of humankind and the need for a world language and a form of global governance. He advocated parliamentary democracy, disarmament, greater spending on education and the poor, and a world security-system in which if any country attacked another the rest of the world's nations would intervene to achieve peace.'[1] Bah'ullah declared that the life and work of all the prophets are the manifestations of God and extended to all religious communities the status of the people of the Book. The theology of religious pluralism is rather complex because of these bold steps but also voicing for the relative nature of all religions as everyone is evolving and progressing. In the practical realm the Baha'is follow the teachings of their leader and relate to people of other faiths with a spirit of friendliness and fellowship. Also they are encouraged to engage in interfaith dialogue in order to understand other religions and thereby understand their own religion better and to comprehend the mystic foundations of the unity of all religions while being aware of the limitations as it arose in the middle of the Semitic traditions. In the 1960s the Baha'i faith took roots in the Indian soil and flourished, and the main reason was that it shared many beliefs with the Parsee (Zoroastrian) community and developed devotion to the Hindu avatars such as Krishna and Rama. Such an attitude and development certainly would be welcome by Hindus, but whether it would lead to a creative engagement in interfaith dialogue is a question.

In the case of ***Christian*** attitudes and approaches toward religious pluralism, there has been a long history and complex developments. It is complex because the Jewish root of Christianity was cut and grafted into Greek and Roman religions. Things became more complicated when Christianity came in contact with other religions such as the pluralistic Hinduism. We have already noted missionary encounters, international events and theological reflections. Efforts to give a reasonable account resulted in voluminous materials, both concise and comprehensive.[2] Elsewhere, I have given a summary following the triple model while acknowledging its limitation and pointing to a fourth way.[3] There is crude exclusivism according to which dialogue is a 'satanic movement' and those who do not accept Jesus as the only saviour, way and name and do not have membership with the Church (Roman Catholic) as the ark of salvation will perish in hell fire. And there is a theological exclusivism which asserts that the divine

---

[1] Coward, op.cit., 86.

[2] E.g. Ibid., 16-60; Jacques Dupuis, *Toward a Christian Theology of Religious Pluralism*, Maryknoll: Orbis Books, 2000.

[3] I. Selvanayagam, "Theological Positions in Christian Approach to Religious Pluralism – The Fourth Way", *Arasaradi Journal of Theological Reflection*, XVII/1, Jan-June, 2004, 1-23; also see "Interfaith Dialogue" (chapter 7) in *A History of the Ecumenical Movement*, Vol. 3 (1968 – 2000), ed. by John Briggs, Mercy Amba Oduyoye and Georges Tsetsis, Geneva: WCC, 2004, 149–174.

revelation in Christ was historically decisive and universally significant (Barth and Kraemer). The inclusivist paradigm includes that Christ was the cosmic Word that enlightens humans everywhere (John, writer of the fourth Gospel, emphasized by Cracknell and others), crown of Hinduism and other religions (Farquhar and others), unknown Christ of Hinduism (Panikkar, based only on the advaita Vedanta), operating grace in the interior of those who seek God who are anonymous Christians even if they have not had a chance to hear the gospel and join the church (Rahner), crucified king of God's reign (Moltmann and M.M. Thomas), universal witness and interior witness (Paul) and so on. The pluralist paradigms on one God/Truth/Faith/Mystery (Hick, Smith and others) and the related relativism bringing together the partial perceptions are more or less the same as in Hinduism and Jainism, and the view of parallel ways and different goals (Heim) which we have already elaborated.

Now, the following form the outline map towards the fourth way. We have already noted Tillich's definition of religion as the ultimate concern and religion of the concrete spirit. For him critical and creative developments in religions are revelatory experiences. He does not find the history of religions existing alongside the history of culture. 'The sacred does not lie beside the secular, but it is its depths. The sacred is the creative ground and at the same time critical judgment of the secular. The sacred is both *inside* and *outside* the secular and therefore God-language is necessary lest secular language absorb the language of religion, which is more enduring in history. Theologians have to break through the two barriers of 'the orthodox-exclusive one and the secular-rejective one.' Any reductionist tendency needs to be avoided, and this is applicable to the understanding of Jesus also, as he is a divine figure or a social figure though a Jesus-centred alliance may be fruitful. All the positive values should be welcome. In every religion there may be decisive moments of change just as the Reformation in Christianity.

Tillich believes that the positive elements and decisive moments have found the highest expression in Paul's doctrine of the Spirit in which the ecstatic and rational elements, love and knowledge, have become united. Intrusion of demonic elements is possible and therefore the secular criticism of religion is indispensable. We can see the whole history of religions in this sense as a fight for the religion of the concrete spirit, 'a fight of God against religion within religion' which could become the key for understanding the otherwise extremely chaotic history of religions. The criterion for Christians to recognise the religion of the concrete spirit is the event of the cross. The church has a critical role to maintain its own affairs according to the demands of this criterion and to welcome goodness, justice, truth and beauty wherever and in whatever form they are found. And it should be critical of the secular 'quasi-religions' because although they originally appeared liberative, 'they are worse, as we have seen in the twentieth century, because they are without the depths and the richness of the genuine religious traditions.' To avoid becoming an all-embracing abstraction the church should continue to define its true uniqueness in the light of religious pluralism.

Stanley Samartha's interesting encounter with Tillich which we described before. He made the latter realize that the Hindu philosopher Radhakrishnan's idea of the 'concrete Spirit' resonated with Tillich's. Parallel to M.M. Thomas's *The Acknowledged Christ of the Indian Renaissance*, Samartha brought out his study entitled *The Hindu Response to the Unbound Christ* (1974) in which, like the former, he pointed out how Hindu thinkers tried to absorb Christ within their all-inclusive framework without taking any pains to understand his uniqueness. His further reflection and actual encounters with representatives of other religious traditions resulted in the production of several books, poems and autobiographical reflections including *One Christ – Many Religions* (1991), *Pilgrim Christ* (1994) and *Between Two Cultures* (1996). It is not surprising that one of the doctoral dissertations on the thought of Samartha by a European scholar is published with the title *Commitment and Openness.*[1]

Samartha placed himself in between uncritical friendliness and fanaticism. He repeated in different terms the view that 'Commitment without tolerance becomes fanaticism. Tolerance without commitment slips into indifference.' He defined dialogue as 'a mood, a spirit, an attitude of love and respect towards neighbours of other faiths' and he applied this to his theological approach also. Dialogue for him was 'not a gathering of porcupines, nor a getting together of jellyfish.' Wishy-washy platitudes and superficial gestures of respect might be a necessary preludes, but he expected the partners in dialogue to move on, taking efforts to understand each other's faith and seeking avenues of interreligious cooperation with proximate goals in the common human life in concrete contexts. Not siding with particular camps he called on both Christians and others to develop 'courage for dialogue.' He was clear about the Christian faith as fundamentally kerygmatic, but warned Christians against 'rehearsing old militant marches using spent bullets' and called them to reinterpret the gospel categories like 'kingdom' as servanthood. At the same time when once Muslim friends in Bangalore propagated that Jesus was only a human prophet, Samartha did not hesitate to declare 'the Christ we adore.'

Theologically, Samartha was unsettled with regard to the triple model, and in some sense one can relate him to each alternatively. For example, he held on the one hand that 'Religions are different responses to Mystery', but on the other warned against 'rudderless boats in the waters of relativism.' He voiced the need for 'theological backbones' to face the question of truth squarely and boldly. For him, issues of religious pluralism cannot be discussed as a concept 'detached from the throbbing of surrounding life and held up for intellectual examination as hardened crystals under the microscope. They are part of the texture of human life, touching the conscience and emotions of people deeply.' He argues that

[1] Eeuwout Klootwijk, Zoetermeer: Uitgeverij Boekencentrum B.V., 1992.

secularism cannot replace religion, and that the religious quest and struggle for justice are not alternatives. 'The basic question is, how our understanding of and obedience to Truth critically illumines and directs our struggle for justice in order that human beings might become free' in a holistic sense. The sensitive question of the place of Christ in the midst of religious plurality, he says, should be regarded both as 'a theological responsibility and a pastoral concern.' He calls Christians to move away from a 'Jesus-cult' and 'Christomonism' and to hold the ultimacy of God being true to the insights of texts like 1Cor. 15:28 (humanity will surrender to the crucified feet of God's Son Christ and Christ himself surrender 'so that God may be all in all').

In actual interfaith encounters with serious commitment and sincere openness, Samartha says, 'participation in truth is enhanced, openings to further dimensions of truth are increased, and the obligation to be committed and loyal to what has been received becomes more compelling.' Recognising that human distortion of the truth received is always possible we need to be open to the lead of the Spirit. 'The Spirit of God cannot be regarded as the monopolistic possession of the Judeo-Christian tradition imprisoned within the steel and concrete structure of Western dogma and a permanent Atlantic Charter.'

Samartha is fond of the images of travel and pilgrimage, but not without commitment and openness. 'We are always *on the way*. Every arrival is a point of departure, and every journey looks for a new destination.' In the case of different scriptures, for instance, they 'should not be regarded as passport documents that divide different nationalities but as signposts that point to a more promising future.' And we need a theology today 'that is not less but more true to God by being generous and open, a theology not less but more loving toward the neighbour by being friendly and willing to listen, a theology that does not separate us from our fellow human beings but supports us in our common struggles and hopes ... a theology that refuses to be impregnable, but which, in the spirit of Christ, is both ready and willing to be vulnerable.' The future remains unpredictable, but for Christians the ultimacy of God who revealed himself in Jesus Christ stands out as paradigmatic. And those who are in the journey of dialogue with proximate goals have a determination to achieve them while sharing the respective views of the ultimate goal.

Although, there is no blueprint about the future there is a biblical vision and hope in Christ that includes the whole humanity. The biblical phrases in this connection are the coming of Christ in his glory, a new creation, unifying everything in Christ, perfect understanding, being filled with the fullness of God and so on. How do these relate to a theology of religious pluralism? Moltmann, a German theologian, known for his *Theology of Hope*, helps Christians to tackle this question in another book. His starting point is the origin of the Christian hope. 'The church's abiding origin in Israel, its permanent orientation to Israel's hope, Christianity's resulting special vocation to prepare the way for the coming kingdom of history – all this will also give its stamp to the dialogue with the world religions. The dialogue cannot be determined by arbitrary and predetermined attitudes, but only by attitudes and judgments which are based on Christianity's special promise and directed towards the universal future of humankind in the kingdom of God.' This is particularly important in the changed world situation marked by interdependence and fast communications which nurture the idea of one world. For him, the only religions that will be enduring as 'world religions' in the future will be the ones that accept the 'one world' that is coming into being and the common world history which can be created today for the first time. This is the new situation for all the religions including Christianity. In true dialogue religions change, the skeptical tolerance will be replaced by productive tolerance. 'Absolutism and relativism are really twins, because both view "everything"from a higher, non-historical watch-tower ... In the open history of potentiality one can only move specifically from one relationship to other relationships in the hope that living relations will enable us to gain "everything" and to combat the threat of "nothingness."'[1] In relationship mutual help is possible, and for Christians the suffering love of God is the motivating factor to be spontaneous in helping others.

Process philosophy/theology provides profound insights on the moving process of life and history as well as God who is the greatest companion and fellow sufferer. Even if one has difficulty in comprehending the twin nature of God, Primordial and Consequent, it is hard to deny the dynamic process of life. Divine initiatives and human deviations and yet the enduring patience of God, trying to persuade with signs and stimulations but not force, is a different language of the core message of the Bible. Those who have the imaginations and inner maturity would see their faith journey not as carrying a package but moving with others on a pilgrimage. On the way the interreligious communities, without exaggeration and manipulation, should be able to share their root stories and inspiring insights. Those Christians who are in a genuine dialogue with others may be frustrated by hearing the familiar stories of creation, revelation, devotions, ethical teachings etc. But at the same time they may be moved to discover their most profound insights such as that God is in solidarity with the victims of injustice as revealed in the Hebrew/Jewish story, demonstrated in the life and teachings of Jesus and commissioned to the disciples of Jesus and the church to follow. If this happens, a Christian may realize suddenly how much time and energy the churches have been wasting in the name of mission.

When Christians thus rediscover the dialogical nature of their faith-tradition and share their story with humility and joy, people of other religious traditions may be stimulated to probe into their own tradition and see decisive moments of God's dialogue in the development of their traditions. The Christian story of divine initiatives and human deviations provides a tool to understand the origin and development of other religious traditions, particularly with reference to such

---

[1] J. Moltmann, *The Church in the Power of the Spirit*, London: SCM Press, 1975, 150f.

decisive moments that reflect 'the struggle of the concrete Spirit within and against religion.' The realism of the Bible hangs not on an 'unmoved mover' but on the one who guides a process and journey, willing to go forward and backward as well as sideways, depending on the turns taken by humankind. The Christ-event was most decisive because it was the story of God's Son or the visible image of the divine humanity who 'humbled himself, and was obedient, even to the point of death, death on a cross.' Though God raised him to the heights, he still stands in solidarity with those suffering for his name's sake asking the persecutors, 'why do you persecute me?' Those who see him as the one having the perfect authority but perpetually being slain, 'slain from the foundation of the world', witness to a unique picture of God. They can affirm with confidence that God is unchanging in his love yet ever changing in his contingent plan. It may look odd in the midst of conflicting images of God or perceptions of Reality. However, it may well be expected that such a self-understanding and friendly approach to people of other faiths will further clarify the fourth way in the theology of religions we have outlined above.

Commitment and Openness: Some Practical Notes

Being nominally religious may not be a problem for the study or research into religion. But it is vital for a person to be committed in interfaith dialogue. Perhaps even the word 'commitment' may not be understandable to all religious people. There may be equivalents such as being self-aware, God-fearing and devoted. Those who are nominal may use their religion for a social identity, a sense of belonging to a group or community. For other people, particularly those in diaspora, the cultural life gives some kind of meaning to their life. This can happen within the religion as well. Christians from other continents living in America and Europe always seek fellowship with fellow Christians of their country, region or language group. Hindus feel at home only when they can visit a temple (mandir), smell the fragrance of incense, listen to Indian music and have a vision of the deities. In public celebrations for religious people it is customary or obligatory to participate and enjoy the *mela*. Sometimes atheists appear in worship places in order to attend a ceremony connected with their dear ones. In such a situation the level of self-understanding, principles in life and helping others may not be evident.

The fact of familiarity and its connection with faith is an important issue to reckon with when we discuss about commitment and openness. In our earlier discussion on the 'meaning of meaning' one perceivable gap is that when a perplexing strange atmosphere becomes familiar there comes a sense of meaning. The immediate picture that comes to my mind is that when a bride in southern Tamil Nadu departs her parental home to the home of the arranged groom, she weeps profusely and the tears fall on her flower garland. In some cases the groom promises publicly 'I will look after you' but that does not console her. But in due course, after a period of struggle with the strange atmosphere, she gets familiar with everything including the neighbours, of whom some become good friends. A sense of belonging to her husband's home and neighbourhood gives enormous satisfaction, and slowly her parents' home becomes strange. The feeling of strangeness and the meaning of being familiar can be applied to several moments in one's life – moving to a new house, joining a college or university, settling in a new place, visiting a worship place of another denomination or sect. Now, the question is whether this kind of familiarity gives full meaning. Is there a guarantee that life in its course will become more and more meaningful? The most confusing and misleading fact is identifying familiarity with faith. I am familiar with a particular way of doing things in a particular worship place where several generations of my family have worshipped! This is my 'faith' which has been tested and tasted by many people. Consequently, faith is understood as adherence to a long tradition or conforming to conservative prejudices. However, as we pointed out, for W.C. Smith 'faith' is the inherent human ability to transcend. Of course he did not discuss the possibility of an 'old faith' replaced by new because of a new experience or conviction. Jesus explained faith as dynamic and liberating, seeking all the time alternatives, 'moving mountains', sprouting to grow and so on. He lamented that there was no faith in his own community that blocked the working of a new thing (miracle) and wondered if there would be faith (to move) when he would come again to the earth. Jesus' understanding of faith is to move on from what is familiar, and it is a challenge for Christians.

Respect and tolerance for other religions has been stressed not only by Gandhi and his followers but also others. These and similar words are repeated in interfaith meetings and protocol speeches. We saw earlier Ashoka's promulgations on this and the danger of unwanted and obscure practices claiming respect and tolerance. When asked about in meetings, the response is a veiled threat of strong reaction and indicating how sensitive the issue of religious practices is. Using this cover adherents of religions may behave in nonsensical ways. For example, in the name of propagating the gospel should we tolerate fundamentalist preachers shouting anti-Semitic views from pulpits through microphones and bearing false witness against their neighbours' faiths? In my context, Hindus and to some extent Muslims, have tolerated this up to a point. But, boosted by the recent Hindu resurgence at the national level, now they have responded with greater noise. The communalized bureaucracy is hardly helpful. More horribly, we hear supportive voices for occasional human sacrifice, child marriage and temple prostitution though they are banned. Further, should we respect and tolerate the popular belief in fate whether it comes in the name of karma, God's will and predestination? When we talk about global ethics, the custodians of law in India should bring out and implement guidelines on codes of conduct in cooperation with the enlightened interreligious groups.

Are Religious Conversions Possible?

It is a most sensitive and intricate question. The answer is not as simple and straightforward as it is to be able to say yes or no. Even the wealth of resources that emerged from studies of various kinds has not helped to un-ravel the claims of experience in one way or other. William James, an outstanding American psychologist of religion did an extensive study of conversion experience, and his source materials included the diaries of nuns and priests. In his famous book (Gifford Lectures) he adopted three subjective criteria for evaluating the value of religious experience: immediate harmoniousness, philosophical reasonableness and moral helpfulness. He describes conversion as follows:

> To be converted, to be regenerated, to receive grace, to experience religion, to gain an assurance, are so many phrases which denote the process, gradual or sudden, by which a self hitherto divided, and consciously wrong, inferior and unhappy becomes unified and consciously right, superior, and happy in consequence of its firmer hold upon religious realities.[1]

James claimed that a certain neurotic temperament is a required condition for receiving inspiration from a higher realm. This led to a recognition in the field of the psychology of religion of healthy mind and weak mind which came to be a subject of much debate.

Though psychology is still of some assistance in understanding the conversion of 'troubled souls' the issue has been looked from many more different perspectives. *Religious Conversion: Contemporary Practices and Controversies*,[2] an informative interfaith volume brings together a detailed introduction ("Conversion: contours of controversy and commitment in a plural world"), two presentations on theoretical perspectives, and eighteen essays by representatives of different religious traditions, new movements, charismatic movements and cults. Each tradition and movement has its own rationale, basis, process, procedures and rituals. This volume is just an illustration here. This and similar works help those who unconsciously generalize. The deviations of original vision and a strange kind of conversion within, need to be acknowledged. For instance, Jesus asked for new openness, a self-transcending faith in action. He condemned those who were engaged in organized proselytism, but called for discipleship which meant a new orientation in life. Paul met the risen Jesus as still suffering in solidarity with a group of victims whom Paul was targeting to persecute. His conversion was not from one religion to another, but from one perception of God to a new

[1] W. James, *The Varieties of Religious Experience: A Study of Human Nature*, London: Longman, Green & Co., 1902, 189.

[2] Ed. by Christopher Lamb and M. Darrol Bryant, London: Cassell, 1999.

perception. It was a struggle for him to distinguish between the Jewish Christians and Gentile Christians.

In the above volume the essay on Hinduism, particularly Gandhi's consistent view on proselytisation, is presented. Gandhi, a devout Hindu, preached tolerance and equal respect for all religions. Although, there is some scholarly appreciation for Gandhi's position,[1] however, it is fair to say that the matter is much more complex. In the Constituent Assembly in preparation for India to become a Republic, one of the most hotly debated issues was religious conversion.[2] A remarkable study of this debate starts its main chapter with a quote of Gandhi: 'Every nation considers its own faith to be as good as that of any other. Certainly the great faiths held by the people of India are adequate for her people. India stands in no need of conversion from one faith to another.'[3] But Gandhi failed to recognise the socio-political-theological implications of conversions in India not only after the arrivals of Muslims and Christians but even before when there were moments of conversion in between different Indian religious traditions. As studies show almost all religions in India are both guilty of forced conversions and victims of conversions by fraudulent means such as emotional manipulation, denigrating of their own religions and cultures, intimidation of hell fire and allurement of heavenly pleasure, and political influence.[4] While genuine conversions in the

[1] A. Pushparajan, *From Conversion to Fellowship: The Hindu-Christian Encounter in the Gandhian Perspective*, Allahabad: St. Paul's Press, 1990.

[2] See Sebastian C.H. Kim, *In Search of Identity: Debates on Religious Conversion in India*, New Delhi: Oxford University Press, 2003.

[3] Ibid., 13.

[4] For the conflict between the Vedic Aryans and Dasas or Dasyus, see *The Rigveda: The Earliest Religious Poetry of India*, Vol. I, tr. by Stephanie W. Jamison and Joel P. Brereton, Oxford: Oxford University Press, 2014, 54-57; there are prayers to gods such as Indra by Aryans to support their cause; probably the subdued Dasas/Dasyus and other indigenous groups were incorporated into the Aryan fold with a distinctive status. For the impalement of eight thousand Jains after failing in a debate, and realignments and conversion between Buddhists, Jainism, and the Saiva and Vaishnava bhakti sects, see Wendi Doniger, *The Hindus: An Alternative History*, New Delhi: Penguin, 2009, 364-369. For conversion in Islam, Sikhism, Christianity and other, see *Religious Conversion in India: Modes, Motivations, and Meanings*, ed. by Rowena Robinson and Sathianathan Clarke, New Delhi: Oxford University Press, 2003; Arun Shourie, *Missionaries in India: Continuities, Changes, Dilemmas*, New Delhi: HarperCollins Publishers, 1999; for Christians (cf. a letter from the Pope) and Sikhs targeting the open-minded but non-literate Akbar the Great, see Rajmohan Gandhi, *Revenge & Reconciliation*, New Delhi: Penguin, 1999, 88, 93; on forced conversion to Islam in the Deccan, 108f.

process of a search for truth[1] or spiritual crisis[2] are not contested, mass conversions are alarming.

The most dramatic mass conversion in the twentieth century was initiated by B.R. Ambedkar (1891-1956), a lawyer and politician from the 'untouchable' community who became the champion of liberation and special privilege for all 'untouchables.' Following a failed truce with M.K. Gandhi about the position of his community in Hindu society and their political privilege and considering other options of religions, he chose Buddhism as he found it to be historically indigenous, intellectually convincing and spiritually satisfying. 'On 14 October, a white-garbed B.R. Ambedkar converted to Buddhism, under the auspices of the Burmese monk, Sri Chandramani, in front of a third to a half-million political followers at Nagpur, in what was then British India's Central Provinces.'[3] In the following ceremony he made a vow in vernacular to follow the traditional values, not to worship the Hindu gods (naming the major ones) and to establish equality. The third and most significant part of the ceremony followed after a few moments of pause:

> Ambedkar now led the assembly of those who had grown to trust him over the three preceding decades, in a mass conversion to the Buddhist path, through a repetition of his twenty-two oaths. It was at this moment and with those words, at what has since been referred to as the great Diksha (initiation), that Navayana Buddhism was put into motion. Two days later, at Chandrapur, 150 kilometres to the south, Ambedkar directed the conversion of hundreds of thousands more, who had gathered for that purpose. Despite passing away only a few weeks later, the total number of converts continued to rise over three million by the 1960 census. By the beginning of the twenty-first century it had grown to over eight million. Though the rate

[1] E.g. Pandita Rama Bai (1858-1922), a Brahmin from Maharashtra, who was exceptional for learning Sanskrit and eloquence, was intellectually convinced about the liberating message of Jesus Christ and became a Christian. She held an independent view on life: she married a low caste man who died after two years; she was confronting the conservative English clerics and unjust administrators, exposed the plight of Brahmin widows and started a mission to shelter and rehabilitate them and to educate the unfortunate people.

[2] Sadhu Sundar Singh (1889-1929?) was first to be hostile to Christian mission in his school where he publicly burned the Bible, and later, following a spiritual crisis and mysterious vision of Christ crucified, despite family opposition, joined the Christian church. He came to be known as the 'apostle of the bleeding feet', moved freely among other religious monks and was appreciative of the Indian spiritual values. See T. Dayanandan Francis (ed.), *The Christian Witness of Sadhu Sundar Singh*, Madras: CLS, 1989.

[3] Gary Tartakov, "B.R. Ambedkar and the Navayana Dilsha", in *Religious Conversion in India*, ed. by Robinson & Clark (ed.), op. cit., 192.

of conversion subsided greatly after the first decade, the number of conversions continues to increase rather than subside.[1]

Thus, a Navayan (new path or Neo-Buddhism) was born with a socio-political-liberational-spiritual combination. Gandhi was no longer alive to make a response. Those who emphasised socio-liberation suggested new attitudes to the fact of religion in people's life. The Hindu reaction to Navayana was not explosive as Hindu-Buddhist identity, and connection was kept fluid. Perhaps this is true of Hindu-Sikh identity.

However, on the contrary, Hindu reaction to conversion to Islam and Christianity, the foreign religions, has been strong. For example, primarily in protest against untouchability, in a village in southern Tamil Nadu State in the early 1980s there was a mass conversion from Hinduism to Islam. The event shook the nation and attracted visits of high officials even from the central government. Once again debate on religious conversion resumed all over the country.[2] Around this time a few States passed a law banning conversion altogether although there are already legal safeguards against fraudulent means and manipulation of juveniles. The tiny Christian minority is often too noisy and exaggerate their dividends of conversion but the Hindu reaction is justifiable. In 2008 August, for example, there was a Hindu riot against Christians in Kandhamal village in the State of Odisha in which nearly forty Christians were killed and property of great worth was damaged. Around that time there were several cases of attacks on churches in the State of Karnataka. But the movement of re-conversion to Hinduism has been continuing unchallenged. More recently, the call for *Garwapsi* (return home/ come back) has been growing louder and action quicker. It may not be unfair to ask if the vast majority of Hindus in India (80%) fear the possibility of conversion to one of the minority religions, what is at stake?

Religious conversion being such a controversial and complex issue, is there any place to use the word in interfaith studies and dialogue? Of course one's religious identity and satisfaction is inauthentic as long as s/he is not knowledgeable of other religions however basic that knowledge may be. But at the same time it is not practicable for every Indian to know about the basics of all religions which would inform the nature, mode and procedure of conversion. We noted before that in countries such as the United Kingdom which is nominally Christian and phenomenally secular, religious education is made compulsory. It requires maturity and fair-mindedness for the religious exponents, thinkers and political leaders to approach the issue boldly without feat of any loss. It is hard to deny that opportunities to study one's religion in comparison with others and interfaith dialogue with commitment and openness would lead to realize if his/

---

[1] Ibid., 193.

[2] See Mumtaz Ali Khan, *Mass Conversion of Meenakshipuram*, Madras: CLS, 1983.

her religious visions and values are intellectually convincing, spiritually satisfying and socially uplifting.

Concluding a remarkable study of religious faiths and human identities in the modern world of which some are dynamic while others are dangerous, Eric Lott makes an appeal to Christians. He uses the phrase 'Ecstatic and Inclusive Christian Identity.' He calls Christians to identify them with Jesus, a Jew who was strongly connected with his religious roots and who became the wanderer without a place to lay his head. He was open to liberating figures in other traditions ('those who are not against us are with us'), offered wholesome healing, ecstatic 'in the sense of "standing outside" the normal boundaries of ego.' He was also 'breaking through the boundaries' of oppressive forces and accepting a new 'transcendent identity' and living with an inclusive outlook.[1] Further he writes:

> The identity of the followers of Jesus, therefore, can never have a once-and-for-all fixed character, and immutable 'body'. Systems and institutions will of necessity be created to serve the transforming intentions of the great Lover; none but that Lover's Spirit, though, can be absolutized. The Christian's grounding givenness is in those clear marks of the character and mission of Jesus ... this givenness can never be more than a revelatory starting point, a continually meaningful reference point, but not a pre-given identity ... To follow Jesus is to set out on the road to a continually new-born identity. And a life of journeying, moving on, with no ever-fixed position, engaging critically with the many cultures, ethnicities, societies, political systems that make up the life of humankind, in turn makes diversity inevitable.[2]

This is not different from the Buddhist position of 'boundless openness'; it is a position-less position without losing the feet. Every religion has core visions, root stories and fundamental values. And to be open for unpredictable change may be the test of their truth and unshakability. This should be as true of a well-informed persons as illiterate masses of diverse and popular cults.

Concluding Remarks

The study of religion, along with the great world events such as the Parliament of World Religions, missionary encounters with religions and new perceptions and approaches, has greatly contributed to the world wide interfaith movement. Theological models emerged, and they are normally grouped under three headings: exclusivism, inclusivism and pluralism. But this triple model does not take into consideration different strands within each. The pluralist paradigms, for example, are grouped under eight: essentialist, monotheistic, relativist, teleological, parallel, ethical, polytheistic and nationalist. However, each religious tradition might

[1] Eric Lott, *Religious Faith and Human Identity,* 401ff.

[2] Ibid., 407f.

have different paradigms and approaches to other traditions. The most helpful and creative approach seems to be that which is based on commitment and openness. This has a backup of a theology which clearly states the core visions and fundamental values and advocates openness to the unfolding nature of the divine. The interpretation of religion as ultimate concern and pathway to mystery that requires a boundless openness but not without critical interaction is convincing. But those who hold that the divine revelation they have received is absolute and unchangeable may find this interpretation intimidating. Further, true interfaith dialogue can take place only between partners who are committed and open. Those who are nominally religious may have some general opinions about human life and the nature of religions, but such persons can spoil the spirit of dialogue. There is a tendency to mistake faith for conforming to a long tradition and certain prejudices. A sense of familiarity gives some kind of meaning, and in religious life that does not mean that there are no further spiritual avenues to explore. Religious conversion is one of the most sensitive and complex issues in dialogue but genuine conversions led by an experience of intellectual conviction, theological persuasion and spiritual satisfaction are appreciated. Fear of genuine conversion is a mark of uncertainty about the validity of one's religion.

In terms of having a fair amount of knowledge about other religions, real interest to know more and firm conviction about the validity of one's foundations of faith and having genuine openness, one may conclude that interfaith dialogue has hardly begun. In dialogue meetings, initiated by representatives of one faith community one normally witnesses that almost everyone wants to project and display their faith, justify their positions and defend their claims. Even within other faiths some claim their knowledge is more correct than that of adherents of that faith. This is not to deny the benefits of some correction, fellowship and friendship. Further the noble ideal of working together on a common mission is put on hold for various impediments though there are events of forced cooperation by governmental and non-governmental departments. Sometimes sensitive issues such as dietary restriction (e.g. beef), restoration of lost heritage and communal conflict, as in the case of India, dash the hopes of interreligious groups. Not only ideas like unity, peace and reconciliation, but also the idea of one essence/truth-many religions are once again sounded from high galleries, which perpetuate interfaith ignorance and nurture prejudice. All such attitudes and actions once again suggest that creative interfaith dialogue can take place only if there is a combination of a daring to know, courage to converse, conviction of the validity of one's faith and boundless openness. Then may well be expected the result of a matured religiosity and common human affection.

Postscript

1. When one looks around and reads around, one fact becomes almost obvious. Humans are religious animals or spiritual beings and they express it in one way or other. Those who are not happy with the word and the structure of 'religion' cannot easily deny an inherent religiosity, spirituality, sacred awareness or transcendental feeling. In sum, a non-material feature in human life is evident where one allows it to come out in questions about the nature, meaning and goal of life, or the questions suppressed. This does not mean that all that religion stands for is spirituality. In fact a kind of spirituality or piety is geared to relentless seeking for safety, wealth, health and peace of mind without bothering about greater values as one finds in all religions.

2. Scientific or objective study of religion in its variety has enriched human understanding of the history and culture of millions of communities around the world. Students of religion may have moments of surprise when they observe how integral religion is to the life of humans in different parts of the world. At the same time some may stop with their methodological parameters, analytical tools and abstract ideals while others approach the adherents of religions with respect and reverence even if certain practices appear to be nonsensical.

3. Religion is multi-dimensional and one dimension should not be allowed to dominate or be projected. Ritual, myth, experience, ethics, sociality, doctrine, change, and non-material factors coalesce in a healthy and integrated religious life. Normally religious persons point out the highlights of their religious life such as ethical ideals and in-depth experiences. Also different dimensions of religion do not carry equal importance in all religions, and therefore the different levels and meanings of practice need to be acknowledged. One may say 'religion is a way of life' in an interfaith sharing but regularly practise what has been given in the tradition.

4. There are different meanings of certain practices and different levels of certain experiences. For example, one ritual followed by a particular village in Africa, Asia and Oceania cannot be universalized even if there are some common features. In this matter some theories of ritual are not applicable to particular practices. Also in some traditions rituals are of intrinsic power and others instrumental. Similarly, the meaning of myths may differ in between different traditions of the same religion. So, also ecstatic outbursts and introspective self-absorption are based on different orientations, methods and personal predispositions. In the case of ethics, one may point out the golden rule 'do to others what you want them to do you', as noted in several scriptures. But when we ask for its social implications there is a wide range from being nice to expressive sacrificial love. We can apply such unique practices and interpretations to all dimensions of religious life.

5. Scriptures play vital roles in literate religious communities. Generally, scriptures teach past stories and traditions, evoke devotion and provide guidance through proverbs and exhortations. There are extreme views about scriptures. Some of them are taken as infallible instructions with perennial value. Some contain mainly devotional poetry in which mythical stories may be referred to. Others have a variety of literary pieces developed over centuries. Consequently, approaches and interpretations have differed, resulting in the development of denominations, sects and new movements. It is observed that the same scripture can nourish some to be saints and others terrorists! One authentic way is to approach them both reverently and critically, watching decisive moments, options, dilemmas and tensions. As such, a level of plurality with openness may be adopted. Moreover, there are thousands of diverse popular cults thriving around the world which do not have written scriptures. Keeping in memory the central story, transmission and reproduction on important occasions are the normal steps. And in some instances the sound of a shaman or drum communicates the message, and the community understands and acts accordingly. The study of religion needs to give more adequate attention to this phenomenon in order to get a fuller understanding of religion.

6. Strict doctrines are often compared to military regimentation without moving. Doctrines cannot be taken as the capsules of eternal truth. They are human made with political entanglement, prejudice and apologetic spirit. The more one knows the limitations the more one makes an attempt to create new creeds, etc. Replacing themes or revising them may be threatening to the 'faithful', and educating them may have to be part of religious education undertaken by every religious community. One refreshing proposal could be to replace doctrines by insights. Insights can be gained by reading, reflection, introspection and interaction. There are profound insights found in each religious scripture, tradition and mission. There may be primary insights and secondary insights. When an individual or group experiments with a set of insights there will be a new realization of the inapplicability of some of them while there is every possibility to perceive new insights.

7. There should be clarity between what is obvious and known and what is unknown. The use of the word Mystery may lead to escapism. 'Mystery is not something to be used to fill the gaps in rational knowledge.' Mystery may be identified with the ultimate Truth or the transcendent centre that remains always beyond and greater than present apprehension or even the sum total of those apprehensions. But can we undermine what is obvious to transform persons and societies? For example, is it legitimate to connect evils such as poverty, untouchability and corruption with mystery? Also there are claims that mystical experiences are ineffable and that the mystics of different traditions speak the same language. Is it unthinkable to expect the mystics or any kind of spiritualists to come to the ground and work for regeneration of life? It stands to reason,

therefore, that while being open to the disclosure of greater visions, religious communities should revisit their existing visions and values that motivate for action.

8. Politicians and fundamentalists exploit religion for their vested interests. We have important stories of political leaders who have claimed to represent their religious community while they themselves are non-practising of their religion. Competing national identities dominate at the cost of exemplary life of a religious community in public life. When new challenges appear and if there is no spiritual shock obserber and intellectual preparedness to make a response, one would tend to drift to a fundamentalist position. From an initial reaction like a porcupine they join a force which becomes dangerous locally, regionally and globally. Such developments bring ridicule after ridicule to religion, and the critics often become cynical and unwilling to explore and compare the motivating forces of religion for a meaningful life.

9. In an ambiguously and religiously pluralistic world, creative space for interfaith dialogue in a secular environment is most important. So far most of the dialogue events are initiated by one religious group, and as hosts they are expected to be restraining and tolerant. Normally the starting and ending points consist of how wonderful are their history, community, scripture and faith. Though such exercises have some merit, the most missing part in the sharing is confessions of failures and blunders in the past, compelling limitations of their community in the present and the misuse of religion for socio-economic exploitation. Those who want to break the mould and change the direction towards a self-critical and truthful sharing are threatening an appeal in the name of sensitivity and imminent explosion. Even in secular and multifaith countries religion is in need of being exorcised for helping persons to come openly as human beings with a religious commitment. Fear of free talk seems to betray uncertainties about one's faith.

10. The clarity and maturity of a religious or secular believer can be measured only by his/her passionate interest in knowing what others believe and enthusiastic engagement in interfaith dialogue. Fundamentally we share a common humanity with all its joys and sufferings. We witness in certain interreligious communities, particularly of illiterate people with non-literate cults, fascinating acts of common human affection. For them, more than intellectual articulation, faith lies in one's ability to welcome both strangers and neighbours, to befriend them and help them, particularly at times of crisis. Also, there are exceptional individuals in all faiths who do not carry a package but join the fellow believers on a pilgrimage. They speak their faiths in terms of visions, values and traditions. They are open to the ever unfolding truth and ready to appropriate new insights. They have anticipation for a better future but no blueprint. The study of religion and interfaith dialogue needs to take into account the experience of such individuals and share them widely.

Bibliography

Abraham, T. P., *Christian Attitude to Non-Christian Religions as it is Reflected in the Discussions of the Int. Miss. Conferences. Edinburgh to Tambaram,* unpublished dissertation, Serampore: Senate of Serampore College, 1971.

Adams, Charles (ed.), *Reader's Guide to the Great Religions,* New York: Free Press, 1977.

Ahmad, Imtiaz (ed.), *Ritual and Religion among Muslims in India,* New Delhi: Manohar Publications, 1981.

Alangaram, A., *Religions for Societal Transformation: Interreligious Dialogue from Subaltern Perspectives,* Bangalore: Asian Trading Corporation, 2006.

Aleaz, K.P., *Harmony of Religions: The Relevance of Swami Vivekananda,* Calcutta: Punthi Pustak, 1993.

-do- *The Gospel of Indian Culture,* Calcutta: Punthi Pustak, 1994.

Allen, Douglas (ed.), *Religion and Political Conflict in South Asia: India, Pakistan and Sri Lanka,* New York: Oxford University Press, 1993.

Allport, Gordon W., *Individual and His Religion: A Psychological Interpretation,* New York: Macmillan, 1952.

Almond, Philip C., *Mystical Experience and Religious Doctrine: An Investigation of the Study of Mysticism in World Religion,* Berlin: Mouton Publishers, 1982.

Anderson, Norman (ed.), *World's Religions,* Leicester: InterVarsity Press, 1975.

Antes, Peter, A.W. Geertz and R.R. Warne, eds., *New Approaches to the Study of Religion.* Volume 1: Regional, Critical, and Historical Approaches, Verlag de Gruyter (Berlin & New York) in the Religion and Reason series 42, 2004.

Ariarajah, A., *Gospel and Culture: An Ongoing Discussion within the Ecumenical Movement,* Geneva: WCC Publications, 1995.

Aurobindo, Sri., *Birth Centenary Library,* Pondicherry: Sri Aurobindo Ashram Trust, 1971, Vol. 1.

Aykara, Thomas A. (ed*),* *Meeting of Religions: New Orientations and Perspective,* Bangalore: Dharmaram Publications, 1978.

Badham, P. (ed.), *A John Hick Reader,* London: Macmillan, 1990.

Bailey, E., *Implicit Religion in Contemporary Society*, Deutscher Student Verlag: Kok Pharos Publishing House, 1997.

-do- *Implicit Religion: An Introduction*, London: Middlesex University, CSIRCS, 1998.

-do- *The Secular Faith Controversy*, London: Continuum, 2001.

-do- *The Sacred Quest for Meaning in Life: Denton Papers in Implicit Religion,* Lewiston: The Edwin Mellen Press, 2002.

Barnes, Michael, *Theology and the Dialogue of Religions,* Cambridge: Cambridge University Press, 2002.

Baum, Gregory, *Nationalism, Religion and Ethics*, Montreal: MacGill-Queen`s University Press, 2001.

Beckerlegge, Gwilym (ed.), *World Religions Reader*, New Delhi: Routledge, 1998.

Beckford, James A., *Social Theory and Religion*, Cambridge: Cambridge University Press, 2003.

Bellah, Robert N., *Beyond Belief: Essays on Religion in a Post-Traditional World,* New York: Harper and Row Publishers, 1970.

-do- *Broken Covenant: American Civil Religion in Time of Trial*, New York: Seabury Press, 2009.

Berger, Peter L., *Social Reality of Religion*, London: Faber and Faber, 1969.

Bianchi, Ugo, *History of Religions*, (trans. by G. Castellani), Leiden: E.J. Brill, 1975.

-do- et al. (ed.) *Problems and Methods of the History of Religions: Papers and Discussions*, Leiden: E.J. Brill, 1972.

Bidwai, Praful, Mukhia, Harbans and Vanaik, Achin (eds.) *Religion, Religiosity and Communalism*, New Delhi: Manohar Publications, 1996.

Billington, Ray, *Religion Without God*, New Delhi: Routledge, 2002.

Bishop, Peter & Michael Darton (ed.), *The Encyclopedia of World Faiths: An Illustrated Survey of the World's Living Religions*, London: Macdonald & Co., 1987.

Bleeker, C. Jouco and Widengren, Geo (ed.), *Historia Religionum: Handbooks for the History of* Religions, Leiden: E.J. Brill, 1969.

Bouquet, A.C., *Comparative Religion*, Mitcham: Penguin, 1958.

Bowman, John (ed.), *Comparative Religion: The Charles Strong Trust Lectures, 1961-1970*, Leiden: E.J. Brill, 1972.

Brown, Fred, *Faith Without Religion*, London: SCM Press, 1971.

Bruce, Steve, *Religion in the Modern World: From Cathedrals to Cults*, Oxford: Oxford University Press, 1996.

Caird, Edward, *Evolution of Religion: The Gifford Lectures Delivered Before the University of St. Andrews*, New Delhi: Cosmo Publications, 2008.

Camps, Arnulf, *Partners in Dialogue: Christianity and Other World Religions* (trans. by John Drury), Maryknoll: Orbis Books, 1983.

Cannon, Dale, *Six Ways of Being Religious: A Framework for Comparative Studies of Religion*, Belmont: Wadsworth Publishing Co., 1996.

Casanova, Jose, *Public Religions in the Modern World*, Chicago: University of Chicago Press, 1994.

Christian, William A., *Meaning and Truth in Religion*, Princeton: Princeton University Press, 1964.

Chryssides, G.D. and R. Geeves, *The Study of Religion: An Introduction to Key Ideas and Methods*, London: Bloomsbury, 2014.

Clarke, Peter B. (ed.), *Oxford Handbook of the Sociology of Religion*, Oxford: Oxford University Press, 2009.

Connolly, Peter (ed.), *Approaches to the Study of Religion*, London: Cassell, 1999.

Coward, H., *Scripture in the World Religions,* Oxford: Oneworld Publications, 2000.

Cracknell, Kenneth, *Justice, Courtesy and Love*, London: Epworth Press, 1995.

-do- *Wilfred Cantwell Smith: A Reader*, Oxford: Oneworld Publications, 2001.

Crawford, Robert, *What Is Religion?,* London: Routledge, 2002.

Crosby, Donald A., *Interpretive Theories of Religion*, Hague: Mouton and Co., 1981.

D'Costa, Gavin, *Theology and Religious Pluralism: The Challenge of Other Religions,* Oxford: Blackwell, 1986.

-do- *The Meeting of Religions and the Trinity*, Maryknoll: Orbis Books, 2000.

D'Souza, Leela, *Sociology of Religion: A Historical Review*, Jaipur: Rawat Publications, 2005.

Daniel, P.S. et al. (eds.), *Religious Traditions of India*, Senate of Serampore College: Indian Theological Library, 1988.

Davies, Brian, *Introduction to the Philosophy of Religion*, Oxford: Oxford University Press, 1982.

Dean, Thomas, *Religious Pluralism and Truth: Essays on Cross-Cultural Philosophy of Religion*, Delhi: Sri Satguru Publications, 1997.

Dehejia, Harsha V. and Makarand Paranjape (ed.), *Soundarya: The Perception and Practice of Beauty in India*, New Delhi: Samvad India Foundation, 2003.

Derrett, J. Duncan, *Religion, Law and the State in India*, London: Faber and Faber, 1968.

De Vries, Jan., *Perspectives in the History of Religions* (trans. by Kees W Bolle), Berkeley: University of California Press, 1977.

Dhavamony, Mariasusai, *Phenomenology of Religion*, Rome: Gregorian University Press, 1973.

Doniger, Wendy (ed.), *Encyclopaedia of World Religions,* Springfield: Merriam-Websters Incorporated, 1999.

Dupuis, Jacques, *Toward a Christian Theology of Religious Pluralism*, Maryknoll: Orbis Books, 1997.

Durkheim, E., *The Elementary Form of Religious Life* (Eng. tr. 1915, 47).

Edwards, David., *Religion and Change*, London: Hodder and Stoughton, 1969.

Eister, Allan (ed.), *Changing Perspectives in the Scientific Study of Religion*, New York: John Wiley and Sons, 1974.

Eliade, Mircea, *Encyclopaedia of Religion*, New York: Macmillan, 1987, Vol. 1-16.

Ellwood, Robert, *History and Future of Faith, Religion Past, Present and to Come*, New York: Crossroad Publishing Co., 1988.

Engineer, Asghar Ali, *Religion, State and Civil Society* (ed. by Parimala V. Rao), Bombay: Vikas Adhyayan Kendra, 2005.

Fenn, Richard, *Key Thinkers in the Sociology of Religion*, London: Continuum, 2009.

Fernandes, Walter, *Caste and Conversion Movements in India: Religion and Human Rights*, New Delhi: Indian Social Institute, 1981.

Fernando, M. and R. Crusz (ed.), *Theology Beyond Neutrality*, Colombo: Ecumenical Institute, 2011.

Flood, Gavin, *Beyond Phenomenology: Rethinking the Study of Religion*, London: Cassell, 1999.

Foucault, Michael, *Religion and Culture*, New York: Routledge, 1999.

Fox, Jonathan, *A World Survey of Religion and the State*, New York: Cambridge University Press, 2008.

Frazer, J G., *Golden Bough: A Study in Magic and Religion*, New Delhi: Cosmo Publications, 2008.

Gandhi, M.K., *Autobiography: Or the Story of My Experiments with Truth*, Ahmedabad: Navajivan, 1927/1991.

-do- *India of My Dreams*, New Delhi: Navajivan Publishing House, 1995 (Collection of articles that appeared in *Young India* in 1930s).

Geertz, C., *The Interpretation of Cultures*, London: Fontana, 1993.

Glenn, Norval, "'No Religion', Respondents to U.S. National Surveys, Late 1950s to Early 1980s", *Public Opinion Quarterly* (1987) 51 (3): 293-314.

Gonda, Jan, *Change and Continuity in Indian Religion*, Delhi: Munshiram Manoharlal, 1985.

Green, Ronald M., *Religion and Moral Reason: A New Method for Comparative Study,* New York: Oxford University Press, 1988.

Gulati, Mahinder N., *Comparative Religions and Philosophies: Anthromorphism and Divinity*, New Delhi: Atlantic Publishers, 2008.

Hale, Rosemary Drage, *Christianity: Understanding Religions*, New York: Rosen Publishing Group, 2010.

Hebblethwaite, Brian, *Ethics and Religion in a Pluralistic Age: Collected Essays*, Edinburgh: T & T Clark, 1997.

Heiler, Friedrich, *Prayer: A Study in the History and Psychology of Religion*, London: Oxford University Press, 1937.

Heim, S. Mark, *Salvations: Truth and Difference in Religion*, Maryknoll: Orbis Books, 1995.

Hellman, E., *Political Hinduism: The Challenge of the Viśva Hindu Parişad*, Uppsala: Department of the History of Religions, 1993.

Hesselgrave, David, *Dynamic Religious Movements*, Grand Rapids: Baker Book House, 1978.

Hick, J. *God and the Universe of Faiths*, London: Macmillan, 1973.

-do- (ed.), *Truth and Dialogue: The Relationship Between World Religions*, London: Sheldon Press, 1974.

-do- *An Interpretation of Religion: Human Responses to the Transcendent*, London: Macmillan, 1991.

-do- *The Fifth Dimension*, Oxford: Oneworld Publications, 1999.

Hick, J. and P. Knitter (eds.) *The Myth of Christian Uniqueness*, London: SCM Press, 1987.

Hick, J. and B. Hebblethwaite (eds.), *Christianity and Other Religions*, Glasgow: William Collins, 1980.

Hinnels, J.R. (ed.), *The Routledge Companion to the Study of Religion*, London: Routledge, 2005.

Holm, Jean, *Study of Religions*, London: Sheldon Press, 1977.

Holm, Jean with J. Bowker, *Sacred Writings*, London: Pinter, 1994.

Hooykaas, R., *Religion and the Rise of Modern Science*, Edinburgh: Scottish Academic Press, 1973.

Honderich, Ted, *The Oxford Companion to Philosophy*, Oxford: Oxford University Press, 1995.

Idinopulos, T. Athanasius, *Comparing Religions: Possibilities and Perils?* Ed. by, Brian C. Wilson, and James Constantine, Hanges: Brill, 2006.

Jakelic, Slavica and Lori Pearson, ed., *The Future of the Study of Religion*, Leiden: Brill, 2004.

Jastrow, Morris, *Study of Religion*, Chicago: Scholars Press, 1981.

Jensen, Jeppe S., *The Study of Religion in a New Key: Theoretical and Philosophical Soundings in the Comparative and General Study of Religion*, Aarhus, Denmark: Aarhus University Press, 2003.

Jordens, J. T. F., *Gandhi`s Religion: A Homespun Shawl*, London: Macmillan and Co., 1998.

Juergensmeyer, M., *Religious Nationalism Confronts the Secular State*, New Delhi: Oxford University Press, 1994.

-do- *Terror in the Mind of God: The Global Rise of Religious Violence*, Berkeley: University of California Press, 2000.

Kadankavil, Thomas (ed.), *Religion and Politics from Subaltern Perspective*, Bangalore: Dharmaram Publications, 1999.

Kärkkäinen, Veli-Matti, *An Introduction to the Theology of Religions: Biblical, Historical and Contemporary Perspectives,* Downers Grove: InterVarsity Press, 2003.

Kaufmann, Walter, *Religions in Four Dimensions: Existential, Aesthetic, Historical, Comparative*, New York: Reader's Digest Association, 1976.

Klootwijk, Eeuwout, *Commitment and Openness: The Interreligious Dialogue and Theology of Religions in the Work of Stanley J. Samartha*, Zoetermeer: Uitgeverij Boekencentrum, 1992.

Knitter, P., *No Other Name?*, London: SCM Press, 1985.

Koenker, Earnest B., *Secular Salvations: The Rites and Symbols of Political. Religions*, Philadelphia: Fortress Press, 1965.

Kramer, Kenneth, *World Scriptures: An Introduction to Comparative Religions*, New York: Paulist Press, 1986.

Kuhn, Thomas, *The Structure of Scientific Revolutions*, Chicago: The University of Chicago Press, 1970.

Kulandran, S., *Resurgent Religions*, Geneva: WCC (Plymouth: Latimer), 1957.

-do- *The Concept of Transcendence*, Madras: The Christian Literature Society, 1981.

Kumar, R. and Ram, S., *Culture and Religion of North-East India*, New Delhi: Arpan Publications, 2013.

Kumar, Nigel, Ajay, *What Is Religion?: A Theological Answer*, Bangalore: SAIACS Press, 2014.

Küng, Hans, *Christianity and the World Religions*, London: SCM Press, 1986.

-do- *Global Responsibility*, London: SCM, 1991.

Küng, H. and J. Moltmann (ed.), *Fundamentalism as an Ecumenical Challenge*, London: SCM, 1992.

Kunin, Seth D. and Miles-Watson, Jonathan (eds.), *Theories of Religion: A Reader*, Edinburgh: Edinburgh University Press, 2006.

Kuriakose, K. K. (ed.), *Religion, Terrorism and Globalization: Nonviolence – a New Agenda*, New York: Nova Science Publishers, 2006.

Kuttianimattathil, Jose, *Practice and Theology of Interreligious Dialogue*, Bangalore: Kristu Jyoti Publications, 1995.

-do- *Tracing the Way: Spiritual Dimensions of the World Religions*, New York: Continuum, 2002.

Larbeer, P.M., *Ambedkar on Religion: A Liberative Perspective*, New Delhi: ISPCK, 2003.

Leeuw, G. Van der., *Religion in Essence and Manifestation*, Princeton: Princeton University Press, 1986.

Lindbeck, G., *The Nature of Doctrine*, London: SPCK, 1984.

Lott, E.J., *Vedantic Approaches to God*, London: Macmillan, 1979.

-do- *Vision, Tradition, Interpretation: Theology, Religion and the Study of Religion*, Berlin: Mouton de Gruyter, 1987.

-do- *Religious Faith, Human Identity: Dangerous Dynamics in Global & Indian Life*, Bangalore: Asian Trading Corporation for the United Theological College, 2005.

-do- M.T. Thangaraj and A. Wingate (eds.), *Discipleship and Dialogue: New Frontiers in Interfaith Engagement*, Delhi: ISPCK, 2013.

Markham, Ian S. (ed.), *World Religions Reader*. Oxford: Blackwell Publishers, 2000.

May, John D. Arcy (ed.), *Pluralism and the Religions: The Theological and Political Dimensions*, London: Cassell, 1998.

McCutcheon, Russell and Willi Braun (ed.), *Introducing Religion: Essays in Honour of Jonathan Z Smith*, London: Equinox, 2008.

McMullen, C. (ed.), *Rituals and Sacraments in Indian Religions*, Delhi: ISPCK, 1979.

Mitri, *Tarek, (ed.), A Christian-Muslim Discussion*, Geneva: WCC Publications, 1995.

Molendijk, Arie, *The Emergence of the Science of Religion in the Netherlands*, Leiden: Brill, 2005.

Momen, Moojan, *Phenomenon of Religion: A Thematic Approach*, Oxford: Oneworld Publications, 1999.

Montefiore, Hugh (ed.), *The Gospel and Contemporary Culture*, London: Mowbray, 1992.

Morris, Desmond, *The Soccer Tribe*, London: Jonathan Cape Ltd., 1981.

Moses, D.G., *Religious Truth and the Relation between Religions*, Mysore: The Christian Literature Society of India, 1950.

Müller, F.M., *Natural Religion*, New Delhi: Asian Educational Services, 1979.

-do- *The Sacred Books of the East*, Oxford: At the Clarendon Press, 1879.

Nehring, A. (ed.), *Fundamentalism and Secularism: The Indian Predicament*, Madras: Gurukul, 1994.

Netland, Harold, *Encountering Religious Pluralism: The Challenge to Christian Faith & Mission*, Downers Grove: InterVarsity Press, 2001.

Neusner, Jacob (ed.), *Religion and the Social Order: What Kinds of Lessons Does History Teach?*, Atlanta: Scholars Press, 1994.

-do- (ed.), *Introduction to World Religions: Communities and Cultures*, Nashville: Abingdon Press, 2010.

Ogden, Schubert M., *Is there Only One True Religion or there Many?*, Dallas: Southern Methodist University Press, 1992.

Otto, Rudolf, *The Idea of the Holy*, Oxford: Oxford University Press, 1928.

Panikkar, R., *Myth, Faith, Hermeneutics: Cross-Cultural Studies*, Bangalore: Asian Trading Corporation, 1983.

Parrinder, G., *What World Religions Teach*, Sydney: George G. Harrap & Co., 1963.

-do- *The World's Living Religions,* London: Pan Books, 1964.

Phan, Peter C., *Being Religious Interreligiously: Asian Perspectives on Interfaith Dialogue*, Maryknoll: Orbis Books, 2004.

Prabhakar, Samson (ed.), *Inter-Play of Religion, Politics and Communalism in India,* Bangalore: BTESSC, 2004.

Pratt, Douglas, *Rethinking Religion: Exploratory Investigations,* Hindmarsh: ARF Press, 2003.

Premawardhana, Shanta, ed., *Religious Conversion: Religion Scholars Thinking Together*, U.K.: W.C.C., 2015.

Pruthi, R. K., Ram, S. and Chaturvedi, Archna, *Buddhism and Religions,* New Delhi: Commonwealth Publishers, 2011.

Rad, Gerhard von, *Genesis*, London: SCM Press, 1972.

Radhakrishnan, S., Radhakrishnan, *The Philosophy of the Upanishads*, London: George Allen & Unwin, 1924.

-do- *Eastern Religions and Western Thought*, New Delhi: Oxford University Press, 2000 (ninth impression).

-do- *Religion and Culture*, Delhi: Hind Pocket Books, 1968.

Raju, T. Swami, *The Study of Religion*, Bangalore: BTESSC/SATHRI, 2004.

Reed, Bruce, *The Dynamics of Religion: Process and Movement in Christian Churches,* London: Darton, Longman & Todd, 1978.

Richardson, Alan, *Religion in Contemporary Debate*, London: SCM Press, 1968.

Ring, N.C. et.al., *Introduction to the Study of Religion*, Maryknoll: Orbis Books, 1998.

Ringgaren, H., *Religions of the Ancient Near East,* Philadelphia: The Westminster Press, 1973.

Robbins, Keith (ed.), *Religion and Humanism: Papers Read at 18th Summer Meeting and 19th Winter Meeting*, Oxford: Blackwell, 1981.

Robertson, S., *Approaching Religion in a Pluralistic Context*, Bangalore: BTESSC/ SATHRI, 2009.

Ross-Bryant, Lynn, *Imagination and the Life of the Spirit: An Introduction to the Study of Religion and Literature*, Chico: Scholars Press, 1981.

Runzo, Joseph and Martin, Nancy M, (eds.*), Meaning of Life in the World Religions*, Oxford: Oneworld Publications, 2007.

Sail, R. and Akshay Sail (ed.), *Selected Speeches on Church and Society* (by A. George Ninan), Mumbai: BUILD & RCDRC, 1999.

Samartha, S. J., *The Hindu Response to the Unbound Christ*, Madras: Christian Literature Society, 1974.

-do- *Courage for Dialogue: Ecumenical Issues in Inter-religious Relationships*, Geneva: WCC, 1981.

-do- *One Christ – Many Religions: Towards a Revised Christology*, Maryknoll: Orbis Books, 1991.

-do- *The Pilgrim Christ: Sermons, Poems and Bible Studies*, Bangalore: Asian Trading Corporation, 1994.

-do- *Between Two Cultures: Ecumenical Ministry in a Pluralist World'*, Geneva: WCC Publications, 1996.

Scott, D. C. and I. Selvanayagam (ed.), *Revisioning India's Religious Traditions*, Delhi: ISPCK (UTC), 1996.

Selvanayagam, I., *Vedic Sacrifice: Challenge and Response*, New Delhi: Manohar, 1996.

-do- *The Dynamics of Hindu Traditions: Teape Lectures on Sacrifice, Gita and Dialogue*, Bangalore: Asian Trading Corporation, 1996.

-do- *A Second Call: Ministry and Mission in a Multifaith Milieu*, Madras: Christian Literature Society, 2000.

-do- *Relating to People of Other Faiths: Insights from the Bible*, Thiruvalla: CSS-BTTBPSA, 2004.

Sharpe, Eric, *Comparative Religion: A History*, London: Duckworth, 1975.

-do- *Understanding Religion*, London: Duckworth, 1983.

Singh, Harbans (ed.), *Approaches to the Study of Religion*, Patiala: Gobindsingh Department of Religious Studies (year not given).

Smart, N. *The Religious Experience of Mankind*, Glasgow: Collins Fount Paperbacks, 1969.

-do- *The World's Religions*, Cambridge: Press Syndicate of the University of Cambridge, 1995.

-do- *Dimensions of the Sacred: An Anatomy of the World's Beliefs*, London: Fontana Press, 1996.

Smith, W.C., *The Meaning and End of Religion*, London: SPCK, 1978.

-do- *Towards a World Theology: Faith and the Comparative History of Religion*, London: Macmillan Press, 1981.

-do- Smith, *Faith and Belief: The Difference Between Them*, Oxford: Oneworld Publications, 1998.

Spencer, Anand, *Understanding Religion: Theories and Methodology*, Patiala: Vision and Venture, 1997.

Streng, F.J., *Understanding Religious Life*, Belmont: Wadsworth Publishing Company, 1985.

Stroup, Herbert, *Founders of Living Religions*, Louisville: Westminster Press, 1974.

Tagore, R., *The Religion of Man*, Boston: Beacon Press, 1961.

Thomas, Owen (ed.), *Attitudes Towards Other Religions: Some Christian Interpretations*, London: SCM Press, 1969.

Thottakara, Augustine (ed.), *Religion and Politics in Asia Today*, Bangalore: Dharmaram Publications, 2001.

Thunberg, Lars et.al. (eds.), *Dialogue in Action: Essays in Honour of Johannes Aagard,* New Delhi: Prajna Publications, 1988.

Tillich, Paul, *Christianity and the Encounter of the World Religions*, New York and London: Columbia University Press, 1963.

Tiwari, Ravi, *Reflections and Studies in Religion*, Delhi: ISPCK, 2008.

Tokarey, Sergoi, *History of Religion*, Moscow: Progress Publishers, 1989.

Vanaik, Achin, *Communalism Contested: Religion, Modernity and Secularization*, New Delhi: Vistaar Publcations, 1997.

Vidyatmananda, Awami (ed.), *What Religion is in the Words of Swami Vivekananda*, Calcutta: Advaita Ashrama, 1998.

Vries, Hent de. (ed.), *Religion, Beyond a Concept*, New York: Fordham University Press, 2008.

Waardenburg, J., *Classical Approaches to the Study of Religion: Aims, Methods, and Theories of Research,* Vol. I: *Introduction and Anthology*, The Hague: Mouton Publishers, 1973.

Wall, O.A., *Sex and Sex Worship in the World,* Delhi: Inter-India Publications, 1979.

Ward, Keith, *Religion & Human Nature*, Oxford: Clarendon Press, 1998.

Weber, Max, *The Religion of India,* New York: The Free Press, 1967.

Whaling, F. (ed.), *Contemporary Approaches to the Study of Religion*, Berlin: Mouton Publishers, 1983 (Vol. I), 1985 (Vol. II).

-do- (ed.), *The World's Religions,* Edinburgh: T & T Clarke, 1984.

Wiebe, Donald, *Religion and Truth: Towards an Alternative Paradigm for the Study of Religion*, The Hague: Mouton and Co., 1981.

Wielenga, Bas, *Introduction to Marxism*, Bangalore: Centre for Social Action, 1984.

Wong, T. P. (ed.), *The Human Quest for Meaning: Theories, Research and Applications*, New York: Routledge, 2012.

Woods, R. (ed.), *Understanding Mysticism,* London: The Athlone Press, 1980.

Zavos, John, et. al., *Hindu Nationalism and Indian Politics*, New Delhi: Oxford University Press, 2004.

Index